American History/ American Film

Of Related Interest

American History/American Television, John E. O'Connor, ed.
And the Winner Is . . . The History and Politics of the Oscar Awards, Emanuel Levy
The Dead That Walk: Dracula, Frankenstein, the Mummy, and Other Favorite Movie Monsters, Leslie Halliwell
Fellini the Artist, Edward Murray
Framework: A History of Screenwriting in the American Film, Tom Stempel
The French Through Their Films, Robin Buss
Hitchcock: The First Forty-Four Films, Eric Rohmer and Claude Chabrol
Italian Cinema: From Neorealism to the Present, Peter Bondanella
Midnight Matinees: Movies and Their Makers, 1978-1985, Jay Scott
Modern European Filmmakers and the Art of Adaptation, Andrew S. Horton and Joan Magretta, eds.
A Project for the Theatre, Ingmar Bergman
Silent Magic: Rediscovering the Silent Film Era, Ivan Butler
World Cinema Since 1945, William Luhr, ed.

American History/ American Film

Interpreting the Hollywood Image

New Expanded Edition

Edited by
John E. O'Connor and Martin A. Jackson

Foreword by Arthur M. Schlesinger, Jr.

A *Frederick Ungar Book*
CONTINUUM • NEW YORK

1988

The Ungar Publishing Company
370 Lexington Avenue
New York, NY 10017

Designed by Stanley Rice

Printed in the United States of America

Library of Congress Cataloging-in-Publication Data

American history/American film.

Bibliography: p.
Includes index.
1. Motion pictures—United States—History.
2. Motion pictures and history.   3.   United States—Civilization—Sources.   I.   O'Connor, John E.
II.   Jackson, Martin A.
PN1993.5.U6A875   1988   791.43'0973   87-31438
ISBN 0-8044-2672-4

FOR
Mary
AND
Jonie

Contents

Foreword

This volume is concerned with the uses of film as a source of historical evidence. Evidence is of course the lifeblood of history. The historian of ancient Greece or China spends months teasing meanings out of a potsherd or a grave rubbing. The historian of the twentieth century has the opposite problem. He faces not a scarcity but an embarrassment of evidence. Much of this evidence, if overwhelming in quantity, remains traditional in form. Scholars feel comfortable, for example, with documents. But some contemporary evidence, because it is absolutely novel in form, poses unprecedented problems both of acceptability and utilization.

Historians are professionally a conservative lot. Movies have had status problems ever since they emerged three quarters of a century ago as a dubious entertainment purveyed by immigrant hustlers to a working-class clientele in storefront holes-in-the-wall scattered through the poorer sections of the industrial city. Conventional history has recorded the motion picture as a phenomenon but ignored it as a source. Social and intellectual historians draw freely on fiction, drama, painting; hardly ever on movies.

Yet the very nature of film as a supremely popular art guarantees that it is the carrier of deep if enigmatic truth. Individuals create novels, plays, landscapes. But the creation of a movie is a mass undertaking, involving directors, writers, producers, cinematographers, players, an army of technicians, the artifact delivered by an intricate assembly line to a vast and anonymous audience. The production process, an unstable merger of commerce and art, dependent on collective effort and collective response, is intimately interwoven with the *mentalité* of the society. If, as Emerson said and cultural historians have always assumed, "No man can quite emancipate himself from his age and country, or produce a model in which the education, the religion, the politics, usages, and arts of his times shall have no share," how much truer this must be for art created by a crowd. What succeeds at the time in the movies, what is remembered later (often two separate things) obviously offer the social and intellectual historian significant clues to the tastes, apprehensions, myths, inner vibrations of the age.

The challenge of the movie is perhaps especially acute for the American historian. Film is the only art where the United States has made a real difference. Strike the American contribution from drama, painting, music, sculpture, dance, even possibly from poetry and the novel, and the world's achievement is only marginally diminished. But film without the American contribution is unimaginable. The fact that film has been the most potent vehicle of the American imagination suggests all the more strongly that movies have something to tell us not just about the surfaces but about the mysteries of American life.

Yet what is the key that will unlock the treasures that movies secrete for the historian? Here we face the question of method— a problem that historians are always reluctant to confront in the abstract. Even if the film is accepted as a legitimate source of historical evidence, how in the world is that evidence to be extracted?

Sociological and literary scholarship has in fact developed a body of theoretical analysis addressed to the relationship between art and society. What Taine wrote long ago about books applies equally, or even more, to films: they do not drop from the sky like meteorites. If Taine's own triad of race, milieu, and moment is too mechanical to be very helpful, it reminds us of the roots all art has in the social environment. And it was Engels who said he had learned more about French society from the novels of Balzac "than from all the professed historians, economists and statisticians of the period together." Following the positivists and the Marxists, scholars have tried in a diversity of ways to show how artistic expression reveals the values and structures of society. The sociology of art and literature remains a relatively underdeveloped field as compared, say, to the sociology of religion, crime, or the family. Yet suggestive work has been done, and historians should know more about it.

The most obvious but perhaps least satisfactory way that historians can use movies is as a mirror of the age. Certainly the Warner Brothers vernacular films of the 1930s, for example, give a graphic impression of the way ordinary people lived, dressed, talked, worked, courted, traveled, and so on. But the documentary approach does not carry us very far. What is more revealing, though harder to ascertain, is the significance of the persisting themes, images, styles, genres, legends that give movies their force and vitality. Here historians have much to learn from literary historians and critics as well as from sociologists of art: from Northrop Frye on archetypes, from Henry Nash Smith on myth and symbol, from Richard Hoggart and Raymond Williams on structures of feeling, from Georg Lukacs on class relationships, from Lucien Goldmann on the homology of artistic and social structures, from Leslie Fiedler and many others on art and the unconscious. They can learn too from sociological studies of the economic situation of the arts, the market conditions of production, the role of the audience, the way in which specific works are received at specific times.

None of this is easy—or rather it is almost too easy to read the times back into the arts. "What films reflect," wrote Siegfried Kracauer, "are not so much explicit credos as psychological dispositions—those deep layers of collective mentality which extend more or less below the dimensions of consciousness." But the deep layers are precisely those most difficult to uncover and verify. Thus Kracauer's own *From Caligari to Hitler*, the most ambitious attempt to use films as an historical source, contended that the German movies of the 1920s predicted Nazism—an interpretation indignantly rejected by artists like Fritz Lang who made some of the crucial exhibits in Kracauer's indictment. Had Hitler not come to power in 1933, what would scholars have read into the German films of the 1920s? In the same way American films of the 1930s are enlisted to display the emotional impact of the Depression. If the films were grim, they reflected the suffering of the time; if the films were screwball comedies or spectacular musicals, they reflected the compulsion to escape the suffering of the time. The use of the social setting to account both for A and non-A reduces explanation to metaphor.

The trouble is that film is a notably ambiguous, even duplicitous, art. Its testimony is hard to decipher. Its manifest content often heads in one direction, its latent content in quite another. Richard Griffith demonstrated this long ago in his elucidation of the way that the contrived happy ending legalized darker messages in the American movies of the 1930s. The implicit meaning and force of a film may often be at war with its explicit moral. Moreover, the audience, supposedly passive in the shrouded theater, is actually an active collaborator, seizing from the movie what it needs for its own purposes of tutelage and fantasy, responding to each movie not as an isolated event but as reverberant with memories of other films, with private lives of stars, with their own private lives.

Ostensibly American movies have been dedicated to the reinforcement of middle-class morality. Certainly they have done their share to strengthen capitalism, chauvinism, racism, sexism, and so on. None the less, as Robert Sklar argues in *Movie-Made America*, movies have had from the start an anti-establishment coloration. They were often made by immigrants whose yearning for respectability could not altogether suppress their own particular experience nor altogether control the personal visions of directors and writers. Crass commercialism conspired with as well as against solitary genius. The film is both an industry that lives by stereotype and an art that often undermines stereotype.

Thus the American movie has provided a common dream life, a common fund of reference and fantasy, to a society divided by ethnic distinctions and economic disparities. At the same time, it may well have excited and even incited the oppressed by displaying the abundance presumably available to their masters. One may guess that movies have generated as much discontent as they have acquiescence. Because society dimly perceived the film as threatening, an elaborate machinery was established to keep it down; the Legion of Decency was only the most notorious example. But the movies somehow eluded the restrictions imposed on them. The visions thrust into circulation—visions of diversity, spontaneity, irreverence, aspiration, passion—prevailed in the end over such requirements as the prohibition of the double bed or the punishment of transgressors in the last reel.

The movies have so much to disclose about the inner as well as the outer life of America—if only historians knew how to coax out the deeper meanings. But the duplicity of the film is not an argument against making the attempt. It is rather an argument for rigor and circumspection in the process of analysis. In their admirable introduction Professors Jackson and O'Connor provide an excellent account of both problems and possibilities. The essays that follow show some of the things historians can discover by careful and specific analysis of particular movies. This is a pioneering work, and pioneering is an adventure in trial and error. In time such pioneers will open up a varied and complex wilderness of evidence for the modern historian.

ARTHUR M. SCHLESINGER, JR.

Preface to the Second Edition

Since the first edition of this book nine years ago, the field of study which brings together the interests of historians and mass media scholars has developed in significant ways. The interesting work of scores of new scholars has been facilitated by the accessibility of new archival collections and by the vastly increased amounts of material available for study in various video formats. By demonstrating the rich potential for the study of films as historical artifacts, analyzing them in their broader cultural context, and paying close attention to their historical content, production, background, and audience reception, the direction of some of the best of that new scholarship was charted in the essays first published here. The essay on *Platoon* by Lawrence W. Lichty and Raymond L. Carroll, which has been prepared especially for this new edition, emphasizes the continuing value of the approach. The promise for the future is that historians who use film in more traditional research and teaching, and communications scholars who are concerned with the historical context of their studies, will continue to learn from one another.

JOHN E. O'CONNOR AND MARTIN A. JACKSON (JANUARY, 1988)

Introduction

It is "history written in lightning." These were Woodrow Wilson's words after seeing D. W. Griffith's newly completed *The Birth of a Nation* in 1915. Wilson came from a generation to which motion pictures were modern marvels. It was understandable, therefore, that he and others of his time would be overwhelmed by the power and scope of such a film. Today the racial bias that pervades Griffith's classic is obvious to every viewer. But Wilson and his contemporaries were likely to accept director Griffith's personal analysis, which, after all, was directly in tune with the then prevalent interpretation of Reconstruction. The television series *Roots* may be seen as the 1970s answer to Griffith's idealization of the Ku Klux Klan as saviors of Southern civilization. But historians are coming to understand better the sometimes subtle ways in which such productions communicate their historical messages and to appreciate the value of motion pictures as tools for teaching and as resources for historical scholarship.

This new visual consciousness has not been born easily. One of the reasons that historians and other serious students of twentieth-century life have for so long ignored film is that, unlike their colleagues in ancient and medieval history who must often piece together their knowledge from scraps of pottery or faded manuscripts, they have so much other evidence to draw upon. Besides, films are difficult to study; there is no other area of research where the historian may be forced to rent his text from a commercial distributor and pay for each screening, and it is difficult (without special equipment) to slow down or stop the film or to go over a section again as one can with a printed document. The tools of visual analysis are different from those with which historians receive training in graduate school. Moreover, till recently much that was written about Hollywood movies was intended primarily for the movie buffs and nostalgia fans. It often lacked rigorous scholarship and rarely related the film to the broader historical and cultural context.

This volume is meant to encourage teachers and students, the professional and nonprofessional historians, to reconsider the Hollywood film as a valid and respectable subject for research. To achieve this goal we have established a format in which, rather than drawing conclusions about whole genres or periods in film history, authors have each concentrated on a specific film to show how its visual text as well as the details of its production, release, and reception, relate to the broader historical and cultural questions of the day. Moreover, the essays are fully documented and annotated to illustrate the benefits that can accrue from the application of traditional techniques of scholarship to the study of film. In short, the films are analyzed as historical documents.

Two parallel threads tie this book together and unite the treatments of each of the films. *First*: the essays seek to understand the way in which each film documents American social history and captures the state of mind of the American people at the time it was released for popular distribution. *Second*: each essay addresses itself to the ways in which the film in question illustrates the development of the American film industry, its business organization as well as its artistic values and production technique, from 1920 to the 1970s. Neither of these threads leads to an ultimate or overall conclusion. It would be impossible to construct a history of Hollywood or its product based on only fourteen documents, much less to attempt an overview of American society using popular movies as the only uniting theme. Though attention has been paid to directors, genres, periods, and the unique scholarly interests of each of our contributors, the films chosen are not intended to typify all of the movies of the eras they represent, and there are scores of other films that might have served as well. Rather, the essays printed here are intended to serve as models for applying historical scholarship to film research and to suggest some of the reasonable conclusions that such a study can yield.

With regard to our first theme, the connections between society and film as a popular art form have troubled generations of scholars and critics. As long ago as 1896 the Polish historian Bronislaw Matezuski wrote of the coming historical value of the fascinating new machine that could project pictures in motion. The earliest filmmakers saw their invention as a record-keeping device, a modern way of recording real events. And it took little thought for historians to realize that pictures of the Kaiser reviewing his troops or of the visit of a President would be tomorrow's archival material. But, as is well known, the potential of movies for providing mass entertainment in expanding industrial cities was soon realized, and film was transformed into a "penny arcade" attraction, and eventually into a cultural force.

It should not be surprising that historians, even those of the 1970s, are quicker to accept the validity of newsreel or documentary film as historical document. There are no actors involved—the newsmakers themselves appear before the camera—and the aura of factual representation is strong. Even after the basic lessons of film language and the first experiences of visual analysis have made it clear that lighting, camera angle, and editing can make such "actuality footage" say whatever the filmmaker desires, there is still strong prejudice to accept documentary films as more relevant to the historian than the more fictional products of Hollywood.

Part of the problem relates to the ways in which forms of evidence are conceived. The value of entertainment films will become more evident if we consider them as we do popular novels, as cultural documents, rather than comparing them with traditional records and archival manuscripts. It is precisely because such films are made for entertainment that they have value for the historian. They tell us what made people of other decades laugh or cry, what made them forget their troubles, and what they believed about their past. The popular movie stereotypes of women, Indians, blacks, and other ethnic and cultural groups, may tell the historian more than any other source can about the subtleties of mass prejudice. And changing tastes in movie fare from decade to decade and year to year may help us to understand the changing values and concerns of people over time.

As one critic noted recently, "All films are ultimately about something that interests and/or bothers the culture they grew out of."* But the validity of the conclusions we can draw from analyzing films—or any historical source material—depends on the questions we ask. Even today, most historians would (and often do) laugh at the suggestion of using the film *Mission to Moscow* for teaching or research. It is so full of falsehoods and misrepresentations that no part of the film can be trusted to present a factual picture of what life was like in Soviet Russia in the late 1930s. But what if the frame of reference is altered? *Mission to Moscow* may tell us nothing of life in Russia, but it speaks volumes about what the Warner Brothers and, through them, the Roosevelt administration wanted the American people to think about Russia in 1943 when the film was released. The worst conceivable source for understanding internal Soviet policy becomes perhaps the most valuable single document for comprehending the patterns of propaganda that World War II introduced to hometown American movie screens. By comparing historical reality with the vision concocted in the Warner studio we can come much closer to understanding which issues were thought more important, and the ways in which appeals were made to change public opinion. Similarly, for an understanding of policies regarding nuclear proliferation and safeguards against accidental Armageddon, the 1964 film *Dr. Strangelove or: How I Learned to Stop Worrying and Love the Bomb* is useless. The proper sources for such an investigation would more likely be found in the State Department or the records of the Joint Chiefs of Staff. But Kubrick's film is a unique mine of information concerning evolving popular attitudes on those issues—attitudes with which Washington bureaucrats may have been out of touch. William Wellman's 1932 film *Public Enemy* is another interesting source for popular opinions on Prohibition. So it goes with each of the essays published here.

As with any other type of historical document—be it a diary entry, a personal letter, a newspaper account, or a public record—the film document must be analyzed with reference to both its sur-

---

* Jack Shadoian, review of *Guest in the House, Film & History*, 4 (1974): no. 1, p. 15.

face content and its deeper implied meanings. It must be considered in relation to the specific conditions which led to its production (studio rivalry, director's taste, star availability, financial limitations), the broader social and political context from which it took shape (the era of prohibition, the cold war, or the bicentennial year), and the audience for which it was intended (the broadest possible commercial market, or perhaps such a specific audience as the segregated black theaters that dotted American cities through the 1940s). As expected, the surface content and implications of some films are by nature more interesting, while others derive their significance from less obvious elements in their production and critical reception. Twentieth Century-Fox's *Drums Along the Mohawk* (1939), for example, is of interest because it represents a 1930s renewal of popular interest in the revolutionary period of American history. But production values are also revealing; the film can be criticized, as the television "docudramas" of the 1970s have been, for paying more attention to the props and costumes than to the validity of the historical events represented on the screen. What makes *Invasion of the Body Snatchers* (1956) an interesting film for historical analysis are the unspoken psychological implications of the characters and story. On the other hand, because of their reliance on unusually complete manuscript source material, the essays on *Mission to Moscow* (1943) and *Viva Zapata!* (1952) tell us more than can usually be found about the production background of most films, and each of these was directly affected by the political climate of the country in the 1940s and 1950s respectively. The special interest of *Scar of Shame* (1927) is that it was one of the best of the "race movies" which were made especially for distribution in segregated black theaters (all the others of course were shown in segregated white theaters).

In relating the film to the audience, historians face the same difficulties involved in any attempt to generalize about popular attitudes. Scholars have grappled with such problems for decades. See, for example, Jesse Lemisch's analysis of broadsides and popular cartoons to establish what might have motivated Jack Tar (the ordinary seaman) in the decade before the American Revolution, or Ruth Miller Elson's content analyses of nineteenth-century schoolbooks to determine what might have been the common cultural perceptions of the mass of Americans at that time.* Each of these historical interpretations, now accepted as valid in their own right, were seeking to discover what went on in the mind of the ordinary American. They therefore focused on sources other than the diaries and other personal observations of the social elite. In the same way such films as *The Big Parade* (1925) and *The Best Years of Our Lives* (1946) can offer sharp insight into popular attitudes in the wake of America's two world wars.

But all efforts to transcend the elite bias of much historical writing and speak of the American "everyman" require a degree of reading between the lines. In most cases it is impossible to discover whether films served more to shape popular attitudes or to reflect them. Sometimes analysis is even more complex. With regard to *Way Down East* (1920), for example, it may be impossible to sort out the images so that it becomes clear whether the film sides more with the traditional view of woman's role or supports the idea of the "new woman" that had grown out of the just completed struggle for women's suffrage. While it may be difficult in such cases to determine the exact opinion that a specific film may proffer, it establishes beyond any doubt that people were concerned about the role that women played; the issue seemed relevant at the time. Moreover, popular reaction to such roles or value systems can be traced over the decades by observing the different ways in which films presented them. The images of "Homeville" in *Steamboat 'Round the Bend* (1935) might have been less acceptable to audiences of the 1920s or the 1950s, but the unique challenges to traditional American values in the 1930s gave the film its special appeal. A film such as *Rocky* (1976) with its subtle characterizations of racism and the problems of ethnic identity might have been impossible to produce at all in an earlier decade.

The second theme, that of analyzing the film industry itself, should require no special explanation. Serious scholarly attention should be paid to the movie business in the same way that historians

---

* See Jesse Lemisch, "Jack Tar in the Streets: Merchant Seamen in the Politics of Revolutionary America," *William and Mary Quarterly*, third series, Vol. XXV, No. 3 (July, 1968) pp. 371–407; and Ruth Miller Elson, "American Schoolbooks and 'Culture' in the Nineteenth Century," *Mississippi Valley Historical Review*, Vol. XLVI (December, 1959) pp. 411–34.

have devoted their efforts to studying the origins and development of oil and steel production, the railroads and automobile manufacturers, banks and insurance companies. Earlier "histories," which did not transcend the popular appeal of fan club trivia and the love affairs of the stars, have made it necessary to argue that point, but there is much of interest here, even for traditional historians not oriented toward visual evidence.

To begin with, the process of invention and perfecting the technology for moving pictures is an interesting and controversial chapter in the history of science. So many amateur and professional inventors were rushing to perfect the mechanisms for photography and projection that doubt still persists over who deserves most of the credit.

The movie industry had its own "robber barons," chief among them Thomas Edison, who tried for years to monopolize the production and distribution of films through his Motion Pictures Trust Company. A later generation of leaders in the industry were interesting too. These "movie moguls" did not enjoy the Anglo-Saxon blood lines or the inborn "Protestant ethic" that motivated other so-called captains of industry. Instead, many of them were Jewish garment manufacturers and theatrical producers from New York who appreciated a new business opportunity and wanted to be in on the action from the beginning. The early film moguls invested in nickelodeon parlors that sprouted up in working-class neighborhoods in every American city and encouraged the widening appeal of movies to middle-class audiences that came with the production of feature-length films such as *The Birth of a Nation* and the construction of the ostentatious movie palaces of the 1920s. There is irony in the fact that these industry leaders, many of them immigrants themselves, presided over the production of films that assumed all of the traditional American values and, in fact, served to ease the assimilation of millions of more-recent arrivals.

The same type of vertical business organization which has concerned historians since Ida Tarbell's *History of Standard Oil* (1904) can be found in the theater chains and block-booking distribution practices developed by the Hollywood studios in the 1920s and 1930s. Moreover, the procedures through which newly emerging technologies such as sound and Technicolor were adopted by the production companies should pique the curiosity of business and industrial historians at least as much as changing processes in the steel and automobile industry have till now.

Students of the government regulation of commerce and industry would also do well to study Hollywood, for the problems there are at the same time subtler and more significant than in many other fields of business activity. The beginnings of control came from middle class reformers of the Progressive era who tried to use local health code violations to close down nickelodeon parlors and little theaters in working-class neighborhoods for fear that the movies were unwholesome and destructive of social stability. Soon state and federal legislatures were involved and, to avoid more stringent government control, the industry began what was perhaps the most vigorous effort at self-regulation in all of American business history—the result was the famous (or infamous) Hays Office and eventually a rating system that persists even today.

The moving-picture business offers a valuable example of an industry adapting itself to declining public demand and the special financial pressures that that brought on. The size of movie audiences reached its peak in the 1946–48 period when ninety million Americans went to the theater every week, but from then on it declined steadily. Some of this was surely the result of new competition with television, but charges of communist influence in the industry and a general decline in the qaulity and interest of the product were also to blame. The changing conditions brought on retrenchment in the studios. Eventually the stockpiles of props and costumes, the back lots with their mock-ups of Western towns, and the huge sound stages themselves were sold off and a new generation of independent producers assumed prominence. With the studios and their theater chains and block-booking contracts gone, the result was a reduction in the number of films produced and a revolution in the methods of financing and distributing them.

The historian of the movie industry has a unique good fortune because much of the product is available for him to study. As the essays in this book will illustrate, the visual dimension can add a great deal to the traditional documentation of studio records, interviews, trade press, and critical reviews, because the visual (and eventually the aural) style of the films was influenced by each new technological innovation and each major change in the organizational structure of the business. Some of these developments brought immediate improvements in the art of moviemaking. For others the changes were less obviously beneficial. But historians are left with a mine of information about the continuing cooperation and conflict between art and industrial "progress."

Finally, and in connection with the first theme of this book, every business or industrial historian must consider the impact which the products of the industry under study may have had on the larger society. Volumes have been written about the influence of the automobile on American mores—from population mobility to sexual practices. The impact of the film (and television) has been certainly no less significant and probably a good deal more. In this regard, of the many books published about Hollywood and its representations of American life, the work of two of our contributors deserves special notice. Garth Jowett's *Film: The Democratic Art* (1976) and Robert Sklar's *Movie-Made America* (1975) offer, between them, the most complete and insightful view of the American film industry. Jowett argues convincingly that the history of communications is a crucial key to the understanding of twentieth-century culture in which film as well as radio and television have buried small-town American values and replaced them with a true national consciousness. Sklar shows in many ways how the developing art of film reflected broader cultural values as well as the hard-nosed devotion of the Hollywood moguls to turning a profit. Both books are indispensable to a complete understanding of the film in American civilization and many of the essays printed in this volume may be viewed as extensions of and further support for their general conclusions based upon close analysis of specific films.

The contributors of the essays that follow have approached their subjects with individual styles and emphases. There are many ways to write history, and the student may find in these fourteen essays examples of different methodologies that historians are able to apply to the study of film and American history. (With one exception, all the essays were written especially for this volume.)

June Sochen, a specialist in the study of women in twentieth-century America, has traced the evolution of women's status by means of her analysis of D. W. Griffith's *Way Down East*. In Griffith's film, the traditional values assigned to women—home, family, obedience to husband, and virginity—were defended and presented as necessary traits in a time of rapid social change. Griffith, the arch-traditionalist, found much to dislike in the sweeping changes brought about during the late 1910s and early 1920s. In this story of betrayal and tragedy, with Lillian Gish as the woman facing the world as an unwed mother, the old values are reaffirmed in a plot that twists and turns under Griffith's legendary directorial hand. At the end, the loose ends are tied together and dawn breaks brightly, but the point has been made: in abandoning tradition and long-settled truths, women face the limitless ruin of self, family, and society.

War, and the American reaction to war, is the subject of Michael T. Isenberg's insightful study of one of the major films of the 1920s, King Vidor's *The Big Parade.* Professor Isenberg, a specialist in the film record of World War I, discounts the traditional wisdom which says that Americans in the 1920s rejected war and were embittered by the experience of World War I. *The Big Parade,* argues Isenberg, more accurately represented popular feelings about military exploits than did the elitist novels and poems that are cited as evidence of the opposite feeling. War, in *The Big Parade,* is not portrayed as degrading or unnecessary, although its inevitable fatalities and loss are conceded. Rather, war, like death, is part of the human experience, able to bestow nobility as well as terror, and for millions of Americans who saw the film during the 1920s, *The Big Parade* better represented their mood about the recent war than any number of Hemingway novels or Cummings poems. The virtues of patriotism, dedication, heroism, and selfless sacrifice for noble ideals were dramatically advanced in Vidor's epic story of young Americans sent far away to defend their nation's dreams. Not that Vidor delighted in war and combat; rather that he grasped the public's feeling a mixture of pride in the warrior's code and sorrow in the human tragedy of war, and so his film became an accurate representation of the American mood in a time that was full of contradictions.

Thomas Cripps offers a unique study not only of *The Scar of Shame,* but of a whole genre of American movies that have all but disappeared from the nation's consciousness: the all-black film, made by black directors, with black actors, and aimed at segregated black audiences. Author of the recent *Slow Fade to Black,* and many articles on blacks in American films, Cripps's analysis of *The*

Scar of Shame reveals the difficult position that many black Americans occupied during the 1920s and early 1930s: on one hand bound by the limits of segregation and racist attitudes, while on the other exhorted to rise in the traditional American manner and join the middle class. *The Scar of Shame* is a story of an upwardly mobile black man—practicing the necessary American virtues of thrift, hard work, and honesty—who finds that his past and his race continue to hold him back. One of the finest black films ever made, its simple and even absurd plot notwithstanding, *The Scar of Shame* was nearly unknown outside the circuit of segregated theaters common in America until the 1940s. Cripps also discusses some of the fascinating details of the black film industry during the 1920s, showing how and why these low-budget films were produced and how they related to the much more prosperous and, of course, better-known Hollywood products of the time.

Garth Jowett, author of the widely respected *Film: The Democratic Art*, focuses on the emergence of the gangster film during the 1930s. In his study of one of the most famous and enduring of the gangster classics, *Public Enemy*, Jowett finds that it was the unexpected success of this movie with its violence and swagger that helped promote Hollywood's decision to reinforce its self-censorship by the creation of the Breen Office. Much of the film's excitement was generated by the performance of the young James Cagney as Tom Powers, the tough ambitious kid who parodies the American dream by becoming a leading gangster—and who is suitably punished by film's end. Since the 1930s, the gangster movie has become a staple of the American industry; in Jowett's informative examination of one of the first of the type we begin to see the relevance of gangsterism to American society, in both good and bad times.

Another perspective on Depression America is offered by Peter Rollins, who has spent considerable time in studying the intriguing figure of Will Rogers. He therefore comes to the film *Steamboat 'Round the Bend* with a deep knowledge of the star and of the period in which the film was made, the 1930s. In a time of depression and spreading international violence (as well as gangster films), the homey and reassuring message of movies such as *Steamboat 'Round the Bend* served to bolster the spirits of the American people. Will Rogers became everyone's favorite uncle, the wise but neighborly symbol of the American folk hero, able to resolve problems and find happiness no matter how unpromising the circumstances. He was a symbol who offered hope in a difficult time and Rogers, the former cowboy and Broadway comic, became one of America's favorite film personalities until his death in 1935.

By the end of the Depression decade of the 1930s, domestic concern receded as the war clouds gathered in Europe and Asia. In 1939, the distinguished director John Ford looked back into American history to make *Drums Along the Mohawk*, an exciting movie that would also be a lesson in courage to the American people facing a dangerous world. John E. O'Connor, a specialist in early American history, analyzes *Drums Along the Mohawk* both as a cautionary tale and as an example of Hollywood's reaction to the larger world. In this story of brave colonial farmers fighting Indians and British invaders to protect homes and families, Ford underlines once again his own vision of the power of individual commitment and the virtues of democracy. These were ideals under attack in that tumultuous time, and the film's success indicated that for many Americans they were still highly valued ideals.

In 1941 the storm broke for the United States and war became reality. In his study of one of the most unusual of World War II films, David Culbert tries to unravel the tangled threads that tied Hollywood to Washington and show how American foreign policy goals were advanced in *Mission to Moscow*. Culbert, who specializes in American diplomatic history, is well equipped to probe the complex nature of Roosevelt's policy toward the Soviet Union during the war, and his creative research into the origins and making of *Mission to Moscow* reveals much about that policy. In addition, Culbert's researches have raised important questions about Hollywood's link to the highest levels of government and suggest that, at least in wartime, the nominally independent American film industry was willing to follow rather closely advice from the White House and the State Department.

The war ended in 1945 but American society did not return to normal; the world had changed since 1941 and for millions of veterans, as well as for those who stayed home, the new era of peace and prosperity was confusing. In *The Best Years of Our Lives*, Hollywood once again responded to the evident concerns of the American people as Martin A. Jackson demonstrates in his essay on this famous William Wyler movie. Fear of a new Depression, concern over unemployment and the atomic bomb, and anxiety about personal relationships strained by war—all these figure in the story of the three veterans trying to reestablish themselves in a nation that was once home but that seemed to have changed while they were away. Professor Jackson seeks to capture the shifting mood of the years following the war, years that were officially "peacetime" but that were often as difficult as war for the American people.

In Howard Hawks's *Red River*, the novel demands of postwar America are again present, although in a less visible manner as Robert Sklar shows. On the surface a Western-adventure story with the always heroic John Wayne in the lead, *Red River* is also a tale of expansion and empire, a tale that said much to the Americans of the late 1940s who looked out to a world that seemed to call out for American domination. The Byzantine complexities of the postwar movie industry are also an important theme in Professor Sklar's essay, as he reveals the mechanisms behind the film's production and release. Sklar, author of *Movie-Made America*, once again demonstrates his skill at combining sophisticated historical analysis with informed film study.

Professor Paul Vanderwood turns to one of the more difficult films of the 1950s as he tries to clarify the relationship between Hollywood and current politics. In *Viva Zapata!*, director Elia Kazan walked a thin line between glorifying the Mexican revolutionary and at the same time avoiding any hint of support for similar radical upheavals in the contemporary world. It was a ticklish and perhaps impossible task that Kazan faced, but he was operating under the twin pressures of a movie industry badly frightened by the anti-communist investigations of the late 1940s and by the public's reluctance to patronize any film that smacked of radicalism. Though the finished product owed much to Marlon Brando's complex portrayal of Zapata and to Kazan's directorial skill, as a whole the film was a product of the multiple influences and mirrored the mood of American life at the time.

Another indication of the shifting temper of the times in the 1950s may be found in Don Siegel's classic science-fiction/horror movie, *Invasion of the Body Snatchers*. As explicated by Stuart Samuels, *Invasion of the Body Snatchers* speaks directly to the unspoken fear of mid-1950s America: the loss of individual identity in a rising tide of conformity. The story of alien beings in the form of giant pods taking control of otherwise normal human beings, and of one man's struggle to alert the world to the danger, is a thinly disguised parable of America in the years of Eisenhower peace. Fear was the operative word in much of American life then; fear of communism, of atomic war, and of disturbing outside influences that might undermine the social order that was (apparently) being erected. In such a low-budget film as *Body Snatchers*, the sort that would usually play at the bottom of a double feature and then disappear, Dr. Samuels finds a rich mine of ideas and insights to help us comprehend the troubling aspects of the nation in the aftermath of McCarthyism and in the high noon of the organization man.

In *Dr. Strangelove*, America's love-hate relationship with the military establishment was subjected to pitiless satire by Stanley Kubrick, and in Lawrence Suid's penetrating study of the film we begin to understand how (and why) the military tries to shape American movies. Suid, author of a recent study of the Hollywood-Pentagon link, is concerned with the movie industry's traditional allegiance to official policy, and that tradition's weakening during the Kennedy years of the 1960s. *Dr. Strangelove* was an important movie, then, not only for its memorable characterizations and mordant humor but because it signaled the emerging independence of the industry and pointed to new directions in American filmmaking.

The 1960s were a period of new directions in other areas as well. In *Bonnie and Clyde*, the movie industry announced its acceptance of the 1960s sensibility, or as some would have it, helped create that sensibility. Lawrence Murray examines this landmark movie of the 1960s as an indicator of the altered awareness that characterized that decade. In its violence, its ambiguity toward the main characters (who were after all criminals and killers), and its skilled evocation of the past, *Bonnie and Clyde* caught the spirit of the new era and became one of the major cultural events of a fertile period. Dr. Murray's research also focuses on the formative period that precedes any film, and it does much to elucidate the new methods and manners as Hollywood went through the culture shock of the 1960s.

That period of change made possible, a few years later, independent films such as *Rocky*, created outside the traditional studio channels, which caught the industry by surprise when it became one of the biggest hits of the 1970s. In his essay on *Rocky*, Daniel J. Leab, author of *From Sambo to Superspade* (1976), studies the film as a statement about ethnic awareness in America. It was, in addition, a restatement of the nearly forgotten American faith in self-reliance, individualism, and courage, as exemplified by the story of the broken-down Philadelphia fighter who gets a chance to fight the champion. Underneath its contemporary language and overt physicality, Rocky is an old-fashioned story of one man's struggle to beat the odds—and along the way find true happiness. It reflected a new sentimentalism that accorded well with the bicentennial atmosphere of 1976 and which, to judge from the film's vast success, many Americans welcomed with open arms.

In 1986, nearly two decades after the events it depicts, *Platoon* became the first major American motion picture to show so vividly and realistically the life of the grunt—the ordinary combat soldier—in Vietnam. The film was released at a time of renewed interest in the Vietnam experience and the plight of the men who fought there. A number of other films on Vietnam were released at about the same time, and there was a TV series as well, but *Platoon* promises to remain for some time the most significant film against which all other visions of Vietnam will be compared. Lawrence W. Lichty and Raymond L. Carroll show how *Platoon* can help us to comprehend the intensity of the battle conditions that existed there, and should add insight to our reading of other more traditional sources concerning the war.

As Arthur Schlesinger, Jr., notes in his foreword to this volume, the type of study attempted here is new and for the most part untried. By bringing the critical faculties of professional historians to the study of film we have endeavored to establish the validity of feature films as historical sources and to experiment with analytical methods for drawing conclusions based upon them. The multiple approaches adopted by our various contributors suggest the richness of this all but untapped resource.

The New Woman and Twenties America:

Way Down East (1920)

JUNE SOCHEN

Lillian Gish lifts her eyes to heaven as she flees across the shifting ice floes. Her performance as Anna dramatized the shifting perception of women in the decade following passage of the women's suffrage amendment.

(Photo courtesy of Museum of Modern Art)

In 1920 America was recovering from participation in its first world war, a conflict that wrought massive destruction and a significant alteration of the world map. The United States found itself in the uncomfortable position of being a world power but undecided as to how that role should be played. At home, a recession followed the war but as the decade of the 1920s began prosperity returned. Key segments of the population, notably farmers and black unskilled city workers, did not enjoy the benefits of the prosperity, but many other Americans found themselves able to buy the new mass-produced goods and appliances coming off the assembly lines. Popular entertainment flourished as magazines, theaters, movies, and, later on, radio all became major industries to satisfy the tastes of the prospering city dwellers.

At the same time, the nation was struggling to adjust to important constitutional changes that people thought would alter social relations tremendously: prohibition and women's suffrage. Women reformers were prominent in both movements: the Women's Christian Temperance Union, one of the largest women's organizations in history, had campaigned on the state and national level for more than fifty years to achieve the prohibition of alcoholic beverages, while the National American Woman's Suffrage Association had been working to extend the right of women to vote for a similar length of time. As a result of their combined efforts, by 1920 Americans could no longer drink liquor legally and adult females were granted full voting rights for the first time in American history.

The right to vote was only one sign of important changes taking place in the social, political, and economic status of women in the 1920s. In D. W. Griffith's classic silent film, *Way Down East*, the rapidly shifting role of America's women forms the central theme, as audiences struggled to make sense of the changes. To many, both male and female, the new circumstances were unacceptable and a threat to social order, while to others the new role granted to women after World War I was long overdue and beneficial. Both attitudes may be found in *Way Down East*, and the film is therefore a valuable example of the interplay between popular culture and deeply rooted social concerns.

In 1920, fifteen percent of all Ph.D. degrees were granted to women, a proportion that began to decline in 1930 and did not turn upward until the 1970s. In the 1920s, women were working in larger numbers than ever, especially young unmarried women who found employment in the new offices and stores of the expanding American cities. Though most young women married and became mothers as before, more than ever worked prior to marriage, and when married they had smaller families, lived in smaller apartments, and spent more time shopping (i.e., consuming) than their mothers had ever done.[1]

The new industrialism begun in the late nineteenth century matured during World War I, and after 1920 its energies were turned to domestic products. Women became the primary consumers of the new household appliances, the new cosmetics, and the new fashionable clothes. Credit buying became the 1920s technique to encourage buying now and paying later. Advertising pages in the popular magazines and newspapers described the advantages of each new product and directed special attention to women. The ideal of the New Woman, first announced during the 1910s as a harbinger of a radically different type of woman, did not fulfill its promise (or fear) in the 1920s. Rather, the 1920s woman became a flapper, a worker, a college student, a wife, and a mother.

The career woman usually subordinated her career to her marriage and few women chose a career over marriage. The elite women went to college and of these few fewer still went to graduate school and entered the professions of teaching and social work. Those who combined a career with marriage did so privately and did not engage in public forums on women's rights. Indeed, the vital feminist movement of the first decade seemed dormant during the 1920s. The public's view of the New Woman was that of the daring young woman who drank and smoked in public, danced all night, and experimented with sex before marriage. The women who broke with tradition included only a small segment of the urban white upper and middle classes. The media made much of the fact that skirts went up and women's hair became stylishly short but there was little examination of the basic social roles each sex played in American society.[2]

Therefore, while American society was changing on one level, basic cultural values remained unchanged. The majority of both sexes still believed that the woman's primary adult role was as wife and mother; the majority still believed in chastity for females before marriage; and the majority still believed that God, self-sufficiency, and hard work were American virtues. Yet the social realities were challenging those beliefs. More women were receiving more education than ever before, the new city living changed the daily patterns of both sexes, and credit buying enabled Americans to purchase the new material goodies without waiting. More and more Americans began to work for large companies while still espousing a commitment to individualism and to rugged self-determination. Rural Protestant Americans who moved to the cities were faced with a heterogeneous population, made up largely of new immigrants who shared neither their values nor their religion. The decade of the 1920s was one in which social values were tested and challenged in a dramatic way in the new urban industrial America.

It is within this context that movies became a mass industry, a big business rivaling the steel, coal, and railroad businesses, by 1920. Both men and women enjoyed the new kind of entertainment, and the reasonable admission price encouraged mass attendance. There were fifteen thousand theaters showing silent movies in 1920 with another twelve hundred under construction. Hollywood had already achieved its position as the movie-making capital of the world with fully eighty percent of the world's motion pictures being made there.[3] One of the key functions of the new mass entertainment industry was to inculcate American values in the new immigrants and the only tried and true values were the old rural Protestant values of self-help, stern morality, a respect for family life, and a commitment to traditional sex roles. Ironically, many of the movie producers were immigrants themselves who accepted the old American values whole and transmitted them to the growing audiences of urban immigrants. Thus agricultural scenes were often glorified and the farmer was still upheld as the most moral of all Americans, but the new city life, replete with gangsters, was also portrayed in the movies. The new and old worlds were reconciled by assuring the preservation of traditional morality: the bad guy was punished at the end.[4]

The story lines of movies borrowed their images of heroes and heroines from popular novels and plays. Directors, writers, and producers generally accepted the stereotypes about each sex, about black Americans, and about such groups as cowboys, Indians, immigrants, gangsters, and showgirls. The movies did not become a daring medium in which new social ideas were explored or old ideas were challenged. Rather, in a continued effort to be popular and profitable, they confirmed the culture's values and assured everyone that their major purpose was escapism and entertainment, not education and uplift. Of course, there were serious artists experimenting with the new movie technology, but most often the only successful and popular experimentation was restricted to photographic effects and technical virtuosity.

One of the best experimenters with the moving picture was David Wark Griffith (1875–1948) who had been making movies since 1907. Indeed, Griffith's greatest movies, *The Birth of a Nation* (1915) and *Intolerance* (1916) were behind him as the decade of the 1920s began. His path-breaking filmic techniques were being widely imitated and applauded, and everyone looked forward to each of his new films with great anticipation. In 1919, he, Mary Pickford, Douglas Fairbanks, and Charlie Chaplin formed United Artists to distribute their independently produced films.

The 1920s did not prove to be as good to Griffith as the past decade of filmmaking had been. While he continued to be fiercely individualistic, the industry was changing rapidly into a collective business with New York bankers playing a larger role in decision making. Small studios were losing out to the larger ones, and individualists found it harder and harder to obtain the needed financing to launch a major movie project. But that future was not known to Griffith when he decided to follow up his successful 1919 *Broken Blossoms* with a popular stage play called *Way Down East*. Griffith bought the theatrical rights from author William A. Brady for a record 175,000 dollars and hired Anthony P. Kelly to write a scenario for the sum of 10,000 dollars. Before *Way Down East* went into production, therefore, it had already cost Griffith more money than *The Birth of a Nation*.[5]

Lillian Gish, Griffith's favorite star and colleague in many movies—including *The Birth of a Nation* (which brought her stardom), *Intolerance*, and *Broken Blossoms*—had been acting in the theater since childhood. She had joined Griffith's company in 1912 at the age of sixteen and was the natural choice for the lead in *Way Down East*. The Griffith-Gish association proved to be immensely successful. Always referring to her as "Miss Lillian," Griffith found her angelic fragile beauty to be a perfect expression of his view of the ideal woman: strong in adversity but essentially at the mercy of men and their selfishness. Griffith photographed Gish with an arc of light, suggesting a halo, around her face and head. Her delicate sweetness, physical slightness, and vulnerable pose made her the perfect Griffith heroine.

Lillian Gish has said, "I think the things that are necessary in my profession are these: Taste, Talent, and Tenacity. I think I have had a little of all three."[6] The evidence suggests that she had more than a little of each. Contemporary critics as well as such recent analysts as Pauline Kael have waxed eloquent about her acting ability, her style, and her magnetic power.[7] Gish's talents included a quickness in capturing the essence of a character and the ability to survive under difficult circumstances. Though she appeared fragile, she was a very tough woman who survived pernicious anemia in childhood and below-zero weather during the filming of *Way Down East*.

When given the story of *Way Down East*, Gish wondered how she was going to make the protagonist believable. "I knew that the whole story depended on my making her plausible."[8] A serious and thoughtful actress, Gish has said, "To play for the pictures is mainly a matter of the face, and of learning to think inside."[9] Since she had been working with Griffith for eight years, Gish was accustomed to Griffith's method and found that he respected her ability and judgment. Griffith described their working relationship as follows: "I give her an outline of what I hope to accomplish and let her work it out her own way. When she gets it, she has something of her own."[10] Nevertheless, Griffith frequently overrode her interpretation. For example, Griffith prevailed on a reluctant Gish to fix her hair and beautify herself for the final scene of this film despite the fact that the scene occurred after a grueling sequence on an ice float.[11]

The plot of *Way Down East* is simple enough: a poor and innocent young woman named Anna Moore (Lillian Gish) falls in love with a wealthy scoundrel named Lennox Sanderson (Lowell Sherman). To assure her complete submission in an age of strict sexual standards Sanderson convinces Anna to marry him and tricks her into a fraudulent ceremony in which his friend masquerades as minister. Anna becomes pregnant, is abandoned by Sanderson, has the baby in a strange town, loses the child, and is forced to become a domestic worker in order to survive. The farm on which Anna obtains a job is owned by Squire Bartlett (Burr McIntosh), a stern puritanical man, whose son David (Richard Barthelmess) falls in love with her. Without explaining, she tries to dissuade him from declaring his love for her as she can "never marry anyone." As fortune would have it, Sanderson's country estate adjoins the Bartlett farm; Anna and Sanderson meet; he tries to convince her to leave, fearing discovery of his rascality; Anna refuses. Eventually, the town gossip reveals the truth of Anna's past and the Squire banishes her from his house.

Before she leaves, Anna reveals that Sanderson is the culprit and he too is expelled from the Bartlett home. It is snowing outside and Anna roams in the snowstorm until she falls faint on the frozen lake. David braves the storm to find Anna in a search sequence famous for its spectacular photography and film editing. Ice floats on the lake break up and begin carrying Anna toward the rushing waterfall. David pursues her, reaches her, and carries her to safety. Squire Bartlett forgives Anna and the final scene is of the wedding of David and Anna as well as two other couples.

The verisimilitude of the snowstorm scene and of the ice floats produced a most exciting climax to a sentimental movie. Griffith had insisted upon filming the real thing and waited for an authentic Vermont storm before filming. Though the oil sometimes froze in Billy Bitzer's camera, thus slowing up production, the scene is a marvel of filmmaking. Tension is built and action is sustained throughout. Lillian Gish noted in her autobiography that her hair froze during the filming of the scene and her hand felt as if it were on flame, an obvious case of frostbite. "To this day, it aches if I am out in the cold for very long."[12] Richard Barthelmess, the young David, had been a sophomore at nearby Dartmouth College a short time before and invited his classmates to watch the filming of the scene. The subzero weather drove them indoors.

Though some critics found *Way Down East* syrupy and sentimental, the public loved both the melodrama and the exciting conclusion. The *Film Daily* declared that the film was "a splendidly treated melodrama rising to the greatest climax ever screened."[13] and contemporary critic William K. Everson has said that Gish's performance "was perhaps her very best for Griffith."[14] Commentator Iris Barry in 1940 judged *Way Down East* to have special merits, and considered Gish's performance as Anna a very convincing portrait.[15]

Griffith booked the movie into a Broadway theater and charged legitimate theater prices. This was an unusual distribution procedure for that time, but it had worked for *The Birth of a Nation*. *Way Down East* wound up playing on Broadway for a year and a half. Griffith also opened the film on a road-show basis, playing it in a small number of major theaters rather than lower-priced neighborhood houses. Despite the high cost of production the film made millions for United Artists, and eventually became Griffith's second biggest box-office success.[16]

Why the tremendous popular success of a rather standard melodrama? Surely the story line was unspectacular and though Gish and her supporting actors did a credible job, the material does not allow for great dramatic acting. Neither could the spectacular photography in the concluding moments of the ninety-minute film account for its great success. I would submit that its popular acceptance was based upon the effective way in which the predictable melodramatic material was presented. Lillian Gish became Everywoman in *Way Down East*. Popular cultural historians have always noted, with some degree of awe, the incredible success of melodrama in every form, be it novel, movie, or television. Melodrama, the exaggeration of dramatic material, sometimes in absurd ways, has always appealed to female audiences. Its plot is always based upon the domestic scene, the woman is the central character, and self-sacrifice and suffering often appear as the woman's fate. Though the particulars change over time, the essence of the abused woman always remains at the heart of melodrama. Further, the heroine is usually an ordinary woman, not unlike her female audience. Thwarted love, seduction and abandonment, or a lover's betrayal generally constitute the major plot of melodrama. Thus, women who saw *Way Down East* either as a play or a movie could respond to the self-sacrificing heroine Anna Moore.

Way Down East fits into this archetypal melodramatic pattern, though it takes on something of a nostalgic quality since it is set in a rural scene. The 1920 audience was an urban one and the heroine's fate was thus acted out in a different setting, though the possibilities for melodrama still existed. As Griffith suggested in the opening note, men are not yet monogamous, and so women continue to suffer; they have no choice. The story, we are told in a prologue, is "A Simple Story of Plain People," just like you and me, the members of the audience. Men and women enter adult relationships but the woman is always at a distinct disadvantage. She seeks marriage, the expected state for all adult women—even the flapper— but is thereby subject to male deception and promiscuity. Her fate is to suffer and to endure. The sexual double standard had not yet been completely demolished. Surely female audiences identified with this theme, knowing of personal experiences when they too had to suffer silently, compromise their wishes, and sublimate their needs to those of husband and family. Though most women's marriages were legitimate, not mock ones like Anna Moore's to Lennox Sanderson, the theme of pain and sacrifice in married life was a universal one.

Griffith introduces the segment before Anna's confinement with the screen title: "Maternity is Woman's Gethsemane." Pregnancy and motherhood become woman's unique experience, burden, and pain. It is her agony, as well as the sign to the world of immorality, if the mother is without a husband. Hawthorne's *The Scarlet Letter* (Gish played Hester Prynne in a fine version of the story a few years later) offers a literary discussion of the same theme. Griffith clearly shows his sympathy for Anna by highlighting her as an innocent victim of male sexuality. He also distinguishes between the good and bad man, David and Sanderson, so that when Sanderson tells Anna at one point that men are expected to sow their wild oats, the audience is led to believe that this is not the accepted view or behavior of all men.

Way Down East is a good melodrama in that we empathize with the innocent Anna, commiserate with her suffering, and rejoice at her final vindication. Audiences are treated to a fallen woman who is not really fallen. Her innocence has not been truly tarnished. Her purity and goodness still intact, Anna marries innocent David at the film's end. Their future will be bright and sure as they are simple and good people. The virginal Mary has not really lost her virginity; she does not descend into the role of the temptress Eve. The villain Sanderson is punished and goodness triumphs. Thus, the melodrama, filled with trials and tribulations, ends happily with the ultimate fantasy being fulfilled: goodness *does* prevail on earth and the pure do achieve happiness. Society can forgive, overlook supposed sins, and include in the fold the mistakenly rejected. Melodrama allowed women the opportunity to cry and clap, to feel sadness and happiness, and to leave the movie theater happy in the knowledge that Lillian Gish, Anna Moore, triumphed in the end.

Another theme of the movie that would be lost on future audiences but which had profound meaning in the 1920s, was the tension between country and city. In Griffith's movie, the pastoral existence of the farmer Bartletts contrasted sharply with the corrupt city life of Sanderson and Anna's city cousins. America was still close enough to its agricultural past and country life in 1920 to appreciate *Way Down East*. Though the population was quickly shifting to the city, the nation's values remained rural ones.

While the audiences of 1920 could still believe in an innocent young woman being deceived into marriage with an unscrupulous man, when *Way Down East* was reissued with a synchronized musical score and sound in 1931, *New York Times* film critic André Sennwald found that the film had lost its power "because the cards are too carefully stacked against winsome Anna Moore."[17] Audiences of 1931 were more experienced in radio and movie melodrama and had become accustomed to more sophisticated treatments of women's seduction. Sennwald reported that the audiences snickered when David valiantly searches for Anna across the ice. What had appeared as extraordinary film editing in 1920 seemed unsophisticated and contrived a decade later, a decade that had witnessed great advances in film adventure stories and melodramas.

Way Down East was remade in 1935 with Rochelle Hudson playing Anna and Henry Fonda in the David role. The *New York Times* reviewer noted a subtle shift in moral values in this version. Though the Hays office, with its censorship code, was already in effect, Mrs. Bartlett suggests to her stern husband, upon discovering Anna's plight, that "unlicensed motherhood isn't nearly the socially embarrassing thing that it was in father's day."[18] A more liberal moral code was already evident and the stern Squire Bartlett seemed an anachronism. The ice-chase scene was rendered comically in this version, thus changing the whole tone of the film. The altered thrust of *Way Down East* and the 1930s audience's reaction to both versions suggests how much the nation had changed in a decade. The simple tale of simple folk no longer appealed.[19]

Way Down East can be fit into a general iconography of women's images in film. Throughout the 1910s and into the 1920s, film audiences were exposed to two totally different feminine images: the Girl-Woman and the Bad Girl. In the first of these, the dominant image—the boyish figures of the actresses, the short haircuts, the bouncy step, the youthful pose—all accentuated the young woman as part girl and part woman, all sweet and innocent, yet already suggesting adult sexuality. This Girl-Woman had many variations; three detectable subtypes are the pure and capable young woman who through spirited activity helps to shape the world around her; the pure but helpless victim; and the pure victim who is strong and enduring.

In the first subtype, the serial films of Pearl White offered audiences a view of a spunky adventuress who wards off dangerous men, pursues assassins, and always emerges victorious. In twenty episodes of the *Perils of Pauline* as well as the very successful thirty-six episodes of *The Exploits of Elaine*, *The New Exploits of Elaine*, and *The Romance of Elaine*, Pearl White regaled her audience with exciting adventures. Between 1914 and 1922 all of these serials reached an estimated audience of fifteen million people.[20] The filmic Pearl White's virtue remained intact, but she was an active and vital person, experiencing dangers and excitements usually reserved for men.

The flapper screen roles played by Clara Bow and Joan Crawford also qualify as pure but spirited types. In *The Wild Party* (1929), Clara Bow plays a flirtatious college girl in love with her professor. She is a tease but never loses her virginity. Joan Crawford in *Our Dancing Daughters* (1928) is also a carefree, rich flapper who dances all night but remains faithful to her one true love. Both the Clara Bow and Joan Crawford characters are energetic leaders who in the movie are admired by young men and women alike. Many of the early flappers, such as Gloria Swanson and Mabel Normand, also always observed society's laws. They played their roles with warmth and humor; they were pals, companions to young men, and in love with life. It was their very combination of purity and gaiety that made them attractive to both sexes.

Mary Pickford's screen roles best epitomized the second type, the pure but passive victim. In the same year that *Way Down East* was released, Pickford appeared in *Pollyanna* as the eternal child. The

New York Times critic asked the rhetorical question: When will Mary Pickford grow up? and answered that neither she nor Peter Pan could ever grow up. "When she stops being a child on the screen," he concluded, "she'll probably just stop. But that time is a long way off."[21] Audiences loved seeing thirty-year-old Mary in her golden curls and frilly dresses stand helpless while the hero destroyed the villain. Indeed, when Pickford tried to portray mature women, audiences rejected the product and clamored for their "Mary" pictures. Pickford's fans never tired of seeing her exposed to danger until at the end she is only just saved by the hero. Mae Marsh and Blanche Sweet, two other Griffith actresses, often played the pure and passive type as well.

Lillian Gish's portrayal of Anna Moore in *Way Down East* and Hester Prynne in *The Scarlet Letter*, displayed the third variation of the type: a victim pure of heart who is also strong and enduring, the melodramatic heroine. Gish suffers at the hands of sensual men but she is ultimately resurrected because of her inherent virtue and her indomitable will. This type is more complex and exciting than the second image; it is multidimensional and suggests that women have hidden reserves that are not apparent on the surface. Anna Moore emerges as an admirable woman who transcends society's view of her; she achieves an heroic stature because of her good works. The woman as survivor, despite ill fate, is an enormously appealing image of women to women. She does not become self-pitying, spiteful, or hostile. She endures and, by so doing, using Faulkner's phrase, she prevails.

In addition to the Girl-Woman image with its subtypes, film audiences were treated to the sophisticated Bad Girl image, the classic Eve, the temptress. Swedish actress Greta Garbo, Polish actress Pola Negri, German actress Marlene Dietrich, and such Americans as Theda Bara (the renamed Theodosia Goodman of Philadelphia) and Gloria Swanson delighted audiences with their portrayals of decadent women, exotic, world-weary, sexual creatures whose lives revolved around the men in the films. Each actress, of course, created a unique interpretation of the image, some with humor and others with pathos, but all operated within the stereotypical framework of the Eve image. Audiences loved (and still love) seeing naughty foreign women lure American Adams into sin. As long as the temptress is punished at the end of the movie, often by becoming the captive mistress of her Adam,[22] the moral code and the double standard are preserved.

Thus, the American penchant for dualisms is encompassed in these two fundamental views of women: as Girl-Woman (good) or Bad Girl (bad), as Marys or Eves. First presented in all their variations to film audiences during the silent screen era, these filmic images of women have not been altered by filmmakers in the past fifty-eight years. During the 1930s, the woman careerist enjoyed great popularity with such actresses as Katharine Hepburn, Rosalind Russell, Bette Davis, and Joan Crawford playing commercial artists, writers, reporters, lawyers, and businesswomen; however, this type could easily fit into the pure but spirited category as most of these women abandoned career for marriage. Giving up adventure for conventional female roles, they also displayed the playfulness and the easy companionship with men that characterized the flapper films as well as the Pearl White adventures. An important part of both Rosalind Russell's and Katharine Hepburn's appeal to men and women was their Girl-Woman ability to be both spunky and feminine, a buddy and a mate.

In the 1950s, the pure victim image was revitalized in movies starring Doris Day and Debbie Reynolds and, a little later, Annette Funicello and Sandra Dee. The third subtype, the strong sufferer remained the essence of melodrama in the movies and, more recently, on television soap operas. *Now, Voyager* (1941), Bette Davis's quintessential tearjerker, shares many qualities with *Way Down East*, as does *Love Story* and *As the World Turns*. The settings, the specific social problems, and the particular female troubles have all changed over time in melodrama, but the themes of woman's suffering and man's dominance in determining her life have remained at its core.

As already suggested, the Eve image of woman continues to thrive; though Jane Fonda saw a psychiatrist in *Klute*, she still remained the classic whore. Despite the Katharine Hepburn and Joan Crawford roles of the 1930s, women characters who convey complex and sophisticated personalities and who do important work are still rare in American film. Independent women who are worthy of respect, and who love and are loved, are only present in the extraordinary movie, one that is long remembered for its exceptional treatment of women. Thus, the filmic images of women developed by D. W. Griffith and the other first-generation filmmakers have continued to define the basic categories for women in American movies.

NOTES

1. There are many important sources that describe the changes in life styles and values in America during the 1910s and 1920s. Among them are William E. Leuchtenberg, *The Perils of Prosperity, 1914-1932* (Chicago, 1958), Frederick Lewis Allen, *Only Yesterday* (New York, 1931), John E. Braemen *et al.*, *Change and Continuity in Twentieth Century America: The 1920s* (Columbus, Ohio, 1960), and Henry F. May, *The End of American Innocence* (New York, 1959). Books that focus on women's rights and lives are William L. O'Neill, *Everyone Was Brave: The Rise and Fall of Feminism in America* (Chicago, 1969), June Sochen, *Herstory: A Woman's View of American History* (New York, 1974) and *Movers and Shakers: American Women Thinkers and Activists, 1900-1970* (New York, 1973), and Lois W. Banner, *Women in Modern America* (New York, 1974).

2. See June Sochen, *The New Woman: Feminism in Greenwich Village, 1910-1920* (New York, 1972) and J. Stanley Lemons, *The Woman Citizen: Social Feminism in the 1920s* (Urbana, Illinois, 1973).

3. Thomas W. Bohn and Richard L. Stromgren, *Light and Shadow: A History of Motion Pictures* (Port Washington, New York, 1975), pp. 116-124.

4. There was a concerted effort afoot to assure that Hollywood films did reflect a healthy moral outlook. Local efforts at censoring the movies had caused tremors of concern in the industry for several years previous to 1920 and two years later the moguls agreed to set up a system to censor their own product, thus hoping to diffuse any efforts toward government regulation of the movie business. See Robert Sklar, *Movie-Made America* (New York, 1975) and Garth Jowett, *Film: The Democratic Art* (Boston, 1976), chapters 4-7.

5. Robert M. Henderson, *D. W. Griffith: His Life and Work* (New York, 1972), p. 215.

6. "Conversation with Lillian Gish," *Sight and Sound*, vol. 27, no. 3 (Winter 1957-1958), p. 130.

7. Quoted in David Shipman, *The Great Movie Stars: The Golden Years* (New York, 1970) pp. 245-246.

8. Lillian Gish with Ann Pinchot, *Lillian Gish: The Movies, Mr. Griffith and Me* (Englewood Cliffs, New Jersey, 1969), p. 230.

9. Romano Tozzi, "Lillian Gish," *Films in Review*, vol. 13, no. 10 (December 1962), p. 580.

10. Ibid., p. 585.

11. Gish, op. cit.

12. Ibid., p. 233.

13. Henderson, op. cit., p. 222.

14. Gish, op. cit., p. 237.

15. Henderson, op. cit., p. 223.

16. Though exact figures cannot be determined, United Artists made a substantial profit. Griffith wrote Gish in the 1940s that Douglas Fairbanks and

United Artists had ". . . robbed him of a million dollars by selling *Way Down East* with other pictures. . . ." (Gish, p. 346) The record shows that Griffith, still in control of the property in 1921, mortgaged the negative of *Way Down East* to finance some of his 1920s films, films that eventually became box-office failures (Henderson, pp. 222–223).

17. Andre Sennwald, *Way Down East, New York Times,* March 16, 1931, p. 25:1.

18. *New York Times,* October 31, 1935, p. 16:2.

19. D. W. Griffith's and Lillian Gish's careers took different turns following *Way Down East.* After *Orphans of the Storm* was made the following year, the two artists split up. Griffith's next production with Gish was running over budget and he refused to pay Gish, so she left. Gish was in great demand at the time; she was offered film contracts by many companies. Tiffany, for example, promised her 3,500 dollars a week if she would sign with them. The 1920s, as already noted, were not good years for Griffith. United Artists grew increasingly critical of his meager productions and retained ownership of many of his properties, including *Way Down East.* Griffith seemed to have lost his touch. He distributed *Orphans of the Storm* in the very same way as *Way Down East* but with dismal results. The neighborhood movie houses offered more features for less money than a high priced theater could. With the number of movies increasing every year, Griffith's techniques no longer seemed so unique or spectacular. Moreover, he did not explore new themes and, by 1925, many critics thought that his creative period had ended.

20. Anthony Slide, *Early American Cinema* (The International Film Guide Series, New York, 1970) p. 176.

21. *New York Times,* January 19, 1920, p. 16:3.

22. Dietrich in *The Blue Angel* and *Morocco* are good examples as are Garbo's portrayals in *Love, Camille,* and *Conquest.*

The Great War Viewed from the Twenties:

The Big Parade (1925)

MICHAEL T. ISENBERG

The title was a product of Laurence Stallings's romantic image of the trans-Atlantic chain of doughboys fighting in defense of liberty. Here Renee Adorée searches the ranks for her lover, John Gilbert.

(Photo courtesy of Museum of Modern Art)

The decade of the 1920s long has stood in the popular perspective as a unity, bounded by the ignoble brackets of war and economic crisis. The customary view of the period, kept alive by dozens of colorful book titles, is that the time was one of carefree hedonism and relentless materialism, in which American society unleashed the pent-up energies of the war years.[1]

The traditional vision sees the war not only as Woodrow Wilson's great crusade, but as the great watershed in modern American history. The war broadened the breakdown of the old moral code, particularly in relation to late Victorian concepts of femininity. It produced a universal social malaise that saw all gods dead, all heroes humbled, all causes exhausted. Americans responded to the Carthaginian peace of Versailles by withdrawing from world affairs and expressing a strong revulsion against war and militarism. The author of the League of Nations proposal died embittered and disowned by his own political party; Wilsonian idealism lay sacrificed on the altar of "normalcy."[2]

With the exception of the unfortunate Hoover and a few others, the decade was almost bereft of first-class political leaders at all levels. The economy, while it seemed to be booming right along, was disastrously uneven. By contrast, the nation's intellectual life flourished, particularly in areas of cultural criticism. The war produced a strong and antagonistic reaction from literature and the plastic arts. The postwar climate shaped by such authors as Ernest Hemingway, John Dos Passos, and E. E. Cummings commonly is regarded as one of disillusionment.[3]

The traditional view is clear. A fatigued society, worn from patriotic exertion and with its almost hysterical idealism shattered, turned away from progressive reform and ran the gamut of self-indulgence. Only with the convulsive shock of the stock market crash and the sickening slide into economic depression did Americans begin to pay for their excesses.

Yet this traditional view of the war-spawned 1920s is drawn largely from the evidence provided by cultural elites dissatisfied with their society. The war itself was at least as much an accelerator as it was a cause of the postwar mood of dissatisfaction and rebellion.[4] Although many Americans doubtless took part in the war-induced climate of cynicism, historians have tended to overlook the continuities of the period. The flaming passions of the jazz age probably held more smoke than fire, for family and church life continued as the hub of social activity for millions. The progressive reform impulse still flickered; Robert La Follette was able to mount a strong third party movement on its base in 1924, and watchdogs like George Norris kept progressivism alive in Congress. Some old progressives were still around to praise the New Deal, although many became as intensely displeased with the second Roosevelt as they had been enchanted with the first.[5]

Especially overlooked has been the fact that in the minds of many Americans the war experience persisted as a legitimate theater for heroism and the display of national idealism. To be sure, this attitude was at a high pitch between 1917 and 1919, when government, organs of public opinion, motion pictures, and popular literature allowed almost no dissent from total and uncompromising support of the war effort.[6] But the public in the years following the war was probably as supportive of this alternative vision as of the pessimistic view that is historically far better known. With the nation in a conservative mood, the sacrifices of wartime met with approbation as well as disapproval. Veteran's organizations hawked their brand of patriotism. The Veterans of Foreign Wars, founded in 1899, gained new life and new blood from World War I, while AEF veterans developed the American Legion in 1919. These organizations had fond memories of the "Great War" and were assiduous in the cultivation of "Americanism" in textbooks and teachers.[7]

While it is fair to say that most of the elitist literature and art was intensely critical of the war and of America's role in it, newspapers, popular magazines, cheap books, and motion pictures did not advance beyond the common sentimentality of daring heroism and noble sacrifice. This was particularly true of the motion picture industry, a young and growing business giant which during the decade advanced to the forefront of popular culture.[8] Americans became habitual moviegoers during these years when the silent film reached its artistic and financial peak. What once had been an inexpensive source of amusement for lower-class urban workers had blossomed into a major recreation for persons of every social and geographic background.

The evidence of the commercial film is useful because of its appeal to a mass audience. Common themes in films often reflect the fears, desires, ideas, attitudes, or beliefs of the mass audience to which they play. Producers depend on this relationship, for profit is maximized in the dead center of audience desires. Such evidence is indirect, but it must be noted that traditional forms of evidence are also indirect in this regard. Historians using novels, memoirs, and other literary productions often make assumptions of effect when they have no audience analysis upon which to depend. The difference between using film and literature as historical evidence is one of degree, not of quality. If anything, film evidence may be more useful because of its wider audience. The American literary public for a Hemingway numbered in the thousands; the movie public for a Chaplin was in the millions.[9]

The motion picture industry generally had done well during the war years. Moviemakers dutifully had cranked out hundreds of one- and two-reel features with war plots, most of which had brought an average return of a few thousand dollars. Many of these films were of the trite heroic genre, although some moved far enough into the fantastic to be remembered today as examples of the extremism of the home front at war. *The Kaiser, The Beast of Berlin* (1918) might be regarded as the quintessence of the latter type. But with the armistice, the hate pictures quickly became ludicrous. All war pictures by November 1918 were falling off as profit makers. Caught with titles like *Red, White and Blue Blood* and *Break the News to Mother*, industry "flacks" hastened to assure distributors that these were not war stories. Movie pioneer Fred J. Balshofer remembered that on Armistice Day he completed final cutting on a "six-reel all-out anti-Kaiser picture." The market was dead, and he lost eighty thousand dollars.[10]

The immediate postwar climate continued to treat the war film as a pariah. Very few pictures with a world war background were made between 1919 and 1925. Almost all sank at the box office. The one major exception, Metro's *Four Horsemen of the Apocalypse* (1921), succeeded largely on the strength of its exciting new leading man— Rudolph Valentino. In general, the industry rode the crest of the broadening wave of materialism, sexual freedom, and sensation.

Riding this crest with everyone else was a young director named King Vidor.[11] Vidor was born in Galveston in 1894, the descendant of a Hungarian grandfather who had emigrated to Texas at the close of the Civil War. By 1918, already a veteran maker of amateur newsreels, he had moved to Hollywood, the new golden land in which the motion picture industry had firmly seated itself during the second decade of the century.

In 1918 and 1919, Vidor did a series of feature films for the Brentwood Corporation, a group of doctors and dentists seeking profits in foreign fields. After a short stint with First National, he formed "Vidor Village," his own independent production company. As was common in those days, he inserted his "Creed and Pledge" in *Variety* in 1920. It was couched in the purplish prose and hyper-idealism of a young man, and an inevitable recession from its extremes soon occurred. But throughout his life Vidor remained committed to film as an art and as a noble device of human expression.

I believe in the picture that will help humanity to free itself from the shackles of fear and suffering that have so long bound it with iron chains.[12]

In 1922 "Vidor Village" folded, and the young entrepreneur moved to the Metro lot. He then worked in "artistically respectable" productions for Louis B. Mayer, going as a staff director with Mayer to the newly formed Metro-Goldwyn-Mayer Studios in 1924.[13] By the age of thirty, Vidor had put a world of moviemaking experience behind him, a background not uncommon in an industry which was still congealing its organizational and bureaucratic patterns. Mayer regarded him as a reliable director of marketable films, and Vidor was entrusted with directing some of MGM's best talent, such as John Gilbert in *His Hour* (1924) and *Wife of the Centaur* (1925).

Irving Thalberg, Mayer's chief of production, was even younger than Vidor, having been born in modest middle-class comfort in Brooklyn in 1899.[14] His father was a lace importer, but Thalberg broke away early from the world of trade and by 1919 was on the coast working for Carl Laemmle in the Universal Studios. For four years he learned about motion pictures from the front office. In February 1923 he amicably left Laemmle to join Mayer. The relationship worked out by the two men, which carried MGM to the leadership of the industry in less than a decade, was for Thalberg to concern himself with the production end and for Mayer to serve as administrator and link to the home office in New York.

Thus Thalberg was the man the restless Vidor approached late in

1924 with an idea for a film which would tackle an important question. As a child of the Progressive Era, Vidor was concerned with the potential of a film on one of three major problem topics: war, wheat, or steel. Thalberg asked if he had a particular subject in mind; Vidor replied vaguely that his story should be about an average young American, neither patriot nor pacifist, caught up in war. Nothing was on paper, and the two men agreed to search for a good story centered on World War I.[15] Both knew of the chilly box-office reception of war stories, yet each felt that a fresh and innovative treatment would find its audience. Thalberg, with production control, was the key to script approval.

Weeks later, Thalberg returned from a trip to New York accompanied by a writer named Laurence Stallings and a story, tentatively titled "The Big Parade," typed on five pages of onionskin paper. Unlike Thalberg or Vidor (who was his exact age), Stallings was an AEF veteran. As a Marine captain, he had lost his right leg in Belleau Wood. When Thalberg met him, the young veteran and Maxwell Anderson had one of the hottest plays of the 1924 season, *What Price Glory?*, running on Broadway.

The ex-marine had recently completed a semiautobiographical novel, *Plumes* (1924),[16] about the painful rehabilitation of a wounded war veteran. Overwritten and consciously tendentious, *Plumes* was a weaker version of the postwar climate of disillusion more artfully limned by such writers as Hemingway and Dos Passos. For Stallings, the sound of the trumpets persisted among the carnage. Despite a shattered leg, his hero, Richard Plume, remained a patriot, albeit a troubled one.`

Until his death in 1968 Stallings retained the love-hate relationship for the war that is so evident in *What Price Glory?* and much of his later work. The memory of his doughboy comrades was constantly with him. "Why write of them at this hour?," he asked rhetorically in 1963. "Why open the door of a room sealed off in my mind for so many years?" In fact the door was never sealed; the stump of his right leg was a daily reminder. "I have my Idaho willow foot to remind me now." As in many aging veterans, romanticism battled horror for memory's hand and won. Stallings claimed in his final testament concerning the earth-shaking adventures of his young manhood that he wrote about the doughboy "conscious of being unable to summon him back in entirety, and heartsick of enduring the melancholy of trying to recover long-buried remembrances of the past. . . ."[17]

In 1924 Stallings's memory of the war was fresh and unencumbered by time. The theatrical realism of his brawling, cursing marines in *What Price Glory?* brought him to Thalberg's attention. The five pages were loosely based on *Plumes*, but what evolved bore little resemblance to the original. While *Plumes* was concerned with a veteran's postwar struggles, the onionskin treatment dealt mostly with the war itself. Both Thalberg and Vidor felt they had their story. Vidor and writer Harry Behn traveled back to New York with Stallings, stayed a week, and returned with the completed script of *The Big Parade*. The title was a product of Stallings's romantic image of the trans-Atlantic chain of doughboys fighting in defense of liberty.[18]

Casting the film presented little problem, since MGM had a growing roster of contract actors from which to choose. Robert Sherwood, one of Stallings's friends at the celebrated Algonquin Round Table, would later claim that Stallings was allowed to select the director and the leads. While Vidor and Thalberg were young, they were not inexperienced in the industry. This was Stallings's maiden voyage in the hazardous seas of film creation, and it is most unlikely that the casting process ever had his veto.[19]

The male lead of the average American boy was cast against type. Thalberg, with Vidor's concurrence, selected John Gilbert, although Vidor supposedly had had difficulties with the actor on the set of *Wife of the Centaur*. Thalberg convinced Vidor that Gilbert, shorn of his mustache, would fit the role of Jim Apperson nicely. The actor had developed a sophisticated, romantic acting style which began to attract public notice after Thalberg offered him a five-year contract with MGM.[20]

The female lead, that of a French peasant girl, went to an unknown with the improbable name of Renee Adorée. The roles of Apperson's two doughboy buddies were filled by raw-boned Karl Dane, who had just stepped up from a job as studio carpenter, and Tom O'Brien, a stocky "Irish" actor.[21]

The story line, a collaboration of Stallings, Vidor, Behn, and perhaps Thalberg, was often modified slightly during shooting by

Vidor, a common practice in the silent film era. What emerged was a tale hackneyed by today's standards, but fresh and engaging to the audiences of 1925.

As the film opens, the three principal characters are seen in their civilian occupations: Slim (Dane) at work as a steelworker on a skyscraper; Bull, or Mike O'Hara (O'Brien), as a bartender; and James Apperson (Gilbert) as a rich wastrel—a departure from Vidor's notion of an average young American. Apperson is persuaded by his sight of a recruit parade to enlist, leaping from his luxury car to join the marching men.

A montage sequence follows the conversion of raw recruits into doughboys, tracing the developing friendship of the central trio. The unit is sent to France, billeted in a small village, and shortly begins to mingle with the local population. Apperson meets a pretty girl, Melisande (Adorée) in the first of a series of light romantic scenes. Rash youth that he is, Apperson's first attempt to kiss her meets with a slap in the face.

The budding romance is postponed by the movement of Apperson's unit to the front, a melee of scurrying soldiers, careening trucks, and hurried goodbyes. The sequence includes one of the most famous separation scenes in cinema, in which Melisande has to be pried apart from her lover by a sergeant. Distraught, she clings to Apperson's leg, then to a chain dangling from the rear of his truck transport, finally collapsing in the dust of the road. Apperson throws her his dog tags, watch, and an extra boot as a rememberance. The fade out is on the peasant girl clutching the precious boot and gazing toward the front.

The battle sequences follow, most prominently a tense march through woods heavy with impending death. Slim ventures into no-man's-land and is killed. The enraged Apperson engages in hand-to-hand combat, but holding a bayonet to a German soldier's throat, he cannot kill him. Instead, he lights a cigarette for the German, who then dies of other wounds. Apperson takes the cigarette and calmly smokes it himself.

A parade of trucks returning from the front disgorges Apperson, minus a leg (like Stallings). The village has been evacuated, and Melisande is nowhere to be found. Apperson is repatriated to America, where his family is shocked by his appearance and his brother is courting his fickle fiancée. Nothing is left but a postwar return to France; he and Melisande are reunited in an open field as the film ends.[22]

Location shooting was rare under the studio system, and the adventures of Apperson and his buddies were mostly recreated on back lots. Many of the sets had an authentic air, a tribute to the talents of an artist named Warren Newcombe. Many of the bombed upper stories of French farmhouses and the top of a cathedral used as a field hospital were expertly painted by Newcombe to match the action taking place in the lower half of the camera frame.

The technical skill behind the picture is not readily apparent today, because the film is usually seen without the original orchestration. The most admired aesthetic aspect was the welding of visual imagery to music. As a young man, Vidor had shot footage of Army maneuvers in Texas; some of these compositions helped him order the crowd shots of *The Big Parade*. In preparation for filming, the director screened almost a hundred reels of Signal Corps war footage. In the process, he was struck by the rhythmic cadence of the soldier images in combat—"the whole pattern spelled death." For the sequence of the doughboys advancing through the woods, filmed in Los Angeles's Griffith Park, Vidor used a metronome for pacing and had a bass drum keep the beat for the actors. In theaters, the orchestra stopped playing during this sequence and only a muffled bass drum kept cadence with the warily advancing soldiers on the screen, a highly evocative suspense mechanism.[23]

Vidor and his assistants also created distinctive orchestral rhythms for the love scenes and the hurly-burly of the movement to the front. Most of the war footage was shot for the film, adhering rigidly to Vidor's visual conceptions gleaned from the Signal Corps material. The director sent an assistant down to Fort Sam Houston to get shots of trucks, planes, and men all moving in a straight line (the "big parade" to the front). While army personnel were most cooperative, they convinced the assistant that the actual conditions on the western front had not encouraged such geometry. Vidor was aware of this, but the convolutions in the resulting footage did not match his vision. Everything was reshot. Thus realism and aesthetic considerations were interwoven, although some of the scenes of trucks moving at night look like model work. The director also at times kept his camera running through three and four hundred feet of film without a cut. This was a considerable innovation at the time, since longer scenes were the later creation of the wider use of synchronized sound and of what Vidor called "panning and perambulating cameras."[24]

During the shooting, Thalberg had looked at the rushes and decided to promote the film into a big feature. Originally, the picture had been intended as a standard production, budgeted at $205,000. An exhibitor named J. J. McCarthy, whose release of *Ben-Hur* shortly gave MGM another box-office hit, viewed the finished print and offered to promote it if more battle scenes and romance were added. Under pressure, Vidor added the weak Apperson family sequences toward the end and created the subplot with Apperson's fiancée. Since Vidor was already involved with his next project, *La Bohème*, director George Hill filmed additional night battle scenes at a cost of $40,000. This tinkering did not enhance the film, but it gave rise to the legend that Thalberg overhauled *The Big Parade* to make it a major release. Vidor later claimed only about seventy feet of additional combat footage got into the final print.[25] Certainly the film is strongest in its recreation of combat and in the romantic bits Vidor dreamed up for Apperson and Melisande. The next-to-closing sequences are conventional domestic soap opera.

With the studio firmly behind the picture, its New York release was heavily promoted. Vidor arrived in the city with a print of 12,800 feet. This running time was a bit too long for the distributor, who claimed commuters in the audience would be put off their schedules by such length. The director was requested to pare 800 feet from his creation. Vidor was naturally averse to letting an editor hack away at the footage, so he took the print back to the coast with him. Each night, after a day with *La Bohème*, Vidor snipped three frames from the beginning and end of each scene, making a loss of six frames at every splice. Upon completion of this labor, he found himself still 165 feet short of the desired length. So he pruned one additional frame on each side of all splices. The total eliminated then came to exactly 800 feet. The whole process would have been impossible with a sound film.[26]

The orchestral scores were written in New York City after the distributors received the truncated version. A full orchestra was in the pit at the Astor Theater, but Vidor's idea of the single bass drum accentuating the foreboding walk into the forest was not used until the film opened at Grauman's Egyptian Theater in Hollywood.[27]

The Big Parade was a money-maker from the beginning. At the Astor alone, the picture took in one and one half million dollars during a ninety-six-week run. By 1930 it had grossed over fifteen million dollars nationwide. In 1931 it was rereleased with a musical score to capitalize on the new sound technology. The final gross was in the neighborhood of twenty million dollars.[28] Vidor personally reaped little of this bonanza. Originally he had owned twenty percent interest in the film, but his own lawyer convinced him that a fixed directorial fee was safer than a box-office percentage. Later in life he sourly remarked, "I thus spared myself from becoming a millionaire instead of a struggling young director trying to do something interesting and better with a camera."[29]

Critics nationwide generally applauded the picture, which played well in urban and rural areas alike. Both Stallings and Vidor burned with the desire to show war realistically, and this realism was the most common point of admiration among the critics. Gilbert Seldes thought the war scenes were magnificent. Stallings's friend Robert Sherwood was amazed that the war scenes actually resembled war,[30] while another admirer expostulated that "in every sense of the word, *it is the war!*"[31] Military organizations also favored the film's vision; the fact that Vidor had used AEF veterans as technical advisors had been widely publicized.

The favorable critical reception reflected several themes infusing *The Big Parade* that were also congenial to Americans. The war was perceived not only as democracy's war, in a righteous sense, but also as an intrinsic leveler of class pretensions. Apperson quickly fuses interests with the steelworker and the bartender; in avenging Slim he is mourning a friend. His romance with the peasant girl furthers the democratization process, and his rejection of his former way of life assures a simpler, unostentatious existence.

The combat sequences did not part substantially from heroic, adventurous patterns. Several critics mistakenly praised the film as antiwar because of the shell-hole incident in which Apperson balks at killing. But Apperson, Bull, and Slim do their share. A publicity still for the picture had the primitive steelworker simultaneously bayoneting one German and decking another with his free hand. Virtually all of the war films of the era preached the litany of commitment-duty-heroism-sacrifice, and *The Big Parade* made no innovations in this regard. The heroics are individualized by dramatic convention. Apperson's war is an intensely personal one: "I came to fight—not to wait and rot in a lousy hole while they murder my pal."[32] His sacrifice (which is double—in friendship and with his own body) is rewarded in the fade out.

In this context, *The Big Parade* offered a most admiring view of the American soldier and his war efforts. The doughboy is a committed civilian who, when aroused, becomes a dominant warrior, only to yearn for the blessings of peace. Here Vidor's humanitarianism, which infused the film, was unable to overshadow the ambiguities of Stallings's relationship to the war. Stallings and most of his comrades could never finally admit the possibility that the whole thing had been unnecessary, meaningless, disastrous. This would have made the loss of life and limb unbearable as well as tragic. So the war became a legitimate theater for the heroics of the democratic fighting man, the New World Cincinnatus.

The general critical tone indicated that the audience response was appreciation of an epic entertainment which was grounded in human emotion. While no one wanted to applaud the fact of the war itself, *The Big Parade* did not indict American war aims or practices nor those of any of the Allies. This statement by an industry reviewer unintentionally keyed the significant qualities of the picture:

> It is the first production that I have ever seen that has caught *the spirit of national pride* that makes the United States Army the greatest fighting organization on earth—that subtle yearning to acquit themselves *honorably* in doing *that which the situation demands*, that brings heroes out of the slums and the mansions of wealth alike.[33]

The themes of nationalism, honor, duty, and heroism are all common to the war adventure genre. Plots threaded with them cannot make a coherent antiwar or pacifist statement, since the focus of such themes is individualistic rather than situational. When another member of the Algonquin Round Table, Alexander Woollcott, viewed *The Big Parade*, he observed among his neighbors in the theater pity for dying doughboys and satisfaction in scenes of German deaths.[34] The individualism of the film is sketched in the positive attributes of friendship and democratic solidarity. Transferred to the emotional level of the viewer, these became the admirable qualities of loyalty, devotion, and dedication to service. Here patriotic impulse overcame the horrors of war, not vice versa.

The mass audience that saw the film probably was unaware of the ambiguities actually underlying the plot. *The Big Parade*'s patina of realism was deemed to be significant comment in itself. Also, many in the audience doubtless shared these ambiguities without any intellectual tensions whatsoever. Thus "war" could be applauded and excoriated at the same time. Thalberg in particular was convinced that his production marked a significant departure from earlier war films:

> The only difference between it and the other war pictures was the different viewpoint taken in the picture. We took a boy whose idea in entering the war was not patriotic. He was swept along by the war spirit around him and entered it but didn't like it. He met a French girl who was intriguing to him, but he wasn't really serious about her. The only time he was interested in fighting was when a friend, who was close to him, was killed. It was human appeal rather than patriotic appeal, and when he reached the German trenches and came face to face with the opportunity to kill, he couldn't do it. In other words, a new thought regarding the war was in the minds of most people, and that was the basis of its appeal. . . .[35]

The producer offered a virtually complete list of mistaken reasons. The basic appeal of *The Big Parade* was adventure and romance. None of its ingredients was new, only packaged differently. The theme of war as a democratic leveler stretched back in movie time at least to Thomas Ince's *Civilization* (1915). Rich boys democraticized by war had been prominent in such earlier films as Edison's *The Unbeliever* (1918) and McManus's *The Lost Battalion* (1919). Apperson reached romantic fulfillment with Melisande at war's end, in spite of being "not really serious about her." Finally, it is difficult to reconcile the audience partisanship observed by Woollcott and applauded by many reviewers with a "human" rather than a patriotic appeal.

The Big Parade was flawed as an antiwar statement by the very individualism Thalberg regarded as its primary virtue. Years later Budd Schulberg would for this reason succinctly call the film "second-rate perfection." While in Gilbert Seldes's terms Vidor gave American audiences the "spectacle of the war," he gave little else.[36] As long as individuals stood apart from the mass and were made *special* through devices of romance or action, the cinema could never come to grips with the nature of twentieth-century warfare.

The protagonists of *The Big Parade* did not lay down their arms and refuse to fight, nor were they left numbed by the potential nihilism of their situation. They dwelt in a rational, if horrible, condition and responded to it in a necessary and rational way. *The Big Parade* was thus a prisoner of dramatic convention and, judging from its reception, so was its audience.

Although English and French viewers naturally tended to resent the film on chauvinistic grounds,[37] its real difficulty lay in a fundamental misapprehension of the war itself. If international combat is conventionally seen as a process with winners and losers, the screen in the 1920s transmuted these into heroes and villains. *The Big Parade* marched in an intellectual arena heavily populated with the ghosts of nineteenth-century romanticism and the American cult of the individual. Here it tapped one of the deepest veins in the national character, and herein lay its success—not in any new conception of the war, for it had none. "No film dare show what [war] resembled," wrote critic Iris Barry. *The Big Parade* "wreathes machine-guns in roses."[38]

Vidor himself later admitted that his love for documentary realism had been dominated by conventional screen action and romance. He saw the picture as late as 1974: "I don't like it much . . . Today I don't encourage people to see the film. At the time I really believed it was an anti-war movie." Even the director conceded that the basic appeal of the film was not the "parade" of masses of young men toward the maelstrom of death, but the romantic bits developed for Apperson and Melisande.[39]

What remains is nevertheless an exceptional piece of screen storytelling. By the standards of its day, *The Big Parade*'s battle scenes were realistic. A few critics derided the forest sequence as militarily inaccurate, but Vidor claimed to have received a letter from the War Department praising precisely these scenes.[40] The basic merit of the film was in Vidor's ability to maintain the action without interrupting overmuch with titles; in this sense the picture is a choice example of mimetic art.

MGM's box-office success inevitably keyed a war-adventure film cycle throughout the industry. The cycle lasted for five years—at least through the release of Howard Hughes's *Hell's Angels* (1930). *What Price Glory?* and its brawling marines appeared in 1926, and William Wellman's aviation epic *Wings* the next year; both spawned dozens of imitators. Vidor's original plot contributions became stale through reiteration, until Gilbert Seldes finally threw up his hands in surrender: "In all American films since *The Big Parade*, if a regiment is marching away, or a thousand trucks roll by, the hero or heroine staggers through the lines, fighting off the men in the trucks, trying to make his or her way to the beloved and departing one."[41] Not until Universal gambled with a screen adaptation of Erich Maria Remarque's novel *All Quiet on the Western Front* in 1930 did the American public see an American film truly antiwar in intent and execution. Even then, films depicting war as a worthy arena for heroic adventure and romance were not extinguished. The genre survived to fuel the build-up to a new and greater war.

Stallings stayed with motion pictures, working as an editor of Fox Movie-Tone Newsreels and turning out journeyman film scripts, several for Vidor. Stallings's documentary film, *The First World War* (1934), was his harshest statement on the experience, but his bittersweet written history, *The Doughboys*, retained the essential ambiguities first developed in *Plumes, The Big Parade,* and *What Price Glory?* Thalberg continued his record of high-quality film production until his untimely death from lobar pneumonia in 1936. John Gilbert's career faded in the late 1920s. His deterioration and early death, which also occurred in 1936, comprise a case history often cited as a classic example of the decline and fall of a star.

Vidor went on to become, by any standards, one of the finest directors in Hollywood history. He tackled a wide variety of projects, from socialist symbolism (*Our Daily Bread,* 1934) to Western epic (*Duel in the Sun,* 1946), before finally closing the books with the routine biblical tale of *Solomon and Sheba* (1959). His original concerns—humanistic, idealistic, freighted with optimism—remained remarkably consistent throughout a career that spanned five decades.

Vidor, Stallings, and Thalberg, all of them thirty or under at the time, bear the essential creative responsibility for *The Big Parade*. The realistic vision of the war is that of Stallings; the aesthetic vision belongs to Vidor. Put another way, the picture was largely a story by Stallings, one which he felt intensely—but the storyteller was Vidor. Their product is symbolic of an American view of the great crusade as seen from the 1920s, a vision alternate from the traditional consensus.

Historian Otis L. Graham, Jr., in a succinct study of continuity and discontinuity in the Progressive reform impulse, has recently restated the traditional view. World War I was "the stimulus to private indulgence and social irresponsibility." To Graham and many others, the war caused the spirit of reaction so evident in many of the social conflicts of the decade.[42] This spirit suffused the debates over fundamentalism, rekindled nativist sentiment, and heightened the tension between urban and rural sectors of American life. Reaction, like almost all American social trends, had no distinctive class basis. Thus films like *The Big Parade* cannot be analyzed as mouthpieces of social thought, either from the left or the right.

Instead, *The Big Parade* is an indicator of a broad, classless climate of opinion, circa 1925, concerning the nature of the Great War. "Consensus" is too strong a word, implying as it does a reasoned decision based on choice.[43] Evidence from films such as this resolves a seeming paradox concerning the historical analysis of the 1920s, which may be stated: How can a decade usually classed as reactionary or conservative also be seen as one of intense antiwar sentiment? To be sure, conservatism and militarism do not always fit snugly, but the instinct for tradition and order implicit in the former camp usually finds a welcome home in the latter. There is sketchy evidence, for example, the empty pacifist idealism of the Kellogg-Briand Pact (1928), to indicate that hostility toward war could encompass reformers and conservatives alike. But such evidence is sparse and does not drive a lasting wedge between conservatism and militarism as patterns of thought and behavior.

The paradox vanishes when the elitist basis of traditional 1920s historiography is recognized. Our evidence of the antiwar and antimilitarist condition of the period is drawn largely from professional cultural critics: novelists, journalists, artists, and others whose business it is to criticize. This is hard evidence and convincing in its sphere; the mistake lies not in accepting it but in allowing this material to dominate the historiography of the decade.

The Big Parade, touching as it did a far wider audience than anything produced by cultural elites in the 1920s, departs from the common view. Its alternate vision, of course, does not stand alone— but neither should that of the antiwar elites. The foggy differentiation between art and entertainment, or high culture and popular culture, should not separate us from the fact that in relying on film evidence to test the nature of American thought concerning the war, we are using precisely the same method as historians utilizing written materials. Only the nature of the evidence is different.[44]

The popularity of the war adventure film of the 1920s strongly indicates that a considerable number of Americans retained an ambiguous relationship to the war experience. For many, the image of war persisted as that of a legitimate theater for heroism and nationalistic endeavor. America had confronted Europe with ancient European wrongs; having righted them on the battlefield (the patricentrism that enraged the English and French audiences of *The Big Parade*), the young giant of the West rejected involvement in the corrupt diplomacy of a decadent continent. Thus the feelings of frustration and disillusion strengthened the climate of isolation, which was indeed strong throughout the interwar period.

But isolationism is not antimilitarism. Intellectual elites might inveigh against the sword, but the qualities of patriotism, service, and social hierarchy implicit in a uniform remained positively symbolic of the essence of national idealism for many Americans. In this sense, the war was perceived as an unwelcome task that had to be done. The passionate excesses of the war years had dampened even before Wilson's debilitating stroke, but the conviction that the war was *necessary* survived in many quarters. The tragedy was thus not only one of lives destroyed and bodies shattered, but also of a task completed with an imperfect ending. Here there was no nation to forge, no sundered union to reunite, no defeated Mexicans or Spaniards waiting to drop vast acreages into the lap of Uncle Sam.

It had been a war fought, in the last analysis, for ideals of the highest order. Human imperfection can suffer this strain so long and no longer, and the resulting disillusionment is compounded by the strength of the original moral fervor. The motion picture theater, however, is the house of dreams. Here ideals may not only achieve perfection, but may endure in screen time forever. The steadily unwinding spools of celluloid may simultaneously reduce a world war to romance and enshrine it as a fit pantheon for heroes. American filmmakers were only beginning to learn the language of tortured ambiguity, and their audiences remained largely unreceptive to this language when it spoke of war.

So Vidor and the others failed, in a sense, to make their antiwar statement. Like all of us, they were culture-bound, working in a medium that relied on broad cultural acceptance for its livelihood. *The Big Parade* inspired no marches to the recruiting station, but neither did the film indict the war itself. An era rich in contradictions blandly ignored one of the most profound contradictions of all: the reconciliation of militancy and pacifism under the symbolic blanket of democratic idealism.

NOTES

1. See in this regard Frederick Lewis Allen, *Only Yesterday: An Informal History of the 1920s* (New York, 1931); Mark Sullivan, *Our Times*, Vol. VI (New York, 1935); Preston Slosson, *The Great Crusade and After, 1914–1928* (New York, 1930). Two excellent general studies of the period are John D. Hicks, *Republican Ascendancy, 1921–1933* (New York, 1960), and William E. Leuchtenburg, *The Perils of Prosperity, 1914–1932* (Chicago, 1958). A shorter, more feisty approach is that of Paul A. Carter, *The Twenties in America* (2nd ed.) (New York, 1975). Attempts to unify the 1920s under colorful conceptualizations include Lawrence Greene, *The Era of Wonderful Nonsense* (Indianapolis, 1939); Isabel Leighton, ed., *The Aspirin Age* (New York, 1949); James Prothro, *Dollar Decade: Business Ideas in the 1920s* (Baton Rouge, 1954); Charles Merz, *The Dry Decade* (New York, 1930); Robert Sklar, ed., *The Plastic Age, 1917–1930* (New York, 1970).

2. George E. Mowry, *The Urban Nation, 1920–1960* (New York, 1965), pp. 24–25, 35, 130–32.

3. For material on 1920s political life, see Robert K. Murray, *The Harding Era: Warren G. Harding and His Administration* (Minneapolis, 1969); William Allen White, *A Puritan in Babylon: The Story of Calvin Coolidge* (New York, 1938); Joan Hoff Wilson, *Herbert Hoover: Forgotten Progressive* (Boston, 1975). For economic insight, George Soule, *Prosperity Decade: From War to Depression, 1917–1929* (New York, 1947) is excellent. Cultural trends are treated in Frederick J. Hoffman, *The 20s: American Writing in the Postwar Decade* (rev. ed.) (New York, 1965) and Harold E. Stearns, ed., *Civilization in the United States: An Inquiry by Thirty Americans* (New York, 1922). For varying interpretations concerning intellectual life, see Roderick Nash, *The Nervous Generation: American Thought, 1917–1941* (Englewood Cliffs, N.J., 1972); Robert H. Elias, *Entangling Alliances With None: An Essay on the Individual in the American Twenties* (New York, 1973). A perceptive contemporary assessment, clouded by pessimism, is that of Joseph Wood Krutch, *The Modern Temper: A Study and a Confession* (New York, 1929).

4. For evidence on this point, see Henry F. May, *The End of American Innocence: A Study of the First Years of Our Own Time, 1912–1917* (New York, 1959).

5. See in particular Clarke A. Chambers, *Seedtime of Reform: American Social Service and Social Action, 1918–1933* (Minneapolis, 1963) and Otis L. Graham, Jr., *An Encore for Reform: The Old Progressives and the New Deal* (New York, 1967).

6. For motion pictures in this regard, see Michael T. Isenberg, *War on Film: The American Cinema and World War I, 1914–1941* (Cranbury, N.J., forthcoming); for popular literature, Charles V. Genthe, *American War Narratives, 1917–1918: A Study and Bibliography* (New York, 1969).

7. Rowland Berthoff, *An Unsettled People: Social Order and Disorder in American History* (New York, 1971), pp. 440, 446.

8. General histories of American film include the still valuable work of Lewis Jacobs, *The Rise of the American Film: A Critical History* (New York, 1968) (Original edition, 1939); Robert Sklar, *Movie-Made America: A Cultural History of American Movies* (New York, 1975); and Garth Jowett, *Film, the Democratic Art: A Social History of American Film* (Boston, 1976). There is no competent history of film in the 1920s, although the final chapters of Terry Ramsaye, *A Million and One Nights: A History of the Motion Picture* (New York, 1926) are still useful. David Robinson, *Hollywood in the Twenties* (New York, 1968) is a sketchy overview. Many excellent insights on the period may be gleaned from Kevin Brownlow, *The Parade's Gone By . . .* (New York, 1968), and Edward Wagenknecht, *The Movies in the Age of Innocence* (Norman, Okla., 1962).

9. This is not to argue that historical impact is measured in numbers alone. The reasons for the mistrust of film evidence by the historical profession are analyzed in Michael T. Isenberg, "A Relationship of Constrained Anxiety: Historians and Film," *The History Teacher*, vol. 6, no. 4 (August, 1973), pp. 553–68.

10. Fred J. Balshofer and Arthur C. Miller, *One Reel a Week* (Berkeley, 1967), p. 139.

11. The best material on Vidor is still his autobiography, *A Tree Is a Tree* (New York, 1953). See also King Vidor, *King Vidor on Film Making* (New York, 1972), and John Baxter, *King Vidor* (New York, 1976). A briefer and highly aesthetic appreciation of Vidor's work is Raymond Durgnat, "King Vidor," *Film Comment*, vol. 9, no. 4 (July-August, 1973), pp. 10–49 and no. 5 (September-October, 1973), pp. 16–51. A bibliography of Vidor, largely of light articles, may be found in Mel Schuster, *Motion Picture Directors: A Bibliography of Magazine and Periodical Articles, 1900–1972* (Metuchen, N.J., 1973), pp. 375–77.

12. Vidor's "Creed and Pledge" is reproduced in Baxter, *King Vidor*, p. 10.

13. A readable history of the Metro-Goldwyn-Mayer Studios is Bosley Crowther, *The Lion's Share: The Story of an Entertainment Empire* (New York, 1957). The creation is described on pp. 79–81. For Mayer, see Bosley Crowther, *Hollywood Rajah: The Life and Times of Louis B. Mayer* (New York, 1960); for Marcus Loew, see Robert Sobel, *The Entrepreneurs: Explorations Within the American Business Tradition* (New York, 1974), pp. 247–88.

14. Bob Thomas, *Thalberg: Life and Legend* (Garden City, N.Y., 1969), is a fair biography. A shorter sketch of Thalberg's background is in Crowther, *The Lion's Share*, pp. 74–90.

15. Vidor, *A Tree Is a Tree*, pp. 111–12.

16. Laurence Stallings, *Plumes* (New York, 1924).

17. Laurence Stallings, *The Doughboys: The Story of the AEF, 1917–1918* (New York, 1963), pp. 1, 6–7. For the play *What Price Glory?*, see Maxwell Anderson and Laurence Stallings, *Three American Plays* (New York, 1926), pp. 5–89.

18. Vidor, *A Tree Is a Tree*, pp. 113–14; Stallings, *The Doughboys*, p. 7.

19. Baxter, *King Vidor*, p. 26.

20. Crowther, *The Lion's Share*, pp. 103–04; Lawrence J. Quirk, "John Gilbert," *Films in Review*, vol. 7, no. 3 (March, 1956), pp. 103–110. A bibliography on Gilbert may be found in Mel Schuster, *Motion Picture Performers: A Bibliography of Magazine and Periodical Articles, 1900–1969* (Metuchen, N.J., 1971), pp. 277–78.

21. Vidor, *A Tree Is a Tree*, p. 115.

22. A convenient summary of the story line of *The Big Parade* may be found in Thomas, *Thalberg*, pp. 332–35. A print of *The Big Parade* is in the Museum of Modern Art, New York City (hereafter cited as MOMA). Frederick James Smith, "Making *The Big Parade*," *Motion Picture Classic*, vol. 23, no. 3 (May, 1926), pp. 26, 71, is a brief presentation of Vidor's comments shortly after the picture was released.

23. Vidor, *King Vidor on Film Making*, pp. 156–57; Vidor, *A Tree Is a Tree*, pp. 115–17.

24. Ibid., p. 120–21; Vidor, *King Vidor on Film Making*, p. 133.

25. Baxter, *King Vidor*, pp. 21–24; Thomas, *Thalberg*, p. 86; G. J. Mitchell, "King Vidor," *Films in Review*, vol. 15, no. 3 (March, 1964), p. 180; Jack Spears, "World War I on the Screen," *Films in Review*, vol. 17, no. 6 (June-July, 1966), p. 351.

26. Vidor, *King Vidor on Film Making*, pp. 134–35; Vidor, *A Tree Is a Tree*, pp. 123–24.

27. Vidor, *King Vidor on Film Making*, p. 142.

28. Vidor, *A Tree Is a Tree*, p. 125; Jim Tully, "King Vidor," *Vanity Fair* (June, 1926), pp. 46, 100; Crowther, *The Lion's Share*, pp. 104–05. The figure for the final gross is given by Baxter, *King Vidor*, p. 24, as eighteen million dollars; by Vidor, *King Vidor on Film Making*, p. 78, as twenty-two million dollars.

29. Vidor, *A Tree Is a Tree*, p. 125.

30. Gilbert Seldes, "The Theatre," *Dial* (February, 1926), p. 169. A convenient collection of reviews concerning *The Big Parade* may be found in George C. Pratt, *Spellbound in Darkness: A History of the Silent Film* (rev. ed.) (Greenwich, Conn., 1973), pp. 397–404. Sherwood's review is on pp. 401–02.

31. Robert M. Finch, "The Big Parade," *Motion Picture Director* (November, 1925), p. 25 (emphasis in original).

32. *The Big Parade*, MOMA; quotation is from the film.

33. Finch, "The Big Parade," p. 59 (my emphasis).

34. "Watching the War From an Orchestra Chair," *Literary Digest* (March 6, 1926), p. 40.

35. Quoted in Thomas, *Thalberg*, p. 129.

36. Budd Schulberg, "Movies in America: After Fifty Years," *Atlantic* (November, 1947), p. 117; Gilbert Seldes, "The Two Parades," *New Republic* (December 16, 1925), pp. 111–12.

37. "'The Big Parade' of British Anger," *Literary Digest* (June 12, 1926), p. 29.

38. Iris Barry, "The Cinema: *The Big Parade*," *The Spectator* (London) (June 5, 1926), pp. 946–47.

39. Baxter, *King Vidor*, p. 21; Vidor, *King Vidor on Film Making*, p. 113.

40. Mitchell, "King Vidor," p. 180.

41. *New Republic* (July 3, 1929), pp. 179–80.

42. Otis L. Graham, Jr., *The Great Campaigns: Reform and War in America, 1900–1928* (Englewood Cliffs, N.J., 1971), pp. 91, 109.

43. For favorable comment on the usefulness of climate-of-opinion historiography, see Robert Allen Skotheim, ed., *The Historian and the Climate of Opinion* (Reading, Mass., 1969).

44. We leave in abeyance the question of causation, which is exceedingly difficult to resolve in the context of intellectual history. This difficulty holds regardless of the nature of the evidence. The contours of this question are examined in Michael T. Isenberg, "Toward an Historical Methodology for Film Scholarship," *The Rocky Mountain Social Science Journal*, vol. 12, no. 1 (January, 1975), pp. 45–57.

"Race Movies" as Voices of the Black Bourgeoisie:

The Scar of Shame (1927)

THOMAS CRIPPS

Louise (Lucia Lynn Moses) considers the difficult world that faces her as she aspires to respectability and security in a white society. The low-budget film raised the artistic level of "race films" designed for black audiences.

(Photo courtesy of Museum of Modern Art)

The depiction of Afro-Americans in Hollywood movies is so well known as to be overstated. One observer of the phenomenon described it in the title of his book: *Toms, Coons, Mulattoes, Mammies, & Bucks*. Unfortunately, in their eagerness to cast blacks as the victims of Hollywood cupidity, some critics present them as passive lambs in an abattoir.

Throughout the history of American movies, blacks with uneven success pressed moviemakers to alter their conceptions of the black characters who appeared on the screen. One of the tactics that persisted throughout the period between the world wars was the production of "race movies" for the consumption of black Americans.[1] Ofttimes these movies were the products of interracial and even white companies with a good ear and eye for the social and aesthetic concerns of blacks.

Because these movies were tailor-made for a specific audience, they often precisely reflected an authentic black morality, social ethic, and point of view. *The Scar of Shame* (1927), a product of a white-owned Philadelphia studio shrewdly named the Colored Players, provides one of the best examples of a movie intended to convey black middle-class social values to a black urban audience.

Race movies grew to maturity simultaneously with the growth of Northern black urban ghettos. The coincidence of visual medium of expression and growing audience contributed to the development of race movies into a distinct genre. Almost every race movie beneath its surface melodrama presented black audiences with sharply etched messages of advocacy, aspiration, group unity, and slogans against racism. *The Scar of Shame* not only stated the messages but also laid the blame for black misfortune at the door of poor environment.

Thus *The Scar of Shame* provides the historian not only with a work of popular art but with a document through which to study the social thrust of a cohesive group who shared a common core of values. In order to appraise the significance of such artifacts they must be seen as tiles in a mosaic—that is as coherent message units set in larger contexts that impart more sophisticated layers of meaning.

The Scar of Shame, and for that matter, all race movies, appeared at the end of a quarter of a century of a black diaspora that spread outward from Southern farms to Northern cities. Indeed, it could be said that race movies signaled the maturing of the consciousness of this black Northern audience, at once more urbane and wealthier than Southern blacks, and more importantly, heavily concentrated in a mass capable of supporting a small film industry. The resulting movies were made for a black audience that had grown in both size and self-consciousness. Therefore the films often depicted half-hidden internal social forces at work within black society. It is through this interaction between moviemaker and presumed audience that the messages are created through which the historian may view group values such as those that permeate *The Scar of Shame*.

In the especially violent decade of the 1890s the black urban migration began in earnest. The white South had seemed to grow more race conscious than ever. The Mississippi and South Carolina constitutions of 1890 and 1895 provided models for disfranchising Southern black voters while at the same time the growing incidence of racial violence moved beyond individual lynchings toward proto-military actions such as the Wilmington race riot of 1898. The press and the pulpit joined in proclaiming a revival of Southern white aggression against blacks.[2]

Between 1900 and 1920, black flight from the South became a social protest movement against this racial savagery. Pushed out by Southern pressures and pulled northward by Northern labor agents, by invitations from such black newspapers as the *Chicago Defender*, and by the promise of higher wages in industrial cities, Southern blacks moved to Northern cities. In those twenty years black Chicago alone grew more than threefold, from thirty thousand to over one hundred thousand. Similar figures marked the growth of Darktowns, Bronzevilles, and Harlems in ten other Northern cities.[3]

Blacks were transformed by the experience from a Southern peasantry into a Northern proletariat. The pyramid of black class structure grew into a broad, flat profile founded upon a vast pool of unskilled, underemployed, recent migrants from Southern farms wracked by sharecropping, boll weevils, and dustbowls. Crowded into noisome, newly formed ghettos beset by crime, violence, and squalor were the disaffiliated, dislocated untutored, unadaptable Southerners who threatened the status of "the old settlers," whose skills had allowed them to eke out stable, if petty, bourgeois lives founded on jobs in proximity to white centers of power and authority. In order to restore the old order the old settlers would have to teach the newcomers "respectable" ways.[4]

This is not to say that sociologists studied or even took note of this cultural basis of social class. On the contrary, as late as the 1950s, most scholars gave undue attention only to skin color as an index of stratification. For example, the distinguished student of Afro-American social class, E. Franklin Frazier of Howard University, was a careful scholar who once broke the constraints of objectivity in a little book so intemperate in its treatment of black social class in Washington that it proved awkward to publish in America. His *Black Bourgeoisie* (1955, 1957) owed at least some of its feisty reputation to its insistence on skin color and descent from the antebellum servant class as the most telling determinants of black social class rather than more eclectic criteria such as antiquity of residence and lineage, stable employment, professional achievement, academic success, West Indian kinship, closeness to whites as in government posts, and clinging to a respectable life style in the face of surrounding trends toward urban decay. Frazier's tour de force diverted historians from seeing a broader basis for determining social class.[5]

Race moviemakers, the authors of movies like *The Scar of Shame*, took a broader view of class and tried to pass on their values to their audiences. The literati of the "Harlem Renaissance" probably included the respectables in their audiences, but certainly not the newly arrived Southerners. Indeed, many black poets and novelists owed their prominence to white patrons and readers with a taste for Negro art. Poor blacks shared little of the literary ferment because of their illiteracy, resistance to urban ways, and isolation from such old-line black institutions as the church. Even black newspapers offered little to the new folk other than advertisements for seers and numerological "dreambooks" that promised "hits" in the daily illegal lottery. The columns ran to heavy fare by the intellectuals, W. E. B. DuBois, Carter Woodson, and Kelly Miller. Only J. A. Rogers's history in cartoon form reached for a popular audience. Clearly, if the old respectables were to reach the newcomers with a usable set of urban values, movies would be the vehicle, much as visually graphic vaudeville had once spoken to illiterate new immigrants from Europe.[6]

Parallel to the northward migration, blacks developed a new

racial consciousness based on a loss of faith in the goals of Reconstruction, the consequent belief that ghettoes were permanent fixtures, and the realization that ambition was possible only within a segregated black world. In this social system, the unchurched, untutored, and unaffiliated could expect little, and rewards accrued to those who learned a skill, cultivated a talent, or provided a service in exchange for a steady, but modest, return. The urban bourgeoisie saw deviations from norms of rectitude as temptations that, if heeded, would cast them into the pit of failure, crime, and improvidence where they would live off women and the public dole. In short, the black bourgeoisie feared becoming lower class, while those on the bottom felt contempt for the middle class's apparent emulation of white social values. Ethel Waters remembered that after her mother became a live-in domestic servant, "she stopped living colored" and despaired of her children who "knew nothing and cared nothing about the better side of life" she had seen as a servant to whites.[7]

By the middle 1920s, those at the top of the middle class became race leaders and self-conscious tutors of—as Booker T. Washington had indirectly described him—"the man farthest down." Alain Locke, a black Harvardian and Rhodes Scholar, described this new leader in his brilliantly edited volume, *The New Negro*, which had grown from the famous "Harlem number" (March 1925) of *Survey Graphic* magazine. If this new Negro had a proximate enemy, it was not white racism but Marcus Garvey, the West Indian whose charismatic Universal Negro Improvement Association threatened to win the black proletariat away from the tutelege of race leaders. Most race moviemakers shared the concern for the uplift of the black lower class and hoped to blunt the threat of Garveyism. Indeed, at the end of the silent era two race movies, *Marcus Garland* and *The Black King* (1932), parodied Garvey as a mountebank who exploited the weakness of the black lower class.[8]

The Scar of Shame and every other race movie of the 1920s retailed a black bourgeois success myth, a manual for those on the make, and a caution to the weak-willed who might be diverted from success by urban temptations. Like a typical Horatio Alger hero, the black hero discovered success rather than plodded toward it. Perhaps because the Southern blacks who were the prospective audiences expected little from the puritanical work ethic and its promise of success, the quick score seemed a more plausible myth. This black myth included tales of discoveries of bonanzas, sports triumphs, the virtues of rural life, and good-bad kids who are redeemed by the benefits of a healthful environment. In only a few cases is credulity strained by having blacks succeed after working hard. In a racist society, luck always seemed to matter more than pluck.

Among the sports legends was *As the World Rolls On* (Andlauer, 1921) in which boxer Jack Johnson teaches a plucky boy both boxing and baseball so that in the last reel he may pitch a game for the all-black Kansas City Monarchs. A year later Johnson himself played a resourceful lad who learns to box in order to win money to pay restitution for his brother's crime in *For His Mother's Sake* (Blackburn Velde, 1922). Boxers Sam Langford and Tiger Flowers also used the fight game as a vehicle for success myths, while black cowboy Bill Pickett starred in *The Bull-Dogger* (Norman, 1923) as a demonstration that "the black cowboy is capable of doing anything the white cowboy does." In at least three more race movies of the 1920s athletic prowess contributed to heroic attainment.[9]

Bonanzas taken from high-risk extractive industries provided another fanciful alternative to conventional success stories. Romances of prospecting, mining, and wildcatting for oil were the most often used. In *Absent* (Rosebud, 1928) a miner and his daughter help a shell-shocked veteran begin a new life. The hero of *The Realization of a Negro's Ambition* (Lincoln, 1916) is a graduate engineer from Tuskegee who strikes oil on his father's farm after losing a job with an oil company because of his race, a denouement similar to that of *The Symbol of the Unconquered* (Micheaux, 1920). The heroes of Oscar Micheaux's *The Dungeon* (1922) and *Smiling Hate* (Superior, 1924) both strike gold in Alaska.

The next best prize was a farm; it provided a source of wealth and symbolized the deep roots that were proof against the demoralization of urban life. In *The Law of Nature* (Lincoln, 1917), for example, the heroine deserts her rancher-husband and child for the high life back East, only to learn in the last reel to prefer the richness of life on the farm. Micheaux's first movie, *The Homesteader* (1919) extolled life on the prairie; *The Colored American Winning His Suit* (Douglass, 1919) used land as the source of tuition for children to attend Spelman and Howard; the hero of *The Virgin and the Seminole* (Micheaux, 1922) uses his reward earned as a Canadian Mountie to buy a ranch; and Micheaux's *The Millionaire* (1927) grows rich ranching on the Argentine Pampas. A treasure map substituted for bonanzas and ranches in at least one movie, Norman's *Regeneration* (1923).[10]

The black hero rarely took up a career that demanded rigorous training; in real life the odds against such black accomplishment were too long. While it is true that characters in *Birthright* (Micheaux, 1924) went to Harvard, in *The Colored American Winning His Suit* to Howard and Spelman, in *The Realization of a Negro's Ambition* to Tuskegee, and the heroes of *Within Our Gates* (Micheaux, 1920), *The Burden of Race* (Reol, 1921), *By Right of Birth* (Lincoln, 1921), and *A Giant of His Race* (North State, 1921), benefited from professional training; eventual fulfillment came not from practicing their craft but from a lucky stroke, or a single event like a gusher. *The Trooper of Troop K* (Lincoln, 1916) bumbles through life until he becomes a hero at the battle of Carrizal. Lawyers make it by winning a single case, as in *The Colored American Winning His Suit* and *A Shot in the Night* (North State, 1922).

Occasionally a race movie, such as *Secret Sorrow* (Reol, 1923), contrasted the lives of a good and a bad kid as a means of demonstrating that environment, and not race, predicted success. One son, raised in squalor by his poor mother, turned wrong, while the other, adopted by a prosperous doctor, became a New York assistant district attorney.[11]

Artists and scientists also achieved single triumphs. The hero of *A Giant of His Race*, a doctor—a child of slaves who has struggled through medical school driven by an urge "to uplift his people"— strikes a bonanza when "yellow plague" visits his village, forcing him to spend days in his lab affecting a cure that brings him a 100,000-dollar prize. In *The Schemers* (Reol, 1922), a "struggling young chemist" attains wealth when he discovers a substitute for gasoline, a story parallelled in the serial, *Zircon* (Norman, 1923). In black movies novelists, filmmakers, bidders for mail contracts, dealers in Brazilian coffee, preachers, detectives, song-and-dance men, musicians all succeeded not through accrual of achievements but through the luck and pluck of Alger's *Jed the Poorhouse Boy* (1899).[12]

The race moviemakers' urge to raise up race pride gave character to their work and distinguished it from white films. Sometimes, therefore, plots turned on the plight of lightskinned people whose black identities seethed below a lifelong camouflage of white skin, a condition that inspired themes of racial pride that grew out of dramatic last-reel revelations. Many of Oscar Micheaux's films were tangled in such dual identities. In *The Homesteader* (1918), the first film of Micheaux's prolific, quarter-of-a-century career, Baptiste, the hero, wins the heart of a "Scottish" girl only to learn in the last reel that she is a Negro. The same plot twist recurred in his 1920s films *Symbol of the Unconquered*, *Birthright*, *The House Behind the Cedars*, and *Thirty Years Later*, always with the result that the hero "becomes proud of his race." Micheaux's rivals took up the issue with equal vigor. In *Loyal Hearts* (Democracy, 1919), the heroes with patronizing tolerance learn to "accept their own people," a denouement shared by *In the Depths of Our Hearts* (Royal Garden, 1920) and *The Call of His People* (Reol, 1922), which ends with hero and heroine together and he "now proud to be one of her people."[13]

But if success and pride were the gospels of the "new Negro," what litanies and epiphanies could black missionaries sing in order to bring the theology to the black masses? Who was to be the black Emile Coué or Bruce Barton, the white acolytes of the success myth in the 1920s? Pivotal in the strategy was the need for a rhetoric that reached the lower class, for the respectable mercantile and meritocratic middle class had little need for more sermons on the theme of ambition, nor did their established churches encourage moviegoing. Thus if race movies were to succeed in the ghetto, their intended audience was necessarily the demoralized poor black on the block. Of all the silent race movies, *The Scar of Shame* most reflected the ambitions of these black respectables.

As early as 1916 black leaders had taken up the issue. Emmett J. Scott, private secretary to Booker T. Washington, attempted to produce a movie version of Washington's autobiography, *Up from Slavery*, as a counterforce to *The Birth of a Nation* (1915) and a celebration "not only of Dr. Washington's personal strivings, but also the strivings of the race climbing up from the tragic period represented by slavery." Like later black filmmakers, he tried to enlist the support of the respectables by appealing to the National Negro Business League. At the same time the Lincoln Motion Picture Company of Los Angeles, led by George P. and Noble Johnson, set out "to picture the Negro as . . . a human being with human inclination, and one of talent and intellect." By the 1920s a host of rivals joined the game, each claiming "to show the better side of Negro life" or "to inspire in the Negro a desire to 'climb higher.'" The black press cheered on the moviemakers, urging readers, in the words of Kennard Williams of the *Afro-American*, to give "sensible support of Negro producers like Micheaux." Lincoln all but formalized this union of moviemen and journalists by using newspapermen as promoters. "Moving pictures," said Robert L. Vann's Pittsburgh *Competitor*, one of Lincoln's hoped-for allies, "have become one of the greatest vitalizing forces in race adjustment, and we are just beginning."[14]

This is not to say race movies enjoyed universal support from black critics. The *Amsterdam News*, for example, charged white theater owners with "a mistaken idea [that] . . . they should exhibit in a colored community [without regard for] the worth of the pictures. With an opportunity of viewing the best things along picture lines, it is hard to expect colored people to accept these Micheaux pictures here in Greater New York." Reviewers insisted on uplift and on "the possibility of individual endeavor and reward of a character of the Negro race," and they took sharp issue when "the story was not elevating." One critic admonished Micheaux: "Society wants a real story of high moral aim that can appeal to the upbuilding of your race." For their part, the moviemakers did their best, but they also believed that audiences preferred "stirring melodrama," "thrilling and realistic" yarns, and lots of "action."[15]

The aesthetic guerrilla war that broke out between the respectables who demanded "uplift" and the unsophisticated moviegoers who demanded "action," may be seen in Micheaux's film of Charles Waddell Chesnutt's *The House Behind the Cedars*. Chesnutt, a staunch black Republican, a civil-rights activist, and a widely praised novelist who earned a respectable living as a court stenographer, opened negotiations with Micheaux in 1920. At first Micheaux, an incredibly primitive writer, merely carped at Chesnutt's writing which "could not very well be filmed" except as "two reel comedies." Poor Chesnutt. "They want to chop it up," he wrote, "and probably change the emphasis of certain characters." He could "only hope that it will be done with reasonable taste."[16]

Micheaux knew his audience. He wished to plunge straightway into the story, delete expository passages in favor of visual incident, change the hero from bumpkin into a "more intelligent" figure so "the girl could have more than passing respect for him," and tack on an uplifting ending designed for the "colored people whom we must depend upon as a bulwark for our business." The result, predicted Micheaux,

> would, I am sure, in so far as our people are concerned send them out of the theatre with this story lingering in their minds, with a feeling that all good must triumph in the end, and with the words 'Oh! want that just wonderful [*sic*]!' instead of a gloomy muttering. . . .

Micheaux was so satisfied with his pastiche of upbeat, affirmative ending, "action, thrills, and suspense," and a plot that hinged on concealed racial identity, that he released it in 1924 and again in 1932 as a sound film entitled *Veiled Aristocrats*. Chesnutt, on the other hand, learned that race movies were like Soviet art that served social rather than aesthetic goals. As his daughter reported: "it was not artistic like the story" and "your beautiful English and the soul of the tale were lacking."[17]

The Scar of Shame sprang from no such distinguished literary source, but its social goals sounded a familiar note. Like so many race movies, *The Scar of Shame* was interracial in origin yet took up black social concerns. Its parent firm, the Colored Players Company of Philadelphia, owed its birth to a fairly common alliance of moviemen: black ideamen and performers, white technicians and crews, and white, often Jewish, entrepreneurs.

Sherman H. "Uncle Dud" Dudley, a black veteran of vaudeville and race movies, first conceived an idea for a black Hollywood outside Washington, D.C. He had learned of films by working on *The Simp* (Reol, 1921) with black stars Edna Morton and Percy Verwayen, and "angel" Robert Levy who later backed Harlem's Lafayette Players. White Philadelphian David Starkman, owner of a black theater, dismayed observer of demeaning racial roles in Hollywood movies, and a visionary who shared Dudley's dream, assumed responsibility for operations, management, and raising capital in white Philadelphia. White journeymen Frank Perugini and Al Liguori directed and shot the film. The actors who came from race movies and black stock or commuted from chorus lines in New York included Harry Henderson, Lucia Lynn Moses, Pearl McCormick, Lawrence Chenault, and Ann Kennedy.

Gradually Starkman, a self-educated immigrant from Austria, and a "little Napoleon," took over. He sold his theater, converted his wife's inheritance to cash, browbeat capital from South Philadelphia lawyers and hardware merchants, wrote scripts, and finally, carried release prints to out-of-town play dates and counted the house in person.

The company had tested its skills with *A Prince of His Race* (1926), a social drama now lost, and with a black version of Timothy Shay Arthur's *Ten Nights in a Bar Room* (1926) starring Charles Gilpin, the original *Emperor Jones* in 1920. As *The Scar of Shame* went into production in 1927, Starkman became demonic, contributing his car, his sister's rooming house as a location, and even his own furniture with which he dressed the set. The effort eventually shattered him. The film opened coincidentally with the debut of sound film, an event that ruined race moviemakers burdened with inventories of silent films, stables of untrained actors, and unwired theaters. The shock changed Starkman from a little engine of ambition into a debt-ridden hanger-on who died of cancer in 1947, his marriage broken and his home foreclosed.[18]

Like many low-budget silent films, *The Scar of Shame* was probably shot without benefit of a fully developed script, which may account for the authentic tone of black social ambience. Even though, the star, Lucia Lynn Moses, remembered that "I never took any directions from anybody colored; it was always the two white fellahs," she knew the life of the black respectables and wove it into her role.[19]

The Scar of Shame, as one of the few survivors of the silent era, provides us with an aspect of the new urban black class system neglected by Frazier's social anatomy, *Black Bourgeoisie* (1955, 1957). Frazier's polemic described the outward appearance but not the engine and driveshaft of the system—aspiration for education and achievement. The need to achieve inspired the broad center of black respectables who earned livelihoods in civil service, proprietorship, preaching, teaching, and social work. Not one title card in

The Scar of Shame mentioned skin color as an index of status, citing instead a need for "the finer things, higher hopes, and higher aims" as middle-class motivations.

The burden of the message was not always evident, but clearly it never included a sermon against color caste. The heroes yearned to be hard-driving and successful black Babbitts, while the heavies compromised this ideal, sold it out for a bottle of booze, or made war upon it to satisfy a criminal ambition. Dark skin and light skin were scattered throughout the ranks of the good and the evil, with, perhaps, a light-skinned bias toward the good guys merely because such a skewing reflected the ways white bias inevitably affected the realities of Afro-American life.[20]

In 1927, blacks struggled to rise above poverty into middle-class respectability. *The Scar of Shame* affirmed and dramatized this new Negro ideal—the grasping after "the finer things, the higher hopes, and higher aims." Throughout the film, visual images symbolize this point: success symbols are good; poverty symbols are bad. Life in the parlor is good; on the street corner, bad. The message is so strong that the hero's success at the expense of his suicidal woman is seen as a tolerable price to pay for a victory over shabbiness and poverty.

From the opening in a Philadelphia ghetto, the hero, Alvin Hilliard, an ambitious black composer, is viewed by the landlady of his "select boarding house" as the eventual "greatest composer of our race." The heavy lives in the same house. Snubbed by the genteel boarders, Eddie is brash, cigar-smoking, and dressed in a loudly checked suit. He is as light-skinned as Hilliard, but his manner, style, and saloon-keeping establish him as the heavy.

The drunken Spike lives in the alley where violence and exploitation are the rule. Louise, his daughter, who marries Hilliard in order to escape her father's brutality, is a heroine as long as she struggles to rise above the ghetto. She must choose between the three men: her dangerous and brutal father, who is broken by alcohol; Eddie, who wants to drag her into a career as a saloon singer; and Hilliard, whose ambition can pull her above the burden of poverty. She is sympathetic as long as she is the victim saved by marriage to Hilliard; she is the heavy once she accepts the compromise with success held out by Eddie's promises. Hilliard's mother symbolizes the prize in the contest. She lives in the suburbs, attended by a butler, reachable only in Hilliard's sporty roadster, as though to tell us that only through the car—the fruit of Hilliard's aspiration—can Louise reach the safe haven of suburbia. Without Hilliard she must rot in the ghetto, exploited by Eddie and beaten by her father.

The stage on which this drama is resolved is the boarding house and its windows looking out on the shabby alley. These symbolic opposites provide the setting for the cluttered plot. Hilliard saves Louise from a backyard beating at the hands of her father; marries her as insurance against future violence; and loses her to Eddie who contrives to win her with the promise of a career on the stage. Hilliard confronts them and in the ensuing affray Louise is shot and marked by her "scar of shame." Hilliard goes to jail, escapes, and takes up the life of a piano teacher in his predestined upper-class niche. He has won the game of life by wanting it badly; Louise has lost because she sold herself cheaply. Desperately, Louise tries to blackmail Hilliard into returning to her, and when he refuses to give up his hard-won life, she poisons herself. One of her rakish lovers reads her suicide note and explains her death to the audience: "Our people," he says, "have much to learn." If only she had aspired to "the finer things" and been raised in a good "environment."

The notion that Afro-American class consciousness was based on color will not entirely fade. Rhetorically, for example, the title cards refer frequently to "caste" when they must mean "class." Visually, when Louise chooses the saloon, she accidentally crushes her brown-skinned doll and mourns it as "a victim of caste." But these symbols only throw the viewer off the trail. By far the imagery of class conflict predominates, and "environment," not color, is seen as the determinant of social status. Low life and respectable life are seen as opposites: the boarding house versus the saloon; Hilliard's cool manners versus Eddie's oafishness; Louise's drab room versus Hilliard's with its portrait of the black Republican Frederick Douglass on the wall. Eddie sneers at Hilliard, not as a "yaller" snob, but as "that dicty sap"—the slang term for *any* pretentious social climber or poseur in black circles. Finally, in the last sequence, Hilliard's musical accomplishments are positively contrasted with Louise's taking up with one of the riffraff who "hit the numbers today." In other words Hilliard's solid accomplishment is set against Louise's settling for the fleeting thrill of a cheap score in the daily lottery. Skin color is never a matter of rhetorical debate or consistent symbolic contrast.[21] As Lucia Lynn Moses remembered her stage directions, she was thrust into her role and asked to improvise. Perugini would call her onto the set and describe the situation. "This man—you're not in the same category with him—you're not in the same league," he would say. "You take it from there."[22] That is, she was asked to play a part in a class, not a color, conflict, in which Negroes of any color were free to contend for success.

No one knows how widely or clearly *The Scar of Shame* spread its message. We have only a bit of advertising copy, some evidence that it played as far south as Virginia, and a few reviews. Apparently it was sold and portrayed as an elegant expression of the need to pursue the best of American culture without regard for race, perhaps as a spreading of the aspirations of the respectables outward to the black proletariat. The advertising claimed that "Race Film is Classic." And an *Amsterdam News* reviewer praised it as a work that "sets a new standard of excellence." Both sentiments were expressions of an assertive, optimistic, middle class speaking to the moviegoer in need of uplift.[23]

All things considered, *The Scar of Shame* exemplified the highest hopes of the black generation of the 1920s who placed faith in individual aspiration as the path to group emancipation. Unfortunately for blacks, history caught up with the modest boom that had given gloss to the ghettos of the 1920s. The Great Crash of 1929 extended into the white world an economic depression that had already tarnished black well being. Race movies in the 1930s grew more collectivist in keeping with the New Deal mood, advocated community organization, and called for race unity. Among the best were *Am I Guilty?* (1940) which featured Ralph Cooper as a doctor who must choose between healing gangsters and opening a free clinic; *Moon over Harlem* (1939) which advocated education and cleaning up of Harlem's rackets; *Murder on Lenox Avenue* (1941) which depicted the struggle to form a "business league" on which to base a "prosperous Harlem"; and *Broken Strings* (1940) which ended with a collective effort to raise money to heal the broken hands of a black violinist.[24]

The Scar of Shame, then, remains a parametric expression of the high point of the self-conscious, individualistic, black bourgeoisie of the 1920s. That its message rang hollow testified to the unyielding forces opposed to black aspiration rather than to the inefficacy of the strategy. For historians the film is a lesson in the need to seek out evidence in every medium of expression of group spirit, and not merely to rely on the traditional media of literature and art.

NOTES

1. The handiest compendia of 1920s race movie titles are Henry T. Sampson, *Blacks in Black and White: A Source Book on Black Films* (Metuchen, N.J., 1977); Kenneth W. Mundin, exec. ed., *The American Film Institute Catalog of Motion Pictures Produced in the United States*, Vol. F2 (New York, 1970); Thomas Cripps, *Slow Fade to Black: The Negro in American Film, 1900–1942* (New York, 1977), VII; and the George P. Johnson Collection, Research Library, UCLA (available on microfilm).

2. A useful bibliography on this period is in Jack Temple Kirby, *Darkness at the Dawning: Race and Reform in the Progressive South* (Philadelphia, 1972).

3. Documents and a brief bibliography are in Richard B. Sherman, ed., *The Negro and the City* (Englewood Cliffs, N.J., 1970) and Hollis Lynch, *The Black Urban Condition* (New York, 1973).

4. This social division is carefully defined in David Gordon Nielson, *Black Ethos: Northern Urban Negro Life and Thought, 1890–1930*, "Contributions in Afro-American and African Studies, No. 29," Hollis R. Lynch, ed. (Westport, Conn., 1977), III. He finds the "respectables" constituted "80 or 90 percent" of the urban population (p. 52) that rested on a base of "undisciplined, unchurched, uneducated riff-raff" (p. 60).

5. Frazier denied that he "had written a book attacking 'upper-class, light-skinned' Negroes," nevertheless he admitted that there were "working-class Negroes who shook my hand for having performed this long overdue service." His intention had been to show that a social system without a true upper class imitated exogenous white norms. E. Franklin Frazier, *Black Bourgeoisie* (New York, 1957), p. 8, quoted in Nielson, *Black Ethos*, p. 176.

6. The intellectuals may be read in, for example, a survey of the *Amsterdam News*. The connection between art, the respectables, and uplift may be seen in David L. Lewis, "The Politics of Art: The New Negro, 1920–1935," a chapter from his forthcoming book. Mss loaned by the author. On literati, see Nathan Irvin Huggins, *Harlem Renaissance* (New York, 1971).

7. Ethel Waters and Charles Samuels, *His Eye Is on the Sparrow* (Garden City, N.Y., 1951), pp. 8–9, quoted in Nielson, *Black Ethos*, p. 182.

8. Alain Locke, ed., *The New Negro: An Interpretation* (New York, 1925). No print of Oscar Micheaux's *Marcus Garland* survives. See Mundin, *AFI Catalog*, p. 492, and Cripps, *Slow Fade to Black*, p. 191. Sampson, *Blacks in Black and White*, p. 137, finds *The Black King* a product of white racists although black musician Donald Heywood received credit for it. See Cripps, *Slow Fade to Black*, pp. 325–26. *The Black King* is an uneven film but the Garvey figure is brilliantly acted as a charismatic leader by A. B. Comathiere. A print is in the film collection of the University of Illinois, Urbana, Illinois.

9. Cripps, *Slow Fade to Black*, VII. Synopses appear in Mundin, *AFI Catalog*, pp. 27–28, 97, 263; Sampson, *Blacks in Black and White*, pp. 99, 115–16, 112–14.

10. Cripps, *Slow Fade to Black*, VII. Synopses and credits in Sampson, *Blacks in Black and White*, pp. 130–32, 95–96, 111–12, 93–94, 127, 90–91, 117–18, 123, 97–98, 115; Mundin, *AFI Catalog*, 2, 207, 514, 643, 782.

11. Cripps, *Slow Fade to Black*, VII. Synopses and credits in Sampson, *Blacks in Black and White*, pp. 150–51, 100–102, 104–105, 118, 92–93, 98; Mundin, *AFI Catalog*, pp. 61, 98, 102, 288, 693, 711.

12. Cripps, *Slow Fade to Black*, VII; Sampson, *Blacks in Black and White*, p. 114; Mundin, *AFI Catalog*, pp. 687–88.

13. Cripps, *Slow Fade to Black*, VII; Mundin, *AFI Catalog*, 104; Sampson, *Blacks in Black and White*, pp. 132–33; 97, 108–11.

14. Emmett J. Scott to Edwin L. Barker, October 18, 1915; November 6, 1915; contract dated December 20, 1915, in Scott MSS, Morgan State University, Baltimore, Maryland; *California Eagle*, July 31, 1915; Tony Langston to George P. Johnson, October 10, 1916, in G. P. Johnson Collection, UCLA, Los Angeles, California; G. P. Johnson holograph memoir, "A Million Dollar Negro Film Deal Fell Through," in Johnson Collection; copies of the *Competitor* are in the Johnson Collection. See Cripps, *Slow Fade to Black*, p. 180 ff. for the sources of the quoted blurbs.

15. *Amsterdam News* (New York), December 23, 1925; *Chicago Defender*, April 2, 1921; "*The Symbol of the Unconquered*, New Play," *Competitor*, January-February, 1921, p. 61.

16. George C. Anderson to Charles Waddell Chesnutt, July 27, 1920; Oscar Micheaux to Chesnutt, January 18, 1921; March 24, 1921; Swan E. Micheaux to Chesnutt, correspondence, September 19, 1921–October 26, 1921; in Chesnutt Papers, Fisk University, Nashville, Tennessee.

17. Oscar Micheaux to Chesnutt, January 18, 1921; Ethel Chesnutt to Charles Waddell Chesnutt, April 25, 1932; in Chesnutt Papers, Fisk University.

18. Cripps, *Slow Fade to Black*, pp. 195–98; Ronald Goldwyn, "The Scar of Shame," *Discover: The Sunday Bulletin* (Philadelphia), November 17, 1974, p. 14 ff.; Ronald Goldwyn to Thomas Cripps, n.d.; William Felker, head, General Information Department, the Free Library of Philadelphia, to Thomas Cripps, July 15, 1974; typescript file under "Scar" in Johnson Collection, UCLA; interview between Lucia Lynn Moses and Cripps, Spring 1973, New York; soundtrack, *Black Shadows on a Silver Screen* (Post-Newsweek TV, 1975); print of *Ten Nights in a Bar Room* (Colored Players, 1926) is in the Library of Congress; *Pittsburgh Courier*, January 2, 1926.

19. Moses's anecdotes recur in two interviews, one with Cripps, Spring 1973, another with Stephan Henriquez, two years later, confirming both her exclusion from the script-writing stage and their urging her to improvise. In addition, she implied that the caste system observed in her day was based at least as much on differences in education as on skin color—which she described with only an oblique assertion that "black wasn't beautiful then."

20. A print of *The Scar of Shame* was viewed several times at the Enoch Pratt Free Library of Baltimore through the courtesy of audio-visual director Helen Cyr.

21. For other samples of evidence against the argument from skin color see *Body and Soul* (Micheaux, 1924) in which the heavy is "Yellow Curly Hines" and the hero is dark brown Paul Robeson as a preacher (print in George Eastman House Museum, Rochester, New York); and *The Girl from Chicago* (Micheaux, 1932), a fragment of which appears in *Black Shadows on a Silver Screen*, in which "the girl" expresses her contempt for low-class people who play the numbers.

22. Moses interviews, 1973 and 1975.

23. *Philadelphia Tribune*, April 16, 1927; Tony Langston to G. P. Johnson, January 15, 1927, in Johnson Collection; *Variety*, August 31, 1927, p. 18; *Amsterdam News* (New York), June 5 and 12, 1927; *Pittsburgh Courier*, June 25, 1927; April 20 and 27, 1929.

24. Cripps, *Slow Fade to Black*, p. 332 ff.

Bullets, Beer and the Hays Office:

Public Enemy (1931)

GARTH JOWETT

Tom Powers (James Cagney) and other aspiring gangsters get the low-down from Putty Nose, in this early scene. Cagney's alert intelligence marks him for bigger things, both in the film and as a future Hollywood star.

(Photo courtesy of Museum of Modern Art)

Against an ominously dramatic rendition of "I'm Forever Blowing Bubbles," and just after the credits have ended, appears the statement that this film is an attempt "to honestly depict an environment that exists today in a certain strata of American life, rather than to glorify the hoodlum or the criminal." We will never know the real reason for this hypocrisy, but there is little doubt that by the end of the film, the principal character, Tom Powers, played with an instinctual brilliance by the very young James Cagney, has left behind one of the key archetypal images in the history of the American cinema. While *Public Enemy* does end with the death of its gangster heroes, thereby conforming to the official dictates of the motion picture industry creed, so powerful is Cagney as Tom Powers, and so deft is the fast-paced direction of William Wellman, that the audience cannot help feeling some envy of the swaggering character, whose brief life is filled with excitement, fast cars, expensive clothes, and beautiful, seductive women. Together with Mervyn LeRoy's *Little Caesar* (1930), and Howard Hawks's *Scarface* (1932), *Public Enemy* is part of a trio that serves as the paradigm of what may be called the "classic" gangster film.[1] But *Public Enemy* can also be used by the historian willing to go beyond its surface plot to provide many clues to the condition of American society and culture during the 1920s and early 1930s.

It is unlikely that any studio other than Warner Brothers could have made *Public Enemy*. After the success of the early talkies, *The Jazz Singer* (1927) and *The Lights of New York* (1928), the studio purchased the Stanley Chain of movie theaters, and had begun to acquire a stable of personable, if not major, film stars. The financial success was short-lived however, and the early years of the Depression were as difficult for Warner Brothers as they were for all the other studios, with the overall loss on the studio balance sheets for the period 1930 to 1933 estimated at $113,000,000.[2] Despite the successful innovation and public adoption of sound films, by 1931 Hollywood was in serious financial difficulty, due in large part to the overoptimistic expansion of the studios in acquiring theater chains throughout the 1920s. Andrew Bergman in his study of Depression films notes that "when the movie public began to stay home, the direct financial impact on movie companies owning theaters was immediate and immense."[3] It was under these trying circumstances that the Warners brought into their Burbank plant an increasing flow of talented young stage actors, writers, and directors in the hope of providing the studio with the properties to ensure its survival.

Writers, in particular, saw promise in the new medium, and, as James R. Silke has pointed out:

> They came with a purpose. Hard times were eroding the nation, eating out its heart, its spirit; but to the literate, educated, thinking man, the Depression was only tearing down the old way to make way for the new. The time was ripe for change, and the socially aware writers needed a stage for their words. One place appeared perfect, Hollywood.[4]

Two of these young writers attracted to Hollywood in 1930 were John Bright and his partner Kubec Glasmon. In Chicago Bright had worked for Glasmon as a soda jerk in a drugstore frequented by gangsters and young hoodlums, and using this as their background, they wrote the novel *Blood and Beer*. Arriving in Los Angeles with the unpublished manuscript, they were able to interest Darryl Zanuck, who had just been made head of production at Warners, in their property. Warners purchased the novel for fifteen thousand dollars, and signed the young writers to a long-term contract.[5] The title of the film was altered to *Public Enemy*, as the Hays Office did not like the use of the word "blood," and the film was assigned to William Wellman to direct.

The original casting of the film called for Eddie Woods to play the role of Tom Powers, and for the relatively unknown Cagney to play his friend Matt Doyle. After three days of shooting Wellman agreed that Bright and Glasmon had been correct in their complaint that the casting was wrong, and that the roles should be reversed. Despite the fact that Woods was engaged to marry the daughter of the powerful Hollywood gossip columnist Louella Parsons, Wellman got permission from Zanuck to make the change. According to all reports, Cagney's image was simply too powerful against the easy-going Woods. Of such things are Hollywood legends made.

For both Wellman and Cagney this film was an important milestone in their careers, while for Zanuck it was one of a series of important films (*Little Caesar, I Am a Fugitive from a Chain Gang, Forty-second Street*) that he oversaw in his brief career at Warner Brothers, which ended in 1933 after a violent argument with Jack Warner.[6] *Public Enemy* was a success in every sense; aesthetically Wellman and his cameraman Dev Jennings created a series of well conceived scenes that moved the narrative along at an ideal pace. There is very little in the film that is not essential to the development of the plot or to providing important clues to Tom's character.

For Cagney the film represented a personal triumph which ensured that from then on Warners would give him star billing. *Public Enemy* was shot in twenty-six days, at a cost of 151,000 dollars, and made well over a million dollars in its initial release. The studio was elated, and in typical Hollywood fashion decided that if this formula had worked once, it would work again. In his perceptive examination of Cagney as "auteur," Patrick McGilligan notes that Cagney's popularity meant "money in the bank," and that "after 1934, none of his Warners' releases grossed less than 1,000,000 dollars."[7] The public eagerly embraced the Cagney "tough guy" image, and he was literally forced to play these roles for the rest of his career, although he was an accomplished song-and-dance man and his only Academy Award came for his performance as the patriotic entertainer George M. Cohan in *Yankee Doodle Dandy* (1942).[8]

The underlying violence in most of Cagney's screen portrayals was a topic for serious discussion among film critics as they attempted to understand the social and cultural significance of his popularity in early-Depression America. Lincoln Kirstein, writing in *Hound & Horn* in 1932, noted that the archetypal American hero had changed from the "lean, shrewd, lantern-jawed, slow-voiced, rangy, blond American pioneer," to "a short, red-headed Irishman, quick to wrath, humorous, articulate in anger, representing not a minority in action, but the action of the American majority—the semi-literate lower middle class."[9] Kirstein went on to make the very important point that Cagney

> . . . is the first definitely metropolitan figure to become national, as opposed to the suburban national figure of a few years ago, or of the farmer before that. . . . No one expresses more clearly in terms of pictorial action the delights of violence, the overtones of semi-conscious sadism, the tendency towards destruction, towards anarchy which is the basis of American sex-appeal.[10]

Whatever the basis of Cagney's personal appeal, the image of the gangster as a "hero" in American popular culture is now well established. (Witness the incredible public response to the morally reprehensible "family" depicted in the novel and films of *The Godfather* [1972] and *Godfather II* [1974].) Robert Warshow has pointed out the curious position of this criminal character in the popular culture of a country that "is committed to a cheerful view of life." He suggests that gangster films do not so much deal with the problem of crime in American life, as with the modern, urban experience of the American people.

> What matters is that the experience of the gangster *as an experience of art* is universal to Americans. There is nothing we understand better or react to more readily or with quicker intelligence. . . . In ways that we do not easily or willingly define, the gangster speaks for us, expressing that part of the American psyche which rejects the qualities and the demands of modern life, which rejects "Americanism" itself.
> The gangster is the man of the city, with the city's language and knowledge, with its queer and dishonest skills and its terrible daring, carrying his life in his hands like a placard, like a club. . . . The real city, one might say, produces only criminals; the imaginary city produces the gangster: he is what we want to be and what we are afraid we may become.[11]

America had become a predominantly urban-based nation according to the 1920 Census, and the resulting demographic shift had also caused an obvious change in the popular cultural pursuits of its people. Newspapers, the motion picture, and, after 1922, radio had each helped to erode the emphasis on local interests and entertainment, leaving in their wake a new *national* "mass culture," with a decided urban cast. In every city, town, or village across the country these images and sounds were taking precedence over the local culture, and precipitating new sources of influence and socialization, especially for the young.[12] The Lynds in their 1925 study of *Middletown* (Muncie, Indiana) devoted considerable effort to an examination of these forces, noting that

> at no point is one brought up more sharply against the impossibility of studying Middletown as a self-contained, self-starting community than when one watches these space-binding leisure-time inventions imported from without—automobile, motion picture, and radio—reshaping the city.[13]

It is against these changes, and the fact of Prohibition that *Public Enemy* is most usefully understood.

Like most of the Warner Brothers films of the early 1930s *Public Enemy* is quite short, lasting slightly under ninety minutes. This relatively short running time proves to be an asset, as the story of the rise and fall of the smalltime hoodlum is told in a series of perfectly conceived sequences. The opening sequence is introduced with the title "1909," and Wellman effectively uses authentic newsreel footage of an earlier period in Chicago to set the mood.[14] These early "atmosphere" scenes also clearly establish the innocent use of alcohol as a pervasive aspect of life in 1909, with scenes of gushing beer taps pouring their contents into buckets, the horse-drawn brewery truck, and a stockyard worker carrying back to his workmates six cans of beer carefully balanced on a long wooden pole; all juxtaposed by the noisy reminder of the Salvation Army Band marching past the saloon—a portent of the legislated prohibition that is to come.

There is an attempt in *Public Enemy* to provide the audience with some sociological and psychological justification for the deviant character of Tom Powers, but while these scenes are interesting, they do not adequately explain why one brother (Tom) becomes a hoodlum and the other (Mike) a war hero, although they both grew up in the same environment.

We first see the young Tom and his friend Matt standing at the "family entrance" of a saloon where they have been sent to buy a pail of beer. Tom, in a gesture which he repeats several times in the film, gives a quick glance over his shoulder, and surreptitiously takes a swig from the family pail, wiping the tell-tale moustache of froth away with his hand. At this point two young girls, also on their way to buy beer, stop to talk to Tom and Matt, and Tom's somewhat callous attitude (in comparison to Matt's anxious enthusiasm) provides us with a clue to his subsequent behavior toward women. In the next scene we see Tom and Matt running through a department store, being pursued by a floorwalker and subsequently a policeman, but they escape capture by sliding down the bannister of the escalator. Tom later steals a pair of roller skates and gives them to Molly, Matt's sister, so that he can cause her to stumble. When Tom's older brother Mike comes to Molly's rescue, he accuses Tom of the theft, and the scene ends with Tom lying across his policeman father's knee receiving a thrashing. This opening "socialization" sequence ends with Tom and Matt entering the Red Oaks "Youth" Club, where the Club organizer, a smalltime hoodlum and fence named Putty Nose is singing risqué ditties to a group of teenage boys. Calling Putty Nose into the backroom, the boys sell him a card of stolen pocket watches for fifty cents each, minus their club dues. And so begins their formal career as petty thieves.

The next sequence of scenes is titled "1915," and opens with the two boys, now in their adult personae, approaching the same club, which they enter after Tom has given his usual suspicious glance over his shoulder. The members of the club are now older, and Putty Nose offers the boys an opportunity to participate in a robbery of a fur warehouse, handing them each a revolver as a Christmas present. The robbery is botched when the nervous Tom fires several shots at a large, stuffed polar bear, and in the subsequent confusion Tom kills a policeman (psychological revenge against his father?). When he learns that Putty Nose has left town rather than "protect" them as promised, Tom vows to kill him when next they meet.

The next title, "1917," is followed by a series of scenes showing the U.S. entry into World War I, and Mike's enlistment. The two brothers have a violent argument when Mike suggests that Tom "spend a little more time at home," and become the man in the family (the death of the father is understood). Tom is clearly unable to understand Mike's values regarding duty and patriotism (no doubt a popular sentiment with many in the 1931 audience), and turns instead to a more systematic life of crime under the tutelage of Paddy Ryan, a local bar owner.

The final time title, "1920," is followed by a montage of actual newsreel footage and studio scenes of the chaos during the hours before the imposition of Prohibition at midnight on January 16, 1920. The advent of Prohibition provides Tom and Matt with the opportunity to rise in the criminal hierarchy, and they become salesmen for an illegal beer operation run by Paddy Ryan, "Nails" Nathan, and a crooked brewery owner, Leeman. They acquire tailored clothes, a big sporty car, and take up with two women they have picked up in a nightclub. Tom has a showdown with Mike at a party given in honor of the latter's return from the war, when Mike destroys a keg of beer that Tom has brought home. Mike shouts at Tom, "You Murderers! It's not beer in that keg! It's beer and blood. Blood of men!" Tom's reply indicates his contempt for his brother's motives, "Your hands ain't so clean. You killed . . . and you liked it! You didn't get no medals for holding hands with them Germans."

It is immediately after this that the famous grapefruit sequence takes place. Tom, obviously fed up with the increasing domesticity of his arrangement with Kitty (Mae Clark) smashes a grapefruit half into the side of her face at the breakfast table.[15] In the next scene Tom picks up Gwen (Jean Harlow) and switches his attention to her. At a nightclub, celebrating Matt's engagement, Tom and Matt spot Putty Nose, and after following him home, Tom shoots Putty Nose as his former boyhood mentor pleads for his life.

Nails Nathan is accidentally killed when thrown from his horse, and Tom and Matt wreak vengence on the horse, Rajah, shooting the animal in its barn.[16] Nails's death precipitates a gangland war with the "Schemer" Burns gang over control of the liquor rackets, and after hiding out, Matt is cut down by a hidden machine gun. Tom, again honoring the code of vengence, singlehandedly attacks the Burns headquarters, and is seriously wounded. Emerging from the building, in the pouring rain, Tom staggers along the street, and collapses in the gutter uttering the famous line, "I ain't so tough!" Tom is taken to hospital, where, swathed in bandages, he is reconciled with his mother and brother Mike. While waiting for Tom to recover and return home, Mike learns that Tom has been kidnapped from his hospital bed by the Burns gang. The end comes swiftly and dramatically, as Tom is "delivered" home, trussed up like an Egyptian mummy, and his body falls into the house as Mike opens the door. The closing scene of Mike walking slowly away from his brother's mutilated remains is played against the sounds of a record of "I'm Forever Blowing Bubbles" clicking to an end on the gramophone. The film closes with yet another title: "The Public Enemy is not a man nor is it a character, it is a problem that sooner or later we, the public, must solve."

There is nothing particularly pathbreaking about the plot or cinematography, both being fairly conventional. Rather, the film's success and importance are based on the way in which the individual elements—story, stars, and production—have been combined into a memorable whole. There are, however, some interesting plot elements worthy of note. Wellman handles the violence in a somewhat curious manner, and only one killing, that of Matt, is actually shown on screen.[17] The point at which Tom cold-bloodedly shoots Putty Nose is indicated by the reaction on Matt's face, and by the sound of Putty Nose's body falling across the keys of the piano he was playing in an attempt to arouse nostalgic sympathy from his former pupils. Cagney's character, as already noted, is a riveting one, made all the more so by such occasional light touches as his loving mock punch on his mother's cheek[18] or his trying out a revolver in a gun shop and using the weapon to hold up the storekeeper.

The gangster film cycle of the early 1930s benefited enormously from the technical improvement of sound quality. (Some film historians suggest that the advent of sound was responsible for precipitating these films.) *Public Enemy* is no exception, and the sounds of gunfire, the snappy dialogue, and the background music are all important elements in the plot. (One scene has Tom indicating his dissatisfaction with their relationship to Gwen with the song "I Surrender Dear" playing in the background.) The movie's sets were typically those of the Warner Brothers art department, and such lower class homes, apartments, and hotel rooms were to be the studio's trademark throughout the 1930s and 1940s.[19]

The authenticity of many incidents in the plot of *Public Enemy* has already been noted, but the film as a whole deals fairly accurately with an event in American social history that is the source of much misunderstanding—Prohibition. The film was, of course, made while Prohibition was still in force, and reflects a great deal of the cynicism toward the morality behind the imposition of Prohibition, and the hypocrisy with which the Volstead Act (the Eighteenth Amendment) was enforced. While there have been many interpretations of the events that lead up to the passing of the Eighteenth Amendment, Joseph Gusfield sums it up best in his study, *Symbolic Crusade.*

> What Prohibition symbolized was the superior power and prestige of the old middle class in American society. The threat of decline in that position had made explicit actions of government necessary to defend it. Legislation did this in two ways. It demonstrated the power of the old middle classes by showing that they could mobilize sufficient politi-

cal strength to bring it about and it gave dominance to the character and style of old middle-class life in contrast to that of the urban lower and middle classes.[20]

In reality this meant the assertion of power by the Protestant, rural, native American, and was directly aimed at the emerging power of the Catholic and Jewish immigrants, and the urban middle class. The Temperance Movement has had a long history in the United States, but it was no historical accident that it should turn its power toward national legislation in the precise decade when urbanism became the dominant mode of American life style. "The result," Gusfield notes, "was that what for one group was a part of its daily existence and a legitimate and welcome source of leisure, was to the dry forces a vice whose eradication was essential."[21]

There are many myths surrounding the failure of Prohibition, in particular that Prohibition's unenforceability created a deepseated cynicism that one could not legislate morality. As Gusfield has pointed out, however, it was the changes in the philosophy of political life precipitated by the Depression which were ultimately responsible. "The Depression had enormously strengthened the demand for increased employment and tax revenues which a reopened beer and liquor industry would bring, and it had made issues of status secondary to economic and class issues."[22] *Public Enemy*, although dealing with incidents in the early 1920s, nevertheless reflects the outlook on Prohibition seen from the first years of the Depression. Tom and Matt have no remorse for their illegal activities, seizing upon Prohibition as a fortuitous chance to get rich as quickly as possible. Their immigrant Irish upbringing could not have made them do otherwise in the face of a law which their culture considered ridiculous. Their open defiance of the law at a family gathering (the beer keg episode) brings tacit approval from all present except Mike, whose objections are on other than moral grounds.

The advent of Prohibition provided the ideal opportunity for criminals of all types to make money by becoming bootleggers. *Public Enemy* deals with this specific period of "individualistic competition" in the years before bootlegging became a highly monopolistic industry like most other large American industries, an organizational development that characterizes much of the criminal activity in the United States.[23] Thus Paddy Ryan and Nails Nathan mobilize immediately, eliciting the assistance of the former brewer Leeman, whose plant is now closed. Their initial meeting to organize the bootlegging operation is worth recalling. Leeman, a small, dapper man in his early sixties, makes a pretense at altruism and says:

> "You can understand, of course, that my desire is merely to furnish a better grade of beer than the working man can now obtain under the present . . . oh . . . unfortunate. . . ."

He is interrupted by Nails, who makes the position of the gang clear:

> "In your hat! I've heard that north wind before. If you're in this, you're in for the coin the same as the rest of us."

Tom and Matt are impressed by Nails's forthrightness and smile knowingly at each other. Leeman has no reply and merely nods agreement. The veneer of piety is shattered.[24]

One factor common to all three of the most famous gangster films of the early 1930s (*Little Caesar, Public Enemy* and *Scarface*), was the immigrant backgrounds of their major characters. Thus Rico Bandello, Tom Powers, and Tony Carmonte are each faced with the same problem of rising from humble origins to attain "The American Dream," a plot line which Philip French has suggested is a grotesque parody of the Horatio Alger myth.[25] Despite what may now appear to be merely conventional plot elements,[26] there is clear historical evidence to support their characterizations as members of ethnic minorities. Mark H. Haller, in his historical study of crime in Chicago notes:

> Crime has had enduring ties with urban political factions, [and] played a crucial part in the social life of ethnic groups struggling upward in urban slums. . . . In Chicago, criminal activity and the criminal justice system were rooted in the city's ethnic neighborhoods and were a means of social mobility for persons of marginal social and economic position in society. (The ethnic political machines served the same purpose.) As a result, criminals, politicians, and enforcement officials often shared experiences and values.[27]

Throughout the 1920s the criminal activities of ethnic minorities had concerned the city fathers of Chicago, and statistics compiled by University of Chicago sociologists William F. Ogburn and Clark Tibbits in 1930 confirmed their worst fears. Of the 108 "directors" of the Chicago underworld, 30 percent were of Italian ancestory, 29 percent were Irish, 20 percent were Jewish, and 12 percent were black. Their report noted that "not a single leader was recorded as native white American of native born stock." The criminal justice system had a similar distribution of groups (except for blacks), and to further underscore the stereotype, 76 percent of the police captains were Irish.[28] Haller's study confirms the validity of the criminal way of life depicted in *Public Enemy*, pointing out that criminals usually worked with a mob, with clearly defined areas of organizational responsibility ("fence," "mouthpiece," etc.). He also notes that the "organized" crime, which was largely precipitated by Prohibition, altered the nature of criminal activity from dealing with victims to dealing with customers. In fact, "the distribution and sale of alcoholic beverages in Chicago during Prohibition brought organized crime to a level of income and customer support that revolutionized the city's underworld."[29]

The reasons for the popularity of the gangster hero during the early years of the Depression are still a matter of conjecture. There has always been room for the antihero in American popular culture (witness Billy the Kid and Jesse James), but these were usually cast in the Robin Hood "rob the rich to feed the poor" mold. The urban, ethnic gangster seldom had any such redeeming qualities in the films of the early 1930s, although by the end of the decade, the second cycle of gangster films, which began in 1935, concentrated on the role of the crimefighters in their war against criminals.[30] It was also in the period 1932–1937 that studios (particularly Warner Brothers) began to turn their attention to films which dealt with the social problems of the day. Wellman's *Wild Boys of the Road* (1933), Mervyn LeRoy's *I Am a Fugitive from a Chain Gang* (1932), and Michael Curtiz's *Black Fury* (1935) were all products of the Warner Brothers studio, which quickly acquired a reputation for producing films about the "working class," and which openly supported Franklin D. Roosevelt's New Deal philosophy.[31]

The mood of the Depression certainly encouraged an intensive examination of American life—what it stood for, its strengths and its weaknesses—in an attempt to hold on to the useful while discarding or altering the useless or outmoded ideas of a previous age.[32] In many ways these early gangster films can be seen as a form of cultural catharsis, which demonstrated the results of a credo that made a virtue of the drive for success at any price, including murder.

The gangster simply ignores the laws and mores of a society which were being questioned anyway; and he establishes his own code of justice and social order within the hierarchy of the criminal underworld. To many in the audience the comparison between the gangster and the grasping, well-organized, business tycoons, who were held to be responsible for the Depression (in the popular culture at any rate), must have been obvious. The gangster embodied both the best and the worst elements of the American ideal, and in these films audiences were given the opportunity to examine these alternatives. In the long run the majority of the moviegoing public opted for the more positive solution, and the movie studios turned their attention to social issues and the fight against crime, rather than its glorification.[33] That these changes occurred after 1933 and the implementation of the New Deal Administration is no mere coincidence, for the new mood of optimism engendered by Roosevelt, although not borne out by any economic reality, was reflected in much of Hollywood's product.[34]

As was noted earlier, *Public Enemy* was a financial success, but it did not arouse any great outpouring of critical acclaim at the time of its release. André D. Sennwald in the *New York Times* called it "just another gangster film, weaker than most in its story, stronger than most in its acting, and like most maintaining a certain level of interest through the last burst of machine-gun fire. . . ."[35] The anonymous *Time* reviewer noted that the film

> . . . is well-told and its intensity is relieved by scenes of the central characters slugging bartenders and slapping their women across the face. U.S. audiences, long trained by the press to glorify thugs, last week laughed loudly at such comedy and sat spellbound through the serious parts. . . . It carries to its ultimate absurdity the fashion for romanticizing gangsters . . .[36]

Dwight MacDonald, a critic who has always been extremely difficult to please, on reviewing the film thirty years after it had first been released, said, "I had remembered it as good, but not as good as it now appears to be . . . [Cagney's] performance is as great as anything I've seen in movies. . . ."[37] Judging from most present-day critical opinion, the quality and impact of *Public Enemy* have now come to be appreciated. However, as has been true throughout the history of the American film industry, critical and public opinion did not coincide, and the approximately seventy million Americans who went to movies every week in 1931 gave their support to this latest gangster offering. It was precisely because of this popularity that the early gangster films were attacked so vehemently by those groups that wanted to see the motion picture industry made more responsive to a public form of social control.[38]

In 1930, after eight years of trying various schemes of self-regulation, the president of the Motion Picture Producers and Distributors of America, Will H. Hays, was finally able to get the studio heads to agree to the *Production Code*, which outlined a fairly comprehensive set of standards for motion picture content.[39] But by 1930 Hollywood was a different place from what it had been in 1922, when Hays resigned as Postmaster-General to accept the role of "Czar" of the industry.[40] The outcries against the "morals of the movies," which had been heard since their introduction in the 1890s, increased in intensity during the early years of the Depression. The advent of sound and the resulting influx of "sophisticated" Broadway actors and playwrights only served to sharpen the focus of moralists who now decried the new "adult" content of Hollywood films. The onset of the Depression, and the economic chaos left in its wake, saw the film studios turn increasingly to themes of sex and violence as a means of attracting audiences to dwindling box-office lines, and the resulting public reaction finally provided Hays with the ammunition he needed to enforce his *Code*.[41]

Historians have disagreed as to why the Depression triggered a new tone of moralism and an increased dependence on religion. Whatever the cause, by 1934 the time seemed ripe for a moral revolution and the motion picture industry, as usual, proved to be a ready and willing target; only this time the industry itself, caught up in a desperate financial struggle for survival, was much more vulnerable to these attacks, and therefore also amenable to change. The increasing public concern with movie morality culminated in the formation of the Roman Catholic Legion of Decency, a powerful pressure group with the full might of the Catholic Church behind it, dedicated to forcing the movie industry to alter its content, and to be more responsive to public demands.[42] The mere existence of the Legion of Decency with its threats of a movie boycott was enough to provide Will Hays with the ammunition he needed to convince the movie industry executives that self-regulation was in their best interests.[43]

Public Enemy was only one of the many films that contributed to the events culminating in the establishment of the infamous Production Code Administration (Breen Office) in 1934. The film stands today as an excellent example of both a genre and a cultural symbol. Its place in the iconography of American popular culture is secure.

NOTES

1. For a perceptive examination of this genre see Stephen L. Karpf, *The Gangster Film: Emergence, Variation and Decay of a Genre, 1930–1940* (New York: Arno Press, 1973); and Arthur Sacks, "An Analysis of the Gangster Movies of the Early Thirties," *The Velvet Light Trap*, no. 1, 1971, pp. 5–11, 32. Surprisingly, *Public Enemy* as an individual film has received very little attention from film scholars.

2. Studio financial statements have always been historical curiosities, and notoriously unreliable. These figures and other extremely useful data come from James R. Silke, *Here's Looking At You, Kid: Fifty Years of Fighting, Working and Dreaming at Warner Brothers* (Boston: Little, Brown and Company, 1976). See also Charles Higham, *Warner Borthers* (New York: Charles Scribner's Sons, 1975); and Ted Sennett, *Warner Brothers Presents* (New Rochelle, N.Y.: Arlington House, 1971). A special issue of *The Velvet Light Trap*, no. 1 (1971) is devoted to "Warner Brothers in the Thirties," and contains many interesting articles.

3. Andrew Bergman, *We're In the Money: Depression America and Its Films* (New York: New York University Press, 1971), p. xxi. For details on the financial aspects of the film industry, see Mae D. Huettig, *Economic Control of The Motion Picture Industry* (Philadelphia: University of Pennsylvania Press, 1944; reprinted New York: Jerome S. Ozer, 1971); the best source for the complex details surrounding the introduction of sound is J. Douglas Gomery, "The Coming of Sound to the American Cinema: A History of the Transformation of an Industry," unpublished Ph.D. dissertation, University of Wisconsin, 1975.

4. Silke, p. 60.

5. In six months Bright and Glasmon wrote four scripts, *Public Enemy, Smart Money, Blonde Crazy,* and *Taxi.* All four films starred the unknown James Cagney, made him into a star, and made considerable profits for Warners. See Silke, p. 61.

6. For details on Zanuck's career, see Mel Gussow, *Don't Say Yes Until I Finish Talking* (New York: Doubleday & Company, 1971).

7. Patrick McGilligan, "James Cagney: The Actor as Auteur," *The Velvet Light Trap*, no. 7 (Winter 1972/73), p. 4.

8. Cagney, of course, played a wide variety of roles in his long movie career, including that of Bottom in Max Reinhardt's movie version of *A Midsummer Night's Dream* (1935). For details of his career, see James Cagney,

Cagney by Cagney (New York: Doubleday & Co., 1976). He was never completely happy in these roles, or with his treatment at the Warners Studio, and this led to a long series of conflicts and many suspensions. He notes, "Actors were considered to be expendable material, just like props or makeup." (Ibid., p. 46).

9. Lincoln Kirstein, "James Cagney and the American Hero," *Hound & Horn* (April-June, 1932), p. 466. (From a collection reprinted by Arno Press, N.Y., 1972).

10. Ibid., pp. 466–67.

11. Robert Warshow, "The Gangster as Tragic Hero," in *The Immediate Experience* (New York: Anchor Books, 1964), p. 86.

12. This question of national vs. local media, especially as it relates to the motion picture, is explored in some depth in Garth Jowett, *Film: The Democratic Art* (Boston: Little, Brown and Company, 1976). For an excellent examination of the irrepressible nature of mass culture, see Arthur J. Vidich and Joseph Bensman, *Small Town in Mass Society* (Princeton, N.J.: Princeton University Press, 1968).

13. Robert S. Lynd and Helen Merrell Lynd, *Middletown* (New York: Harcourt, Brace & World, 1929), p. 271. When they returned to Middletown in 1935, they found that cosmopolitanism had greatly increased. See *Middletown in Transition* (New York: Harcourt, Brace & World, 1937).

14. The exact date of this footage is unknown, but judging by the number of automobiles present on the street, and the fashions, it appears to be a few years later than 1909; probably 1912–1915.

15. The grapefruit scene is undoubtedly one of the most famous in the history of the American cinema. As one would expect there is disagreement as to how it originated. Darryl Zanuck has claimed that it was his idea; but so has William Wellman, who claims that he had Cagney perform an act which Wellman wanted to perform in real life on his own wife. The truth, more likely, is the claim that the scene was based upon a real incident when a Chicago hoodlum, Hymie Weiss, shoved an omelet into his loquacious girlfriend's face. Cagney notes: "It was just about the first time . . . that a woman had been treated like a broad on the screen instead of like a delicate flower. . . . That bit of business became so identified with me that years afterward when I'd go into a restaurant, people would send me half grapefruits with their compliments. . . ." Interview in *Saturday Evening Post*, July 14, 1956, p. 51.

16. This scene is not as far-fetched as it may seem, and was based on a similar incident after Samuel "Nails" Morton was killed by his horse. See Richard Whitehall, "Crime Inc., Part Three: Public Enemies," *Films and Filming* (March, 1964), p. 42.

17. An interesting point here is that in 1931 the special effects were unable to simulate machine gun fire, and a real machine gun, manned by an expert named Bailey, was used. Cagney notes that this made for some hair-raising experiences, but the scene itself is graphic evidence that real bullets were fired into the wall above the actor's head. See Cagney, p. 44.

18. Patrick Gilligan has noted that Cagney's films often showed his character's relationship with his mother: "No other actor has been so closely haunted by his nearest kin." This recurring motif reaches its climax in the complex Freudian dependence on his mother in his role as Cody Jarrett in *White Heat* (1949). See Gilligan, pp. 9–10.

19. Calvin Pryluck has noted that, "In the 30s Warner Brothers sets were cheaply constructed, their directors of photography were under instructions

to avoid lighting the corners of the set so as to mask the shoddy construction." Calvin Pryluck, "The Aesthetic Relevance of the Organization of Film Production," *Cinema Journal*, vol. 15, no. 2 (Spring, 1976), p. 4.

20. Joseph R. Gusfield, *Symbolic Crusade: Status Politics and the American Temperance Movement* (Urbana: University of Illinois Press, 1963), p. 122. For other useful studies of Prohibition see Charles Merz, *The Dry Decade* (New York: Doubleday, Doran and Company, 1930); Andrew Sinclair, *Prohibition: The Era of Excess* (Boston: Little, Brown and Co., 1962); and James Timberlake, *Prohibition and the Progressive Movement* (Cambridge, Mass.: Harvard University Press, 1963). The best overall discussion of the long-term effects of Prohibition on American society is Joseph R. Gusfield, "Prohibition: The Impact of Political Utopianism," in *Change and Continuity in Twentieth-Century America: The 1920s*, edited by John Braeman, et al. (Columbus, Ohio: Ohio State University Press, 1968), pp. 257–308.

21. Gusfield, "Prohibition," p. 294.

22. Gusfield, *Symbolic Crusade*, p. 127.

23. For further thought on the nature of criminal activity, see Daniel Bell, "Crime as an American Way of Life," in *The End of Ideology* (Glencoe, Ill.: The Free Press, 1960), chapter 7.

24. Leeman's name is obviously European, possibly German. While this is not explored in the film itself, German immigrants have always been strongly connected with the brewing industry in the United States. During World War I this was the source of much popular outcry by the drys, again a reflection of the status argument suggested by Gusfield.

25. Philip French, "Incitement Against Violence," *Sight and Sound* (Winter, 1967–68), p. 3. He goes on to point out that later gangster heroes (John Dillinger, "Baby Face" Nelson, Bonnie Parker and Clyde Barrow) are all "fourth or fifth generation WASPS from rural communities of the Mid-West and South-West," who actively sought publicity. Bergman suggests that *Little Caesar*'s Rico is following Andrew Carnegie's "The Road to Business Success, An Address to Young Men," only to fail when he strays from this advice. *We're in the Money*, pp. 7–10.

26. The concept of conventions in popular culture is examined in depth in a brilliant study, John G. Cawelti, *Adventure, Mystery, and Romance* (Chicago: The University of Chicago Press, 1976). Cawelti notes of the 1920s and 1930s urban gangsters: "These new formulas made protagonists or heroes out of lower-class figures characterized by crudeness, aggressive violence, and alienation from the respectable morality of society." (p. 61).

27. Mark H. Haller, "Urban Crime and Criminal Justice: The Chicago Case," *The Journal of American History*, vol. 57, no. 3 (December, 1970), pp. 619–620.

28. Quoted in Ibid., p. 620.

29. Ibid., p. 623. Haller's study also confirms the truth behind other scenes in the movie, such as the lavish floral tributes to dead gangsters, the open association with segments of Chicago upper society in the night life of the city, and the general tolerance of the police for these activities.

30. Warner Brothers was also in the forefront of this new cycle with such films as William Keighley's *G-Men* (1935), *Show Them No Mercy* (1935), *The Petrified Forest* (1936), and *The Wrong Road* (1937).

31. Harry Warner was one of the few Hollywood "moguls" to actively support Roosevelt in his 1932 election campaign, and he issued a directive to this effect to his employees. Russell Campbell has noted that the Warner

production chiefs (Hal Wallis, Darryl Zanuck, and Jack Warner) had, in fact, been receptive to "social realism" long before the directive. See Russell Campbell, "Warner Brothers in the Thirties: Some Tentative Notes," *The Velvet Light Trap*, no. 1 (1971), p. 3.

32. William Stott explores this topic in an excellent study, *Documentary Expression and Thirties America* (New York: Oxford University Press, 1973).

33. It can be argued, of course, that even the crime-fighter films glorified the gangster. However, the marked shift in the mid-1930s cannot be ignored. It is interesting to note that the release of Arthur Penn's *Bonnie and Clyde* (1967) started a new cycle of gangster or criminal "hero-worship."

34. No consideration of the cultural mood of this period would be complete without a serious examination of the insightful analysis by Warren I. Susman, "The Thirties," in Stanley Coben and Lorman Ratner, eds., *The Development of an American Culture* (Englewood Cliffs, N.J.: Prentice-Hall, 1970), pp. 179–218. For a useful overview of the historical literature of the period, see Otis L. Graham, Jr., "The Age of the Great Depression, 1929–1940," in William H. Cartwright and Richard L. Watson, Jr., eds., *The Reinterpretation of American History and Culture* (Washington, D.C.: National Council for Social Studies, 1973).

35. *New York Times*, April 24, 1931, p. 27:1.

36. Quoted in Homer Dickens, *The Films of James Cagney* (Secaucus, N.J.: The Citadel Press, 1972), pp. 50–51.

37. Ibid., p. 50.

38. The issue of social control and the motion picture industry is explored at length in Garth Jowett, *Film: The Democratic Art*. The questions surrounding the problems of movie censorship are discussed in Ibid., Ira H. Carmen, *Movies, Censorship and the Law* (Ann Arbor: University of Michigan Press, 1966); Richard S. Randall, *Censorship of the Movies* (Madison: University of Wisconsin Press, 1968), and Douglas Ayer, et al., "Self-Censorship in the Movie Industry: An Historical Perspective on Law and Social Change," *Wisconsin Law Review*, no. 3 (1970), pp. 791–838.

39. The *Code* was explicit when it came to the treatment of crime on the screen. "General Principle" no. 1 read:

Crimes Against the Law: These shall never be presented in such a way as to throw sympathy with the crime as against law and justice or to inspire others with a desire for imitation.

1. Murder
   a. The technique of murder must be presented in a way that will not inspire imitation
   b. Brutal killings are not to be presented in detail
   c. Revenge in modern times shall not be justified.
2. Methods of crime should not be explicitly presented
   a. Theft, robbery, safe-cracking, and dynamiting of trains, mines, buildings, etc., should not be detailed in method
   b. Arson must be subject to the same safeguards
   c. The use of firearms should be restricted to essentials
   d. Methods of smuggling should not be presented.

Obviously, not only were these rules being ignored, they were being openly flouted by the studios in the period 1930–1934. For a detailed examination of the failure of the *Code*, see John A. Sargent, "Self-Regulation: The Motion Picture Production Code, 1930–1961," unpublished Ph.D. dissertation, University of Michigan, 1963.

40. In reality Hays was never a "Czar," as he lacked the basic power to force the studios to adhere to MPPDA regulations. It is also quite clear that Hays's appointment was based upon his close connection with the Republican Administration and was made in the belief that he would be able to thwart the introduction of federal censorship. In this role he was very successful.

41. The complaints about movie content came from all sources, but religious groups were usually in the forefront. An editorial in *The Commonweal* in 1931 noted that a recent meeting of the New York State Chapter of the Knights of Columbus had considered a resolution that the gangster film "creates a criminal instinct in our youth." The editorial continued: "The gangster movies . . . are often brilliantly acted and directed. Their detail is conveyed with a vividness almost hypnotic." "Gang Films," *The Commonweal*, June 10, 1931, pp. 143–144.

42. Unfortunately limitations of space prevent a full discussion of the circumstances surrounding the formation of the Legion of Decency, its tactics, and its ultimate effect. See Jowett, *Film: The Democratic Art*, pp. 246–256; and Paul W. Facey, *The Legion of Decency: A Sociological Analysis of the Emergence and Development of a Pressure Group* (New York: Arno Press, 1974).

43. In July, 1934, less than three months after the formation of the Legion, the MPPDA agreed to the establishment of the Production Code Administration (PCA), to be headed by Joseph Breen, a Catholic. It was also agreed that no member company of the MPPDA would distribute or release or exhibit any film unless it received a certificate of approval signed by the PCA. These regulations were strengthened by the provision for a 25,000 dollar penalty for failure to comply—the first time such a "punishment clause" had ever been agreed upon by members of the industry organization. It was this infamous *Code* that would dictate the content of what was seen on American movie screens until the late 1960s. There are no really good examinations of the Production Code Administration. For an anecdotal account, see Jack Vizzard, *See No Evil* (New York: Simon and Schuster, 1970).

Will Rogers and the Relevance of Nostalgia:

Steamboat 'Round the Bend (1935)

PETER C. ROLLINS

Doc Pearly (Will Rogers) ties up the loose ends in a complicated plot by overseeing the marriage of Fleety Belle (Anne Shirley) and Duke (John McGuire). The film was released after the actor's death.

(Photo courtesy of Museum of Modern Art)

On August 15, 1935, Will Rogers and his pilot Wiley Post were killed in a plane crash at Point Barrow, Alaska. One week later, the offices of Fox and Universal Studios closed at noon so that office workers could attend a special memorial service at the Hollywood Bowl "where over twenty thousand gathered to pay tribute to the memory of the beloved humorist."[1] That evening, twelve thousand motion picture theaters across the country observed two minutes of respectful silence before beginning their evening programs.

Just before leaving for Alaska, Rogers had completed two films. Previously, Hollywood had observed "an unwritten law forbidding the release of a picture after the death of a star,"[2] but in the case of Will Rogers, there were obviously other factors to be considered. In fact, the rationale behind the release of *In Old Kentucky* and *Steamboat 'Round the Bend* gives us a glimpse of the special relationship between Will Rogers and his American audience. After a long conference, Joseph Schenck (chairman of the board of directors) and Sidney R. Kent (president) of Fox determined that the release of these last two pictures would not have the same morbid overtones that might have accompanied a similar posthumous release of films by other actors: "Rogers was totally different from Valentino, Wallace Reid and Lon Chaney, where audiences appreciated their work. Rogers was loved as a man, as a national character, as the greatest of all home philosophers."[3]

Joseph Schenck was right about the unique place of Will Rogers in the hearts of Americans. Although he never held political office, the popularity of his daily syndicated columns, his books, and finally his movies made him one of the most important molders of opinion in America from 1922 until his untimely death in 1935. As public person, as journalist, and as film star Will Rogers confronted and subdued many of the pressures and anxieties affecting his audience. A typical Will Rogers fan had very special ideas about Rogers's behavior as a private individual; he derived a special pleasure from the style of Rogers's journalism. With these elements in mind, he attended and surrendered to the seductive nostalgia of films like *Steamboat 'Round the Bend.*

Some of the material in this essay first appeared in *Journal of Popular Culture*, 9 (1976).

In the last stage of his Hollywood career, Rogers became the film industry's best paid and most popular male movie attraction (225,000 dollars per film). From 1933 until 1935, he portrayed a film character who deeply moved his American audience. If correctly interpreted, his nostalgic rural dramas document the spirit of the 1930s as accurately as *I'll Take My Stand* (1930),[4] in which "Twelve Southerners" protest against progress, "sophistication," the city, and a declining estimate of man. Like that famous anthology, the late films of Will Rogers portray an alternative society in which the best traditional elements of the American national character could have free play. Will Rogers was important to Americans in the 1920s and 1930s because he addressed his humor to their basic sense of rootlessness and loss. As a cowboy version of Rip Van Winkle, Rogers passed through this era of change, judging new developments by the standards of the 1890s. And despite the criticism he delivered, he somehow bridged the gap between the old and the new. Franklin Delano Roosevelt was not alone in concluding that the sanity of Americans in the turbulent early decades of the twentieth century had been preserved because of the sympathy and humor of this complex companion of the American people.[5]

Will Rogers's first film, *Laughing Bill Hyde* (1918), showed him twirling his rope on the stage of Ziegfeld's *Follies*. Not surprisingly, he soon found himself cast as a cowboy in various melodramatic and comic roles. Yet Rogers had real problems with his audience in these first films. New York critics who knew Rogers from the *Follies* brought an understanding of his humor to the films and this preparation helped them relate to the silent film character. The general public, however, was indifferent because it had not yet been exposed to the Oklahoman's satires. Records show that Samuel Goldwyn lost at least forty thousand dollars on these early films.[6]

After a short time as a cowboy, Rogers developed a second film persona. Called "Jubilo," the figure is a rural clown, a perpetual loafer who floats through society getting himself into trouble and avoiding work whenever possible.[7] Jubilo is an eccentric figure whom we love despite his numerous flaws. He is distinctly unlike the philosophical Rogers persona of the 1930s: Jubilo can fall in love and even has a few (rather athletic) fist fights.

During Rogers's middle film period (1929–1932) he developed

still another screen persona, one which would have been readily recognized by his daily readers. In these portraits of an Innocent Abroad, Rogers plays a simple down-to-earth figure (usually from Claremore, Oklahoma) who is forced to travel outside his provincial world to Washington (*Going to Congress* [1924]), New Orleans (*Handy Andy* [1923]), or Europe (*They Had to See Paris* [1929]). The Innocent is usually forced out of his normal environment by his wife, who aspires to be a sophisticated and "broad minded" citizen of the twentieth-century city. In at least three films, some local political faction accidentally elects the Innocent to Congress.[8] The humor in all of these films about the Innocent Abroad derives from the interplay between the central character and the corrupt people of the urban centers which he is forced to visit. In most cases, Will Rogers overwhelms the cosmopolites by the sheer force of his ebullient personality. In playing these roles as the Innocent, Rogers began to show that he was more than merely a good actor. One reviewer discerned that Rogers tapped deeper themes. In speaking of Pike Peters (a character portrayed by Rogers in *They Had to See Paris*), the reviewer noted that "Will Rogers has become a national character, infinitely more characteristic of America than the grotesque figure of Uncle Sam. It would be an artistic and patriotic crime to let such a film character [i.e., the Innocent Abroad] die."[9] The reviewer and his public were not disappointed, for *So This is London* (1930) placed Rogers in a similar ironic contrast between the solid provincial and an effete society.

America's new place in the international world determined the strong response to Rogers in this role. America had refused to enter the League of Nations, but the facts of international life could not be denied—the United States was the most powerful nation in the world, but was still unsure of its role. Rogers's Innocent Abroad films gave Americans a confident sense of poise. The message of these films was that older civilizations may have posted their claims to preeminence before the United States, but postwar realities dictated that the United States was the only country whose spirit had not been broken by World War I. As one discerning reviewer, reported, Rogers not only gave Americans a positive self-image, he also communicated a better picture of American character and values to the outside world:

There was always the quiet homely voice and the lovable smile to keep us in touch with the things we knew and understood. He was a Westerner talking to Westerners in a language and with an awkward grace readily comprehended. He was the epitome of the spirit of the West: open-handed, free and easy, loquacious, oddly philosophical, genuinely sentimental with a smile ever within reach—one of the boys. And we liked to think that this was the picture of us that he carried to other and far corners of the world, where people, not knowing us too well, were apt to think of us as uncouth and six-shooting.[10]

The advent of sound films effected a transformation in what Rogers could convey to his audience. Prior to sound, viewers missed much of Rogers's special humor. With sound, it was impossible to miss his radiating humanity. Speaking of this power to project a lovable personality, a reviewer of Rogers's first talkie, *They Had to See Paris*, noted that:

This picture changes all [the difficulties of communication in the silent films]. Rogers's shadow is almost a living thing. The wit is spontaneous and droll . . . the disarming humanness of the man envelopes the screen, the orchestra and the auditorium with one surging feeling of brother-hood.[11]

What was now needed in the era of sound was the proper screen vehicle for the Rogers personality. Of importance in selecting that role was the awareness that the camera could supply much of the atmosphere for the Rogers persona, that Will Rogers in a film could say less and still actually personify the values that had guided his "private" life and his journalistic commentary. The final Rogers films portray him as a small-town figure. He is no longer the cowboy, the clown, the satirist, nor even the innocent abroad, but a very different symbol of a harmonious America before the turn of the century.[12]

Actually, Rogers had experimented with the small-town role during the 1920s. One critic was extremely impressed by its possibilities. In a review of *Jes' Call Me Jim* (1920), he noted the kind of effects which would later be attributed to the Rogers of sound films—that he was not merely amusing his audience, but conveying a refreshing perspective on human possibilities. In this way, Rogers was showing that his films performed a social function:

Will Rogers's . . . good natured personality seems to spread throughout the world a sense of happiness and kindness. I suppose a man like this, acting as he does before almost countless millions, does more good to this old earth than scores of preachers and philanthropists; able to reach more hearts than can be reached through any other medium.[13]

In *State Fair* (1933), Rogers returned to this role. Audiences, executives at Fox, and critics all recognized immediately that this was the ideal role for Rogers because it placed him "in a day when American village life was far more isolated than it is today."[14] Celebrating the fact that "Will Rogers Restored Picture Themes to Provincial Subjects," a reviewer captured the essence of this universally positive response: "*State Fair* taught Rogers his correct *métier* and it taught the industry that pictures concerning inland, provincial characters were more appealing than penthouses and gun-spattered pavements." The reviewer concluded that Rogers's nostalgic pictures had tapped a "forgotten public" which "had lost interest in crime and so-called 'smart' films [and had] stayed away entirely from cinema."[15]

At least in the beginning, both the film critics and this "forgotten public" shared a common enthusiasm for these rural films. Some critics thought that they saw in Rogers a "complete metamorphosis from amusing philosopher into character actor."[16] Other critics thought that Rogers, after being a cowboy, clown, and innocent abroad, had finally stumbled upon the right character for the screen. But while film critics tired of the rural vehicle and quickly stopped applauding Rogers's films, the American public swarmed to them in ever-increasing numbers. Film rentals for Fox averaged about 2.5 million dollars per film. The irony was that Rogers had begun his film career as a darling of the critics but a box-office failure; in these late films, Rogers was obviously appealing to real and profound popular emotions that could easily be overlooked by a critic interested in film as an art form.

If we ignore the artistic merits of the late films and keep a clear focus on the response of the viewer, we begin to see why Rogers refrains from commenting directly on current events. The world of the later Will Rogers film is insulated from contemporary strains and pressures. For this reason the viewer's psychological "pay-off" from these rural dramas was the opportunity to escape temporarily from the world of ethical confusion, Depression, and impending war. In *David Harum* (1934) this place is called "Homeville," a term which will be used hereafter to describe the nostalgic, pre-industrial world in all of the late films of Will Rogers. Economic breakdown, the separation of a democratic society into rigid classes, and the professionalization of knowledge may exist in this world of the later films, but in a special form. In Homeville, all of these threats are reduced to human proportions. They may challenge the wits of Homeville's citizens, but they never seem to be overwhelming. Because the challenges to happiness and fulfillment have been reduced, the Will Rogers persona in Homeville, hereafter called "Uncle Will" because of his avuncular role, can deal with them. In a few instances, Uncle Will enlists the aid of the threatened, but most often he is capable of solving the problems by himself. He is really more than just an inhabitant of Homeville: he is its super-intending consciousness. Uncle Will has a special insight into the human heart. Because of this special power, and because every problem in Homeville has a human face, Uncle Will is a master of this world. The best metaphor for the perspective given the viewer of the late Rogers films is probably that of a telescope which we look through backwards. The result is that everything appears smaller and therefore less challenging.[17]

What has been said about Homeville and Uncle Will applies to the Rogers persona and the community portrayed in *Steamboat 'Round the Bend* (1935). *Steamboat* drops Uncle Will into a characteristic *fin de siècle* setting: the main title is followed by a montage showing a paddle wheeler steaming down the Mississippi; the river is broad and the banks are lined with timber. Just in case viewers might be inattentive to details of rustic *mise en scène*, descriptive titles clearly identify that we are back in Homeville: "*Time: 1890s . . . Place: The Mississippi Valley.*"

At the bow of the *Pride of Paducah*, we listen to an orotund evangelist (Burton Churchill) who claims to be "The New Moses." By means of a dissolve (indicating a short passage of time), we move slightly aft where we find "Doctor" John Pearly (Will Rogers) selling patent medicine of high alcoholic content. Contrasts could not be more extreme: The New Moses preaches against Demon Rum and Sloth; Doc Pearly promises that his Pocahontas remedy will exempt consumers from work, "especially at plowing time." Viewers should expect that all characters in this nostalgic tale will be equally eccentric and that the action will contain similar implausibilities.

After selling his entire stock Doc Pearly climbs to the bridge of the ship to talk with Captain Eli (Irvin S. Cobb), master of the *Pride of Paducah*. In a series of unscripted lines, the two aging humorists introduce the action. Captain Eli learns that Doc Pearly has purchased "an old mud scow" which he plans to name the *Claremore Queen*.[18] When Captain Eli claims that he will beat him in the annual steamboat race to Baton Rouge, Doc Pearly takes up the challenge: a bet is made, winner take all. Captain Eli then drops Doc Pearly and his engineer, Efe (Francis Ford, brother of the director), at a jetty. A short distance away is the deserted *Claremore Queen*, a backwheeler in considerable disrepair.

Plot complications are soon introduced. After sundown, Duke (John McGuire) comes aboard secretively, bringing with him a "swamp girl" named Fleety Belle (Anne Shirley). Doc Pearly is dismayed to learn that Duke has recently killed a man while fighting for the "honor" of this ragamuffin. When Doc Pearly hears that the homicide was in self-defense, he counsels Duke to surrender in order to clear himself. Duke follows this sensible advice, but an ill-tempered judge condemns the young man to be hanged. Duke's only hope is that Doc Pearly will find the New Moses, sole witness to the fight, before the scheduled hanging. The law's delays and the challenge of the elements provide Doc Pearly, in the persona of Uncle Will, with a number of opportunities to work his magical powers.

In *Steamboat*, as in the other late films of Will Rogers, plot complications are never as important as atmosphere. Early in the film, Duke finds that even the jails of Homeville are hospitable. When Doc Pearly and Duke present themselves to Sheriff Jetters (Eugene Pallette), they are received as friends seeking lodging. The agent of law and order throws Duke the keys, inviting his "guest" to select any jail cell that looks comfortable. During Duke's incarceration, the prison guards permit other domestic functions expected in Homeville: Duke and Fleety Belle conduct a lover's tryst while a chorus of black prisoners serenade them with a mellow rendering of "There's No Place Like Home." Prior to Duke's departure for execution at Baton Rouge, the sheriff and his family do their best to provide the young lovers with a proper wedding. That the sheriff's sermon is ungrammatical and unnecessarily emphatic about the phrase " 'til death do us part," and that his daughter can only play "Listen to the Mocking-bird" as a processional, only contribute to the quaint atmosphere. Affirmation of authority so pervades the mood of this segment that Duke refuses to escape when Fleety Belle plucks a rifle from the sheriff's hands.

Doc Pearly's attempts to find the New Moses become more desperate as Duke's execution approaches. When the *Claremore Queen* heads toward Baton Rouge, Fleety Belle and Doc Pearly become embroiled in the annual steamboat race. Fortunately, the *Claremore Queen* happens to pass a landing where the New Moses is declaiming against Booze. Drawing on his cowboy skills, the favorite son of Claremore lassos the prophet and drags him abroad. The evening watch also finds use for the improvised lasso: in an effort to conserve fuel, Doc Pearly ropes a capstan on the stern of the *Pride of Paducah*; with a tow line firmly affixed to the bow of the *Claremore Queen*, Doc Pearly is able to bank his fires. Not until the next morning does Captain Eli discover ("Holy jumpin' catfish") that he has been pulling a competitor all night.

During the closing miles of the race, the *Claremore Queen* runs so low on fuel that the New Moses proclaims, "Nothing will save us now but the power of prayer." Recapitulating the contrasts of the opening scene, we discover that not prayer, but the potent power of Pocahontas will bring victory over the *Pride of Paducah*. Bottles of Doc Pearly's long-forgotten patent medicine are cast into the flames: humorously, flashes from the wonder-working elixir are shown spurting from the twin smokestacks of the vessel, propelling the *Queen* at unwonted speed. Throughout the excitement, black comedian Stepin' Fetchit, cabin boy for the *Queen*, expostulates while others stoke the fires which will bring victory. A concluding reaction shot of Captain Eli shows us that he has been completely overwhelmed by this *deus ex machina*.

Although completely devoid of verisimilitude, this conclusion has the virtue of tying up a number of loose plot elements: Duke is exonerated moments before his scheduled execution; Stepin' Fetchit gets the victory cup; most importantly, boy gets girl. In the final shots of *Steamboat 'Round the Bend*, Doc Pearly lounges on a "back porch" aft of the *Claremore Queen*'s pilot house, smoking one of Captain Eli's favorite cigars. Our avuncular protector deserves his rest: he has resolved the discord around him; life in Homeville will return to its normal placidity.

In playing the role of Captain Eli, Irvin S. Cobb probably assumed that audiences would bring a knowledge of his Kentucky regional style to a viewing of *Steamboat 'Round the Bend.* It would have been difficult for a contemporary to be ignorant of Cobb: his articles were syndicated in the daily press and scores of his stories had found their way into the pages of the *Saturday Evening Post* and other magazines. Will Rogers fans would have seen *Judge Priest* (1934), a film that had been adapted from a story by Cobb.[19] Whatever the reasons, a marvelous ancedote conveys the insouciance of the two major actors as they approached the shooting of *Steamboat.* Here is Cobb's memory of the first meeting between the two regional writers and their young director, John Ford:

> So we went out to make *Steamboat 'Round the Bend.* We had a grand director, John Ford, an emotional Maine Yankee-Irishman, one of the authentic geniuses of the movies. The first morning of "shooting," Will and I were to have a scene together.
>
> "Do either of you two gentlemen by any chance happen to have the faintest idea of what this story is about?" inquired Ford, with his gentle, Celtic sarcasm which can be so biting.
>
> "I don't for one," confessed Rogers, and grinned sheepishly. "Something about a river, ain't it? Well, I was raised at Claremore, Oklahoma, where we don't have any rivers to speak of, so you might say I'm a stranger here, myself."
>
> "I thought so," murmured Ford, who had directed Rogers before. "And I don't suppose, Mr. Rogers, you've gone so far as to glance at the script?"
>
> "Been too busy ropin' calves," admitted Rogers. "Tell you what, John, you sort of generally break the news to us what this sequence is about and I'll think up a line for Cobb to speak and then Cobb'll think up a line for me to speak and that way there won't be no ill feelin's or heart burnin's and the feller that kin remember after it's all over what the plot was about—if there is any plot by then—gets first prize, which will be a kiss on the forehead from Mister John Ford."
>
> As heaven is my judge, that is how we did the scene, with Ford sitting by, as solemn as a hoot owl.[20]

Director John Ford had good reasons for being so indulgent: what these two regional figures said was not as important as what, in their accents and colloquialisms, they *represented.* Cobb and

Rogers were simply more important as relics of a bygone era than as actors playing roles. For this reason, the script was designed to be little more than a framework within which these regional humorists could be seen and heard. The Fox studio was alert to the monetary rewards for such hokum. The American audience was actively interested in seeing more "family films," and Fox was eager to please. Both the general audience and the critics were in agreement about the appeal of films about Will Rogers's "Homeville": "Audiences thanked him for his contribution to clean, family diversion. The more analytical saw him as a social factor and a godsend to a stagnant theater."[21] Thus, there were solid economic reasons for allowing Rogers and Cobb to clown on the set.

During location shooting near Sacramento, California, Rogers and Cobb continued their repartee on one of Rogers's regular Gulf radio broadcasts.[22] Audience expectations as to the characters' "innocence" can be extrapolated from the following radio dialogue. Rogers and Cobb here portray themselves as men from the heartland who have succeeded in Hollywood without becoming tainted by it:

> *Rogers:* Do you feel yourself, kind of going Hollywood in any way? You know, we all kind of do. It kind of gets us down there. Do you feel yourself kind of?
> *Cobb:* Well, I find that I am talking to myself, and worse than that, I am answering back. And I have been cutting out paper dolls at odd times.
> *Rogers:* And saying your own yesses, Hey?
> *Cobb:* Yes, I'm living in yes-man's land, which is worse than no-man's land was during the war. I haven't worn slacks yet. I'm still sticking to my first wife. I guess I haven't gone Hollywood.
> *Rogers:* Do you find that this censorship that Will Hays has got in on us now, does it kind of interfere with you, kind of cramp your emotions in any way?
> *Cobb:* Well, I noticed as a result of Will Hays' campaign they no longer talk about putting a tax on raw film.[23]

The role of innocent had dual functions: over the airwaves, Cobb and Rogers posed as Innocents Abroad in America's most liberated city; in *Steamboat*, John Ford was doing his best to establish them as innocents at home in a simpler, rural past.

The contribution of Stepin Fetchit (Lincoln Theodore Perry)

to *Steamboat 'Round the Bend* is difficult to evaluate because it is almost impossible to separate his work as an actor from the deplorable history of racial stereotyping in American film. Peter Noble, for example, accuses Fetchit of helping to perpetuate the "popular myth that the American Negro was a happy, laughing, dancing imbecile, with permanently rolling eyes and widespread, empty grin."[24] In a famous CBS documentary, *Black History: Lost, Stolen, or Strayed?* (1968), Bill Cosby similarly codemned Fetchit: "It is too bad he did it so well. It has been planted on the minds of Americans like the memory of a bad auto accident."[25] Criticism along these lines constitutes the conventional wisdom at this time.

A close study of *Steamboat 'Round the Bend* yields additional information. Fetchit's role is not unlike those of other supporting actors: he is a humorous eccentric. Looking directly at performance rather than role, one student of the Fetchit-Rogers films has observed that:

> To determine the *why* of laughter, one might first examine Fetchit's physical appearance on the screen. His image can be described without reference to his race. His bald head, his tall, thin, and angular body, always garbed in torn clothing, always seeming to be in motion, though Fetchit may be sleeping through his own trial. Fetchit's outward image is one of the clown of any color. When Fetchit does move it is in jerks and bounces. His most frequent movement is to lift one arm to his bald head and scratch in bewilderment. Fetchit's maneuvers puts one in mind of a trained pantomimist.[26]

Fetchit was thus an actor whose humor was not based solely upon racial characteristics.

Fetchit injects a number of incisive remarks as he helps to remodel a wax museum that Doc Pearly has acquired from the local sheriff. While preparing new exhibits, Fetchit notes that "Little Eva goes with Uncle Tom; she doesn't belong with Napoleon"; when told to move a statue of General Grant, he remarks that the Northern general's uniform "would fit me." That it is Fetchit who plays "Dixie" for a tribute to General Lee seems to classify him as one of the hucksters of the film rather than as a witless underling. When Doc Pearly fishes a choking New Moses from the river, Fetchit asks him if he is thirsty. This remark has subtle overtones: to a casual viewer, it appears that Fetchit is merely conforming to the stereotype of Uncle Tom, the fawning menial; the attentive observer will note that Fetchit is actually satirizing Uncle Tomism by exaggerating it. All such lines and ploys were of Fetchit's own invention, not the work of scripwriters, and all comment on black history and black aspirations. As a character actor of economic value, Fetchit was given considerable freedom for extemporaneous utterance: his contributions were frequently left unscripted, with a general indication that the black comedian should invent "Fetchit stuff" appropriate to the scene.[27] Thus, while Fetchit wears the costume of a black menial, he uses physical and verbal comedy to expand his role beyond the stereotype.[28]

The love match between Duke and Fleety Belle takes up a considerable amount of screen time early in *Steamboat*, but, as the film progresses, we discover that the most significant emotional tie in the story is the filial bond between Doc Pearly and the swamp girl. Doc Pearly is at first scornful but gradually discovers that she is "a spunky rascal." The last of his doubts are dispelled after a confrontation with her "people" from the swamp. In the wake of this test of character, Doc Pearly supplies Fleety with a feminine costume in place of her rags, making her a true "Belle". Throughout subsequent attempts to save Duke, Doc Pearly and the young girl work together as a father-daughter team.

If her function in the film is properly understood, Anne Shirley performed admirably as Fleety Belle. Proponents of women's liberation could easily brand the character as just another clinging vine since she is transformed into womanhood with the help of a man (Doc Pearly) and she seems to require masculine guidance. Another view would stress her function as an alter ego for viewers. Like many in the Depression audiences for *Steamboat*, Fleety Belle is poor, an outcast longing to be valued for her inherent worth. An accident of birth may have labeled her a swamp girl, but we have the opportunity to learn that she is really a sincere and sensitive young person who needs help.

A close observer of the Depression era and Will Rogers's role in it might venture a few additional speculations. Like the audience, Fleety Belle needs the guidance of a kindly uncle or father figure. This protector must be above personal or selfish concerns. How much alike Will Rogers and Franklin Roosevelt were in the eyes of theatergoers cannot be determined; but it is certain that many who have studied films of the era agree with Andrew Bergman that movies of the 1930s conveyed "that the federal government was a benevolent watchman, that we were a classless, melting pot nation."[29] Certainly the Homeville movies communicated a sense that American character (as embodied by Will Rogers) was sustaining the spirits of the Fleety Belles and the Dukes of this world. And the "forgotten public," viewers who had suffered economic setbacks, or had felt the stigma of class, could find reassurance through Uncle Will that the American Dream was still viable.[30] Coming back to the performance of Anne Shirley, it seems clear that she was not merely conforming to a screen stereotype, but serving as a developed symbol representing the needs of a weak and confused nation.

Executives of Fox pictures seemed to understand that anecdotes about Rogers's off-screen benevolence toward Shirley were good for the picture. According to a release repeated endlessly in the press, Rogers allowed the novice to steal scenes from him. Supposedly, Rogers took John Ford aside one day and told him that "I'm gettin' the star's billin' and drawin' down the star's salary, but the star of this picture, man or woman, is the one that can steal it. Come on, John, and have a heart—give the kid a chance."[31] Whether this "real life" scene came from reality or from the Fox publicity department does not really matter: either way, we have proof that there was an appetite for vicarious participation in the protective influence of Will Rogers. Scenes in the pilot house of the *Claremore Queen* concretize this theme of benevolence: both Will Rogers and Anne Shirley wear hats inscribed with the word "Captain"; both share the wheel of the ship, a traditional symbol; there is even a bit of bussing from time to time. An involved viewer of these moments of tenderness could interpret that Uncle Will is helping us to steer a course through difficult times, and that he is concerned because our normal hopes and desires have been thwarted by impersonal forces.

Although *Steamboat 'Round the Bend* is hardly mentioned in most studies of John Ford's career, there are obvious connections between the two men and their work which warrant discussion.[32] John Ford was born near Portland, Maine, just before the turn of the century. Students of Ford's life and work agree that his formative years in rural New England gave him an outsider's view of twentieth-century developments. Like the Oklahoma humorist, Ford felt an attraction for rural life, especially the strong ties cultivated by small communities. Ford also shared Rogers's concern about the future of the American family; as a result, Ford films celebrate the virtues of family life and portray the effects of lack of family support upon atomized individuals. Ford is also known for his interest in American history—not for antiquarian purposes, but to find a source of affirmation for traditional values.[33]

After Will Rogers's death in 1935, Ford would articulate his world view in such classic films as *Stagecoach* (1939), *The Grapes of Wrath* (1940), and *How Green Was My Valley* (1941). Study of the films made with Will Rogers reveals that Ford must have understood the affinity between his goals and those of Rogers. In *Dr. Bull* (1933), Ford helped Rogers bring to the screen the character of a rural general practitioner who has an excellent bedside manner but a distrust of new-fangled ways; *Judge Priest* (1934) was a nostalgic portrait of the old South.[34] In all the films made with Will Rogers, Ford devoted considerable attention to evoking mood through *mise en scène*. Although they may seem ludicrously sentimental by Age of Anxiety standards, the jailhouse segments of *Steamboat* stress the social harmony of an organic society. Characterizations throughout the film emphasize the quaint: Ford treats rural eccentricities with the same affection found in the regional novels of Harriet Beecher Stowe or the delicate tales of another Maine artist, Sarah Orne Jewett. Without Ford's precise tuning of mood, the ripostes between Rogers and Cobb would have fallen flat.

More difficult to explain is the *laissez-faire* attitude that Ford took toward his principals. Ford would later become known as an auteur who planned his films so carefully in advance of shooting that he was said to edit in the camera. Such a director should not have been happy with stars who appeared for a day's work without their lines memorized. Ford must have known that the subtle obligato of happiness which Rogers and Cobb generated could not be obtained through normal means: only if these two entertainers were allowed to play against one another extemporaneously would the right spirit be communicated. Since the goal of most scenes was to evoke a general atmosphere, precision of lines was unimportant. But the right tone (supplied by the actors) within the right setting (supplied by carefully planned photography and painstaking editing) was essential. By allowing Rogers and Cobb to perform without restraints, and by keeping his own presence unobtrusive, Ford achieved the desired directorial objective.

Students of John Ford have ignored his Will Rogers films. *Dr. Bull, Judge Priest*, and *Steamboat 'Round the Bend* have been seen as "bits of work" performed so that Ford could go on to make his auteur films. A closer reading of these rural dramas shows that Ford themes are prominent—the peacefulness of rural life and the simplicity of rural people, the importance of tradition and the family—but they are messages also associated with Will Rogers. In fact, the films are more effective because of the overlapping interests and concerns of these two artists.

Will Rogers and his audience were aware that their world was becoming increasingly perplexing and violent. The most important factor about the imaginary world of Homeville created by a Will Rogers film was that the forces and the people were entirely malleable under the workings of the spirit of Uncle Will. Millions of Rogers fans must have watched such resolutions of conflict with satisfaction. They must have been impressed by what one contemporary noted was Rogers's power "to set right all the troubles of the impulsive people around him."[35] Given a sympathetic understanding of the forces affecting Americans in the 1920s and 1930s, it is difficult to vouchsafe them their inner need to love such a symbolic man. He meant so much to his people in a time of change and deprivation because he presented them with an image of what Americans had been told to believe was the best in their national character. In preserving this image of humanity and love, Rogers was making no small contribution to the sanity of Americans in a world rushing toward international violence.

A reviewer of *In Old Kentucky* hit upon some of the essential positive factors of Rogers's contribution as man and as film image. These late Homeville movies reassured Americans (especially frenzied New Yorkers) "about the solidity and innate common sense of this country." While the reviewer granted that Rogers was probably playing himself, he felt compelled to add that, as a representative figure, Rogers supplied welcome reassurance in an era of bad news: "Will Rogers has a curious national quality. He gives the impression somehow that this country is filled with such sages, wise with years, young in humor and life, shrewd, yet gentle." Most importantly for the reviewer, "He is what Americans think other Americans are like."[36] After the erosion of values in the 1920s, after the economic disaster of the 1930s, Americans were indeed fortunate to have such a public person to keep a hopeful image of American values and optimism bright.

NOTES

1. Fred Stone Scrapbook No. 3, Will Rogers Memorial and Museum, Claremore, Oklahoma. Most of the contemporary responses to Rogers the man and film image have been taken from the numerous 2-ft. by 3-ft. scrapbooks collected and preserved by Robert and Paula Love of the Will Rogers Memorial. Whenever possible, the article's title will be given along with scrapbook and page numbers. Many of these fascinating popular reactions are unidentifiable in any other way. All of these scrapbooks have been microfilmed and are on deposit in the University Library, Oklahoma State University, Stillwater, Oklahoma. Hereafter, they will be referred to as Memorial Scrapbooks, Fred Stone Scrapbooks, or Homer Croy Scrapbooks.

2. File Box No. 14, Will Rogers Memorial and Museum, Claremore, Oklahoma. Hereafter referred to as File Box No. 14.

3. *Ibid.*

4. *I'll Take My Stand* (New York: Harper and Brothers, 1930).

5. Memorial Scrapbook No. 14, p. 32. A letter dated October 15, 1938, from President Roosevelt to Walter M. Harrison, Secretary of the Will Rogers Commission, reads in part: "There was something infectious about his humor. His appeal went straight to the heart of the nation. Above all things, in a time grown too solemn and somber, he brought his countrymen back to a sense of proportion." For a detailed study of Will Rogers as a journalist and social commentator, see Peter C. Rollins, "Will Rogers: Symbolic Man, Journalist, and Film Image," *Journal of Popular Culture*, 9 (1976), 851–77. Of use in the classroom is a short documentary by Peter C. Rollins and Cadre Films, *Will Rogers' 1920s: A Cowboy's Guide To the Times* (Los Angeles: Churchill Films, 1976).

6. "Series R" Goldwyn Contracts, December 29, 1923, indicate that Goldwyn lost $40,102.23. Most biographers of Will Rogers claim that Rogers was a failure in silent films, but a success once sound was introduced. In terms of box-office receipts this is true, but Rogers's biographers also believe that he was a poor actor in these films. *New York Times* film reviews indicate that Rogers's early silent films were very much admired by those who understood Rogers's style of humor. The real problem for Rogers was to make the nation aware of that style. This he did from 1922 onward as a public person, public speaker, and syndicated journalist. Most students of this period are unaware of the writing churned out by Rogers. The statistics are impressive: a daily article syndicated from 1926–35; a weekly article syndicated from 1922–35; special book-length assignments for the *Saturday Evening Post*; convention articles covering both presidential nomination conventions, 1920–32. All of these journalistic efforts are now being reprinted as the *Writings of Will Rogers* (Stillwater, Oklahoma: Okla. State Univ. Press).

7. Some of the films of this persona are *Jubilo Jr* (1924), *Too Busy to Work* (1923), *Honest Hutch* (1920), *Boys Will Be Boys* (1921), *The Headless Horseman* (1922), *Fruits of Faith* (1922), and *Don't Park There* (1924). Stepin' Fetchit assumes this role in *Steamboat 'Round the Bend* (1935).

8. Some of the films of this persona are *Strolling Through Europe with Will Rogers* (episodes) (1926), *Going to Congress* (1924), *A Truthful Liar* (1924), *A Texas Steer* (1927), *They Had to See Paris* (1929), *Lightin'* (1930), *So This Is London* (1931), *Young as You Feel* (1931), *Connecticut Yankee* (1931), *Ambassador Bill* (1931), and *Business and Pleasure* (1932).

9. Memorial Scrapbook No. 8, p. 204.

10. "Chatting With the Editor," Fred Stone Scrapbook No. 3.

11. *Beverly Hills Citizen*, September 19, 1929, Fred Stone Scrapbook No. 3.

12. In this final role, Rogers plays a variety of small town figures: in *State Fair* (1933) he is a farmer anxious to see his pig take first prize; in *Dr. Bull* (1933) he is a small-town doctor who is resistant to new-fangled ways; in *David Harum* (1934) he is a small-town banker who is more interested in fishing and horse trading than gain; in *Handy Andy* (1934) he is a small-town druggist who runs amuck when he tries to become part of the leisure class; in *Judge Priest* (1934) he is a small-town judge in the post-Civil War South; in *County Chairman* (1935) he is a frontier politician in Wyoming about the time that Wister's hero, the Virginian, would have been settling down to make his bundle; in *Life Begins at Forty* (1935) he plays a small-town newspaper editor with his hand on the pulse of the community; in *Steamboat 'Round the Bend* (1935) he is an avuncular captain of a renovated steamboat, the *Claremore Queen*; *In Old Kentucky* (1935) tells the story of the world of the Kentucky Derby before the syndicate moved in. During the 1930s, many Americans looked back to the 1890s as a lost Eden from which the America of their own postwar era had departed. As nostalgically recalled by these unsettled people, that earlier America had been a face-to-face society, a comprehensible world painted in primary colors. As William E. Leuchtenburg notes in his *Perils of Prosperity: 1914–1932* (Chicago: Univ. of Chicago Press, 1958): "By 1932, the prewar years had taken on a luminescence that they did not wholly have at the time. In retrospect, the years before World War I seemed like a lost Arcadia. Men remembered county fairs and church socials, spelling bees and sleigh rides, the excitement of the circus train or the wild dash of firehorses from the station house, the cool smell of an ice cream parlor and the warm fragrance of roasted chestnuts. . . . They remembered people: the paper boy with his off-key whistle, the brawny iceman sauntering up the walk with his five-cent cake of ice, the Negro stable boys, the printers and devils in the newspaper offices. They recollected general stores: the bolts of calico and muslin, the jars of cinnamon and gunpowder tea, bins of dried peaches and cornmeal, kegs of mackerel, canisters of striped candy. From the vantage point of 1932, it seemed as though they had danced endlessly at tango teas and strummed mandolins every evening" (p. 213).

13. Memorial Scrapbook No. 20, p. 37.

14. Homer Croy Scrapbook No. 24, p. 90.

15. John Rosenfield, Jr., "Screen Loses Star at Peak of Influence," *Dallas Texas News*, August 17, 1935. Memorial Scrapbook No. 53, p. 27.

16. Memorial Scrapbook No. 1, p. 46.

17. The desire to look back at a simpler past is not new in American thought. In the 1970s people are learning to "groove" on the good old 1950s, forgetting in the process the atomic bomb, air raid drills, the Korean war, and

the rampage of Senator Joseph McCarthy. In the 1860s and 1870s, Harriet Beecher Stowe held her inverted telescope up to the religious and social history of New England and discovered the nostalgic and peaceful towns she describes in *Oldtown Folks* (1869) and *Poganuc People* (1878). Still earlier, Royall Tyler wrote probably the first work of nostalgia in *The Contrast* (1787), a play about a country squire and his man in the corrupt city of New York.

18. Audiences in the 1930s would have noted the aging of these two syndicated humorists: Rogers was fifty-six, Cobb was fifty-nine. Also apparent to audiences would have been the significance of the ship names: Paducah is a city located on the Ohio River where it joins with the Kentucky; Claremore is the major city of Rogers County, Oklahoma, where Will Rogers was born and where the Will Rogers Memorial and Museum now stands.

19. Cobb tells his story in an autobiography entitled *Exit Laughing* (New York: Garden City Publishing Co., 1941). Like Rogers, Cobb saw himself in the tradition of Mark Twain, for his regional humor as well as for his journalistic commentary on the times.

20. "His Last Precious Days With Friend Will Rogers Recalled by Irvin Cobb," File Box No. 14.

21. "Screen Loses Star at Peak of Influence," *Dallas Texas News*, August 17, 1935. Memorial Scrapbook No. 53, p. 27.

22. Contrasts between Rogers's journalism and his films could be no better illustrated than in this broadcast. While *Steamboat* takes us away from contemporary events, the nationwide radio program addressed such issues as unemployment, a proposed California state tax on the movie industry, prejudice against Indians, the CCC, and the national debt.

23. Gulf Radio Broadcast, May 19, 1935. Both tapes and transcripts of these broadcasts are available at the Will Rogers Memorial.

24. *The Negro in Film* (London: Skelton Robinson, 1947), p. 49.

25. This excellent documentry is available from most audio-visual centers for a minimal rental fee.

26. Harry Menig, "Stepin Fetchit in Will Rogers' Films," an unpublished paper presented at the national meeting of the American Studies Association in 1973, p. 14.

27. Information concerning the treatment of Fetchit was obtained from a Boston College faculty seminar on the black image in film, sponsored by the American Studies Association in Spring 1977.

28. Close viewing of *Steamboat 'Round the Bend*, suggests that future scholarship dealing with the black image in film should attend more closely to specific dramatic contexts, since typed roles can be transformed by gifted actors, among whom Stepin Fetchit must be counted. A recent study by Thomas Cripps, *Slow Fade To Black: The Negro in American Film, 1900–1942* (New York: Oxford University Press, 1977), is unique for its attention to performances.

29. *We're In The Money: Depression America and Its Films* (New York: New York University Press, 1971), p. 149.

30. Students are invited to explore the relationship between American heroes of the period (on screen, in real life) and the ability of traditional institutions to weather those troubled years. A more extended version of the above quote from Bergman might stimulate discussion and writing: "Movies of the Thirties made a central contribution toward educating Americans in the fact that wrongs could be set right within their existing institutions. They

showed that individual initiative still bred success, that the federal government was a benevolent watchman, that we were a classless melting pot nation."

31. "Cobb Bares Secrets on Film Lot," *Tulsa Daily World*, 5 Sept. 1935, p. 7, col. 7.

32. Charles Maland's *American Visions: The Films of Chaplin, Ford, Capra, and Welles, 1936–41* (New York: Arno Press, 1977) is an excellent study which makes no mention of films made with Rogers. John Baxter, *The Cinema of John Ford* (New York: A.S. Barnes and Co., 1971) lists the Rogers films in a filmography, but does not discuss them in the text. Other studies bearing the title *John Ford* by Peter Bogdanovich (London: Studio Vista, 1967), Phillippe Hardiquet (Paris: Editions Seghers, 1966), and Jean Mitry (Paris: Universitaires, 1954) all slight the Ford-Rogers collaborations. Andrew Sarris substantiates my analysis of the Rogers-Ford relationship in his *John Ford Movie Mystery* (Bloomington: Indiana Univ. Press, 1976), pp. 51–59.

33. In preparing this portion of the essay, I have been particularly informed by Charles Maland's *American Visions*, pp. 99–190.

34. Adaptation of regional tales for Will Rogers is examined closely in Peter C. Rollins and Harry Menig, "Regional Literature and Will Rogers Film Redeems a Literary Form," *Literature/Film Quarterly*, 3 (1975), 70–82.

35. Memorial Scrapbook No. 1, p. 31.

36. Review of *Life Begins at Forty*, *New York Sun*, File Box No. 14.

A Reaffirmation of American Ideals:

Drums Along the Mohawk (1939)

JOHN E. O'CONNOR

The grim realities of life on the New York frontier in the 1770s are faced by Henry Fonda and Claudette Colbert in this patriotic film which stressed the bond between the people and the land.

(Photo courtesy of Museum of Modern Art)

Drums *Along the Mohawk* (1939) was one popular example of a series of feature films released in 1939 and 1940 dealing with American history. Historical spectacles about America were hardly a new genre, but during these few years they did enjoy a spurt of popularity. Why did Hollywood producers choose this time to deal with the American past, and especially the Revolutionary era? Why did audiences respond so well, choosing *Drums Along the Mohawk** and another such film, *The Howards of Virginia*, as two of their favorite movies of the 1939–40 season? The answers to these questions lie buried deep in the changing national consciousness as the Great Depression drew to a close and another world war loomed on the horizon.

Even at the end of the decade, the vast majority of the American people were still caught up in the malaise of the 1930s.[1] Many suffered from a psychological depression brought on by the harsh economic realities of everyday life. Americans who had grown up in the "free-wheeling" and "free-spending" 1920s and felt they had had every reason to look forward to success in life were forced to reshape their image of America and their image of themselves. For some it was a trauma they would carry with them for the rest of their lives.[2]

As Europe turned toward fascism to confront the economic crisis, American disillusionment and despair increased. The American dreams of democracy and individual success seemed unrealistic in a crisis-ridden world. In this climate of tension and insecurity panaceas became more appealing: Huey Long proposed to "Share our Wealth"; Father Charles Coughlin promised to expose those who conspired to betray America's economic interests; and Francis Townshend explained that pensions for the elderly would straighten everything out by boosting consumer spending. When F.D.R. sought to defuse such popular movements by coopting some of their suggestions into his administration's proposals for a social security program and a progressive income tax, a storm of indignation arose from those who still held dear the gospel of "rugged individualism" which Herbert Hoover had preached so successfully a decade before. Even supporters of the New Deal were unsure where the

---

* Henceforth referred to as *Drums*.

new, seemingly uncharted, course would take the nation. People felt the need to reassure themselves that traditional American ideals were still alive and that the United States would not follow Europe headlong into radical antidemocratic experiments.[3] This thirst for reassurance reached a new intensity in 1939 and 1940 as friends and allies overseas were caught up in another total war that threatened, like the last one, to drag in the United States.

One manifestation of this concern of the 1930s was the passion for rediscovering the roots of our national heritage. During the 1920s, an era marked by extraordinary confidence in America, the trend in historical writing had been toward a debunking of the legends of the founding fathers and a cynical attitude toward the ideals for which they supposedly stood: James Truslow Adams condemned seventeenth-century Puritans for being repressed autocrats, and Charles Beard accused the authors of the United States Constitution of being concerned with pecuniary gain rather than the public good.[4] In his three-volume biography of George Washington, Rupert Hughes pulled the legendary general off his pedestal and tried to set the record straight with regard to all those supposedly loyal patriots in the struggle for independence:

> The fact [was] that the generation of Americans which coincided with the Revolution, was far from being the supremely virtuous race its descendants have been pleased to pretend. . . . A few soldiers, a few statesmen, a few devoted men did all the work, suffered all the hardships, and saved the country in spite of itself, while the majority ran away or kept aloof, grew fat and looked on.[5]

The task of rebuilding the reputation of the colonists began in 1930 with Samuel Eliot Morison's respectful new look at seventeenth-century New Englanders, and was continued by such others as Clifford Shipton and Perry Miller.[6] An interesting index of popular history can be found in the guides prepared in the 1930s by the WPA, including historical surveys of every state and major city in the nation. By cataloging the historic sites that related to the experiences of ordinary Americans, as well as the homes of the great and the famous, the guides helped to restore a recognition that the people made history as well as their leaders.[7] By the late 1930s, a significant body of literature sought to reaffirm the virtues of American heroes and to resurrect positive images of them. Even radicals and communists, who before had devoted their efforts to pointing up the flaws in American society, now turned to highlighting the traditional American values that united people of diverse backgrounds in opposition to fascism[8]—thus American leftists who went off to Spain in 1936 and 1937 to struggle against Franco and Hitler were called the Abraham Lincoln Brigade.

Popular novels and their cinematic adaptations brought this new positive portrait to a mass audience. Margaret Mitchell's *Gone With the Wind* received special attention when it appeared in 1939, but there were a series of similar films adapted from novels: Kenneth Roberts's *Northwest Passage* (RKO, 1939), Elizabeth Page's *Tree of Liberty* (released by Columbia pictures in 1940 under the title *The Howards of Virginia*), and Walter Edmonds's *Drums Along the Mohawk* (Twentieth Century-Fox, 1939). Each novel and each film stressed the underlying vigor of the national character and served to comfort the populace in an age of chaos and uncertainty by reassuring them that the nation had overcome hardships before and could do so again.

Drums Along the Mohawk, published in 1936, is a pastoral novel. A man builds a home for himself in the wilderness, then marries a pretty young girl and takes her to live with him there. They farm the land in an idyllic setting (the Mohawk River winds right past the door of their cabin) and survive with the rest of their agrarian community of simple folk. Their greatest challenge comes in the form of savage attacks by Indian "destructives" who remained loyal to the British after 1776 and threatened frontier settlements all during the war for independence.

Novelist Walter Edmonds had stressed his reverence for the historical facts to the extent that in a foreword he indicated which of the characters were fictional and which real, and almost apologetically pointed out a few of the occasions where the stories of actual persons had been altered out of necessity for dramatic emphasis. Moreover, he acknowledged his debt to specific historians, encouraged interested readers to study further, and recommended primary as well as secondary sources for the period. But the novel owed its popularity to more than its romantic interest, its bucolic atmosphere, its excitement and suspense, and its aura of historical veracity. The characters in the book were moved by the same types of concerns which preoccupied Americans in the 1930s. The challenges of everyday life on the frontier were complicated by the military struggle for independence, in which neither continental troops nor state militia could be relied upon to defend tiny settlements on the fringe of civilization, and in which the hopes and dreams of ordinary people were shattered as families were terrorized and homesteads destroyed. The Depression had shattered hopes and dreams now too and, as in revolutionary days, it seemed that the solutions that were proposed from above sometimes made things worse. As Edmonds explained:

> These people of the [Mohawk] valley were confronted by a reckless Congress and ebullient finance, with their inevitable repercussions of poverty and practical starvation. The steps followed with automatic regularity. The applications for relief, the failure of relief, and then the final realization that a man must stand up to live.[9]

Here was the relevant and comforting message of the novel: through reliance on their personal inner strength and traditional American ideals, twentieth-century Americans could live to prosper and to dream again about the future just as the colonists had. The public responded so well to the book that it seemed only a matter of time before it would be put on the screen.

Darryl F. Zanuck at Twentieth Century-Fox had purchased the movie rights to the book in 1936, even before it went into circulation. As Zanuck explained a few months later: "It was our original idea that if the book became tremendously popular, we would make the picture, as there is no doubt in my mind but what [sic] very successful novels usually make very successful pictures." The book's sales had moved slowly at first, but in the first month of 1937 there were five printings of 10,000 each and *Drums* became a bestseller. Still Zanuck described himself as "not terrifically enthused" about the project and, when several other companies made offers, he considered disposing of the property.[10] Only the continuing popularity of the book (it went into thirty-one printings by 1939) encouraged him to stick with the story.

Zanuck's primary concern was with the story treatment completed by screenwriter Bess Meredith in January 1937. He thought it was too long and confused, with too many characters to follow, overly complex characterizations, and too much overt emphasis on the patriotic theme. Like his competitor David O. Selznick at M.G.M.,

Zanuck prided himself on his historical and period dramas such as *The House of Rothschild* (1934), *Les Miserables* (1935), *Clive of India* (1935), *Lloyds of London* (1937), and *In Old Chicago* (1938). They were successful because the producer realized that audiences did not plunk down dollars at the box office to learn a history lesson. They came to be entertained, and Zanuck was particularly conscious of how the story developed in the screenplay would appeal to a mass audience. He personally supervised revision after revision in a process that eventually involved William Faulkner (who tried to simplify the story in a short narrative treatment dated March 15, 1938), Sonya Levein (who did two dialog treatments and a first-draft continuity script with specific shots, angles, and cuts spelled out in detail), and Lamar Trotti (who polished Levein's work making more changes to satisfy Zanuck and completed the shooting script in May, 1939). At every stage along the way Zanuck maintained close contact with the writers, dictating detailed conference notes on several editions of the screenplay in which he specified places to tighten the story and techniques to heighten the drama. In response to Levein's first-draft continuity of December 2, 1938, he responded:

> In the first place, let us get it understood that we do not want to make a picture portraying the revolution in the Mohawk Valley. We want to tell a story about a pioneer boy who took a city girl to the Mohawk Valley to live and we must tell the story of what happened to them—their ups and downs, their trials and tribulations—the same as it was told about the Chinese couple in *The Good Earth* [1937]. In *The Good Earth* the producers wisely discarded chapter after chapter of the book and concentrated on the personal story and on one spectacular trick with the locusts. We must follow this example. We have in the script practically all of the necessary ingredients to accomplish this but now they are dissipated and lost in a rambling jumble of historical and revolutionary data.[11]

After giving another writer three months to work on the project he was again dissatisfied, especially with the still complicated plot development. Zanuck's reactions as written up by one of his assistants ran to eleven pages, but a few sentences carry the gist of his feelings:

> We must not let ourselves be bound by the contents of the book—but simply retain the *spirit* of the book. We must concentrate our drama,

tighten what plot we have and make it more forceful—so that we build and build to a big sustaining sock climax where we let everything go with a bang. So long as we capture the general line, the characters, the period—we can and should forget the book. Mr. Zanuck could not be emphatic enough in bringing home the fact that we are in the business to *Give A Show*—that our first job is to *Make Enter-tainment.*[12]

The "final script" of April 24, 1939, was better, but Zanuck and John Ford who had been chosen to direct the picture still found seven pages of corrections to suggest. All through the writing process Zanuck looked to Julian Johnson, chief story editor for the studio for insight and reassurance. As Johnson later observed to him:

I think the thing that gave us the fine script we shot was, as much as anything else, your own constant revision and elimination, revision and elimination, every time a new treatment showed its head. The shoot-ing final was a triumph of *perspiration* as well as *inspiration.*[13]

In their final form, the plot characters and dramatic elements of *Drums Along the Mohawk* seemed tailor-made for the special talents of John Ford. Ford's skills as a director were well known, but they had resulted in only a few really memorable films: *Iron Horse* (1924), *The Informer* (1935), and *Hurricane* (1938). It was in 1939 that Ford began to turn out hit after hit with *Young Mr. Lincoln,* *Stagecoach* (his first Western since the introduction of sound), *Drums Along the Mohawk,* and finally, in 1940, *The Grapes of Wrath.*[14] Each of these films, like his 1941 classic *How Green Was My Valley,* gave him the opportunity to develop characters based on common people. Ford's best films shared with those of Frank Capra a populist view of American society.[15] Although Capra's plot situations were usually farces in contrast to Ford's popular dramas, the two men shared a special talent for portraying ordinary people who struggle to preserve significant human values challenged by forces far more powerful than themselves. In Ford's *The Grapes of Wrath,* for example, the values are those of the family threatened by dual catastrophes—dust bowl and Depression. In most of his Westerns the simple virtues of frontier life are seen challenged by the unremitting advance of "civilization," usually symbolized by the railroad.[16]

Drums Along the Mohawk offered a rare opportunity. Here Ford could depict an idyllic early-American agrarian community in more explicit terms than in any of his other films. That this idealized life style was menaced by barbarous Indians who would not hesitate to rape or torture innocent victims served to accentuate the virtuous qualities of the God-fearing settlers. In dramatizing the life of New York's Mohawk Valley in the 1770s, the film strikes a careful balance between the individualism and the mutual interdependence that typify the frontier ideal. It is punctuated with scenes that celebrate the simple agrarian life: weddings, births, harvests, and a barn-raising scene in which neighbors come from miles around to help Gil Martin (Henry Fonda) clear his land. The frontier people are outgoing and friendly. Some are comical, such as Christian Real (Eddie Collins), who forgets to respond to his own name while calling roll for militia muster, and the Scotch-Irish parson (Arthur Shields), who works an advertisement for a local dry-goods store into his Sunday sermon. Gil's bride, Lana (Claudette Colbert), a girl raised in a comfortable home in Albany, is heartbroken at her first glimpse of his cabin on the fringe of the wilderness and demands that he take her back home. But soon the beauty of the surroundings, the sense of accomplishment in seeing their own farm take shape, and the feeling of belonging to the open and congenial community of settlers, bring her to love their simple life. Ford paints this picture in such appealing terms that the audience understands perfectly when she prays, "Please God, let it go on like this forever." Unfortunately the American Revolution disturbs their serenity.

Thanks to Zanuck and his screenwriters, the story that reached the screen was a fine example of movie drama with three carefully paced climaxes, each increasing in intensity until the final climax of the film. Shortly after the first crops are harvested, the colonists meet their first challenge as bloodthirsty Indians come whooping through the woods and, under the direction of a Tory leader named Caldwell (John Carradine), destroy the Martins' farm, sending the settlers scurrying to the nearby fort to find safety for the women and children. When Gil returns from chasing the Indians, he finds his house burned to the ground and his wife barely surviving the miscarriage of their first child. Gil is disheartened by their bad luck and now it is Lana's turn to sustain the pioneering couple. They go to work for a wealthy widow named Mrs. McKlennar (Edna May Oliver) and begin planning their family once more. But, as if on cue, the second crisis arises. It is reported that Indians and loyalists are gathering at the head of the valley in preparation for a major attack, and the militia marches off to meet them. This time we do not see the Indians themselves, but we do see the human cost of their "war fever" as the men are pictured, weak and wounded, straggling back from Oriskany. In a daze, Gil explains how the militia force had been ambushed and nearly wiped out, but how they had rallied and finally sent the Indians running. As Gil sleeps off the exhaustion of battle, General Nicholas Herkimer (Roger Imhof) is outside in Mrs. McKlennar's parlor, dying in the hands of a young doctor performing his first amputation.

For a year after the Battle of Oriskany, the Martins and their newborn son live happily with Mrs. McKlennar, hoping someday to be able to rebuild their cabin. Then, on the day after they have celebrated a bumper crop, a party of hostile Indians sets fire to the McKlennar house and all the neighboring farms. The terrified colonists, huddled in the fort at German Flats, find themselves besieged by an overwhelming force. The plot becomes more active as the situation at the fort becomes more desperate. Heavily outnumbered by their attackers, the women take weapons and join the men on the walls. Mrs. McKlennar is the first to be hit. She takes an arrow in the chest and dies. Things look bleak. Ammunition is getting dangerously low. In desperation Joe Boleo (played by Francis Ford, the director's brother) resolves to escape and run to Fort Dayton for aid. Unfortunately Boleo is captured by the Indians who tie him atop a wagon loaded with hay and, in full view of the fortress, set the wagon aflame. It is left to Gil to make another try and, assuring Lana that he can outrun any redskin, he lowers himself through a portal in the fort wall and takes off with three Indians close at his heels.

Gil's escape is the most memorable action sequence of the film as Ford drags out the chase for almost five minutes. As the sun comes up a vivid orange in the background Gil finally does leave his pursuers gasping behind. In the next shot we see the Indians breeching the fort walls and Lana shooting one at point blank range. Just in time the Continental reinforcements arrive to rout the savages. Fortunately the fighting will not recur. In the last scene an officer arrives with the news that Washington has defeated Cornwallis at Yorktown and the war is over.

From the outset it was obvious that, because of the sets and locations required, *Drums* would be a very expensive picture to make. Still, Zanuck decided to raise costs much more when he slated this to be one of the seven Technicolor features produced by Fox that year. His philosophy was that the investment in producing quality pictures was worth risking because of the profits that were likely to return. In the summer of 1939, just as his studio was readying to shoot *Drums*, Zanuck announced his intention to eliminate several low-budget pictures from their 1939–40 production quota and replace them with an equal number of more expensive, quality productions.[17]

Twentieth Century-Fox was eminently qualified to provide the sophisticated services that were necessary for such a production. After twenty years of development the studio system had emerged as a complex of specialists in every craft associated with filmmaking, from scenario- and scriptwriting to set design and construction, from casting and makeup to feeding the actors between takes, from maintaining the intricate photographic equipment to editing the individual snippets of celluloid into a finished product, and finally from planning publicity campaigns to seeing that the film was distributed in a way that would maximize profits.

The establishment of the giant studios had been necessitated by the burgeoning popular demand for movies through the 1920s and 1930s.[18] Another factor was the Depression, which finally hit the movie business in 1933. By the mid-1930s money troubles had forced several of the largest movie companies to merge into still larger conglomerates. Such problems had allowed Zanuck's company, Twentieth Century, to take over the Fox studio in 1935. The business suffered another slump in 1938;[19] studio organization continued to provide the most efficient use of manpower and talent, and, finally, there was the need for increasingly specialized technical expertise as such innovations as sound and Technicolor were introduced. By 1939 the studio system was at its peak, and it was used to the fullest in the production of *Drums*.

The greatest problems were logistical. The open spaces called for in the script required shooting on location. Any thought of shooting in the Mohawk valley itself was quickly rejected because industrialization had transformed almost every inch of the landscape. Moreover, Zanuck's decision to film in Technicolor led them to search for special atmospheric conditions to maximize the quality of the photography. They finally chose a high plateau in the Wasatch Mountains near Cedar City, Utah, where the lack of haze in the morning allowed vast distances to be photographed with perfect clarity and beautiful cloud formations appeared on schedule every afternoon to accent the panoramic views.[20]

Once the site was chosen, the studio hired a local contractor to supply 1,400 logs and put 125 of the local unemployed to work constructing four sets, including a full-scale stone and log fort and a two-story farmhouse and barn. Utah residents were happy to have their area chosen for the production, and company executives must have been pleased to capitalize on local workmen who could be paid far less than the unionized Hollywood professionals.[21] But there was some controversy when, according to a local paper, commissioners from Kane and Washington Counties complained that Iron County men seemed to be getting all the jobs.[22] Perhaps they were most concerned that their people get some of the two hundred additional positions which the studio was expected to create to augment the three-hundred-member crew brought in from California on a special train. The Hollywood personnel were housed in specially-built tent-cabins, fully equipped with modern plumbing and electricity, and fed out of a fully-staffed kitchen transported to the shooting site.[23]

As with its previous historical films, Twentieth Century-Fox was scrupulous about details. The studio claimed to have searched all over Hollywood for genuine Iroquois Indians to play in the film. All they could find were two, and one of them was thought to be too short and fat for the part. The other was a seventy-two-year-old man named Chief Big Tree who was purported to have posed for the head on the buffalo nickel. He was given the role of Blue Back, a friendly but rather dull-witted native who had been christianized and now fought on the side of the colonists. Great attention was also given to the uniforms the men were to wear and the weapons they would use. In a paean of praise to her enterprising agents abroad, the studio boasted that the flintlock muskets employed had been purchased in Africa, where their anachronistic ineffectiveness had been proven in Ethiopia's attempt to ward off Mussolini's modernized army in 1935.[24]

The publicity campaign mounted for *Drums* illustrates some of the ways that Hollywood in its heyday tried to appeal to its audience. The studio issued a pressbook for theater owners suggesting a number of ploys. For example, Grosset and Dunlap, publishers of the novel, were willing to have the book sold in theater lobbies at a discount of almost fifty percent. And since female vanity was always a good angle, even in connection with a frontier saga, Westmore cosmetics, a company formed by the famous Westmore family of Hollywood makeup artists, mounted a special campaign featuring Claudette Colbert. More energetic exhibitors were encouraged to play up the colonial theme: box offices could be decorated as blockhouses and ushers costumed as colonists. Contests might be set up through the local newspapers with free tickets as prizes. In a special pitch for the school-age audience, posters and charts were provided for distribution to classrooms, and Indian headbands were handed out to youngsters at Saturday matinees.[25]

The highlight of the studio's publicity efforts was the film's gala opening. When Kate Smith devoted her network radio program to an interview with Henry Fonda and some of the other principals the night before the Hollywood premiere, she guaranteed the film national attention. But the simultaneous opening planned for the Albany-Mohawk Valley area was less successful. A half-hour radio broadcast from the lobby of the Palace Theater in downtown Albany was poorly coordinated: announced celebrities, including New York's Governor Herbert Lehman, never even arrived. In desperation, an announcer filled dead air by reading page after page of publicity releases for the picture. Quick to recognize a flop when it saw one, *Variety* described the evening as "a big yawn."[26]

Critical response to the film was mixed. Louella Parsons called it "unexcelled entertainment." Most reviewers were impressed with the action scenes such as the Indian attacks and Gil's dash for reinforcements. Almost all liked Fonda and Colbert. Several noted approval for Arthur Shields and Edna May Oliver, especially for the scene in which she browbeats the two Indians who have just set her house on fire into carrying her and her bed through the flames to safety.[27] Herbert Cohn, the movie critic for the *Brooklyn Daily Eagle*, who saw the film at the Roxy in New York (along with a stage show featuring "Bobby May, the juggling jester"), was more perceptive than better-known reviewers. He noted that the film needed "dramatic tightening" and more "fluidity of plot." As it stood, the action proceeded "in fits and starts from battle to battle and fire to fire, in brilliant but episodic flashes."[28] Indeed some of the transitions

are jarring—from summer to dead of winter with a fade, for example
—but recurring formulas and cliches are almost as disconcerting.
Rain storms are used to set the tone for several downbeat scenes, and
there is at least one instance of dramatic foreshadowing that is just
too improbable: when Gil and Lana stop at an inn on their wedding
night they are approached by a mysterious one-eyed stranger who
emerges from the shadows by the fire (he later turns out to be the
infamous Caldwell); he asks their political position and warns that
the Indians may be likely to cause trouble on the frontier.[29]

Some of the secondary characters, such as Arthur Shields and
Eddie Collins, could have played the same role in many other
pictures—and did time and again. They added nothing but comic
relief to a story which might have been too "serious" without them.
The image of the Indian in the film was terribly stereotyped: "He
slaughters, he dies, or, as in the case of Big Tree, becomes a friend
to the whites." There was no in-between.[30] Moreover, Ford might
have encouraged Colbert not to faint to the floor in emotional
exhaustion quite so often. On the other hand, the director's eye for
using the camera did save several scenes that might otherwise have
turned out unbearably dull. Take, for example, the point at which
Gil is preparing to march off with the militia to Oriskany. He kisses
Mrs. McKlennar, who gives him her dead husband's canteen, hugs
and kisses his wife, then hurries off to his place in line. Lana clutches
apron to breast and follows along beside the troops until she
dramatically slumps to the ground on a hillside and watches as they
disappear into the distance. In the hands of a lesser director such a
sequence would likely be presented as maudlin and overly sentimental
melodrama. Ford's movement of the camera along with Lana in a
long tracking shot, stopping her just at the point where the road can
be seen stretching off for miles, is an example of how a skilled
director and his cameraman (in this case the much respected Bert
Glennon)[31] can sometimes lift the conventional to the level of art.

Not without a touch of condescension, the editors of *Time* magazine predicted that *Drums Along the Mohawk* would appeal to "Fans
who like their warpaint thick, their war whoops bloodcurdling, and
their arson Technicolored." For this and other, more significant,
reasons *Drums* was successful at the box office.[32] It appeared on the
"honor roll" of *Film Daily*'s critics poll for 1940, and local polls
showed *Drums* to have been much more popular with the audience

than the critics. Those who responded to questionnaires in twenty-six newspapers across the country ranked *Drums* highly—only three other films stood between it and the top ten.[33] The studio was pleased enough with the film's profits to rerelease it in 1947 for another successful run.

While most of the reviewers praised *Drums* for its adherence to historical fact,[34] the film differed significantly from the history portrayed in the novel. As noted above, the foreword to Walter Edmonds's book had stressed his reverence for the facts, and historical scholarship confirms the overall veracity of his story. The Battle of Oriskany did take place exactly as described in the novel, there was a loyalist named Caldwell who led Indian raids, General Herkimer did lose a leg and die, and there is a documented case of a colonist who, like the character in the book, spent hours outrunning a party of nimble Indians to bring news of an attack.[35] However, there are significant points at which the film differs from both the novel and the historical record. For example, the real run as described in the novel was made by a man named Adam Helmer (a character played by Ward Bond in the film), not Gil Martin (a fictional character whom Edmonds had been careful not to credit with Helmer's achievement). The run was actually made to the fort at German Flats, not away from it. And his warning, instead of bringing continental reinforcements, frightened the colonists and their militia into hiding within the walls of the fort from which they watched their homes and barns being burned while making no effort whatsoever at self-defense. As portrayed in the novel, this episode was one of dozens of confrontations with the "destructives," none of which was truly conclusive. Victory and peace in the novel—as in historical reality—came only after the British were completely defeated and stopped provoking the Indians to attack. The dramatic siege and the victorious battle which culminate in the closing minutes of the film never actually took place.[36]

The original screenplay and several of the subsequent revisions had retained the veracity of Edmonds's narrative. It was Julian Johnson and Zanuck who insisted that the movie end with a stirring climax, even if the novel and the historical record did not. The run did not appear in the early scripts. In a memo of March 13, 1939, Johnson suggested using it as a device for heightening the final climax. At first he thought that both Adam and Gil should run, but

Zanuck later specified that Gil should do it alone. Once this was decided the rest of the story had to be altered to fit.[37]

Under watchful eyes from the executive offices, the screenwriters had also seen fit to alter significant fictional aspects of the book. For example, Edmonds was much more sensitive to the plight of the frontier woman. Although she works side-by-side with her husband in the fields, Lana, as played by Claudette Colbert, begins the story as an essentially weak character. While the film has Lana totally hysterical at her first sight of an Indian, her reaction in the novel was not fear, but disgust at the native's "greasy smell." Colbert as Lana does become acclimated to the frontier life and even finds the courage to shoot an Indian near the end of the film, but she has little of the depth and complexity possessed by Edmonds's heroine. This simplification of her role was dictated by Zanuck who feared that otherwise the audience would not see how far she had grown by the close of the story.[38]

Gil's character, on the other hand, was polished for the film. Early in the novel Gil takes part in burglarizing the home of a suspected loyalist, and later he joins a party of Americans that deliberately seeks vengeance against a Tory settlement by setting torch to the homes and raping the defenseless women there. In each case Gil's participation was only half-hearted, and he was plagued by second thoughts, but there were no circumstances under which Henry Fonda's Gil Martin could take part in such atrocities. Neither the production code nor the patriotic tone of the film would permit it.

Another significant character in the novel never made it to the screen at all. John Wolfe was a storekeeper, a decent man who happened to believe in his loyalty to the king and therefore found himself sentenced to death by a local revolutionary court. Gil had testified against the prisoner, but, self-confident and forthright, Lana went behind her husband's back to plead for the man's life. Through the intercession of influential friends Wolfe was sent to a prison in Connecticut instead of his eternal reward. But the only loyalists represented in the film were Caldwell and his heathen followers— and Caldwell himself does not show much respect for the Indians.

These changes reflect evident pressures at work on the producer, writer and director in converting a story from one medium to another, but they also suggest how the huge investments required to make such movies as *Drums* influenced producers into taking

liberties with the facts in their striving for universal audience appeal.[39]
By studying the characters and situations that Hollywood observers
thought most likely to generate audience approval, we can gain
some insight into the spirit of the times. The changes made in *Drums*
suggest a few of the basic rules which film producers have followed
either consciously or unconsciously in preparing "Hollywood history" over the years:

Rule one: For a film to be successful with a mass audience, there
must be scenes and characters with which the broadest possible group
of people can identify—therefore the roles played by Eddie Collins
and Arthur Shields and therefore the accent on weddings and births,
experiences which everyone encounters at some time in his or her
life. The opening scene of the film, for example, the wedding in
Lana's spacious and comfortable Albany home, does not appear in
the novel. It was added by the scriptwriters in an evident attempt
to provide a colorful contrast to the stark life of the frontier and to
allow the audience to relate immediately to Gil and Lana. This type
of scene, of course, was the stock in trade of John Ford, and such
sequences may have had special meaning for him, but their most
basic function in a film such as this was in making the audience feel
at home.

Rule two: Characters who are meant to have broad appeal cannot
be too intellectual or too radical, their personalities should be simple
and their loyalties unconfused—therefore the characters of Lana
and Gil Martin are altered in their transformation to the screen and
John Wolfe never makes it into the movie at all. Audiences were
comfortable with stereotypes. Indians were expected to be faceless
savages; women were consigned to serve their men and keep their
mouths shut (as Mrs. McKlennar notes: "politics isn't women's
business"), and blacks (like Mrs. McKlennar's slave girl) were seen
as loyal and submissive. Time and time again the minister in *Drums*
reminds us whose side God is on. Wolfe is deleted partly to simplify
the story, but also to simplify ideological alignments and to avoid
confusing the audience by introducing a sympathetic Tory figure.
There are no troublesome subtleties for moviegoers to dwell upon.

Rule three: Events and characters might have to be rearranged
to heighten the excitement and sharpen the climaxes—therefore Gil
makes the run instead of Helmer and a cavalry-to-the-rescue type of

Western ending is grafted onto the story to achieve the desired emotional crescendo.

At the outset of the film, when Gil and Lana are leaving their wedding en route to the Mohawk Valley, the minister reassuringly turns to the sobbing mother of the bride and explains, "It's always been like this since Bible days. Every generation must make its own way—one way or another." As this implies, on one level the film, like the novel, was a reconstruction of the same kind of concerns which preoccupied Americans in the late 1930s. The nagging economic troubles were reflected in Gil and Lana's struggle to rebuild their financial security and their hopes for a future that was threatened by forces beyond their control. The fear of impending war, more real in 1939 than it had been three years before when the novel first appeared, was obviously translated into the anxious waiting for the next Indian attack. To this extent the film seemed to support continued isolation by showing the frontier colonists rising to fight only when their farms and homesteads were wantonly attacked. The studio was well aware of the delicate international situation at the time. One piece of inter-office correspondence pointed to possible difficulties with distributing the film abroad. By implying to the Axis Powers that there was still a lingering resentment against England because of the American Revolution, the film might weaken England's stance in her war of nerves with Germany. Ordinarily they would consider the film innocuous "but now the international situation is so delicately balanced, that the powers that be in England weigh feathers and might find the picture injudicious."[40]

As noted above, Edmonds was interested in showing the settlers surviving on their own. By twisting the story so that the Continental troops are shown coming to the rescue, the screenwriters may have upset the novelists intended parallel with the politics of the 1930s, but the more pertinent message was too powerful to be set aside— the colonists had faced hardships far more challenging than the ones of 1939 and they had survived because of their devotion to basic American values. As if the parallel had to be reinforced, part of the studio's publicity campaign suggested local exhibitors sponsor essay contests in which they ask housewives: "Is the modern economic frontier as hard to combat as the primitive one of 1777?"[41] In the film, when Mrs. McKlennar is breathing her last, she explains that Gil and Lana have become like flesh and blood to her. She bequeaths her large farm and stone house to them, and the film ends with the Martins secure—even comfortable—financially. Apparently those at Twentieth Century-Fox responsible for determining popular taste decided that it was better to leave the story there than to follow the conclusion of the book, which has the farm confiscated by the State of New York for nonpayment of taxes and Gil and Lana returning to their burned-out cabin in the woods.

As far as reaffirming the American dream is concerned, although *Drums* may not be quite so explicit as some other popular movies of 1939–40,[42] it is no less effective. In John Ford's rendition of traditional American values, the simple and uncomplicated virtues of ordinary people provide the vitality that enables the society to prevail. As one recent observer has said of his films: "Ford is the keeper of a folk memory compounded of the ideals of America's founding fathers, the legends of her past, the aspirations of her immigrant peoples."[43] A recurring scene in many of Ford's films is the ritual celebration of family and community ties which hold the society together. There are several such sequences in *Drums*. One that was suggested by Zanuck shows Gil sneaking away from a combined wedding feast and harvest ball to go upstairs and gaze at his infant son resting peacefully in his cradle. As Lana quietly follows and observes the scene, we are struck by the depth of Ford's (and Zanuck's?) belief in the family as the repository of American ideals.[44] The closing scene of the film shows a detachment of Continentals marching into the fort with the Stars and Stripes unfurled. A colonist remarks, "So that's our new flag—the thing we've been fighting for." Lana turns to Gil to say "It's a pretty flag, isn't it?" as the men pass it hand to hand and proudly raise it over the fort they had defended so valiantly. A montage of shots shows us in order: a teary-eyed black woman (Mrs. McKlennar's slave), a determined-looking blacksmith pausing over his fire, an intent Chief Big Tree signaling "How," and a tightly-knit family grouping (Gil and Lana with baby in arms), all looking up to admire the new symbol of nationhood as the tune "My Country Tis of Thee" builds in the background. Finally Gil turns to his wife and says, "I reckon we'd better be gettin' back to work; there's gonna be a heap to do from here on." Such a statement had both eighteenth- and twentieth-century applications. With the economy at last starting to reawaken, with America's role in world affairs entering a new and critical phase, moviegoers of 1939 and 1940 were encouraged to maintain faith in the traditional ideals.

The underlying message of *The Howards of Virginia* emphasizes similar themes.[45] Columbia's publicity people belabored the obvious when they suggested that audiences who saw the *Howards* respond to the question: "Which decade do you consider more important and critical to American life, 1765–75 or 1931–41?"[46] Most viewers could do nothing but react internally and automatically to each of the series of films about the American past that they saw in 1939 and 1940. The nation that could conquer the wilderness (*Allegheny Uprising* [1939], *Northwest Passage* [1940], *Brigham Young* [1939], *Union Pacific* [1939]), could win independence and establish a democratic republic (*Drums Along the Mohawk, The Howards of Virginia*), could give birth to great leaders (*Young Mr. Lincoln* [1939], *Abe Lincoln in Illinois* [1940]) who held the country together during its severest trials (*Gone With the Wind*), and could conquer the environment with science and technology (*Young Tom Edison* [1940], *Edison, The Man* [1940], *The Story of Alexander Graham Bell* [1939]) would surely continue to survive. The nation's ideals were renewed in the hearts of many Americans, and the depressing uncertainties of real life were forgotton—at least until the lights went up.

NOTES

1. The best surveys of American life and public issues in the 1930s are: William Leuchtenberg, *Franklin D. Roosevelt and the New Deal, 1932–1940* (New York, 1963); Frederick Lewis Allen, *Since Yesterday* (New York, 1940), and Dixon Wechter, *The Age of the Great Depression* (New York, 1948). For a community perspective see Robert S. and Helen Lynd's *Middletown in Transition* (New York, 1937). On 1930s culture, see Warren Susman, ed., *Culture and Commitment, 1929–1945* (New York, 1973) and the same author's essay "The Thirties," in Stanley Coben and Lorman Ratner, eds., *The Development of an American Culture* (Englewood Cliffs, N.J., 1970).

2. See, for example, Studs Terkel's published interviews with people who lived through the Depression, *Hard Times* (New York, 1970). The utter hopelessness of many Depression families can be seen perhaps most clearly in the faces of the rural poor recorded at the time and published in such volumes as *Let Us Now Praise Famous Men* and *You Have Seen Their Faces*. For

analysis, see William Stott, *Documentary Expression and Thirties America* (New York, 1973).

3. The temper of the times was clearly reflected in the popular literature and the popular films of the time. The specter of fascism in America was perhaps most clearly drawn by Sinclair Lewis in his 1935 novel *It Can't Happen Here*, but Lewis, of course, was afraid that it could. Films that dealt with similar fare included *Gabriel Over The White House* (1933) and *The President Vanishes* (1934). See Andrew Bergman, *We're In The Money: Depression America and Its Films* (New York, 1971), pp. 110–120. Incipient fascism in America remained an issue through the 1930s. As late as 1941 it was the theme of Frank Capra's *Meet John Doe*.

4. See James Truslow Adams, *The Founding of New England* (Boston, 1921) and Charles Beard, *An Economic Interpretation of the United States Constitution* (New York, 1913). The work of Vernon Parrington, *Main Currents of American Thought*, 2 vols. (New York, 1927), fits into the same school of thought.

5. Rupert Hughes, *George Washington III* (New York, 1930), pp. 691 and 694.

6. See Morison's *Builders of the Bay Colony* (Boston, 1930), Shipton's "The New England Clergy in the 'Glacial Age,'" in Colonial Society of Massachusetts *Publications*, XXXII (1933), pp. 24–54, and Miller's *The New England Mind: The Seventeenth Century* (New York, 1939). For a discussion of the historiographical debate, see Wesley Frank Craven, *The Legend of the Founding Fathers* (Ithaca, 1955), chapter 6.

7. See analysis in Stott, *Documentary Expression in Thirties America*, pp. 111–118.

8. Richard H. Pells, *Radical Visions and American Dreams: Culture and Social Thought in the Depression Years* (New York, 1973) pp. 314–317. This is by far the best work on the intellectual life of America in the 1930s.

9. Foreword to Walter Edmonds, *Drums Along the Mohawk* (New York, 1936).

10. Memo, Darryl F. Zanuck to Earl Carroll, Ray Griffith, Kenneth McGowan, Nunally Johnson, Gene Markey, Lawrence Schwab, and Harold Wilson, March 3, 1937. Story Editor's Correspondence File, Twentieth Century-Fox Archives, Hollywood, Ca.

11. Darryl F. Zanuck, Comments on First Draft Continuity of December 2, 1938, dated December 30, 1938, 9 pp. Story File, Twentieth Century-Fox Archives, Hollywood, Ca. The Story file also contains copies of all the other script editions, Faulkner's 26 page treatment, and a final dialog and continuity script as taken from the screen.

12. Conference notes (on Temporary Script of March 11, 1939), dated April 5, 1939, 11 pp. Story File, Twentieth Century-Fox Archives, Hollywood, Ca.

13. Julian Johnson to Darryl F. Zanuck, July 31, 1939, Story Editor's Correspondence File, Twentieth Century-Fox Archives, Hollywood, Ca.

14. According to Andrew Sarris, Ford's latest biographer, it was *The Grapes of Wrath* that earned his title as "America's cinematic poet laureate." *The John Ford Movie Mystery* (Bloomington, Indiana, 1975). For further information on Ford, see Peter Bogdanovich, *John Ford* (Berkeley, 1968).

15. The contributions of these two giants are cogently discussed in Charles Maland, *American Visions: The Films of Chaplin, Ford, Capra and Welles, 1936–1941* (New York, 1975).

16. See Ralph Brauer, "History and Myth in the Films of John Ford and Sam Peckinpah," *Film & History*, vol. 7, no. 4 (December, 1977), pp. 72–84.

17. The decision to use Technicolor is an indication of Zanuck's commitment to big-budget pictures, for there were only 17 Technicolor features produced in the entire industry in 1939 (*Variety*, January 3, 1940). As Robert Sklar has recently explained: ". . . most medium-priced pictures, in the 1930s as in the 1920s, simply were not good enough to attract sufficient customers in the first-run market, and they could not make up their expenses in the neighborhood and small town theaters. If a picture was expensively produced, with handsome sets and costumes, big-name stars and plenty of ballyhoo, it was likely to make out all right even if it was mediocre—and if it was good, it could make a fortune." *Movie-Made America* (New York, 1975), p. 191. For more information on Hollywood and the industry at this time see John Baxter, *Hollywood in the Thirties* (New York, 1968). On Zanuck's plans for the 1939–40 season see *Variety*, July 26, 1939.

18. Between 1929 and 1940 approximately 600 to 800 feature length films were released for distribution each year in the United States. Of these some 350 to 400 were produced by the major Hollywood studios. *Film Daily Yearbook*, 1941.

19. See Sklar, *Movie-Made America*, Chapter 10. For an interesting treatment of the studio system at work see Gerald Mast, *Short History of the Movies* (New York, 1971), chapter 11.

20. *Drums* pressbook, Library of the Performing Arts of the New York Public Library. This point was also made in *Variety*'s year-end survey of the industry, January 3, 1940.

21. The unions were not yet securely entrenched in the movie industry, but the threat of strikes and walkouts in Hollywood was perennial. Sklar addresses the development of labor organization in the 1930s in chapter 10 of *Movie-Made America*.

22. *Iron County Record* (Cedar City, Utah), June 29, 1939; July 6, 1939. Also *The Salt Lake Tribune*, May 19, 1940.

23. *Drums* pressbook. Press material from the studios must often be presumed to be unreliable as a historical source; it clearly reports only what the studio wants known. When the question at hand, however, concerns the ways the studio sought to publicize its product, the press material is crucial. In this case Twentieth Century-Fox thought it would help to draw an audience to the film if people were impressed with the lengths to which they went in producing it. It is possible, of course, that they exaggerated. While the local papers wrote of two hundred positions for local people assisting the Hollywood crew, the pressbook suggested they had given work to over a thousand.

24. *Drums* pressbook.

25. *Ibid.*

26. *Variety*, November 8, 1939.

27. *New York Times*, November 2, 1939; *New York Sun*, November 8, 1939; *New York World Telegram*, November 4, 1939; *Variety*, November 9, 1939; *New York Post*, November 4, 1939, *Los Angeles Examiner*, November 3, 1939.

28. *Brooklyn Daily Eagle*, November 4, 1939.

29. It should be noted that this first meeting with Caldwell was an episode drawn directly from the novel and that this was one of the points where Edmonds had allowed his imagination to take the place of actual events. There was a real Tory leader named William Caldwell, and he was active in

the Mohawk Valley in 1777, but in 1776 when Gil and Lana stopped at the inn on their first trip together Caldwell was fighting for the king in Pennsylvania hundreds of miles away. Dale Van Every, *A Company of Heroes: The American Frontier, 1775–83* (New York, 1962), p. 155.

30. Ralph and Natasha Friar, *The Only Good Indian: The Hollywood Gospel* (New York, 1972), pp. 162–64 and passim. It should be noted here that Ford became more sensitive to Indians in his later films.

31. It is clear that this scene was the creation of director and cameraman because it does not appear in the final shooting script. Glennon was listed as one of the ten best cameramen in *Variety*'s end-of-year anniversary roundup, January 3, 1940.

32. *Time*, November 20, 1939.

33. *Film Daily Yearbook*, 1941. Weekly reports of grosses in *Variety* indicated that *Drums* was holding its own in the first-run theaters around the country, earning the appellation "Heavy coin getter" from at least one reporter; *Variety*, November 8, 15, 22, 29; December 6, 1939.

34. The one audience, of course, that was impossible to please were the local residents of the Mohawk Valley. One Mohawk Valley historian was especially concerned that the Borst homestead where Lana's wedding took place was presented as too pretentious for Albany of the 1770s, and that according to the film the first American flag seen in the Mohawk Valley was brought in by Continental troops. As any local D.A.R. member could have explained to Zanuck, the first flag in the valley was actually made by local militiamen besieged in Fort Stanwix near the present site of Rome, New York. Another local notable pointed out that the parson (played by Arthur Shields) was supposed to be a Palantine German, not an Irishman, and that the run, as it appeared on the screen, was in the wrong direction—evident from the position of the rising sun. *New York Herald Tribune*, February 18, 1940. It is interesting to note that none of the locals seemed bothered by the more serious twisting of the historical events noted below.

35. See, for example, John Alden, *The American Revolution, 1776–1783* (New York, 1962), and Dale Van Avery, *A Company of Heroes: The American Frontier, 1775–1783* (New York, 1962), pp. 159–161.

36. Van Avery, *A Company of Heroes*, pp. 159–160. The historians record the runner's name as John Helmer, but in the novel and the film the character bears the name Adam.

37. Julian Johnson to Darryl F. Zanuck, March 13, 1939, Story Editor Correspondence File, and Zanuck, Conference Notes, April 5, 1939, Story File, Twentieth Century-Fox Archives, Hollywood, Ca.

38. Zanuck, Conference Notes, April 5, 1939, Story File, Twentieth Century-Fox Archives, Hollywood, Ca. One scene in the film has Blue Back congratulating Gil on his choice of a bride and offering a stick with which he recommends she be beaten into submission. Gil thanks his friend, but instead of throwing the stick away, he looks at it for a moment and then places it on the mantle—close at hand. John Ford later filmed a similar scene in *The Quiet Man* (1952).

39. Other films of 1939 and 1940 drew critical attention for this too. For example, two articles were published in the *New Masses* criticizing *Gone With the Wind* for its treatment of, among other matters, slavery and "carpetbaggers." The filmgoer is left at the end of the movie, the author noted, feeling sorry for Scarlett who has suffered from little more serious than increasing real estate taxes, while the real poor and the blacks go ignored. *New Masses*,

January 23 and January 30, 1940. The *New York Times* Sunday magazine ran an article on August 4, 1940, commenting that "There is evidence that historical truth is not at a premium at the box office"—there was an understatement. Under the title "Hollywood goes Historian," the author went on to compare two recent films: "Consider the contrasting receptions given *Abe Lincoln in Illinois* and *Young Mr. Lincoln*. The latter starred Henry Fonda and was no more than a chronologically inaccurate merger of several episodes of Lincoln's life, but it did commendable business. The former was enthusiastically received by the critics as a conscientious and moving account of a transitional period in the career of the Great Emancipator. But though Raymond Massey had played the original stage role in New York to standees night after night, the vast hinterland movie audience knew him only as an occasional supporting player. The Massey film accounts were written in red ink," pp. 6–7. The people were not particularly concerned with the reliability of the historical details. Perhaps it was, as the *Times* author suggested, the popularity of the actor. Perhaps it had more to do with the effectiveness of the film in creating and perpetuating the "historical myth" which helped to reassure the nation that its ideals were too strong to be destroyed overnight.

40. Captain Lloyd Morriss to Col. Jason Joy, June 27, 1939, Story Editor Correspondence File, Twentieth Century-Fox Archives, Hollywood, Ca.

41. *Drums* pressbook.

42. In Frank Capra's *Mr. Smith Goes to Washington*, for example, the audience starts out chuckling along with savvy secretary Jean Arthur at the naiveté of Jimmy Stewart playing boy ranger turned U.S. Senator. By the last third of the film, however, viewers found themselves transformed along with the reporter into believing again in the patriotic ideals. A measure of the greatness of this film is that the transformation still takes place in audiences today.

43. Jeffrey Richards, *Visions of Yesterday* (London, 1973), p. 270.

44. Zanuck, Conference Notes, May 3, 1939, Story File, Twentieth Century-Fox Archives, Hollywood, Ca.

45. In this case it is a Virginia frontiersman played by Cary Grant who marries a Tidewater belle played by Martha Scott. The characters are developed in more interesting ways in this film, and more traditional historiographical issues are raised, such as colonial class barriers and sectionalism. But the basic outlines of the film are the same. Notably, in *The Howards of Virginia*, instead of archvillain Carradine, the loyalist sympathies are represented by a prissy and effeminate Sir Cedric Hardwicke.

46. *The Howards of Virginia* pressbook, Library of Performing Arts of the New York Public Library.

Our Awkward Ally:

Mission to Moscow (1943)

DAVID CULBERT

A kindly, pipe-smoking Joseph Stalin (Manart Kippen) greets Joseph Davies (Walter Huston) in this scene from the controversial Warner Brothers film based on the American ambassador's years in Moscow.
(Photo courtesy of Museum of Modern Art)

Faced with widespread popular distrust of the Soviet Union, our awkward ally in the war against Germany (1941–45), the United States government asked Hollywood to make feature films with pro-Soviet themes.* The results included Sam Goldwyn's *North Star* (1943), MGM's *Song of Russia* (1943), and the official *Battle of Russia* (1943), part of Frank Capra's *Why We Fight* series made for the United States Army.[1] The Warner Brothers contributed *Mission to Moscow*, a feature-length film glorifying Stalin, releasing it on April 30, 1943.[2] The film purported to be a factual record of Ambassador Joseph E. Davies's years as diplomat in the Soviet Union, 1936–38, and could be considered an example of the feature film as documentary.[3] It also has much in common with the genre of *film noir*, for the film explores an "interior landscape of mind and emotion."[4]

Because the film is the most extreme example of official attempts to create support by distorting history, it commands the serious attention of those interested in propaganda and wartime censorship. Its fictions require detailed refutation, however, for today's viewers can hardly be expected to know enough of foreign affairs in the 1930s to see the film without a good deal of explanation. The story of the making of the film provides small comfort for those who see conspiracy wherever they look—there is no cast of villains; rather we see a tale of zeal gone awry, of misplaced enthusiasm, of government officials at cross-purposes, a story of the buck never stopping anywhere. While *Mission to Moscow* may not deserve to be considered a Frankenstein's monster, its extreme fabrications make it a significant document of World War II America. It is hard to imagine a more obvious example of the state's desperate need, in time of total war, to wed the home-front citizen to official war aims. All of Hollywood's skills were used to subvert an entertainment medium to sell a message in a risky and highly controversial fashion.

When Hitler invaded the Soviet Union on June 22, 1941, most Americans assumed that another Nazi victory was imminent. Public opinion polls showed that, while a majority of those questioned hoped Russia would win, the overwhelming majority believed the

* I would like to thank the Woodrow Wilson International Center for Scholars, Smithsonian Institution, Washington, D.C., for support in preparing this essay as a Fellow, 1976–77.

Nazis would gain another quick victory.[5] Franklin D. Roosevelt recognized that the war in Russia was a line of defense for America, so he extended Lend-Lease aid to Stalin in the fall of 1941.

Public dissatisfaction with the Soviet Union went back to 1917, the date of the Bolshevik revolution. Woodrow Wilson sent an American army to Russia to help put down the Bolsheviks, and formal diplomatic relations were broken. To many Americans it seemed that the Soviets intended to foment revolution in the rest of the world. Franklin Roosevelt reestablished diplomatic relations with the U.S.S.R. in 1933, but only a small group of Americans, mostly intellectuals, ever found themselves enthusiastic about the Soviet experiment. The majority felt no sympathy for Stalin and when the Nazi-Soviet Non-Aggression Pact of August 23, 1939, was signed, even most intellectuals turned against the Soviet Union.[6]

Internal events within the Soviet Union strained the credulity of even the most enthusiastic friends of Russia. First Stalin embarked on a policy of collectivization in 1928. Peasants by the millions were ordered to give up their private land and made to live communally on collective farms. Millions of persons died in the first years of the program while additional disruption stemmed from a five-year plan for massive industrial development.

Still more unsettling to foreign observers was an internal purge of suspected enemies of the state, which began with the assassination of a Leningrad Communist leader in December 1934. From 1933 to 1938 Stalin removed over 850,000 members of the Communist Party; it is estimated that approximately one million Russians were executed while twelve million more died in labor camps.[7] Those who already distrusted anything with the name "communism" attached to it considered these purges ready proof of Soviet barbarism; to such persons the name Stalin was synonymous with Genghis Khan or Ivan the Terrible; the purges reinforced the stereotype of Russia as a land of half-civilized beasts.

Friends of the Soviet Union abroad had a hard time explaining the severity of the purges, particularly when Stalin chose to stage public trials of high-ranking Bolsheviks. Foreign observers attended these showcase trials in Moscow in August 1936, January 1937, and March 1938. In addition, with no public trial at all, in June 1937 a massive purge of the Red Army led to the execution of Marshal Tukhachevsky; by 1938 Stalin had removed fully ninety percent of the Red Army's generals and eighty percent of its colonels. Such a massive turnover left the Army ill-prepared to fight the Germans in 1941.[8]

The movie version of *Mission to Moscow* conflated four major purges into a single trial and had Tukhachevsky (shot in June 1937) testifying with Nikolai Bukharin (tried in March 1938) and Karl Radek (tried in January 1937). Tukhachevsky made statements which represented a Hollywood screenwriter's inspired idea of what a Marshal might have been expected to say when he realized his last days on earth had arrived. The other major figures in the film said pretty much what they had actually been compelled to say publicly. Much controversy attended the decision to put all of these trials into one, though touching up reality is a Hollywood tradition. Jack Warner blurted out the truth at a hostile House Committee on Un-American Activities (HUAC) hearing in 1947. HUAC was investigating charges of Communism in Hollywood and *Mission to Moscow* was a prime target. "If you ran the two trials it would go on for 20 reels," Warner declared.[9] Certainly the decision to turn several trials into one can best be explained by dramatic considerations, not the desires of unnamed Hollywood Communist sympathizers.

Those looking at the film today should be aware of what is now known concerning Soviet politics in the 1930s. The purge trials in the film are represented as a device whereby Stalin rid himself of a massive plot to destroy Russia from within. Leon Trotsky, Stalin's arch-enemy, in exile since 1927, is described as employed by both Nazi Germany and Japan. For enemy gold he foments sabotage inside his native land and plans to dismember her in fulfillment of German and Japanese territorial ambitions. The actual purge trials themselves were a propaganda device for Stalin. Leading Bolsheviks stood up and confessed to being in league with Trotsky to commit treason. The purge trials asked foreign observers to believe that the Soviet equivalents of the American Secretary of State, the Secretary of Defense, the Chief Justice of the Supreme Court, and the Chairman of the Joint Chiefs of Staff had all plotted to destroy the United States from within.

Today the reality of the situation is no longer in doubt. There never was any Trotsky plot aided by German and Japanese gold. The purge trials were fabrications from start to finish. In actuality the purge trials demonstrate, in combination with collectivization of agriculture, a "revolution from above." By 1940 Stalin had killed off virtually all of his political opponents, even arranging to have Trotsky murdered with an axe in Mexico City.

To speak so confidently in hindsight is the good fortune of the historian who now has abundant documentation for the fictional quality of the purge trials. More interesting to modern film audiences, however, is why the film portrayed the purges as representing the response to a "clear and present danger" to the Soviet Union. Was *Mission to Moscow* a Stalinist tract? If so did it prove that Communists had taken over in Hollywood and were inserting Bolshevik dogma into feature scripts? In particular why did *Mission to Moscow* dwell on the purge trials? No other wartime Hollywood film said a word about the purges; why did this single film accept so uncritically the official Stalinist line?

To many the explanation has seemed simple: conspiracy. In 1947, for example, when HUAC held hearings about the infiltration of Hollywood by Communists, leading actors and actresses testified that there were Communists in Hollywood and that they had been forced to create pro-Communist films to subvert American audiences. But in 1947 the congressional desire was not to prove that *Mission to Moscow* told falsehoods about the purge trials; instead the aim was primarily to get at a supposed conspiracy on the part of the Soviet Union to subvert Hollywood by putting Bolshevik ideas into innocent scripts. The scriptwriters became the villains; in addition many insisted that Franklin D. Roosevelt had surrounded himself with Communist sympathizers and that the New Deal had subverted American ideals. To prove that *Mission to Moscow* had been ordered up by Roosevelt would prove, so many felt, that America had been endangered from within by a Communist conspiracy to destroy the country through state-directed programs that limited the rights of the individual and enabled the shiftless to live off their working neighbors (for example, Social Security and unemployment compensation).

By 1946–47, war's awkward allies found themselves ideological opponents; the Cold War had begun. President Harry Truman, in the Truman Doctrine, pledged American aid to governments in Europe resisting Communist aggression. Winston Churchill had spoken of an "iron curtain" descending across Europe, while inside the United States the hunt began for alleged Communist sympathizers. In such a time *Mission to Moscow* seemed a piece of Communist special-pleading. Congressional hearings merely confirmed what all could see; Hollywood promised to purge itself of so-called Communists. Warner Brothers made amends by releasing *I Was a Communist for the FBI* (1951), in which Soviet spies try to subvert American steel unions from within.[10]*Mission to Moscow* stayed in film vaults unseen for twenty years, an embarrassment to all who had anything to do with it. Only a renewed interest in American society during World War II, an interest which dates from the early 1970s, in combination with a reduction in Soviet-American tensions, has allowed us to look at the film with more scholarly detachment now.[11] These days the film is occasionally shown on television and it finds increasing use in the classroom. Yet even today the film's producer, Robert Buckner, takes "no pride" in what he did. "It was an expedient lie for political purposes," he says, "glossily covering up important facts with full or partial knowledge of their false presentation."[12] And Jay Leyda, the film's technical adviser, claims that "many lies were told."[13]

The film's plot can be summarized briefly. After a rolling title, Ambassador Joseph Davies personally addresses the movie audience. He assures us that what we are about to see is fact, pure and simple, that his "sainted mother was an ordained minister of the gospel," that he "came up the hard way," and "is glad of it." The point is to establish the credibility of the film and Davies's personal involvement in its production, and to dispel any thought that Davies has been tainted with Communist doctrine. Following the credits we see Walter Huston (considerably more handsome than the real Ambassador) who tells us again that what we are to see is fact, pure and simple, and that the key to understanding foreign policy between 1919 and 1939 is the principle of collective security. This of course was Woodrow Wilson's hope at Versailles—the idea that an attack on any member of the League of Nations would lead to mandatory use of force to stop the aggressor. The story begins in Geneva, in 1936, where Ethiopia's Emperor Haile Selassie tells the League that only collective security can prevent world aggression. We cut to Washington where President Roosevelt asks Joseph Davies to go to Moscow as Ambassador. Davies first agrees to take a disarmament plan to Hitler, but in Berlin discovers that the Nazis are already bent on world conquest.[14] Saddened, he moves on to Moscow.

Inside the Soviet Union Davies discovers much that impresses him: industrial progress, the fact that communism in practice is strikingly similar to capitalism, the necessity of massive purge trials to rid the country of fifth-columnists, and the enthusiasm Stalin and other Russian leaders have for both America and collective security. Before leaving Moscow he is granted a private interview with a kindly, smiling Stalin who talks about the need for collective security.[15]

Davies pays a visit to Britain's Winston Churchill on the way home from Moscow. Churchill tells Davies it will take a war to make England realize that appeasing Hitler is hopeless. Back in America Davies tells a group of isolationist senators that America must do more. He is brushed off with a prediction, a few weeks before the Nazi invasion of Poland in September 1939, that there will be no war. Once war begins Davies accepts a second mission from Roosevelt, and makes a swing around the country promoting friendship for Russia and the need for America to intervene in the European war. At a giant rally in New York's Madison Square Garden, Davies answers questions from audience hecklers (each with an ugly contorted face); Davies refutes each of their several objections with a combination of innuendo and visual image which makes it seem that all isolationists are probably paid agents for Nazi Germany. Davies shows America why it must fight; the film ends with a plea for collective security, an end to war, and the necessity of force to stop aggression.

Mission to Moscow is filled with factual errors, some because of the necessity of dramatizing history for the screen, some because of an interest in portraying the Soviet Union in a favorable light, some because of the desire to show Roosevelt in a favorable light. The viewer should be aware of what is not true, though it is arguable that an excellent method for studying the history of the 1930s comes from discovering what is factually incorrect about the film rather than simply reading a standard survey textbook. Here are the major inaccuracies.

1. *Joseph Davies is superhuman; he correctly predicts the outcome of every single foreign crisis from 1936 to 1941.* A soon-to-be-

published study indicates that Davies spent much of his time in Moscow collecting art and was so often out of the country that he hardly had time to learn what was going on. The Davies 123 File in the State Department shows he was inside the Soviet Union for about five months in 1937 and for four more in 1938.[16]

2. *Roosevelt is superhuman. He saw World War II coming, did everything in his power to stop it, but was thwarted by an isolationist Congress at home.* Documents published in the last decade indicate that Roosevelt gave comparatively little attention to foreign affairs before 1939 (with a Depression at home this is scarcely surprising) and had himself urged passage of the first Neutrality Act in 1935.[17]

3. *Unlike Britain and France, the Soviet Union was the one unswerving supporter of collective security at the League of Nations.* It is true that Litvinov paid lip service to collective security from the time Russia joined the League in 1934, but nobody could be sure Stalin would actually send an army across hostile territory. Taking a chance on what Stalin might or might not do was complicated by the fact that the United States was not a member of the League at all.

4. *The purge trials were totally justified. Trotsky really sought to destroy Russia with a fifth column and actually received full support from Hitler and Hirohito.* Recently published studies have established absolutely that the purge trials were a fabrication from start to finish and represented Stalin's device for ridding himself permanently of all conceivable opposition. Nor is there any evidence of German or Japanese involvement in a plot to destroy Russia from within.[18]

5. *Stalin signed the Nazi-Soviet Pact in August 1939 to give himself time to prepare for the German attack he knew was coming; there was no opportunism involved.* It is now clear that the Soviet Union signed the pact in part to seize part of Poland. Right up to June 22, 1941, in spite of repeated warnings of an imminent Nazi attack, Stalin refused to believe that Hitler would invade Russia.[19] Such behavior does not suggest that Stalin had been preparing for an "inevitable" war since August 1939.

6. *The Soviet invasion of Finland was no invasion at all.* The film never says Finland invaded Russia but it stoutly denies that Russia attacked Finland. It is an incontrovertible fact that the Soviet Union

seized a considerable piece of Finland in the spring of 1940. This action, and the taking of eastern Poland as a result of the Nazi-Soviet Pact, made a mockery of the principle of collective security.[20]

7. *The Soviet Union bears a striking resemblance to the United States; its leaders are happy, down-to-earth folk just like you and me.* Actually considering the massive purge of political and military leaders, and the internal police apparatus, it is unlikely that any Soviet leader would speak frankly the first moment he met an American Ambassador. And given the perceived necessity of a five-year plan and collectivization, it is improbable that Moscow shops would be filled with luxury goods and that everyone would be as well-dressed and well-fed as they are in the film.

8. *Collective security is a practical method for ensuring world peace.* Actually the plan involves sacrifices never mentioned in the film. In 1945 the replacement of the League of Nations, the United Nations, recognized the basic problem inherent in collective security —getting a powerful nation to behave when it does not want to— and set up a Security Council with a veto for great powers. In part because of the Security Council provision, the United States joined the United Nations.

By looking at the production of the film we can lay some conspiratorial ghosts to rest. In 1947, lest it seem that his studio was part of a New Deal-Communist plot, Jack Warner denied that Roosevelt ordered him to make the film. Sympathetic HUAC investigators let the statement go unchallenged. In reality there was administration support from start to finish. There was no explicit conspiracy, but a film that depicted the President of the United States, the Premier of the Soviet Union, and the Prime Minister of Great Britain, and that told such controversial "truths" required, in wartime, full cooperation between Washington and Hollywood.

Such cooperation began, as might be expected, with Davies's book, an edited series of dispatches. Since Davies was no writer, he got some professional help.[21] The selections for his book were made by Jay Franklin Carter, while Spencer Williams and Stanley Richardson, both journalists in Moscow during the 1930s, put the final product together. Formal approval to publish State Department dispatches came from Undersecretary of State Sumner Welles in July 1941.[22] It seems clear that Roosevelt and Davies, reasonably good friends since they had served in Washington together in World War I, talked over the possibility of such a book following the Nazi invasion of Russia in June 1941. An unpublished Davies manuscript indicates Roosevelt asked him to do the book but it seems more likely that he approved Davies's idea rather than thinking it up by himself.[23] Aides selected only those passages which showed aspects of the Davies mission which seemed appropriate in 1941. As one would expect, most references to the furious art collecting that was going on were deleted, and there was no indication of how rarely Davies was in Moscow. Most important, Davies added a postscript dated 1941 in which he admits that he never realized in 1937 that the purge trials were to rid Russia of fifth-columnists under Trotsky; this 1941 hindsight is made even more explicit in the film.[24]

The publication of *Mission to Moscow* by Simon and Schuster on December 29, 1941, was preceded by other special publicity. Selections from the book appeared as the lead article in the *New York Times Magazine* on December 14 (a week after Pearl Harbor); *Times* editor Quincy Howe rewrote an introduction to give further point to the Davies material.[25] The book sold over 700,000 copies in English and was translated into thirteen foreign languages.[26] A special Gallup poll, commissioned by Davies and completed in October 1942, showed that readers believed the information about the purge trials to be the book's most important contribution.[27]

The decision to turn the bestseller into a movie also involved explicit administration approval. There is no evidence to suggest that Roosevelt ordered the film though he did write, rather portentously, in his own copy, "This book will last." It seems more likely that Davies the publicist saw the possibility of doing such a film and again got Roosevelt's approval rather than the other way around.

Why did Warner Brothers decide to do the film? In 1947 Jack Warner testified that Davies asked Warner Brothers to make the film. Warner then changed his testimony to say that Harry Warner read *Mission to Moscow* and afterwards contacted Davies.[28] Howard Koch, scriptwriter for the film, says in his forthcoming memoirs that Jack Warner went to a dinner at the White House and was asked by Roosevelt to do the film.[29] But this is testimony from a genre (the Hollywood memoir) notoriously prone to error. The best evidence is probably a detailed letter Davies sent to HUAC in 1947 in which he states:

I knew of the great war film in War No. 1 which Warner Bros. had produced in filming Ambassador Gerard's great war book. They had also fought a bold and courageous fight against the Nazis before Hitler's war and in the production of *Confessions of a Nazi Spy*. . . . I therefore called Harry Warner up and told him of the approaches which were being made to me with reference to filming *Mission to Moscow*. I told him frankly that I would prefer his company should do it.[30]

Davies really did know Harry Warner and the latter was a sometime guest at Davies's immense mansion in Washington. Davies told Harry Warner that Roosevelt wanted such a film, but the Warners were already aware that something had to be done to boost public support for the Soviet Union. It is also true that a very dull book (surely not ghost-written), Ambassador James Gerard's *My Four Years in Germany* had been a great financial success as a film when the then-struggling Warners made it in 1917.[31] Davies had seen it during World War I and recognized that his experience might be dramatized as well. It is possible that Hollywood should never have let appeals for wartime unity lead to production of pro-Soviet films but the capacity of the federal government to declare film production nonessential and deny film stock made it a virtually certainty that Hollywood would go along with what was asked.[32] Though we cannot be certain what Roosevelt demanded of Hollywood, in a sense it does not matter. Warner Brothers sincerely believed that they were making the film at Roosevelt's personal insistence, and Joseph Davies took every opportunity to further such an impression.

Davies signed the contract with Warner Brothers in July 1942. Not only did he get a good price (ever the businessman) but he retained final authority over the script.[33] Thus the film's message must be credited to Joseph Davies and not to unnamed Communist-inspired screenwriters. The first writer assigned was Erskine Caldwell, just back from reporting the Nazi attack on Russia for magazines and CBS radio.[34] Caldwell produced part of a script which Robert Buckner, the producer, considered unacceptable. Certainly the Caldwell treatment, as far as it went, was discursive but it is hard to say that the next writer was able to put much more excitement into a format in which Davies talked to or was talked at by an endless number of persons.[35]

Michael Curtiz was assigned to direct the film. He had just finished *Yankee Doodle Dandy* (1942), a screen version of George

M. Cohan's patriotic songwriting career, and *Casablanca* (1942). Both films contained explicit appeals for wartime unity. Still Curtiz was an unusual choice for a "message" film.[36] His favorite theme was swashbuckling romance, including *The Charge of the Light Brigade* (1936) and *The Adventures of Robin Hood* (1938), both vehicles for Errol Flynn's simple approach to problems of right and wrong. Certainly Curtiz was no Communist sympathizer, which may well explain his choice as director. In any event there is nothing to suggest that Curtiz tampered with the political content of the picture though his expertise with back lighting gives many of the film's sinister or portentous moments particular effectiveness (for example, the scene when the purge victims are arrested, or the opening when Davies [Huston] is shown in his study in a high angle shot). The film was completed while Curtiz directed another Warner Brothers film, *This is the Army* (1943), an enormously popular stage show featuring seventeen of Irving Berlin's songs.

Caldwell was replaced by Howard Koch as screenwriter in August 1942.[37] Koch had no background in Soviet affairs, had never visited the country, and was not particularly interested in politics, though he admired Woodrow Wilson and the principle of collective security.[38]

Koch had just come from helping write *Casablanca* and was an experienced, if not senior, writer for Warners when he got the assignment for *Mission to Moscow*. A skillful craftsman but not an original or brilliant thinker, he had to produce a script which was overseen every step of the way by Joseph Davies—the latter not only having final script approval but also able to insist that his preferences were also Roosevelt's. Koch got a copy of an English translation of the 1937 and 1938 purge trials from Davies, a copy of *Mission to Moscow*, a few other basic references, and set to work.[39] He also profited from the Caldwell script as indicated by similar devices in each of the various drafts.[40]

Jay Leyda served as technical adviser. He had worked with Sergei Eisenstein in Moscow in the 1930s and had an excellent knowledge of newsreel footage at Artkino, the Soviet film agency in New York City. Much of the compilation footage in the film is the result of Leyda's expertise. In fact it is arguable that the extraordinary reliance on montage composed of stock newsreel footage gives the finished film a genuine documentary flavor. There is no evidence that Leyda had any control over the political content of the film; he claims that even decisions for look-alikes to play Churchill and Stalin were "reserved for higher-ups." Max Steiner provided a bombastic score based mostly on *Meadowlands* (a Russian folksong and a juke box hit of 1942), Mussorgsky's *Pictures at an Exhibition,* and similar fare.

Davies invited Soviet Ambassador Maxim Litvinov, his English wife Ivy Low, and Robert Buckner to the Davies "camp" in upstate New York before the film went into production. Though this does not necessarily mean that the exact content of the film can be attributed to direct Soviet supervision, it is unusual, even in wartime, for an ambassador to spend an entire week discussing the content of a film to be made by another country. Davies reported to Roosevelt in October and November 1942 about the progress of the film, made sure that a suitably laudatory picture of Roosevelt emerged, and helped with casting. He even tried, unsuccessfully, to bring Litvinov's daughter from Moscow to play herself.[41]

The Davies papers prove that it was Davies himself who made sure that the film's political content ended up as it did. He was in Hollywood in December and January 1943, along with members of his family, to watch the shooting. The decision to have Davies appear as himself in a prologue was at Davies's personal insistence and over the strenuous objections of Koch; the ending, unlike the one Koch wrote, was specifically the way Davies wanted it.[42]

Further evidence of government involvement in the writing of the script comes from the records of the Hollywood Office, Bureau of Motion Pictures, Office of War Information (BMP, OWI). The script was read by OWI staff members in several drafts. The final film was previewed by BMP head Lowell Mellett and his staff who came from Washington for a special screening in Hollywood in March 1943.[43] It also seems likely that staff members of the Soviet embassy in Washington read the actual shooting script though evidence for this procedure exists only for other pro-Soviet feature films and not for *Mission to Moscow.*[44] The OWI did not demand changes in the political content of the script; in its final version they felt the film would make "an outstanding contribution" to wartime unity.[45] When Jack Warner screened the film at a Hollywood sneak preview, every single comment card Warner passed along to Davies praised the film extravagantly.[46]

Warner Brothers went all out on publicity. A gala preview for over 4,000 persons in Washington, D.C., made page one of the *Hollywood Reporter* for April 29, 1943. "Before a tough, hard-boiled audience of . . . newspaper men," the glowing account began, and then listed a goodly number of those present. Warner Brothers announced an advertising budget of 500,000 dollars, a handsome figure by the standards of 1943.[47] In short, a lot of people liked the finished product for what it said about wartime unity.

No sooner was the film released on April 30, however, than a roar of protest developed in some quarters. Daniel Bell's *New Leader*, a pro-Trotsky New York newspaper with a small but vocal national readership, had published a number of attacks on the film during its production. And it turns out that the newspaper had indeed gotten quite accurate information about various scripts and what the film planned to say.[48] More damaging was a lengthy letter that philosopher John Dewey published in the *New York Times* in May. Dewey had headed an independent commission of inquiry concerning the Moscow trials and had already written to the *New York Times* in January 1942 to condemn the distortions of Davies's book. The film called forth his special rage. *Mission to Moscow*, he began, "is the first instance in our country of totalitarian propaganda for mass consumption—a propaganda which falsifies history through distortion, omission or pure invention of facts."[49] The following Sunday he was answered in the *Times* by Arthur Upham Pope, who had also replied to Dewey's attack on Davies's book in 1942. Pope had been chairman of the Committee for National Morale and was a recognized scholar, though not in Dewey's league. He defended both film and book on the grounds that the purge trials really were a response to a Trotskyite conspiracy and, besides, in the middle of a war in which Russia was our ally, it was unseemly to argue over the content of the film.[50]

Other reviewers dealt with the dramatic appeal of *Mission to Moscow*. Bosley Crowther, critic for the *New York Times*, had measured praise; James Agee, in the *Nation*, found much of the film dull but said he neither believed nor disbelieved the claims about the purge trials—an interesting position given what we know in retrospect about that subject.[51] The most skillful roasting was by Manny Farber in the *New Republic*. A few excerpts suggest his attitude:

Now I'm ready to vote for the booby prize: I have seen *Mission to Moscow*. . . . Mr. Davies' book was a stale, innocuous melange of the fewest and most obvious facts that Soviet interpreters . . . had been reporting on Russia for years. . . . The movie, as a movie, is the dullest imaginable. . . . To describe Davies' tour of Russian heavy industry, one device is used five times without break—Davies talking to a mechanic, a coal miner, an engineer, a farmer—until you expect a flashback to the October Revolution and Davies talking to Lenin (obviously like this: "Just what do you think of your chances, Mr. Lenin? I'm a capitalist myself . . .).[52]

Though Mr. Pope had scholarly credentials and liked the film, and though some like Mr. Crowther and Mr. Agee straddled the fence, the critics who hated the fabrications in the film were more vocal. No one looking at the film today should imagine that this film reflects what was universally thought about Russia in 1943.

Estimating audience response to the film is as hard for *Mission to Moscow* as for most feature films. The best gauge is the box-office gross, a rough index at best. In January 1944 *Variety* listed the top grossers of the season; *Mission to Moscow* was eighty-fourth out of ninety-five. This meant it grossed 1.2 million dollars from commercial distribution in the continental United States in calendar year 1943.[53] Since out of this figure comes the exhibitor's share, the distributor's share, distribution expenses, the cost of prints, and the advertising budget, it seems unlikely that the film made any money or even paid for itself.[54]

The film, then, was not the hit of the season but neither did it collapse after the Dewey letter or any other public criticisms. It was shown to servicemen on posts throughout the country as well as overseas, as part of the Army Motion Picture Service. And a Gallup poll reported that eleven percent of those questioned had seen the film in 1943 at a time when each percentage point represented 750,000 persons.[55]

Popular opinion polls suggest that there was no great upswing in trust for the Soviet Union, but *Mission to Moscow*, and the other Hollywood films like it, certainly kept anti-Soviet feeling from growing.[56] The United States Army embarked on a *Why We Fight* series (with the *Battle of Russia* being released to a commercial public in October 1943) precisely because so few inductees knew anything much about overseas political events of the 1930s. *Mission to Moscow* filled in the gaps for the uninitiated. Certainly to the degree a feature film can change attitudes, *Mission to Moscow* was the most significant overt example of Hollywood's attempt to intensify support for an awkward ally.

In Nazi Germany the appearance of *Mission to Moscow* did not pass unnoticed. Propaganda minister Joseph Goebbels recorded in his diary on May 19, 1943, that the film was so overboard in its praise of Stalin that it had aroused protest "even" from the American public. A week later he described a report from a source inside the Soviet Union regarding Davies, back again on a diplomatic mission. Goebbels called Davies a "dangerous ignoramus," and a "type of salon bolshevik." In other entries for this period Goebbels, incorrectly, assumed that the film's release had been coordinated by Roosevelt to accompany Stalin's announcement that he was dissolving the Comintern, the official organization charged with spreading Communist ideology in other countries. In July Goebbels arranged for a harsh attack on Davies and his film to appear in *Das Reich*, unusual attention considering that *Mission to Moscow* was scarcely scheduled for release in all German theaters.

Finally the film deserves special attention because of its impact on the Soviet Union itself. Between 1939 and 1945 only twenty-four American films were purchased by the Soviet Union for commercial distribution within its borders.[57] Stalin was himself chief movie censor and personally approved every foreign film before it was distributed within the country to as many as 21,000 movie theaters.[58] Joseph Davies went to Moscow in May 1943 and took a print of the film with him. Roosevelt agreed that the film might put Stalin in a more pro-American mood. Diplomatic records reveal that Stalin, Vyshinsky, Molotov, and others sat down together and viewed this film when Davies arrived in Moscow for a diplomatic reception.[59] We also know that the film did go into commercial distribution within the Soviet Union, though probably minus the Davies prologue, and, if newspaper accounts can be trusted, with a scene about bugging the American embassy omitted as well.[60] The Russian narration followed the original closely; the purge scenes were left as they were. It seems of considerable significance that this film, with its Stalinist distortions, was so widely seen in the Soviet Union. It is one of the few examples one can point to of Roosevelt's being able to show Stalin that America had experienced a change of heart and that friendship and understanding were the new watchwords of the day.[61] This was the real message of the film. It was intended not so much to reinforce or somehow legitimize a specious account of domestic Soviet politics in the 1930s as to convince Americans and the rest of the world that the United States really cared about her Russian ally.

Why did Warner Brothers risk their name in making a film that is a history lesson? And why did they make so distorted a picture? The answer lies in the desperate plight of Russia and the feeling that perhaps a film of the right sort could make the Soviet Union look better in American eyes. Clearly the extreme nature of the film offers compelling evidence of just how critical the Russian situation seemed to Davies, Roosevelt, and Warner Brothers in 1942–43.

Those concerned with changing public attitudes can learn something from *Mission to Moscow* of a more general nature. Effective propaganda reinforces that which is true.[62] *The Battle of Russia*, the Frank Capra-*Why We Fight* film, never said a word about the purge trials or Finland; it tried to pretend that the Nazi-Soviet pact had not happened. It focused instead on historic enmity between the Germans and the Russians and used superb Russian footage of the defense of Leningrad, Moscow, and Stalingrad in 1941–43. Telling of Russian heroism in wartime, not rewriting of history in a ludicrous fashion, is an effective strategy for the propagandist. The audacity of *Mission to Moscow* may entitle it to a certain sort of respect though the falsehoods still seem disturbing.

Perhaps the most unsettling aspect of the film is what its content says about the federal government's control over Hollywood in wartime. The Hollywood Office of the Bureau of Motion Pictures, Office of War Information, established in the summer of 1942, monitored the content of every feature film coming out of Hollywood.[63] But the OWI never really had the confidence of Roosevelt and, in the end, the President let an idea of his old friend Davies run away with itself. Davies used his personal fortune and claims of "inside information" to club the opposition into silence.

Roosevelt never thought through what the film was supposed to say and the OWI was, from a practical administrative point of view, powerless to impose its will on the President. So a government agency giving the illusion of censor turned out to have no real power when it mattered. A film seen by millions of persons throughout the world and, because of its political content, presumed by the knowledgeable to represent Washington's intent, actually came into being without anyone really having given serious thought to the matter of ends and means. It is a disturbing aspect of how media events occur in the modern world that this is often the case.[64] It suggests that in the making of this film independent moral judgment deteriorated as a result of everyone's easy adjustment to bureaucratic procedures.

Screening *Mission to Moscow* today requires returning emotionally, as best we can, to the world of 1943 while at the same time bringing some historical perspective to bear on the film. Thanks to the immense surviving documentation we can avoid exaggeration and still say that this film is the most significant example of official attempts to promote wartime unity through manipulating the content of an entertainment medium. Today's lessons are not necessarily those of 1943: to the degree that we can recognize the false "facts" of the film we escape its power to force us toward emotional or subjective conclusions. It should serve as a warning to those who would use media technology to manipulate what we think—there is a limit to what the traffic will bear.

NOTES

1. For an overview of films with pro- or anti-Soviet themes, see Melvin Small, "Buffoons and Brave Hearts: Hollywood Portrays the Russians, 1939–1944," *California Historical Quarterly*, vol. 52 (Winter, 1973), pp. 326–37. For those who seek additional background concerning American diplomatic and political history, 1933–1945, the following are helpful: James MacGregor Burns, *Roosevelt: The Soldier of Freedom* (New York, 1970), an overview of wartime diplomacy and domestic affairs; John Lewis Gaddis, *The United States and the Origins of the Cold War, 1941–1947* (New York, 1972), a sound account; George F. Kennan, *Memoirs, 1925–1950* (Boston, 1967), beautifully written by the diplomat who served in Moscow in the 1930s; Geoffrey Perrett, *Days of Sadness, Years of Triumph: The American People 1939–1945* (Baltimore, 1974), the best account of American society during the war; Bruce Russett, *No Clear and Present Danger: A Skeptical View of the United States' Entry into World War II* (New York, 1972), an important revisionist interpretation; Forrest C. Pogue, *George C. Marshall: Organizer of Victory, 1943–1945* (New York, 1973), an excellent volume about the military direction of

the war. For those interested in a fuller documentary record, see Department of State, *Foreign Relations of the United States: The Soviet Union, 1933–1939* (Washington, 1952) and the many volumes of the *Foreign Relations* series covering 1933–1945.

2. Joseph Davies, prologue to the film. I have edited the filmscript, *Mission to Moscow: The Feature Film as Official Propaganda*, to be published by the University of Wisconsin Press in 1979. As part of that project I had a print of the film for several weeks in order to select frame enlargements. I have checked all dialogue with the final shooting script and the continuity, a verbatim recording of the release print's soundtrack submitted for copyright purposes.

3. The definition of documentary is notoriously difficult. Here is one attempt: "All methods of recording on celluloid any aspect of reality interpreted whether by factual shooting or by sincere and justifiable reconstruction, so as to appeal either to reason or emotion, for the purpose of stimulating the desire for, and the widening of human knowledge and understanding, and of truthfully posing problems and their solutions in the spheres of economic, culture, and human relations." On June 23, 1977, a colloquium on Davies and the making of *Mission to Moscow*, organized by Professor Robert C. Williams and myself, was held at the Woodrow Wilson International Center for Scholars, Smithsonian Institution, Washington, D.C. The film's screenwriter, Howard Koch, spoke before an audience including several diplomats who served with Davies in Moscow in the 1930s. There are several doctoral dissertations on Davies, none of which discusses the film. Two thorough articles by Thomas R. Maddux carefully assess Davies's service in Moscow: "American Diplomats and the Soviet Experiment: The View from the Moscow Embassy, 1934–1939," *South Atlantic Quarterly*, vol. 74 (Autumn, 1975), pp. 468–87; and "Watching Stalin Maneuver Between Hitler and the West: American Diplomats and Soviet Diplomacy, 1934–1939," *Diplomatic History*, vol. 1 (Spring, 1977), pp. 140–54. Unflattering references to Davies as a diplomat may be found in Kennan, *Memoirs*, and Charles E. Bohlen, *Witness to History, 1929–1969* (New York, 1973), in particular, p. 123.

4. Though *film noir* refers specifically to the psychological thriller, it applies in many respects to *Mission to Moscow:* "its sense of people trapped—trapped in webs of paranoia and fear, unable to tell guilt from innocence, true identity from false." Robert Sklar, *Movie-Made America: A Cultural History of American Movies* (New York, 1976), p. 253.

5. Ralph B. Levering, *American Opinion and the Russian Alliance, 1939–1945* (Chapel Hill, N.C., 1976), p. 43.

6. For Americans who favored the Soviet Union, see Daniel Aaron, *Writers on the Left: Episodes in Literary Communism* (New York, 1974), in particular, pp. 334–42; and Richard H. Pells, *Radical Visions and American Dreams* (New York, 1973); more generally, see David Caute, *The Fellow-Travellers* (London, 1973); pp. 203–24.

7. The most significant works on the purges are Robert Conquest, *The Great Terror: Stalin's Purge of the Thirties* (rev. ed., New York, 1973); Roy A. Medvedev, *Let History Judge: The Origins and Consequences of Stalinism* (New York, 1971); and Stephen F. Cohen, *Bukharin and the Bolshevik Revolution: A Political Biography 1888–1938* (New York, 1973), in particular, pp. 337–81.

8. Conquest, *Great Terror*, pp. 666–67. For Soviet policy, see Max Beloff, *The Foreign Policy of Soviet Russia* (2 vols.; London, 1947–49); on Nazi-

Soviet relations see Gerhard L. Weinberg, *The Foreign Policy of Hitler's Germany: Diplomatic Revolution in Europe* (Chicago 1970). See also Adam B. Ulam, *Expansion and Coexistence: The History of Soviet Foreign Policy, 1917–1967* (New York, 1968).

9. U.S. Congress. House Committee on Un-American Activities. *Hearings Regarding the Communist Infiltration of the Motion Picture Industry.* 80th Cong. 1st Session (Washington, 1947), p. 33 (hereafter HUAC, *Communist Infiltration*). Warner's testimony will be included in the documentary appendices to my edition of the filmscript.

10. Russell E. Shain, "Cold War Films, 1948–1962: An Annotated Filmography," *Journal of Popular Films*, vol. 3 (Fall, 1974), pp. 365–72.

11. On this topic see Perrett, *Days of Sadness, Years of Triumph*; for popular films in World War II there is a useful discussion in Richard R. Lingeman, *Don't You Know There's a War On?: The American Home Front 1941–1945* (New York, 1970), pp. 168–233.

12. Buckner to author, January 1, 1978.

13. Interview with Leyda, New York City, May 2, 1977.

14. The final shooting script called for a montage of newsreel stock shots at this point with substantial emphasis on Soviet assistance to Spain. In the end all references to Spain were omitted. For information about how Warner Brothers got a print of Leni Riefenstahl's *Triumph of the Will*, used in the film to depict Nazi regimentation, see telegram, Karl MacDonald, Motion Picture Division, Office of Inter-American Affairs, to Francis Alstock, December 15, 1942, Central Files 3, Box 211, Record Group 229, Records of the Office of Inter-American Affairs, Archives Branch, Washington National Records Center, Suitland, Maryland (hereafter WNRC).

15. The favorable depiction of Stalin accords exactly with the description in Joseph E. Davies, *Mission to Moscow* (New York, 1941), pp. 356–7, though it bears little similarity to what we now know about Stalin's actual personality.

16. Dr. Gerald K. Haines, Diplomatic Branch, National Archives, Washington, D.C., kindly provided me with a copy of the complete Davies 123 file, 1936–1941, part of the Records of the Department of State, Record Group 59 (hereafter NA). On Davies's art-collecting mania, see the forthcoming book by Robert Williams of Washington University concerning the entry of Russian art into the United States. Davies was actually inside the Soviet Union January 19–March 26, June 24–July 30, and October 4–November 24, 1937; and February 23–June 11, 1938. For illustrations of the Davies paintings, see John E. Bowlt, "Soviet Paintings in the Joseph E. Davies Collection," *Elvenjem Art Center 1976–1977 Bulletin* (Madison, Wis., 1978), pp. 34–42.

17. See the documentary record in Edgar B. Nixon, ed., *Franklin D. Roosevelt and Foreign Affairs* (3 vols., Cambridge, Mass., 1969) and Robert A. Divine, *The Illusion of Neutrality* (Chicago, 1962).

18. This is proved in exhaustive detail in Conquest, *Great Terror*, and Medvedev, *Let History Judge*.

19. See Ulam, *Expansion and Coexistence*; A. J. P. Taylor, *The Origins of the Second World War* (New York, 1966).

20. Concerning Finland, see William L. Langer and S. Everett Gleason, *The Undeclared War, 1940–41* (New York, 1953).

21. In 1944 Edmund Wilson wrote an essay likening Davies's prose to that of Warren G. Harding: "Mr. Joseph E. Davies as a Stylist," *Partisan Review*, reprinted in Wilson, *Classics and Commercials: A Literary Chronicle of the Forties* (New York, 1950), pp. 98–104.

22. Davies admits this in his "Author's Note," p. xxii; the Welles letter of July 20, 1941, is reprinted in facsimile following p. 14; both in *Mission to Moscow*.

23. "Preface," Missions for Peace, 9, Box 109, closed section, Joseph E. Davies Papers, Manuscript Division, Library of Congress, Washington, D.C. (hereafter Davies MSS).

24. Davies, *Mission to Moscow*, pp. 271–4. The selection process may be seen by contrasting a letter Davies wrote to Stephen Early, April 4, 1938 (pp. 317–19) regarding the trial of Bukharin. In the book one gets only information arguing that there was a conspiracy. In the original letter Davies also said: "Here there was no issue left—the guilt had already been determined by the confessions of the accused. . . . There is scarcely a foreign observer who attended the trial but what arrived at the conclusion that while there was a great deal that was untrue; that it was established that there had been a great deal of plotting on the part of many of these defendants to overthrow Stalin. It was a case of the 'outs' against the 'ins'." Original in "Davies folder 38–41," Box 3, Stephen Early Papers, Franklin D. Roosevelt Libary, Hyde Park, New York (hereafter FDRL).

25. "Moscow Notebook—An Ambassador's Report," pp. 12–13 et seq. The excerpts include the 1941 postscript about the purge trials being a Trotsky plot and the cordial interview with Stalin. The editorial assistance by Quincy Howe is described in Howe to Davies, Box 97, Davies MSS. An extreme example of Davies's support for the Soviet Union is *Life*'s March 29, 1943, issue devoted to Russia. Davies answered twenty-one questions about "The Soviets and the Postwar: A Former Ambassador to Moscow Answers Some Perplexing Problems," and included a plug for the film.

26. The various editions are described in Davies's diary entry, November 20, 1942, Box 12, Davies MSS.

27. The poll, whose results fortified Davies's determination to say certain things in the film, is found in Box 97, Davies MSS. It will be reprinted in its entirety in the documentary appendices to my edition of the filmscript.

28. HUAC, *Communist Infiltration*, pp. 32–33.

29. Howard Koch kindly sent me material relating to *Mission to Moscow* from his forthcoming memoirs, *As Time Goes By*, to be published by Harcourt, Brace, Jovanovich.

30. Davies to Chairman, HUAC, June 10, 1947, copy enclosed in Davies to Koch, October 1, 1947, Howard Koch MSS, Film and Manuscripts Archive, Wisconsin Center for Film and Theater Research, State Historical Society of Wisconsin, Madison, Wisconsin (hereafter WCFTR). This material was kindly sent to me by Professor Tino Balio, Director. This story is exactly the same as that given in George Bye to Jay Franklin Carter, August 3, 1942, copy in "Davies 42–49" folder, Box 3, Early MSS, FDRL.

31. Warner offered a review of his 1917 film in HUAC, *Communist Infiltration*, pp. 22–24. Its success no doubt encouraged Warner Brothers to try again with Davies's book.

32. See, as a representative example, Edgar Dale, Bureau of Motion Pictures, Office of War Information, to Iris Barry, Museum of Modern Art Film Library, May 10, 1943, "War Production Board" folder, Central Files, Museum of Modern Art Film Library, New York, New York. I am grateful to Eileen Bowser for opening these files to me.

33. Davies to George Bye, August 11, 1942, "Davies 42–49" folder, Box 3, Early MSS, FDRL; see also Koch, *As Time Goes By*.

34. Caldwell had been in the Soviet Union with his wife, photographer Margaret Bourke-White. See his *All-Out on the Road to Smolensk* (New York, 1942) and *Moscow Under Fire* (New York, 1942).

35. Copy of Caldwell script, August 21, 1942, in WCFTR.

36. Buckner says that Davies at first "wanted a 'bigger' name," but settled for Curtiz (by 1942 clearly one of Warner's most successful directors) after discovering how ill-suited his first choice for screenwriter had been. Buckner to author, January 1, 1978.

37. See treatment by Koch, August 28, 1942, WCFTR; Koch, *As Time Goes By*. For Curtiz's career, see Jack Edmund Nolan, "Michael Curtiz," *Films in Review*, vol. 25 (November, 1970), pp. 525–48.

38. Both were honored in *In Time to Come: A Play About Woodrow Wilson* (New York, 1942), in particular, pp. 57, 92–94. Koch specifically thanks John Huston and John Houseman for help "in research and in the writing of this play." Otto Preminger was the producer.

39. Koch, *As Time Goes By*; statement by Koch, colloquium at Wilson Center, June 23, 1977; Davies to Koch, December 4, 1942, Box 98, Davies MSS.

40. This is spelled out in detail in my introduction to the filmscript. As examples, Caldwell used an isolationist senator named Hightower who lasted into the final shooting script but not the release print, and Caldwell and Buckner also decided on conflating the purge trials into one before Koch came on the scene. Indeed the development of the first thirty-one sequences of the film is virtually identical with Caldwell's ideas.

41. Interview with Leyda, New York City, May 2, 1977; Davies to Tania Litvinov, September 18, 1942, Box 125; Davies diary entry, October 16, 1942, Box 12; Davies diary entry, November 20, 1942, Box 12, all in Davies MSS. Buckner to author, January 1, January 14, 1978; interview with Mrs. Lowell Ditzen, Washington, D.C., April 1, 1977.

42. The planning of the film is suggested in a twenty-four-page memorandum Davies sent Curtiz in September 1942 after reading scripts by Caldwell and Koch: "The original discussion between Mr. H. M. Warner, Mr. Buckner, and myself involved one of three forms of treatment. (1) An attempt to dramatize conventionally the *Mission to Moscow* and sugar-coat the facts, by bringing in the human interest, accommodating an emotional impact to be the supreme moment in the screen play. (2) To dramatize it by making it the life story of a typical American, whom from modest beginnings, achieves success, and bring in the message from Moscow as part of a movement, this along the line of *Knute Rockne*, or *George M. Cohan* or possibly, *The Fighting 69th*. (3) Make it primarily a factual script, covering the main features with as much dramatic quality as the material in and of itself produces. This treatment would be somewhat like Gerard's *My Four Years in Germany*, or *March of Time*. It would be addressed primarily to the intellect and would be more or less based upon the purpose of bringing information which would appeal more to the mind than to the emotions." (September 23, 1942, Box 98, Davies MSS.) See also Koch, *As Time Goes By*; final shooting script, copy in WCFTR; Buckner to Davies, March 15, 1943, Box 98, Davies MSS.

43. See notation relating to completed film plus synopsis, Hollywood Office, BMP, OWI, April 29, 1943, Box 1434, entry 264, Record Group 208, Office of War Information Records, WNRC; see also Nelson Poynter to Buckner, December 3, 1942, Box 16, Lowell Mellett MSS, FDRL.

44. Mellett to Warren Pierce, OWI, January 9, 1943, Box 3517, entry 567, RG 208, WNRC; Mellett to Davies, April 19, 1943, Box 11, Mellett MSS, FDRL. Both of these memoranda will appear in the documentary appendices to the filmscript.

45. Statement with synopsis of film, April 29, 1943, BMP, OWI, Box 1434, entry 264, RG 208, WNRC.

46. Jack Warner to Davies, May 3, 1943, Box 98, Davies MSS. If there were any negative responses, none seem to have been passed along.

47. *New York Times*, May 7, 1943, p. 33. The Library of Congress, among other places, has copies of the *Hollywood Reporter*.

48. *The New Leader*, copies of which are also available at the Library of Congress, carried articles condemning *Mission to Moscow*, generally on page 1, on the following dates: March 20, April 10, April 24, May 1, May 8, and May 15, 1943, and had run an attack on Jay Leyda and the film on December 26, 1942.

49. Dewey and Suzanne La Follette to *New York Times*, May 9, 1943, IV, p. 8; the Dewey letter is discussed in *Time*, May 17, 1943, pp. 19–20.

50. Pope to *New York Times*, May 16, 1943, IV, p. 2; see also Dewey to *New York Times*, January 11, 1942, IV, p. 7; and Pope to *New York Times*, January 18, 1942, IV, p. 7; Pope also defended the film in Soviet Russia Today, June 1943, pp. 8–9. Koch himself defended his film in a letter to the *New York Times*, June 13, 1943, II, p. 3. Dewey had already written to the head of the OWI to protest the treatment of Trotsky in the film, Dewey to Elmer Davis, September 24, 1942; Davis responded: "I have talked with Mr. Harry Warner and with Mr. Davies and am assured by both that the treatment of Trotsky . . . will not be the sort to justify your fears." Davis to Dewey, October 5, 1942, both in Box 1433, entry 264, RG 208, WNRC.

51. *New York Times*, April 30, 1943, p. 25; Crowther ran a second article about the film on May 9, 1943, II, p. 3. *The Nation*, May 22, 1943, pp. 749–50.

52. May 10, 1943, p. 636.

53. January 5, 1944, p. 54; Hadley Cantril and Mildred Strunk, *Public Opinion 1935–1946* (Princeton, N.J., 1951), p. 485; see also reports on weekly grosses for the film in selected cities in *Variety* and *The Hollywood Reporter*. For the former see May 19 (pp. 13, 15–16); May 26 (pp. 9–11); June 2 (pp. 7, 9, 10–11); June 23 (p. 10); June 30 (p. 13). For the latter see May 3 (p. 1), and December 29 (p. 2), where the rebooking of the film is credited to the Tehran conference; see also April 30 (p. 1), and July 13 (p. 1).

54. This is Buckner's opinion. "*Mission to Moscow*," he writes, "was not a financially successful film. It did not return its negative cost, although the publicity released by the studio insinuated otherwise. I could never obtain the exact figures (few ever can in any studio), but I had a good friend in the accounting department who confided to me years later that the film was a financial failure. Not a disaster, just that it never broke even. I can assure you that you'll never get any closer to the fact." Buckner to author, January 14, 1978.

55. Hadley Cantril and Mildred Strunk, *Public Opinion 1935–1946* (Princeton, N.J., 1951), p. 485.

56. The film's impact—its immensely rosy picture of Soviet history—was significant because other devices for creating pro-Soviet feeling in the United States had little effect. Poll data on the basic question of whether one trusted or distrusted the Soviet Union from March 1942 to December 1943 showed that trust never received more than 51 percent and that in the spring of 1943

trust was on the downward swing. Such data are generally correlated to specific events overseas and it seems fair to conclude that the December 1943 meeting at Tehran between Roosevelt and Stalin, not pro-Soviet films, explains increased public trust in Russia. See Levering, *American Opinion and the Russian Alliance*, pp. 116–17; see also Warren B. Walsh, "What the American People Think of Russia," *Public Opinion Quarterly*, vol. 8 (Winter, 1944), pp. 513–22.

57. Unpublished *Tagebücher*, May 19, 23, 25–26, 1943, pp. 2419–20, 2474, 2476, 2493–94, 2509, 2511–12, all in F12/25, Institut für Zeitgeschichte, Munich, Germany. A bowdlerized version of some of these entires may be found in Louis P. Lochner, ed., *The Goebbels Diaries, 1942–43* (Garden City, N.Y., 1948); *Das Reich*, July 25, 1943. "Motion Picture Production in the U.S.S.R.," John Paton Davies to Secretary of State, February 18, 1946, 861.4061, RG 59, NA.

58. Ibid. Concerning Stalin's addiction to film and his role as censor, see Nikita Khrushchev, *Khrushchev Remembers* (Boston, 1970), pp. 318–19; and his *Khrushchev Remembers: The Last Testament* (Boston, 1974), p. 407.

59. Roosevelt to Stalin, May 1, 1943, copy in Koch MSS, WCFTR; Ambassador Standley to Secretary of State, May 25, 1943, Box 13, Davies MSS; Robert E. Sherwood, *Roosevelt and Hopkins: An Intimate History* (New York, 1948), pp. 705, 733; Davies diary entry, May 23, 1943, Box 111, Davies MSS.

60. Standley to Secretary of State, July 27, 1943, Box 3273, 811.4061, RG 59, NA; *New York Times*, July 28, 1943, p. 18. Professor Stefan Sharff of Columbia University, who saw the film in Moscow in 1944, says the Davies prologue was cut; comment following my lecture on the making of the film for University Film Seminars, Museum of Modern Art Film Library, December 8, 1977.

61. Averell Harriman states that the Russians loved *North Star*, MGM's pro-Russian film with a screenplay by Lillian Hellman; and Zina Voynow, Eisenstein's sister-in-law, told me that *Mission to Moscow* was much appreciated by the Russian people who nevertheless recognized the often ludicrous Hollywood-style characterization of their own country. Harriman to author, March 14, 1977; telephone interview with Zina Voynow, June 22, 1977. The Soviet government proposed to give decorations to two films, *North Star* and *Mission to Moscow*, that had helped strengthen Soviet-American relations. The State Department suggested that the Capra-unit *The Battle of Russia* would be better since *Mission to Moscow* "aroused undesirable and heated controversy . . . concerning the Soviet Union and Soviet-American relations." Ambassador Harriman to Secretary of State, January 22, 1944; Secretary of State to Harriman, January 29, 1944; Box 4943, 861.4061, RG 59, NA.

62. The problem of defining what is propaganda and what is not lies outside the scope of this essay though the subject bears directly on how we interpret the film. The more thought one gives to the struggle between ends (increasing support for one's ally) and means (distorting reality) the more slippery the concept of objective truth becomes; the less easy to say with certainty what the contextual significance of any fact is. Education assumes the rational man as attainable ideal; given sufficient facts or sufficient perception of objective reality, so the argument goes, it is possible to know the truth about public issues of the day. But propaganda lies behind every opinion we hold on public issues. No moral or religious code arms the citizen sufficiently in the quest for separating what is true from what is not. A working definition of

propaganda is as follows: "The controlled dissemination of deliberately distorted notions in an effort to induce action favorable to predetermined ends of special interest groups." Michael Choukas, *Propaganda Comes of Age* (Washington, D.C., 1965), p. 37. A brilliant book on the subject is Jacques Ellul, *Propaganda: The Formation of Men's Attitudes* (New York, 1973), in particular, pp. v-xviii, 52–90. I will deal further with the relation of propaganda to *Mission to Moscow* in my introduction to the filmscript. I have learned a great deal about propaganda from many arguments with John E. O'Connor.

63. See Clayton R. Koppes and Gregory D. Black, "What to Show the World: The Office of War Information and Hollywood, 1942–1945," *Journal of American History*, vol. 64 (June, 1977), pp. 98–99.

64. See Thomas Cripps and David Culbert, "Persuasive Film and Racial Attitudes During World War II: *The Negro Soldier*," to appear in *The American Quarterly* in 1979, for an example of this process.

The Uncertain Peace:

The Best Years of Our Lives (1946)

MARTIN A. JACKSON

In this film about the uncertain peace, former Captain Fred Derry (Dana Andrews) walks among the stripped corpses of wartime aircraft and wonders about his own continued usefulness in a changed world.

(Photo courtesy of Museum of Modern Art)

In the summer of 1946, as Sam Goldwyn's latest production was being prepared for the screen, the American people could well say, as Dickens did about the French Revolution, that "it was the best of Times, it was the worst of Times." It was a time of virtually limitless world power for America, coupled with a nagging inability to find comfort or joy in the brave new postwar world. In its mirroring of the nation's mood in those first years of peace, *The Best Years of Our Lives* remains an important piece of evidence regarding that moment in American life when the past had been irretrievably lost but the future had not yet taken a clear form. The subtly ironic title of the film captures the atmosphere of fear mixed with optimism of that year, and in its plot, *Best Years* pins down the mood of the American people as they tried to adjust to the novel demands of a strange new world. For the historian, *Best Years* offers an opportunity to grasp the public mood of the mid-1940s, and to measure the way in which commercial movies both reflect and create the consciousness of a generation. The film can tell much about the mechanics of Hollywood and about the insistent demands of the public during the years of Truman's presidency and changing world conditions.

Best Years opened in New York City in November 1946, fourteen months after V-J Day, but its origins extend back to 1944, to the living room of Sam Goldwyn.[1] According to the unusually intense prerelease publicity for the film, Sam and Frances Goldwyn were spending a quiet Hollywood evening at home when Frances asked Sam to read a story in *Time* magazine about a group of returning Marine veterans.[2] The article described the readjustment problems faced by these men and, by implication, raised questions that would soon have to be answered on a much larger scale by the millions of GIs who would be making that homeward journey.[3] As World War II moved toward its conclusion, the problems of reconversion and readjustment were already in the public consciousness.[4] The memories of the haphazard policies of 1918 were fresh enough in 1944, and it was firmly resolved by all concerned to avoid the same dismal story of unemployment and disillusion after this war. The returning soldiers would be greeted as heroes this time, their postwar future assured by a grateful nation.[5] Goldwyn, with that acute feel for the public mood that had made Hollywood the world's film capital, knew a story hook when he saw one. That same evening he placed a long-distance phone call to Mackinlay Kantor, a novelist who had done some writing for Hollywood and who Goldwyn thought could handle the delicate issue of the returning veterans.[6]

The transcontinental phone call in 1944 resulted in an assignment for Kantor: ten thousand dollars for a treatment based on the *Time* story. What Goldwyn expected was a story outline that, if workable, would then be fashioned into a full-length script for filming. Kantor, however, perhaps stimulated by the subject, allowed his creative instinct full play and produced one of the more unusual story treatments in Hollywood history: a novel in blank verse that ran to 434 pages and was eventually published under the title *Glory for Me*.[7] Perhaps it was the length that put off Goldwyn, or the greater urgency of other films then underway, but, for whatever reason, Kantor's "treatment" was shelved shortly after it was delivered in January 1945. Goldwyn paid the writing fee but did not pursue the film; not an unusual episode in the film business, but the cavalier handling of his work annoyed Kantor. He had labored long and hard on the idea and later insisted that Goldwyn had given him freedom to write as he wished, including blank verse although he conceded that it might have been done differently. "If the form happened.to be a mistake," Kantor admitted, "I have only myself to blame."[8] After the success of *Best Years*, there would be a public dispute over authorship, with both Kantor and Goldwyn claiming credit for the idea, and arguing over the importance of the blank verse treatment as an inspiration for the film. Kantor declared that while "I didn't get much satisfaction out of it. . . . There's such a thing as pride of authorship. . . . After all . . . it was my idea and my book. Sam Goldwyn just put up the dough to produce it."[9]

There was no question, however, that Goldwyn had the legal right to kill the project if he wished, and during that winter of 1945 the treatment remained unused in Goldwyn's files. A year later it was resurrected under different circumstances and under the insistent prodding of William Wyler, one of Hollywood's most successful directors, who had returned from the war seeking the right material for his next film. Under the terms of a prewar contract with Goldwyn, Wyler owed one picture to the Goldwyn Studios and was anxious to complete it quickly, to be free for more important work. Wyler had spent the war years as an Air Force cameraman and director, responsible for such acclaimed work as *Memphis Belle*; he won a Distinguished Flying Cross for bravery while filming the B-17s over Germany.[10] An established name in Hollywood before the war, Wyler returned from combat with a revised outlook on art and life. "The war had been an escape into reality," Wyler observed, "in the war it didn't matter how much money you earned. The only thing that mattered were human relationships; not money, not position, not even family."[11] It was, then, a more serious director who came home from the war, one who sought stories that dealt honestly and responsibly with the human condition; Wyler had no interest in making another Hollywood fantasy movie—he wanted to make a statement.

Goldwyn had managed to interest Wyler in a film biography of Dwight D. Eisenhower, the immensely popular wartime commander of Allied armies in Europe, and Wyler was at work during early 1946 with playwright Robert Sherwood on a script about Ike. The project was going slowly, however, without much enthusiasm from Wyler who wanted something more important than a traditional screen biography of a famous person. In the interim, Kantor's novel, based on his original treatment for Goldwyn, had appeared and while its form militated against popular success, it had won critical notice. Wyler read the book and was impressed; when he found that Goldwyn already owned the screen rights he urged that the Eisenhower script be abandoned and Kantor's idea be substituted. Goldwyn was unhappy about this change in plans and tried to interest Wyler in several other properties, but to no avail. [12] Robert Sherwood, one of that group of New York playwrights and authors lured to Hollywood in the 1930s and 1940s and well respected in the industry, agreed with Wyler's decision and was also impressed by the theme of Kantor's book. Faced with the combined reluctance toward the Eisenhower film, Goldwyn gave the two men a go-ahead to produce a script based on *Glory for Me*.

In that spring of 1946, Goldwyn was not taking a very big gamble on the Kantor story. With attendance at a record high, movies were the nearest thing to a guarantee of sure profit available anywhere and Goldwyn could rest easily in the expectation of a fair return on his investment.[13] He ultimately spent three million dollars on *Best Years* but Goldwyn was a Hollywood veteran, willing to take big risks for big profits and, in this case with the seasoned William Wyler behind the cameras, his money was well protected.[14]

Sherwood was a skilled dramatist and with Wyler's help the two men had a script ready for shooting by April 1946. Kantor played virtually no part in the scriptwriting and never even saw a rough cut of the film until August, and then was not invited to change anything he saw.[15] The final script, however, followed Kantor's novel to a substantial degree, indicating that Sherwood and Wyler were satisfied with the broad outlines of the story as plotted by Kantor two years before. In the novel, as in the film, the central characters are three returning veterans who meet on the homeward journey and whose lives continue to intersect: Fred Derry, a former drugstore clerk turned air force hero; Al Stephenson, a banker who spent the war as an infantry sergeant; and Homer, a fresh-faced boy who served in the navy and suffered severe wounds. In the novel Homer is portrayed as a spastic, a victim of shell shock. In the film, of course, Homer's wounds are more visible; he is a double amputee. The change from a mental wound to a physical one was momentous; it involved finding an actor capable of playing a veteran with no hands, and this required a crucial decision on Goldwyn's part.

Filming had already begun with the part of Homer remaining unfilled, when Wyler remembered a training short he had seen featuring a young soldier who had lost both hands in an accident being fitted with hooks. It occurred to Wyler, and Sherwood agreed, that the only person capable of playing an amputee was, in fact, an amputee—it was a role that could not be acted but had to be lived. Wyler and Sherwood traced the soldier from the training film and thus the brief but spectacular career of Harold Russell was launched. Goldwyn, however, was stricken at the thought of using a real double amputee, it being traditional Hollywood wisdom that audiences wished to be entertained, not depressed. His mind was changed, however, after he did some audience research and found that people were indeed concerned about wounded veterans in that year and would probably react well to screen portraits of real wounded men.[16] Goldwyn's willingness to accept Harold Russell, an untried

and unprofessional actor, in the important role of Homer was rewarded when Russell won an Academy Award for his moving portrayal as the handicapped veteran.[17]

By April 1946 the cast was ready and, under Wyler's customary
vigorous direction, rehearsals began. Fredric March (Stephenson)
and Dana Andrews (Derry) were well-known film actors and good
box-office names; Myrna Loy was also a box-office attraction but
she was reluctant to play Al Stephenson's wife, the mother of grown
children, feeling that it cast her in a role that was too mature. But
with Goldwyn's celebrated persuasive skill and the admired Wyler
in the director's chair, Miss Loy accepted the part. Others in the
cast included Virginia Mayo as Fred Derry's philandering wife—
a part that gave Mayo the chance to rise above the usual B-movies
she inhabited—Teresa Wright as Al Stephenson's daughter, and
Cathy O'Donnell as Wilma, Homer's loyal girlfriend. It was an odd
assortment of veteran actors, bright newcomers, and amateurs, but
the assembled cast found the elusive chemistry and the result was
a film that remains a showcase of Hollywood acting.

Goldwyn knew better than to interfere with the day-to-day
shooting, being careful to avoid Wyler's wrath, but he had insisted
upon certain rules before production began. First, the film would
not be an attack upon America or its institutions although Goldwyn
accepted a certain amount of social criticism. Second, Wyler had
to bring in the completed film according to budget. To achieve the
latter, Wyler had agreed to curtail his normal practice of endless
rehearsals, a directorial method that had earned him the nickname
"Forty Take Wyler" and that usually raised emotions on his sets to
fever pitch.

Even before the cast began reading, Wyler had dispatched film
crews to shoot the background scenes, especially the aerial photography that would form some of the film's most memorable scenes.
Cincinnati was selected as the sort of typical American town en-
visioned by Sherwood in his script and later much location shooting would be done there, in itself an unusual decision in 1946 when
almost all of Hollywood's output was filmed on back lots or in
studios. Wyler considered this an important film, both personally
and artistically, and he went to great lengths in assembling the cast
and crew.[18] Wyler remembered his feelings twenty years later:

"I had just come out of the service," he said, "I was a veteran. I knew how these people felt. I knew all about them. I never had to ask myself, how would these people feel under the circumstances?"[19] To assure the best possible outcome, Wyler (with Goldwyn's support, of course) spared no expense in material or crew. As cameraman, Wyler employed the skilled and innovative Gregg Toland, already known for his pathbreaking work in Orson Welles's *Citizen Kane* (1940) and who was to win an Academy Award for his razor-sharp black and white photography in *Best Years*. Toland's camera work won the admiration of many critics, including James Agee who said, "I can't remember a more thoroughly satisfying job of photography in an American movie since *Greed*."[20] *Best Years* was Toland's final assignment; he died soon after the film opened but it remains a suitable monument to his career.

Wyler took pains with every detail, including costumes and makeup. In order to heighten the realism of the film, for instance, Wyler ordered male members of the cast not to wear makeup at all, an unusual device for any Hollywood director in those years. Wyler even insisted, if we are to believe the studio press releases, that every member of the crew be a veteran.[21] To increase the film's sense of reality, Wyler and the costume designer ignored the studio costume department and instead purchased clothes in a Los Angeles department store, and then had the cast wear the clothes for several days prior to shooting. The result of this careful attention to detail and realism was a film that was rooted in the feel of the times; the audience had no trouble identifying with the characters on the screen, for not only was the story about concerns of the day but the *look* of the scenes was right also.

By August 1946, working on a tight schedule, the shooting stage of the film was completed. There remained long weeks of editing, dubbing, and polishing under the combined attention of Wyler, Goldwyn, and Toland. Goldwyn wanted to exercise his producer's privilege and cut the film down to an hour and a half, although in its final release form *Best Years* ran for nearly two hours, a remarkably long movie for those years. While final editing was proceeding, Goldwyn had unleashed his publicity machine and the word was spread in industry circles that a major event was in the offing. Arrangements were made for a world premiere in Hollywood in

January 1947, to be followed by first runs in New York and other major cities. Wyler, however, reminded Goldwyn that in order to qualify for an Academy Award a film had to be released prior to the end of the year and he urged therefore an earlier premiere. "Do you really think it has a chance to win anything?" Goldwyn asked his director. When Wyler ventured that it might, Goldwyn revised his schedule and found a New York theater that would take the film in November, in time to qualify for the Academy Awards of 1946.[22]

On November 22, 1946, at the Astor Theatre in Times Square, *Best Years* went on public view.[23] For weeks before stories had been appearing in the *Saturday Evening Post*, *Colliers*, and *Life*, while Goldwyn hmself had appeared on radio shows to promote the film. Prerelease publicity was lavish, much of it extolling Goldwyn's foresight, wisdom, and courage in terms that would embarrass anyone but a Hollywood producer.[24]

Still, the heavy publicity expenses were rewarded the day after the opening, when the New York film critics gave the film excellent reviews. Bosley Crowther of the *New York Times* wrote that it "gives off a warm glow of affection for every-day, down to earth folks."[25] He was sufficiently impressed by *Best Years* to write yet another review the next day, praising the film's treatment of veterans' problems and noting that "the routine mechanics of Hollywood could never do the job."[26] In the *Herald Tribune*, Howard Barnes was even more taken with the movie: "rarely have the potentialities of a medium been so dazzlingly disclosed as they are. . . . The result is a work of provocative and moving insistence and beauty."[27] *Best Years* was, then, a certified hit, at least with the critics for the daily newspapers.

The more thoughtful, or slower working, critics for the weekly and periodical press found time to express some reservations. James Agee in the *Nation* wrote a two-part review, describing the film as "a long pious piece of deceit and self-deceit embarrassed by hot flashes of talent, conscience, truthfulness and dignity."[28] He rated Wyler one of the "few great" directors and had kind words to say about Fredric March, Harold Russell, and especially Theresa Wright, but Agee was clearly not swept away by the popular chorus over *Best Years*. Robert Warshow was even less overwhelmed by the film's content, and he offered a bitter critique in the liberal/left *Partisan Review*.

This review appeared six months after the film's opening, but it remains an important analysis of its political theme, or rather lack of any political theme, which was Warshow's major complaint. "The chief means of concealing the reality of politics is to present every problem as a problem of personal morality," said Warshow. Like Agee, he was able to admire Wyler's technique but insisted that the skill had been put too little effective use: "he [Wyler] sees how everything must look but frequently he cannot see what it really means."[29] In another generation and a far different cultural context, Andrew Sarris echoed these sentiments by labeling *Best Years* a work of "humanitarian blackmail" and wondering how badly the film had aged.[30] In 1968 Charles Higham and Joel Greenberg, in their *Hollywood in the Forties*, labeled *Best Years* "a banal, occasionally cynical tribute to the American way of life" and went on to criticize Wyler's directorial style as being "so tepid and attenuated that it reduces the film's visual interest to practically nil."[31]

The serious cinema critics, particularly the Europeans, found much to admire in Wyler's style. André Bazin wrote a long essay on *Best Years* and ranked Wyler, as a director, even higher than the reigning European prince, Orson Welles. "The immense talent of Wyler," Bazin announced, "lies in his knowledge that to simplify is to clarify and in his humility toward both subject and audience."[32] Jacques Sadoul, a leading French critic of the late 1940s was, like Bazin, deeply impressed by the cinema style of Wyler and by the social message of *Best Years*.[33] In America, the European-born critic and film historian Siegfried Kracauer praised Wyler as a director while criticizing the film's message. Wyler "never makes his audience believe, as Capra does, that human decency is alone sufficient to change the existing state of things," wrote Kracauer in 1948; "His film is not a fairy tale, but an attempt however limited to promote social progress."[34] Kracauer was not pleased with the overall theme of *Best Years* and several other "social message" films of those late 1940s, finding in them a resigned acceptance of corruption, despair, and weakness; ". . . our postwar films present a common man reluctant to heed the voice of reason and a liberal spokesman unable to run the emotional blockade around him."[35]

What Kracauer labeled as "ideological fatigue" was in fact a widespread affliction of those postwar years as the promises of the early 1940s gave way to the troubled and puzzling world at the end of the decade. *Best Years* may indeed exhibit the cynicism and lack of hope that Kracauer finds so repellant, but in doing so the film accurately mirrored the feelings of the American people at that moment. After several years of patriotic war films, in which the forces of good (i.e., the United States) inevitably triumphed over evil, *Best Years* came as a sharp and not unwelcome corrective with its sombre tone and lack of overt propaganda.

In 1946 the American people faced, with varying degrees of equanimity, a strange world. It was, as Henry Luce declared in a famous editorial, "the American Century." The United States emerged from World War II with its industry intact, its political influence paramount in every corner of the world, and its economic weight felt in shattered nations from Japan to France. The sense of nearly limitless opportunity runs through *Best Years* and serves as a balance to the otherwise bleak tone of the film. The three returning veterans who are the film's central characters respond differently to the postwar world they find back home. Al Stephenson finds the emphasis on business and profit distasteful. "Last year it was kill Japs—this year's it's make money," he says with anger, wondering if the sacrifice of wartime was justly rewarded at home. Al is the most well placed of the three, a banker with his job waiting for him and his future apparently bright, and it is significant therefore that he reacts most strongly against the grasping atmosphere of peacetime America.[36]

Fred Derry is the veteran who has the hardest time in finding his niche in the expanding economy. A drug-store clerk before the war, Derry returns a decorated air force captain and the film makes much of the irony of his being forced back behind the soda fountain. His bitterness at the lack of job prospects, combined with an unhappy marriage to an unfaithful wife, results in violence, divorce, and Derry's decision to leave Boone City forever. At the last moment, as he prepares to board a plane to anywhere, Fred is saved by a job offer from a salvage crew and so finds his place in the American dream. The irony is redoubled here, for Fred's new job involves dismantling the very planes that made him a hero and will now presumably assure his future. For Homer, the armless navy veteran, America's economic problems take second place to his personal dilemma: Homer, as many other wounded veterans in those years, has to make the radical adjustment to life with a handicap; he must deal with his girlfriend Wilma (Cathy O'Donnell) and with the clumsy good-will of his family, who mistake pity for support.

The three veterans meet on their way home to Boone City, and a solid friendship grows between them based on their military experiences and the impossibility of mere civilians ever understanding those experiences. They are markedly different in background and age: Al the banker is middle-aged, Fred the former clerk is in his twenties, and Homer is barely old enough to drink—yet the three find comfort in each other's company and gravitate together at Butch's Bar when the pressures of civilian life become too intense. The bar is the focal point for much of the film—it serves as an arena for their stories and a dark comfortable retreat from the outer world. Butch's is seedy and friendly, operated by Homer's uncle (Hoagy Carmichael) and—as Homer pointedly remarks—has hardly changed at all since the war. Butch himself is the familiar Hollywood deus ex machina, the wise but cynical observer of the human comedy.

When Fred Derry becomes dangerously infatuated with Al's daughter, Peggy, it is Butch's Bar that provides him a place to confront Al about the matter. In one of the film's most elegant bits of camera work, Fred makes the decision to call Peggy and break off their romance, while Al, Homer, and Butch continue their conversation in the bar. The frame is complex and a tribute to Toland's artistry: Homer and Butch are in the foreground, Al in midground watching Fred talking on the phone in the background. Toland's use of deep-focus is never better demonstrated than in this shot, as the camera takes in the whole panorama, balancing three distinct focal areas connected by the characters' eye movements—it is a dazzling piece of filmmaking.

Fred's encounter with Peggy emerged naturally from Fred's own bad marriage and Peggy's sympathetic nature. The love interest between the married Fred and the virginal Peggy gave Wyler and Sherwood their most difficult scriptwriting chore, for it would have been impossible, in 1946, to have the affair consummated, and yet the sexual attraction between the two characters had to be clearly delineated. Equally, it would not have passed the Production Code restrictions of those years to have Fred abandon his legal wife, no matter how destructive the marriage, in order to wed Peggy. The problem was solved by having Fred's wife leave *him*, the innocent victim of an immoral woman, free to marry Peggy someday.

It was altogether fitting, in 1946, that marriage played a central role in *Best Years*. The audiences of that year were sensitized to the issue of marriage and divorce among veterans, and to the matter of women's role in the postwar world. Although some recent critics have dismissed *Best Years* as a film that belittles women,[37] the female characters are, in fact, centers of strength and wisdom. The story focuses on the male characters, true enough, but the women are not mere accessories to their husbands or comic figures. Wilma, Homer's loyal girlfriend, is almost alone in regarding his wounds as bearable as she strives to convince him that their planned marriage should not be put off. In a delicately handled scene, Kathy helps Homer remove his clumsy harness and puts him to bed, a demonstration to Homer (and the audience) that their future sexual relations will not be male dominated or male initiated. Similarly, Al's daughter, Peggy, helps the tipsy Fred Derry to bed following a beery reunion with her father. The visual contrast between the uniformed Fred, sprawled on Peggy's lacy and utterly feminine bed, is highly suggestive of the sexual electricity between these two. There is a wry comment on Fred's usual relations with women when he awakens, realizes he is in a strange bed, and hurriedly checks for his wallet before remembering he is safe in a "nice girl's" room. The overseas sex life of the GI was a disturbing matter to many wives and mothers after demobilization, and magazines were full of stories about the wild misconduct of sons and husbands while in foreign lands. *Best Years*, in suggesting this delicate issue, albeit in a roundabout way, offered the women in the audience a glimpse into a highly charged dilemma.

Fred Derry's wife, Marie, is the analog to the misbehaving GI: she is the unfaithful wife who let down the boys overseas. Swiftly portrayed as a shallow grasping woman, Marie abandons her veteran husband for a slick war profiteer and announces her intention to divorce Fred. Just as wives and mothers were worried about their men's behavior overseas, the men in turn feared for their wives and girlfriends left unprotected back home. Marie symbolizes the worst fears that the GI had about his wife, but she is so unmistakably "bad" that the point is blunted. It would have been more meaningful, although infinitely more difficult, to portray an ordinary housewife as the unfaithful partner.[38]

Best Years did not limit itself to examining the purely personal or human problems of those years: it stepped boldly into political and social areas that Hollywood had treated tenderly, if at all, in preceding years. Wyler and Sherwood, with Goldwyn's often reluctant support, probed some of the most pressing world and domestic issues of the postwar years. There was a long list of problems confronting the American people.[39] Most visible, perhaps, was the new face in the White House, coupled with the disturbing knowledge that Franklin Roosevelt no longer guided the nation's affairs. When Harry Truman became President in April 1945, he had been a largely unknown Senator from Missouri who had been made Vice President out of political necessity and who was generally considered unsuited to the tasks confronting him.

But Truman rapidly adjusted to the demands of his office and even began to win favorable comments for his lack of pomp; his early morning walks and acerbic temper made him seem a far more friendly and understandable figure than FDR. Still, the shock of Roosevelt's death and the widespread sense that the country lacked strong, or at least proven, leadership was evident throughout 1946. Truman grappled with the immediate postwar domestic problems of price control and labor strife. In the case of the former, the demands for the immediate end of the Office of Price Administration (OPA) were resisted, but after an unedifying struggle with Congress, Truman was forced into a clumsy compromise that satisfied neither business nor consumer. When price controls were finally lifted in October 1946, the resulting inflation and price spiral fulfilled Truman's worst fears. The fall and winter of 1946, when *Best Years* opened, was a time of meat shortage, bizarre price increases, and bitter discontent. The labor movement, its demands held in check during the war, was in a restive state by 1946. As early as September 1945, Ford was hit by strikes and in 1946 General Motors was struck by the United Auto Workers. American labor was in full rebellion during 1946, and Truman found the nation near paralysis with strikes in the rubber, oil, textile, and electronics industries. The complex plans for reconversion were put in jeopardy by the labor unrest, and while Truman was by no means unsympathetic to labor, he was determined to preserve order and proceed with healthy economic growth. The breaking point came in May 1946, when the railroads were struck and Truman's temper overwhelmed his political caution. He announced the federal takeover of the nation's rail system and threatened, in a coast-to-coast broadcast, to draft the strikers into the Army, making them subject to military law if they refused to work. It was a drastic, almost unprecedented, action. But it worked. The striking train unions collapsed under the awesome federal pressure and the railroads were back at work. Truman suffered the obloquy of labor for his actions, but he probably won the respect of even larger numbers of citizens, who were grateful for his decisive steps and for his very human display of temper.

America's overseas problems were, if anything, even more difficult and unexpected than the knotty domestic agenda. The wartime alliance with the Soviet Union had collapsed in disarray even before Roosevelt's death. Americans found to their discomfort that the defeat of Hitler and Tojo had not brought universal peace, and newspaper readers learned a new vocabulary that included such names as Tito, Ho Chi Minh, and DPs. Europe was, in Churchill's words, "a charnel house"; the outlines of recovery were not even dimly seen in that winter of 1946. In Asia, the collapse of the Japanese empire was followed by political chaos and the ineffectual anachronistic attempts by the French and Dutch to restore their rule over peoples who were obviously not receptive. In China, the brief cooperation between Nationalists and Communists was rapidly turning to civil war, despite the best efforts of the Americans to bring the two sides together. No part of the world was truly peaceful, and in some parts warfare continued unabated, as though the global conflict had never ended. Greece, Turkey, Iran, and Korea were under Soviet pressure, while Soviet troops sat unmoved in eastern Europe. It was, as the American people had been promised, a new world. But was it a better one?

In the background, underlining each of the world's political and economic troubles, was the new force that had been released over Hiroshima in August 1945. Atomic energy had come to stay, and even in that dawn of the atomic age, no particular insight was needed to understand that the world had changed, permanently and probably for the worse. In *Best Years*, the atomic theme appears several times. Once when Al is questioned by his teenage son about the Hiroshima bombing and about atomic energy in general. It becomes obvious that Al does not really know as much as his son about this new force, and that what he does know does not please him. Just as Al, the returning army veteran, does not want to probe too deeply into the implications of the atomic bomb, so too the American public preferred to think about the beneficial use of the atom. But the mushroom cloud refused to dissipate—it hovered over the late 1940s and cast a shadow over the emerging American ascendancy.

The question of jobs and economic conditions was a vital one to the audiences of 1946. Many in those years had vivid and painful memories of the Depression, and while the war period provided full employment, there was the nagging thought that once the war factories closed and the boys came home, hard times would return with them. Truman's proposal for a Full Employment Act was one effort to avoid the postwar crash, by involving the federal government in economic planning. Nevertheless, as is made plain in *Best Years*, the best informed forecasters were not sanguine about future growth. Homer is greeted with the prediction that "hard times are coming, boy," and all three veterans confront the very real suspicion that returning GIs will replace those already employed. Thirty years later we can dismiss these fears of impending depression, knowing that they were groundless, but to the public in 1946, *Best Years* touched on a sensitive issue in revealing the depth of unease that existed in those years.

Wyler, however, was no pessimist about America's future. Despite Fred Derry's employment difficulty and Al Stephenson's despair over the nature of the banking business, the film ends on a bright note. In the justly renowned airplane graveyard scene, as Derry walks down the eerie rows of scrapped bombers, the past and future come together and a turning point is reached. Not a word is spoken as Derry wanders amid the broken and abandoned planes, used and thrown away just as he was by the nation that could find no further use for either. His reverie is broken by a voice, a workman who ejects him from the B-17 where he had been reliving his combat experience. At this juncture the long arm of Hollywood coincidence reaches out to save Fred Derry: the man is a junk dealer who offers Derry a job in what should be a growth industry, for the planes are being converted into badly needed homes for the veterans. In reality, therefore, neither Derry nor the planes are junk; they both will have their uses in the postwar economy and Derry's life is swiftly transformed. He is employed, rid of his evil wife, and soon to be free to marry the delightful Peggy. The veteran, in other words, has actually come home to prosperity and happiness, and while it may have taken the skill of the scriptwriters to solve Derry's fictional problems, he was an accurate representation of millions of real GIs who also faced the fears of unemployment, unwise marriage, and their own futures; they also emerged into a better world. For many of those veterans, and their families, the late 1940s were in fact "the best years" and they look back to those days with deep affection. In 1976, Harold Russell, now a Massachusetts businessman, reflected:

> I could give you a long lecture on what went wrong. But the important thing is that the postwar years *were* a great period for our country, and you had a tremendous feeling just being alive. Periods of adjustment are always difficult, but they are also interesting. We had problems, sure, but they didn't dominate us; we face the same things now, and we despair.[40]

Best Years became one of the major events of 1946 and has since passed into American folklore, an integral part of the memories of all the millions who saw it in 1946 and who have seen it in the years since. The film swept the Academy Awards in that year, winning no fewer than seven Oscars, including Best Picture, Best Director, and Best Actor (Fredric March). Audiences responded as eagerly as members of the Academy. *Best Years* was a commercial success, thanks in large part to the nearly unprecedented publicity granted to the film. Part of the publicity was of course the result of Goldwyn's heavy spending on advertisement and his energetic peddling in the best Hollywood tradition, but the film was a genuine news item in its own right and was given considerable free coverage in the media. There was particular interest in the story of Harold Russell: his amateur status, his courage in the face of severe wounds, and his unfailing good nature made Russell one of the more familiar faces before the American public in 1946.

European critics and audiences were as receptive as their American counterparts, with *Best Years* being greeted as one of the first major American films released in postwar Europe. The film ran for sixty weeks in London, seventeen in Stockholm, and was seen in nearly every country open to American movies in the late 1940s. By 1977, according to *Variety, Best Years* had gross rentals of 11.3 million dollars, as compared with its initial cost of three million dollars.[41] In 1953, with the war in Korea and a new group of veterans making the adjustment to civilian life, Goldwyn decided to rerelease the film; it was critically and financially successful, although it failed to arouse the same excitement it did in 1946. *Best Years* continues into the 1970s as a television feature and is a standard part of many university film courses and revival programs. Its stature as one of the great American films seems secure, with millions unborn in 1946 finding much that is moving and important in the story of the three soldiers trying to find their way in a nation that is at once enticing and foreign to them. Few Americans can forget the picture of Homer putting his artificial hands through the garage window in frustration or of Fred wandering through the ghostly airplane field—*Best Years* is so bound up in the memories of millions that it is hard to separate the film from real life. There could be few better examples of the power of the motion picture to become part of the lives of the audiences, and a critical factor in the cultural/political life of the nation.

NOTES

1. See the press kit for *The Best Years of Our Lives*, Museum of Modern Art (MOMA) Library, New York.
2. Arthur Marx, *Goldwyn* (New York, 1976), p. 305.
3. *Time* magazine, August 7, 1944. The article described the cool reception given these marines, some of whom were badly wounded, and the fears they held about returning to civilian life.
4. By the summer of 1944, Allied armies had landed in France and Soviet forces were making rapid gains against Germany in the east. To many Americans the war had taken a decidedly favorable turn and victory was coming in view, at least in Europe, so that plans for the reconversion were no longer considered unnecessary or unrealistic.
5. See especially David Ross, *Preparing for Ulysses* (New York, 1969) for a complete study of veterans' policy during and shortly after the war.
6. Marx, op. cit., pp. 305–06.
7. The book is long out of print, considered a rarity, and was not one of Kantor's better efforts.
8. *New York Herald Tribune*, November 25, 1946.
9. *Variety*, January 22, 1947.
10. Axel Madsen, *William Wyler* (New York, 1973), pp. 256–261.
11. Marx, op. cit., p. 307.

12. Wyler had a reputation in Hollywood as a "difficult" director, tough on his cast, crew, and studio superiors but worth all the trouble. Goldwyn was not anxious to provoke Wyler's temper by insisting on the Eisenhower picture; he wanted Wyler's name on *any* picture.

13. Weekly attendance in American movie houses reached an all-time high in 1946, more than ninety million *every week*. The GIs were anxious to catch up on such peacetime pleasures as moviegoing, there was ample money available, and there was little competition from television yet. All these factors combined to make Hollywood films a highly profitable commodity.

14. Goldwyn's studio, an independent, had not fared well during the war but was on the rebound, in part due to Goldwyn's popular new star Danny Kaye. Wyler's name on the credits of a new film made it easier for Goldwyn to raise financing, and the generally prosperous state of the industry in 1946 made the whole venture a good investment. See Marx, op. cit.

15. *New York Herald Tribune*, November 25, 1946.

16. Marx, op. cit., p. 311.

17. Russell never made another movie. He remained a recognizable figure in American life, however; in 1956 he was invited to address the Democratic National Convention and in 1976 he was one of the guests at the American Film Institute's Life Achievement Dinner for William Wyler.

18. Madsen, op. cit., pp. 262–264.

19. *Andy Warhol's Interview* magazine, March 1974.

20. *Nation*, December 14, 1946.

21. *Best Years* press kit, MOMA Library.

22. Marx, op. cit., p. 314.

23. Goldwyn fought hard to get the Astor, one of New York's most desirable theaters, and agreed to a $2.50 top price, unusually high in 1946 (Marx, op. cit., p. 315).

24. For example, *Life*, December 16, 1946; *Newsweek*, November 25, 1946; *New York Times Magazine*, November 17, 1946.

25. *New York Times*, November 23, 1946.

26. Ibid., November 24, 1946.

27. *New York Herald Tribune*, November 23, 1946.

28. *Nation*, December 7, 1946.

29. *Partisan Review* (May-June, 1947), reprinted in Warshow, *The Immediate Experience* (New York, 1962), pp. 107–112.

30. *Village Voice*, July 15, 1965.

31. *Hollywood in the Forties* (New York, 1968), pp. 84–85.

32. Bazin, quoted in Masden, op. cit., p. 275.

33. Ibid., p. 271.

34. Kracauer, "Those Movies With A Message," in *Harpers* magazine (June, 1948), p. 568.

35. Ibid., p. 571.

36. Al's criticism of banks and bankers was later cited by congressional investigators as evidence of radical influence in Hollywood films. See Masden, op. cit., pp. 262–263.

37. See Molly Haskell, *From Reverence to Rape* (New York, 1974) and Marjorie Rosen, *Popcorn Venus* (New York, 1974).

38. The divorce rate in 1945 was extraordinarily high: 31 out of every 100 marriages for a total of 502,000 over the year. The strains of wartime marriage and long separation were widely felt, as well documented by Joseph Goulden in *The Best Years* (New York, 1976), chapter 1.

39. Among the useful surveys of the period are: William E. Leuchtenburg, *A Troubled Feast: American Society Since 1945* (Boston, 1973); Carl N. Degler, *Affluence and Anxiety* (New York, 1968); Eric F. Goldman, *The Crucial Decade and After—America, 1945–1960* (New York, 1961). Chester E. Eisinger, ed., *The 1940's: Profile of a Nation in Crisis* (New York, 1969) is a compendium of source material and statistics, while Richard S. Kirkendall, ed., *The Truman Period as a Research Field* (New York, 1967) collects important essays about the mid-1940s and about Truman's administration. A well-written study of the period, in a more popular vein, is Goulden's, *The Best Years*, cited above. Truman's own memoirs *Years of Decision* and *Years of Trial and Hope* (Garden City, 1955–56) are curiously lifeless and self-serving but valuable nonetheless. Another side of Harry Truman appears in Merle Miller's *Plain Speaking* (New York, 1974), in which Truman reviews his career with considerable frankness. Caball Phillips, *The Truman Presidency* (New York, 1966) provides a solid overview of the Truman years in the White House. David Riesman's *The Lonely Crowd* (New Haven, 1950) remains an important statement about the American character in the postwar world, as does C. Wright Mills's *White Collar* (New York, 1951).

40. Quoted in Goulden, op. cit., p. 6.

41. *Variety*, May 7, 1977. By way of comparison, *The Exorcist* earned 82 million dollars and *Gone With the Wind* more than 76 million. *Best Years* was not a box-office miracle but it returned a comfortable, and continuing, profit.

Empire to the West:
Red River (1948)

ROBERT SKLAR

Rich in social significance, *Red River* is as teeming with messages as it is with meat on the hoof. The inevitable encounter between Tom Dunson (John Wayne) and Matthew Garth (Montgomery Clift) as the cattle drive is completed.

(Photo courtesy of Museum of Modern Art)

Red River is one of the curiosities in American film history. Nearly everyone pays homage to it, almost no one pays attention to it. Howard Hawks's first Western—incredibly, after two decades of directing and nearly thirty films, this was his first Western—was hailed on its release in September 1948 as an archetypal Western, the quintessential Western, the kind that tingles all the nerve endings but never touches the brain. A rattling good outdoor adventure movie, was *Time* magazine's assessment. Peter Bogdanovich in *The Last Picture Show* caught the core of its iconographic value by showing the commencement of the cattle drive on a small-town Texas theater screen. "Take 'em to Missouri, Matt," crusty Tom Dunson says, the music flares, and we see that classic sequence of cowboys in closeup yelling, "Ya hoo. Hi yaa. Ya hoo. Whoopee. Yaa. Ya hoo. Yaa Yaa." A magnificent horse opera, Pauline Kael called *Red River*, and there is no denying that a chorus of "ya hoos" does not address the deeper issues of that time, our time, or any time.

"When things get tough in Hollywood they start the horses galloping," wrote Kyle Crichton, in the midst of the backlash from the blacklist, in his 1948 *Collier's* review of *Red River*. "Nobody can yell 'propaganda' at a motion picture full of cows, horses, gun play, brave women and daring men." It became the central theme of *Red River* criticism, that here was a motion picture happily innocent of ideology, and the great French critic André Bazin a few years later gave this attitude toward *Red River* its definitive expression.

"Howard Hawks, indeed," Bazin wrote, "at the height of the vogue of the superwestern should be credited with having demonstrated that it had always been possible to turn out a genuine western based on the old dramatic and spectacle themes, without distracting our attention with some social thesis, or, what would amount to the same thing, by the form given the production. *Red River* (1948) and *The Big Sky* (1952) are western masterpieces but there is nothing baroque or decadent about them."

Ultimately the critical consensus on *Red River* succeeded too well. It enshrined the film on a pedestal, a masterpiece of old-fashioned movie entertainment, a spectacle without, thankfully, social significance; it rendered the film irrelevant. Some of the most penetrating interpretations of Hawks's career ignore *Red River* completely. Those who aspire to complete coverage generally notice *Red River* for its *mise-en-scène*, its spectacular (what else?) set-pieces, the stampede, the river crossing, the final confrontation between Dunson and Matt.

No one noticed that there might have been a motive in the dual gesture of honoring and dismissing *Red River*, that there is a curious note of overkill in Bazin's and the reviewers' remarks—that they protest a little too much *Red River*'s mindlessness, as if trying too hard to keep us from seeing some things they prefer us not to see. No one noted that film criticism as much as any other intellectual or artistic pursuit has its ideological foundation, even when its ideological project is to deny the presence of ideology. No one observed the most obvious fact of all: that *Red River* is rich in social significance, is as teeming with messages as it is with meat on the hoof.

Red River announces itself, in fact, boldly. It is a film about the issues of empire. It is a film about the territorial expansion of one society by the usurpation of land from others, and the consequences arising therefrom—in the relations between men and women, in the relations between men and other men, in the social compact that binds people together for a common purpose. And these human themes, important as they are, are subordinate to even more fundamental issues of economic survival, of commodity production, above all of the need to find a market for one's goods. *Red River* is a film about cows, horses, gun play, brave women, daring men—and capitalism.

When Matthew Garth brings Tom Dunson's herd into Abilene, opening the Chisholm Trail route for Texas cattle to reach a Kansas railhead, Chicago stockyards, and distant consumers, the *Red River* dialogue continuity script has a voiceover line (later eliminated from the completed film) spoken by Groot the cook: "It was just the first of thousands of such drives bringin' beef to the world." That the issues *Red River* raises of empire and markets were also central issues of American economic power and expansion after World War II should come as no surprise to anyone, except those film critics who prefer their masterpieces to be meaningless.

Red River is not only about capitalism; its form and its destiny were also the products of capitalism, specifically of the changing economic structure of the Hollywood film industry in the postwar years. The film's director and producer, Howard Hawks, was a man not unlike its hero Thomas Dunson, a man with a vision, a man leaving the ordinary ways and trying to establish himself independently, struggling to find a market and gain a return on his investment of time and toil. He was to face as many challenges as Tom Dunson in reaching his goal.

Hawks was among the half dozen or so long-time studio directors —Frank Capra, William Wyler, Leo McCarey, Preston Sturges, and George Stevens were others—who aspired after World War II to work independently of the Hollywood factory system. They wanted to break away from assembly-line studio production methods, to develop their own properties, and maintain control of the filmmaking process from beginning to end. What they wanted was soon to be commonplace in posttelevision Hollywood, but for some of them the desire was a few years premature. Hawks was actually one of the few to accomplish what he set out to do.

In December 1945 Hawks took part in establishing a corporation, Monterey Productions, Inc., with himself as president. *Red River* was Monterey Productions' only product. The last one hears about Monterey Productions is some six years later, when Pathe Labs tries to sell the negative and sound track of *Red River* to recover four thousand dollars it claims Monterey still owes them. The intervening years are replete, as Hawks himself delicately put it, with "unforeseen production difficulties."

The genesis of *Red River* was an original story by Borden Chase, later published in *Saturday Evening Post* as a serial, "The Chisholm Trail." Chase wrote the first *Red River* screenplay and Charles Schnee was called in to tighten Chase's somewhat unwieldy and rambling narrative. The story of Tom Dunson and his cattle drive seems straightforward enough, but Hawks obviously came to feel the plot needed more explanation than the shot continuity provided. At some point in postproduction he added a voiceover narration, and as late as the dialogue continuity script those lines were to be spoken by Groot. The cutting continuity script, however, dated the same time as the dialogue script, lists the shots of the "Early Tales of Texas" manuscript, the narrative backbone Hawks finally chose to use.

There may be no such source with the precise title "Early Tales of Texas," but at least one of many first-hand accounts of cattle drives was almost surely used by Chase in developing his story. Joseph G. McCoy was an Illinois businessman who set up a shipping center for Texas cattle in Abilene in 1867 and wrote *Historic Sketches of the Cattle Trade of the West and the Southwest*, published in 1874. McCoy seems clearly to have been the model for Melville, who greets Matthew Garth in Abilene with the words, "Matt, I'm the Greenwood Trading Company of Illinois." Around the basic economic tale of a commodity finding its outlet to markets, the screenwriters and director wove their stories of men with and without women, of tyranny and rebellion and reconciliation, of a man and a boy grown up.

Hawks cast John Wayne as Dunson, Walter Brennan as Groot, and a young New York stage actor, Montgomery Clift, as Matthew Garth. Joanne Dru replaced Margaret Sheridan in the role of Tess Millay at the last minute when the latter actress became pregnant and left the cast. Location shooting began early in September 1946 at Rain Valley Ranch and other ranches south of Tucson, Arizona, and production ended in December 1946 after more than seventy shooting days. *Red River* was budgeted at approximately 2.4 million dollars, much of it provided as a production loan by Motion Picture Investors Corporation, a firm established to channel funds from individual investors into independent productions.

Rain Valley Ranch unfortunately lived up to its name, and bad weather was the first of the "unforeseen production difficulties" to beset *Red River*. Extra location days began to drive up the picture's cost, and years later an outfit called the Arizona Wranglers, the men who cared for the cattle, was still trying to collect 32,000 dollars in wages from Monterey Productions for the additional days. "As you know," Hawks wrote to Donald Nelson, president of the Society of Independent Motion Picture Producers, in May 1947, "unforeseen production difficulties have caused this picture to cost far beyond what was originally intended," and there were "difficulties which still have to be met in finishing this picture." Ultimately *Red River* was estimated to cost 4.1 million dollars, including prints and advertising.

Hawks's letter to Nelson may have had something to do with his efforts to get out of his distribution deal with United Artists and seek a distributor who would guarantee him a larger minimum return, to compensate for the additional production costs. *Red River* was completed by October 1947 but it sat on the shelf for nearly a year while Hawks wrangled and finagled. At one point there was talk of having the Motion Picture Investors Corporation foreclose on Monterey Productions and have its assets placed in the hands of a trustee; the trustee, in turn, would be free to find a new distributor.

United Artists succeeded in holding on to *Red River* through an arbitration hearing. It was the only picture that troubled company had at the time that was believed capable of realizing substantial profits. Hawks continued to balk, however. He resisted UA's plan to open the picture at its four Los Angeles Music Hall theaters, then acquiesced when Fox West Coast theaters rejected UA's offer to turn over the picture for a fifty-fifty split of the box office (*Red River* also opened at 265 theaters affiliated with the Interstate Circuit in Texas, Oklahoma, and Kansas—Chisholm Trail country).

Then *Red River* was hit with an unforeseen postproduction difficulty. In August 1948, a few weeks before the picture's scheduled opening, Howard Hughes, through the Hughes Tool Company, sued Monterey Productions for plagiarism. Hughes maintained that the climactic battle between Dunson and Matt had been copied from his controversial Western, *The Outlaw* (1943), where Billy the Kid refuses to reach for his gun though he is nicked in the ear by a shot fired by his one-time friend Doc Holliday. It so happened that Hawks had developed *The Outlaw* for Hughes and had directed at least part of the film, receiving, however, no screen credit. Within a week a settlement was reached: twenty-four seconds were cut from the *Red River* fight scene.

At last *Red River* made it to market. United Artists promoted it by a perhaps unfortunate comparison to two earlier historical epics of the West, *The Covered Wagon* (1923) and *Cimarron* (1931), dull, earnest films, much honored but quickly forgotten. Reviews were generally strong but box office was soft. *Variety*, reporting the final 4.1-million-dollar total cost for the picture, set a figure of

5 million dollars gross as its break-even point. The trade paper predicted a gross of between 4.5 and 5 million dollars from domestic box office and 2 million dollars from overseas bookings (the term "gross" in the language of motion picture economics generally refers to rentals paid to the distributor, not total ticket sales). Though information about actual motion picture revenues is notoriously unreliable, it is estimated that *Red River* earned just under 4.5 million dollars domestically; foreign revenues are not recorded. Monterey Productions disappeared—leaving behind, as noted, several disgruntled creditors—but Hawks's "unforeseen production difficulties" on *Red River* did not deter him from further capitalist ventures. He was to produce, through his own companies, nearly two-thirds of the dozen or so films he directed during the remainder of his career.

Themes of contract and compact are central to *Red River*. The social use of contracts goes back a long way, of course, but in modern society contracts denote economic relationships, exchanges, promises, or commitments enforceable by law; they are how business gets done in a capitalist economy. Compact, though sometimes a synonym for contract, generally has a wider meaning, as in Mayflower Compact: an agreement among many to pursue a common purpose, a tacit community of shared goals enforceable more by moral or social suasion than by law. In Hawks's visual style contract relationships are presented in closeups and two-shots, compact situations in medium and long shot, panoramas not of spectacular events but of men in groups, standing or sitting horse, talking or silently observing. On one fundamental level *Red River* is a film that asserts the superiority of compact over contract in the achievement of economic and social goals.

Tom Dunson is a man who believes in contract. The opening shots of the film define him. He is leaving the wagon train. The colonel rides up and says, "You can't do that. You signed on. You agreed with the others." Dunson replies, "I signed nothing. *If I had, I'd stay.* (Emphasis added.) If you'll remember, I joined your train after you left Saint Louis." In Borden Chase's original script Dunson *had* signed a contract and broke it to set off on his own, but Hawks and Charles Schnee wisely changed that because it destroys the grounds for his later actions.

The sanctity of contract animates Dunson's behavior throughout *Red River*. He makes his cowboys sign a contract and is willing to kill those who break it. He makes a contract with Matt to add the boy's initial to the cattle brand when he has earned it. And he contracts with Fen to come and get her. The climactic conflict in *Red River* is ultimately founded not only on the opposition between contract and compact, but between two kinds of contracts Dunson and Matt have made—one between each other and one that each of them has with a woman.

The role of women in *Red River* disconcerted many of the film's contemporary reviewers. "This is a movie about men, and for men," *Time* magazine insisted, and both the *New Yorker* and the *New York Times* complained that the film was spoiled by Tess Millay's intervention in the fight between Dunson and Matt. For some spectators, the final scene of Millay stopping the fight does not seem to work; in fact, however, without that scene *Red River* would not hold together as it does. Instead of spoiling the film, Millay's act serves to unite its many themes.

For *Red River* also asserts the importance of women to the society and economy of the expanding American empire. After Dunson has announced his intention to leave the wagon train, he must tell Fen that he does not want to take her with him. "Oh, you'll need me!" she argues, in her desire to go along. "You'll need a woman. Need what a woman can give you. To do what you have to do!" Much of this scene of parting is shot so that we see only the back of Dunson's head, hiding his emotions from us. "But you're wrong," Fen cries, the first of many times Dunson is told that. He puts the snake bracelet on her wrist, a gift that binds him to her, emblem of his promise someday to rejoin her.

The next time Dunson sees that bracelet it is on the wrist of an Indian he has just fought and killed. "Oh, I wish. . . ." he whispers to himself, and we can complete the sentence for ourselves. The Indian raid that took Fen's life had broken Dunson's contract with her, but the snake bracelet continues to embody that obligation. The shot of the bracelet on Fen's wrist is duplicated three more times in the film—Dunson's shock of recognition exemplified in the gesture of his hand grasping another person's wrist: once it is the dead Indian's, once it is Matt's, the last time it is Millay's. This final view of the bracelet reveals a contract between Matt and Millay with which Dunson, with his views on the sanctity of contract, must come to terms.

Fen had insisted on the importance of a woman in Dunson's life. After seeing the bracelet on the Indian's wrist his face contorts momentarily, on the verge of tears. That is the first and almost the only expression of emotional vulnerability John Wayne portrays. Otherwise he plays Dunson as cold, hard, stone-faced. The second time he breaks this mask comes after Dan Latimer is trampled to death in the stampede. With his wages from the cattle drive Dan was planning to buy presents for his wife, including the red shoes she always wanted. After Dan's burial, Dunson makes arrangements for the widow. "And . . . uh . . . get her . . . ah, anything you can think of," he instructs Matt. "Like a pair of red shoes, maybe?" Matt replies. Dunson blinks, as if again about to cry. He turns his back to the camera and says, "That's the way he wanted it, wasn't it?"

Dunson's separation from the company of women also separates him from the company of men. Perhaps he would not have been so ruthless and successful a rancher and empire-builder if Fen had been along to divert and restrain him; but his human feelings would not have so atrophied that he becomes a tyrant, believing only in contractual relations, with himself as their enforcer. Yet *Red River* makes clear that even without a woman Dunson is dependent on the feminine for his achievements. In the Indian attack on Dunson and Groot the bull is spared but both his cows are slain. No cows, no herd, no ranch—a blasted dream. Before this fact has time to register on the spectator, however, the boy Matthew Garth appears with a cow; the cow had strayed and Matthew had gone searching for it, and thus escaped the slaughter of the wagon train. Matthew restores to Dunson the indispensable feminine.

Matthew serves as bearer of the feminine principle in a society of men without women. This is one of the most subtle aspects of *Red River*, brilliantly achieved by the choice of Montgomery Clift to play Matthew, and by Clift's performance. But Clift did not completely create the ambiguous elements of Matthew's character; some of those elements are even stronger in Borden Chase's original script than in the film itself. There, Cherry Valance several times tells Matthew he has the look of a man who needs a woman. He also tells him he's "as tender as a mother and child."

How are we to understand Matthew Garth? On one side he is a superb gunfighter, and he went off to fight in the Civil War. The boy Matthew shows his toughness when Dunson confronts Don Diego's men after crossing the Red River into Texas. Knowing a gunfight is at hand, Dunson waves the boy to step back. Matt shakes his head, no. Dunson says, "Get away, Matt." The boy remains by Dunson's side, and draws his gun when Dunson does.

But on the other side is the Matthew who is sensitive, virginal, soft. One of the film's most revealing moments is the first shot when Wayne and Clift appear together. Dunson has been sitting, Matt standing with one knee bent. Preparing to rise, Dunson put his hand on Matt's knee, Matt reaches out to help Dunson straighten up. Then he rolls a cigarette, lights it, and hands it to Dunson. This is no longer the hard, slightly-crazed, boy Matthew; as Clift plays him, he is more like an androgynous Matthew.

It is the "feminine" side of Matthew that supports Dunson, literally and figuratively, in Dunson's rise to become a powerful rancher. It is this "soft" side that reluctantly drives Matthew to side with the cowboys against Dunson, to preserve the compact that is their hope for survival, as Dunson insists ever more cruelly on enforcing the terms of contract. But after Matthew becomes a leader of men, he must become fully a man. Hence the appearance of Millay and her seduction of him, hence the need to fight it out physically with Dunson.

"It's gonna be all right," Groot cries when Matt at last fights back. "For fourteen years I've been scared . . . but it's gonna be all right." Was Groot scared that Matthew's androgyny was going to tip to the feminine side? Perhaps part of Dunson's pleasure at Matt's violent manhood, as well, is relief, a release of sexual tension aroused by the youth's feminine role in his life. Finally, with Matt fully a man, and Dunson and Matt able to express an asexual love for each other, Millay assumes the feminine influence and imposes part of what a woman, in the terms of *Red River*, can give—reconciliation between men and the promise of a normal social order.

The taming of Tom Dunson's tyranny, the proving of Matthew Garth's manhood, the assertion of Tess Millay's feminine will: these are the human elements that critics refer to, along with the spectacular scenes of the cattle drive, of course, when they speak of *Red*

River as a magnificent horse opera, as a "genuine" Western without "some social thesis" to bother our minds. But these human struggles and events take up only the foreground of *Red River*'s larger canvas, only part of the foreground at that, and the film's critics have rarely stepped back for a wider look, for a complete view of *Red River*, seeing the human stories and the spectacle within their given frame. That frame, as *Red River* insists we recognize, is the history of American westward expansion. But many critics and spectators find it hard to recognize, because we have learned to accept the westward movement as, well, a darn good excuse for a movie, in the same class with a haunted house.

The westward movement was, of course, a series of historical events: the Indians actually were defeated and driven onto reservations, Texas actually was wrested from Mexico, Texas cattle actually did meet the railhead at Abilene. But we know all this already. That is one of the reasons we pay attention to the human and not the historical drama; the individual's destiny appears more contingent, more open, more uncertain, than the national destiny. Hawks in *Red River* is interested, however, in more than individual destiny. One of his major themes is the values and behavior of men in groups. His human concerns in *Red River* are as often social as they are individual, and the social theme inevitably links men to the process, to the contingency, to the actual events of history.

First and foremost in the historical process of the westward movement was the taking of the land. *Red River*, typical of its time and genre, could not care less about the Indians' claim to the land. The Indians appear as no more than cruel savages, obstacles to be overcome. But the Spanish-Mexican claim to the land is something else: a European title, a legal document. How can Dunson, the believer in contract, usurp the land from Don Diego, who holds land grants from a Spanish king? Groot supplies the justification: "That's too much land for one man. Why, it ain't decent. Here's all this land aching to be used and never has been! I tell you, it ain't decent."

The seizure of the land has a larger social purpose than personal wealth or aggrandizement: morality and utility are invoked. Dunson endorses these wider aims in his narration behind the montage sequence depicting the building of his personal empire: "Wherever they go, they'll be on my land. My land! I'll have the brand on enough beef to . . . to feed the whole . . . country. Good beef for hungry people. Beef to make 'em strong . . . make 'em grow." The hesitation in his voice suggests he is just discovering, indeed creating, the link between his personal empire and the nation's imperial future. It is one of the classic American visions—to do good by doing well.

And we in the audience learn that our own fates are linked with Dunson's: it was his beef, or beef from someone like him, that fed our forebears. When historical forces intervene, clouding Dunson's dream, we know that more than one man's success hangs in the balance. The Civil War impoverishes the South, leaving Texas rich in commodities—cattle—but poor in capital. Without a market, all of that meat on the hoof is not worth a cent. "He learned that a ranch ain't only beef, but it's money," says Groot of Dunson. "But the war took all the money out of the South. He never knew about money, Matt, he never had none. He . . . he didn't know what to do." Dunson begins to realize that his personal destiny is linked not only to hungry consumers, but also to Northern and Eastern capital.

Matthew makes a significant reply to Groot's explanation. "You mean," Matthew says, "he just doesn't know who to fight." Dunson's skill is as a fighter—he fought the Indians, he fought Don Diego's emissaries, he fought the men who lie in seven graves on his ranch. He never knew about money, because he never had money. He is a feudal lord, and Texas is preparing to undergo the transition from feudalism to capitalism. His cowboys are not mere hired hands. They are, or once were, landowners and cattle ranchers too, though their properties were destroyed, scattered, or stolen by war and postwar "carpetbaggers." For them the cattle drive is not simply a way to earn a living, it is their opportunity to accumulate capital, to qualify for full participation in the rewards of the new capitalist era. Their need for solidarity, for an effective working compact, is no abstract or sentimental thing, it is essential for their economic advancement.

Nowhere in *Red River* is this theme presented more vividly than in the shot that precedes the stampede. In the background of the frame, in deep focus, stands Buck Keneally, the sugar thief, pots falling all around him. In the foreground are six men in closeup, expectation and fear on their faces, looking not toward Buck but away from him and off screen, looking toward the herd. This economic theme also gives meaning to the many shots in *Red River* of men in groups, standing around, looking and listening as other men talk. Hawks in fact frames many shots with men in profile on both sides of the frame, witnessing conversations or confrontations. They are not casual observers, they are part of the compact, their futures are involved.

Far more is at stake here, for example, than a husband's wish to buy a present for his wife, "a pair of red shoes." Dunson's sentimentality over Dan Latimer's widow is a welcome sign of humanity but it also reveals his limitations. The loss of his woman seems in fact at times so to control his feelings that he cannot even recognize the larger issues at stake for his men. Perhaps he thinks all they want to do with their earnings is buy presents for their families, rather than what they actually do want—land, cattle, income-producing property. "I'll do the thinking," Dunson says, but it becomes clearer and clearer that his mode of thinking is inadequate. "Don't tell me what to think," Matthew at last tells him. "I'll take your orders about work but not about what to think."

The critical turning point comes after Teeler, Laredo, and Bill Kelsey run off. Estranged from Matt, completely drained of human feelings for his men, Dunson sends Cherry Valance to bring them back. He returns with Teeler and Laredo, having killed Kelsey. "I'm the law," Dunson says, preparing to hang them, marking the extreme point of his tyranny. Teeler then speaks for the compact among the men. "You're crazy. . . . This herd don't belong to you. It belongs to every poor hopin', prayin' settleman in the whole wide State. I shouldn't have run away. I should have stayed and put a bullet in you. I signed a pledge, sure. But you ain't the man I signed it with."

As Teeler speaks, Matt edges slowly away from Dunson's side— the opposite of the boy Matthew's behavior when Dunson tried to wave him off in the confrontation with Don Diego's men. Matthew rebels against Dunson, and Cherry Valance, the gunfighter whose last name means an ornamental piece of drapery, sides with Matthew. Ornamental Cherry may be, particularly for his taunting of Matt and his threat to get Matt's gun (symbol-readers may do what they will with the fact that a man named Cherry wants another man's "gun"); but he understands the capitalist imperatives as well as any other of the men.

The cattle get to Abilene, Northern capitalism makes its appearance ("I'm the Greenwood Trading Company of Illinois"), and Thomas Dunson, by proxy, is introduced to capitalism by means of a bank check for his cattle. The heroes and heroines of the American West have suffered their struggles and tribulations, have made their legends, in service of a larger social purpose. Texas beef will make Americans strong in body; sold to the world, it will make America strong in balance of payments.

Red River was an imperialist film for an imperialist era in American life. That it ends with a woman firing a gun at two brawling Texas gunmen, who, it turns out, are expressing their love for each other, only serves to remind us, after all, how benign the behavior and purposes of Americans really are.

NOTES

The Howard Hawks Collection in the Arts and Communications Archives, Harold B. Lee Library, Brigham Young University, contains considerable material on *Red River*, including the original Borden Chase script, final dialogue continuity and cutting continuity scripts, and files pertaining to production, advertising copy and strategy, correspondence, and newspaper reviews. I wish to express my thanks to James V. D'Arc, Curator, Arts and Communications Archives, for his aid in my use of this material. A useful file of materials on *Red River*, mainly clippings, is in the Margaret Herrick Library of the Academy of Motion Picture Arts and Sciences, Los Angeles.

Red River dialogue quotations are taken from the dialogue continuity script in the Harold B. Lee Library and checked against the actual film.

Information on *Red River* reviews comes from the Academy files. Dates of cited reviews are as follows: *Time*, October 11, 1948; *Colliers*, October 9, 1948; *New Yorker*, October 9, 1948; *New York Times*, October 10, 1948.

Information on *Red River* production and postproduction, as well as financial data, comes from the Production and Correspondence files in the Howard Hawks Collection, and from clippings in the Academy file, including the following: *Variety*, July 30, August 16, August 23, and December 7, 1948; *Daily Variety*, August 3, 1948; *Hollywood Reporter*, August 16, 1948; *Los Angeles Times*, August 20, 1948; *New York Times*, February 2, 1948; *Hollywood Citizen-News*, August 18, 1952.

Hawks's letter to Donald Nelson, May 9, 1947, is in the Correspondence file of the Howard Hawks Collection.

André Bazin's remarks on *Red River* appear in his essay, "The Evolution of the Western," in *What Is Cinema?*, *Volume II*, essays selected and translated by Hugh Gray (Berkeley, Calif., 1971), p. 154. Pauline Kael's description of *Red River* is in *Kiss Kiss Bang Bang* (Boston, 1968), p. 338. An extensive treatment of *Red River* is in Donald C. Willis, *The Films of Howard Hawks* (Metuchen, N.J., 1975), pp. 43–55. Among other writings on the film see Robin

Wood, *Howard Hawks* (Garden City, N.Y., 1968) and Leo Braudy, *The World in a Frame* (Garden City, N.Y., 1976). A significant critique of Hawks that does not mention *Red River* is in Peter Wollen, *Signs and Meaning in the Cinema* (Bloomington, Ind., 1969). George N. Fenin and William K. Everson, *The Western* (New York, 1962), consider *Red River* "pedestrian," p. 331. Information on Hawks's dealings with United Artists is in Tino Balio, *United Artists: The Company Built by the Stars* (Madison, Wis., 1976).

An American Cold Warrior:

Viva Zapata! (1952)

PAUL J. VANDERWOOD

Bound but unbowed, Emiliano Zapata (Marlon Brando) is led away to
prison. He is soon freed and on his way to revolutionary greatness. In
reality, Zapata was no democrat, nor was he the land reformer he is popularly considered to be.

(Photo courtesy of Museum of Modern Art)

Confronted by the realities of militant totalitarianism in Europe, the United States had by mid-1938 begun to budge from its passive isolationist stance. Hitler's persecutions and racial discrimination grated against the nation's Christian morals and distate for dictatorship.[1] While President Roosevelt still faced substantial opposition in his determination to get the country more actively involved in European affairs, most Americans, even the staunchest isolationists, agreed that strong measures should be taken to preserve the Western Hemisphere as democracy's fortress. And the film industry, always restive in its marriage of convenience with the government, was anxious to make a contribution.

Roosevelt planned to strengthen commitments between the hemispheric nations at the Inter-American conference scheduled for December, 1938, in Lima, Peru. Hollywood, through the Producers Association, joined the strategy sessions at the highest level.[2] Meanwhile, individual studios looked to recruit Latin American historical heroes to the cause of democracy. Jack Warner, a vociferous patriot and personal friend of the President, turned to Mexico's President Benito Juárez, who had in the 1860s repulsed French imperial designs on his country. Carefully imbued with Lincolnesque characteristics and thoroughly aware of current (1939) events, Paul Muni as Juárez embodied the determination of the Americas to resist European fascism.[3] At the same time the possibility of Hollywood's enlisting the agrarian rebel Emiliano Zapata in the fight for democracy was also underway. Zapata, in reality, was no democrat, nor was he the land reformer he is popularly considered to be. But he did fight doggedly and against great odds to see to it that land taken by prospering sugar-growing capitalists was returned to its traditional owners—Zapata's humble compatriots in the state of Morelos; he joined the Mexican Revolution of 1910. The essence of his struggle has been co-opted by succeeding governments to legitimize their politics, and today Zapata stands tall in the pantheon of Mexican heroes. How much land the peasants of Morelos got back is another question. In any case, revolutionaries do not sit well with the bourgeoisie, and for cinema Zapata proved much more difficult than Juárez to control. It took another dozen years of nervous hesitancy, until 1952, before he finally emerged in movie theaters, by then a somewhat bedraggled victim of Cold War tensions.

Plans for a Zapata movie emerged in 1938 from the desires of a Zapatista to publicize his hero in the United States and from the ambitions of a romantic socialist to crown his long-term study of the Mexican revolution. The Zapatista was Gildardo Magaña, close associate of Zapata during the rebellion and now governor of the state of Michoacán. He had collected materials pertaining to the agrarian movement and had produced in Spanish a two-volume biography of the guerilla chieftain. Magaña wanted Zapata introduced to North Americans through an English translation of his work. Edgcomb Pinchon was the romantic leftist who intended to chronicle, as he put it, "Mexico's 100 years of struggle for a democratic government."[4] To date he has produced three books on the subject, including *Viva Villa!* from which the 1933 movie was adapted. Pinchon saw in Magaña's documentation the means of completing his project, and as potential book royalties were limited, he hounded Metro-Goldwyn-Mayer to purchase the screen rights to his work.[5] In his hard-sell to the studio, Pinchon stressed the supposed contemporary value of a motion picture about Zapata. Such a movie, he predicted, would both reinforce democracy in Mexico and assure United States hegemony in Latin America. Pinchon's enthusiasm for the movie was unbounded.

The World is teetering between the enticements of dictatorship and democracy. Show in the film a dictatorship at work—and Porfirio Díaz had Hitler and Mussolini backed off the map! Show what happens—the final, mad desperate, heroic revolt. Then show the denouement—peace and home and happiness, freedom to be a man, go one's way and speak one's mind. Show smashed the terrible link between governmental power and capitalist interest—for that is Fascism that must depend upon actuating the vilest impulses of humanity for its existence—

Show that—and you [will] have . . . a world document of immense preachment at this moment.

And I say—do it big. Make it the answer! Done in gay skirts, big hats and brown skins—it is again the story of [the] Magna Carta on which all democracy is based.

. . . It could revivify the waning flame of Democracy in the English speaking world (witness England—and Fascism here [in Mexico]). It could light, like a torch, the almost unkindled fires of democracy in Latin America. It could be the answer—beautiful, sweeping, unanswerable to Mr. Hitler and Mr. Mussolini. . . . Done in Spanish it could take Latin America for the U.S.A.! Let's do it right.[6]

MGM leaped at the bait. Pinchon wrote his eulogy—*Zapata, the Unconquerable*—and the studio planned its film adaptation. Then World War II intervened. With Europe engulfed by Hitler's blitzkrieg, Roosevelt on August 16, 1940, created by executive order the Office for Co-ordination of Commercial and Cultural Relations between the American Republics, later to become more simply the Office of Inter-American Affairs.[7] Its mission was to root out Axis trade and propaganda penetration in Latin America and to replace them with heavy U.S. doses of the same. Nelson A. Rockefeller headed the new agency with John H. (Jock) Whitney his assistant in charge of the motion picture division. Hollywood eagerly joined the team. In what must have been one of Rockefeller's earliest decisions about motion picture potential in Latin America, he ordered the study of a movie about Emiliano Zapata.[8]

The research assignment fell to Addison Durland, a Latin American specialist with the Motion Picture Producer's Association, which enthusiastically cooperated with the government's wartime intentions. History proved to be not very generous. After research in New York's Public Library and other resources, Durland reported Zapata far too controversial in Latin America to chance cinematic treatment in this hemisphere. He cited a number of specific dangers. First, no movie could say or imply anything negative about the man. Most Mexicans considered him a hero. Second, the Catholic Church probably considered the guerilla one of its greatest enemies. Others had referred to him as "The Attila of the South," "The Scarlet Monster," and an "Anti-Christ." Some saw him as a communist, or at least a radical land reformer. In addition, the Mexican government discouraged movies about the nation's bloody revolution, and finally, in summary:

> Countless problems will unavoidably arise when dealing pictorially with such controversial characters as Zapata and his followers, and dangerous issues as his revolutionary activities, not to mention the difficulties of achieving an historical interpretation of the man and his times that would be generally satisfactory or the practical problems created by the demands of authenticity of characters, historical facts, and all other Mexican elements.

Durland counseled the Office of Inter-American Affairs to forget about Zapata as film material, and during the succeeding war years he gave similar advice to several studios considering a movie about the rebel.[9]

Soon after the war the idea for a Zapata movie was regenerated through the spirited endeavors of Jack Cummings, one of MGM's premiere producers and the nephew of Louis B. Mayer. Cummings possessed a warmly romantic view of Mexico and in 1946 had made several short pictorial movies which the Mexican government credited with increasing tourism in the country. The president, Miguel Alemán, wanted to repay the favor. Cummings asked to do a picture about Zapata, and in mid-1947 he went to Mexico City with the screenwriter Lester Cole to arrange the details. Cole carried along his proposed outline of the picture, which, with its rather radical and decidedly altruistic bent, evidently pleased the Mexicans. Ranking members of Mexico's cinema industry and the government agreed to cooperate on the project.[10] Cummings and Cole returned to MGM ready to go to work, but under Cold War influence the national temper had begun to change and, sensing their opportunities, the politicians had determined to play rough. Many streamlets fed the torrent of anticommunism which swept the country and one branch, the House Un-American Activities Committee (HUAC), dusted off old machinery first used in 1938 and remounted its attack on Hollywood. The Committee's yawning net soon caught Lester Cole.[11]

The strategy behind and the results of HUAC's attack on the movie industry are reasonably well known and, at any rate, go beyond the intentions of this essay. It suffices to say that the Producer's Association promised the federal government that the industry would not release movies which did not accurately portray American life and institutions, a deliberately vague catch-all that permitted arbitrary control of picture content and production. The State Department ordered its foreign missions to report on audience response to American films. Hollywood could then pitch its material accordingly. The industry also established a clearing house to furnish filmmakers with information about foreign sensibilities and to review screenplays and movies with an eye toward the elimination of material that might be offensive to foreign viewers.[12] Hollywood had always engaged in assertive self-censorship in order to avoid outright federal government restriction. However, HUAC was not to be deterred. Cole claims that MGM's management had always been queasy about its Zapata movie. Eddie Mannix, the studio's manager, had once exclaimed: "This bastard Zapata is a goddamn commie revolutionary." But the Mexican drama seemed to have box-office potential, so MGM had determined to proceed. Then HUAC subpoenaed Cole, and MGM became convinced that Zapata had to go. Cole went on to defend himself as one of the Hollywood Ten, and on February 8, 1949, for some sixty thousand dollars, MGM sold all its rights to the Zapata materials to Twentieth Century-Fox, which for several years had itself been considering a movie about Zapata, temporarily titled *The Beloved Rogue*.[13]

Fox immediately employed John Steinbeck to write the screenplay. The novelist was paid twenty thousand dollars to deliver a script to the studio by January, 1950. Fox would then take it under advisement with an option to purchase within eight months. If indeed the studio made the film, Steinbeck would receive an additional seventy-five thousand dollars.[14] From the beginning, Fox Studios approached the Zapata project with reservations and restraints uncommon in an industry fueled by glitter and enthusiasm. Steinbeck had for a number of years been interested in writing a Zapata screenplay. While he was in Mexico in mid-1945, a film company approached him to prepare just such a script, but the novelist was already committed to other work. Still he liked the idea, but said he would only write it if the Mexican government assured him that he could accurately portray the historical events.[15] Somewhere along the way Steinbeck lost his zeal for historical accuracy.

As vice president in charge of production, Darryl F. Zanuck guided Twentieth Century-Fox motion pictures with tight control and a strong hand. His influence pervaded the studio's movies from their overall point of view down to the smallest details. Zanuck's job was to make movies that made money, and with him commercial considerations almost always superseded artistic desires. He found *Viva Zapata!* a particularly troublesome picture to produce.[16] Although he engaged the highly regarded Elia Kazan to direct the movie, questions concerning content, financial potential, possible public criticism, and McCarthyite pressures continued to worry him. In fact, Zanuck's waning enthusiasm for the movie soon after its release, led to its early withdrawal from distribution.[17] But like the Zapata myth, the movie now seems immortal, at least as resurrected for continuing replays at colleges and on television.

There stands Zapata (Marlon Brando) in the opening sequences, demanding land relief from his national patron, the dictator Porfirio Díaz (Fay Roope), who advises the petitioners to substantiate their claims legally. But the property owners meet the peasants' search for land markers with machine guns and drive Zapata and his brother (Anthony Quinn) into rebellion. His movement is soon part of the overall revolution headed by Francisco Madero (Harold Gordon), which in 1910 engulfs the nation. Though urged on by a mysterious intellectual dressed in black (Joseph Wiseman), Zapata remains a somewhat reluctant rebel, mainly because of his urge to marry a local middle-class village girl (Jean Peters). Madero triumphs but fails to implement the immediate land reform that Zapata demands, so Zapata resumes the struggle. At one point in the internecine war that follows, he has the opportunity to become acting president of the republic. However, after momentarily accepting, in sudden recognition of his commitment to the people of Morelos, he returns to his home state to continue the fight for land. The search for military supplies leads Zapata into a trap and his assassination, but he has foreseen his death and has previously assured his followers that they no longer need leaders; they are now a united people destined to win their fight. So much for the storyline as it finally emerged; more significant is the tortuous path it took to get there.

Steinbeck and Kazan began to collaborate on the screenplay in late 1949. Steinbeck wrote and Kazan rewrote. During his recent years in Mexico, the novelist had collected, mostly through interviews, a mass of material about Zapata which he molded into a storyline. Kazan and scenarists translated Steinbeck's prose into movie language.[18] No documents better reveal the problems of political focus which beset the intellectual left in postwar America than the succession of Steinbeck/Kazan screenplays which preceded the filming of *Viva Zapata!* What began as an endorsement of revolution with determined leadership as the means to social change ended up as a rejection of power, strong leadership, and rebellion in favor of a grass-roots democracy which promises little, if any, change at all.[19] Kazan in analyzing his shifting mind of the time says today, "I was bewildered. I was anti-Stalinist and anti-McCarthy at the same time. It was difficult to reconcile the two."[20] Such a position now appears to be standard with the unglued leftists of the 1950s.[21] For certain, Kazan was vociferously pro-American and not noticeably anti-McCarthy during that period. Anyhow, Lillian Hellman calls his 1950s stance "pious bullshit."[22]

When he was working on the script in 1949, Kazan saw Zapata as a social-climbing "snob" with a New Deal mentality, a man who is early on "brought down to the bedrock of human circumstances. The very meaning of conscience today is responsibility for the unfortunate or the less fortunate of our fellow man." As the film develops, Zapata "meets the spectacle of injustice with silence." Finally, he is propelled into action, and becomes the leader in his people's struggle for land and freedom.[23] Three years later Kazan talked about his completed movie in terms of power—how leadership corrupts; it corrupted Zapata. Genuine power, he had decided by then, resides in the "people," and the values of democracy.[24] Kazan believes today that Zapata was a flawed human being, complex and beset by contradictions. Of course, he was heroic, because he tried, even if he failed. Mexico's Revolution wrought no change, according to Kazan. But then progress everywhere, he believes, comes slowly and in small increments.[25]

In the climactic sequence of Steinbeck's earliest script, a well-meaning hacendado, who had at first scorned Zapata's violence, says to the guerilla: "You know, Emiliano, caught up in business, perhaps I did not think about things clearly. . . . You were right Emiliano." Zapata's head jerks up and he stares at the hacendado, who continues:

> I know now you had to fight. You see, Emiliano, because the world moves on slowly and majestically, I forgot the thousand little agonies that make it move. Just as a man may rise from a chair because a single nerve twitches on his body, so perhaps is progress in the world stimulated by aching Emilianos. I know this now. And so I think you are a good man.[26]

In later treatments the hacendado is eliminated and in the final version Zapata tells his countrymen: "You've looked for leaders. For strong men without faults. There aren't any. There are only men like yourselves. They change. They desert. There's no leader but yourselves—and a strong people is the only lasting strength."[27] Hail the blessings of democracy for Mexico's downtrodden.

If violence does not lead to change, Zapata, the violent, had to be cast as a failure at the end of the movie. Steinbeck eventually did just that. His original finale took place in an unspecified future. Townspeople filled their water jugs at a fountain topped with a small bronze bust of Zapata. In the background was a school called "Escuela Emiliano Zapata," and inside the children sang: "And so he was not dead. And no one was beaten anymore. And no one dared to steal the land again. And the crops grew freely. And the people were not afraid. And so he's alive."[28] But in the finished movie there is no such assurance of progress. Zapata is no more than a memory in the guise of a white horse retreating into the mountains. The people are miserable. The federal army is intact and readily able to crush them, despite their newfound defense in democracy. It is a desperate time for the campesinos of Morelos.[29]

Steinbeck and Kazan continued to wallow in ideological confusion: It was late into December 1951, and filming was scheduled to begin the following spring. Maybe the entire project should be canceled. Zanuck asked the writers: "What are we trying to *say* in this story? Why are we particularly making this picture? What do we *finally* say when the story is over?" "Frankly, I do not know." Then the real Zanuck concern followed: "I hope people don't get the impression that we are advocating civil war as the only means to peace."[30]

The producer doubted that the movie should terminate by conveying the impression that "Mexico turned into a very nice place devoid of political corruption." Mexico, he understood, had progressed. "Some of the recent elections sound almost like they are on the level. And whether it is true or not, I am certain we can attribute some of this to Zapata."[31]

Noting that he had a particular stake in the financial consequences of the movie, Zanuck found the ending too bland. "I want to have the audience rooting for us [first] and rooting for Zapata [second]." While the hero dies, his ideals live. But what were Zapata's ideals? Zanuck had the answer:

"Certainly it isn't communism, and we want to make this very clear because, frankly, in the present script there is inadvertently a peculiar air about certain speeches which might be interpreted by the Communists to claim that we are subtly working for them." It seemed to Zanuck that Zapata had a few well-informed companions.

One was Pablo, who had earlier been to Texas to see Francisco Madero. "Pablo must have told Zapata about a little country known as the United States of America," Zanuck surmised. "It seems to me that Zapata must have heard about free elections and a government run by the people, for the people." Zanuck wanted emphasis put on "free election." "It seems to me that Zapata has a pretty good pattern for a democratic government in his neighbor, the United States— only one civil war in 170 years. I am sure that Zapata must have asked the question many times: 'How do they do it in the United States?'"[32]

The producer's design for the intended message for *Viva Zapata!* was quickly inserted into the script. For sure, in visiting Madero Pablo had learned the lessons of democracy as evidenced in the United States. North Americans, it is explained, protected political refugees like Madero. "Up there the Government governs, but with the consent of the people. The people have a vote. . . . They also have a President, but he governs with the consent of the people. Here we have a President—no consent. Who asked us if we wanted Díaz for thirty-four years?"[33] Zapata's brother responds, "Nobody ever asked me," and in this manner Darryl F. Zanuck formulated the goals of his Mexican Revolution. These democratic ideals are confirmed by Zapata himself just before he rides to his death at the end of the film.

Still Zanuck had serious reservations about featuring a Mexican revolutionary hero during such tense times in Hollywood and the nation. He did not believe audiences would apply the movie's plot directly to contemporary world conditions, or that they would learn any subversive lessons from it. Yet, the film, as history, would carry some significance for the viewers—and that could result in difficulties for the studio.[34] "Of course," he said, "I suppose if it is a very great entertainment, loaded with theatre, and if the audience sits on the edge of the seats in the last act, and if underneath it all it has a small cry for democracy, audiences will love it and not ask any questions."[35] Producers customarily disdain their audiences. Zanuck then told Steinbeck and Kazan to ponder his remarks and to help him decide whether or not the production should continue.[36]

The writers blended their producer's handiwork into the belabored script, and despite mounting obstacles, the picture moved ahead. The Mexican government in concert with the recommendations of the country's cinema industry refused to permit any part of the Zapata story to be filmed in Mexico. It simply did not appreciate the ambivalent Zapata designed by Steinbeck and Kazan.[37] The studio also had difficulty in deciding whom to cast in the film. Should the major parts be played by Mexicans speaking through dubbed English, or by North Americans with an occasional dubbed Mexican accent?[38] Furthermore, Mexican censors forced numerous changes before approving its showing in Mexico. They wanted the title changed from *The Tiger* to *Viva Zapata!* because *The Tiger* suggested a bloodthirsty Zapata. The Mexicans also rejected the gala procession sequence near the start of the movie. (The campesinos had been told by their supreme patron, President Díaz, to verify the boundaries of their village lands. They do this in a festive mood, led by their local priest.) Any inference that their countrymen were less than soberly determined rebels, or that the Church had a stake in land reform, is anathema to the official rhetoric of the Mexican Revolution. Zanuck agreed to remove the priest from the Mexican prints, but not from the U.S. version of the movie. The censors further indicated their nation's official attitude toward the Catholic Church in discussing the early scene where Zapata proposes to Josefina inside a church. Twentieth Century-Fox wondered if such manners might not be considered irreverent, but the censors assured them that such behavior was appropriate in Catholic Mexico.[39]

The studio was also uncertain about its portrayal of Francisco Madero, the inspiration and promulgator of Mexico's Revolution. Madero is shown to be weak and vacillating in governmental affairs and even corrupt when he offers Zapata a choice hacienda in reward for his military services. The censors said they were not concerned with the depiction of Madero, as he was a secondary character in the movie. In fact, they wanted him to appear even less humane. In the scene where Madero gives his watch to a Zapatista woman who has lost her husband and sons in the fighting, the censors suggested that Zapata replace Madero as the donor. Zanuck, however, believed that the event added an important dimension to Madero's character, and the censors did not press the issue. Yet for the historian of Mexico, the propensity of the censors deliberately to downgrade the image of Madero in 1952 is surprising.[40]

For the most part the studio and the foreign censors traded compromises, but they deadlocked over the crucial dialogue which compares democracy in the United States and Mexico—specifically, that in the United States it is the people who name their president, but in Mexico, no choice. The censors feared that Mexican audiences might forget that the film was set in 1910 and would relate the picture's comments to the contemporary status of democracy in their country. In fact, 1952 was a restless election year in Mexico, and the ruling clique had already announced their hand-picked presidential successor. The movie definitely could not be shown in Mexico unless the entire reference to democracy was deleted. But Zanuck had pegged the whole sense of the picture to Zapata's discovery of American democracy, a theme purposefully developed to keep the red-baiters in check. No trade-off was possible. The democratic statement remained the crux of the American version of *Viva Zapata!* and was removed from the prints exhibited in Mexico.[41] Despite the adjustments, the movie failed badly in Mexico, where it played for one week and then was withdrawn.[42]

Characterizations of major figures in the movie underwent continuing adjustment as the filmmakers struggled to fit them into an ideologically safe and dramatically sound framework. Emiliano's brother, Eufemio; the rebel's major intellectual prop, Pablo; Zapata's wife and mistress, and his president, Madero, all experienced changing interpretations as the writers suffered from one draft of the screenplay to the next.[43] None of them, however, underwent as much manipulation as the figure "Bicho," alias "Fernando," that mysterious and sinister opportunist in black who surfaced periodically at the elbow of power. Bicho became Fernando only in the final stage of the film's production. Zanuck preferred the name Bicho, because it sounded cruel and tough-minded. But when the Mexican censors explained that "bicho" in Spanish meant "bug" or some kind of vermin, the producer retreated to Fernando.[44] There was no such character in Steinbeck's original treatments of the Zapata story. When Fernando first appeared, he was an insignificant character in the plot, but as Cold War concerns increased along with HUAC pressures, Fernando grew in stature—as a villain. The studio felt that the public had to be assured beyond question that Zapata (liberal democrat) was right and that Fernando (opportunistic totalitarian) was wrong. The argument had been virtually the same with Warner Brothers' *Juárez* in 1939. The Mexican heroes were consistently portrayed as good democrats, only by 1952, Stalin replaced Hitler as the malevolent dictator.

In the script of August 1950, Fernando favors a strong Mexico. He is not a republican but believes Mexico could edge toward democracy after an interim period of strong executive control. When Madero becomes president, Fernando is disappointed to find the executive romantic and weak. He therefore turns to Zapata: "Unless you consolidate your victory now and rule with a hand of iron, all this will have been for nothing." Zanuck thought Fernando's position absolutely right on this point, but Zapata still declined to rule. So Fernando turned to Carranza, the arch-enemy of Zapata. Still Zanuck remained sympathetic to Fernando saying, "While we may not go along with him one hundred per cent, we will at least understand what makes him tick."[45] Zanuck was no smitten liberal; he appreciated the uses of power, especially his own.

Six months later the filmmakers enlarged Fernando's presence, turning the character into a greedy individual driven by his lust for power. Fernando seeks power for Zapata only because that would increase his own power. When Zapata rejects the presidency, Fernando turns on him. Zapata responds: "Now I know you. No field. No home. No wife. No woman. No friends. No love. . . ."[46] Disillusioned liberals of the early 1950s sought solace where they could find it. Politics dismayed them, so they drifted into sentimentality hoping for the fog to clear. Socialism as an alternative to harsh, impersonal capitalism still attracted them, but the tyranny of Stalin had wrecked their model. Social revolution might still lead to progress, but it could also lead to totalitarianism. The Cold War further rattled their assumptions about power and progress. Steinbeck and Kazan sculptured and remodeled Zapata through a series of scripts seeking a cornerstone for their liberal orientation, but none appeared. Even the invention of Fernando did not help. In the end Zapata is assassinated, Fernando thrives at the elbow of the presidency, and the people's power is an illusion. Zanuck's patience was finally exhausted. The movie was mired in an inescapable intellectual morass. But Twentieth Century-Fox aimed to recoup some of its production expenditures, which meant that despite the ambiguities, the movie had to be sanitized and released.

Zanuck also had immediate political and personal concerns about the movie. He objected to its verbal slurs against military generals in the movie. Political acumen invited discretion. "Our next President of the United States," he noted, "is very apt to be a General named Dwight Eisenhower, and this picture is apt to be out at that time. . . . In addition, I myself am still a colonel in the reserve, and I may have to be taking orders from generals."[47]

Before approving the U.S. release of *Viva Zapata!*, the Breen Office demanded cuts in scenes it considered too violent, vulgar, or immoral.[48] Zanuck himself ordered further deletions. In a major sequence that places Zapata in the presidential palace, a long-time compadre and general in Zapata's army advises his chief to make peace with his enemies, meaning Venustiano Carranza. "We can't wipe out the opposition," says the weary old-timer. "We must learn to live with it." Zanuck eliminated that entire scene. Locked in a Cold War with the Soviet Union, compromises, he explained, are not possible. "I don't pretend to know the answer," Zanuck said, "but it seems to me we are having a difficult time both in living with the Communists and in wiping them out. It seems to me that when the opposition decides to devour you, you have to do a little devouring yourself—or submit."[49] Zanuck clearly reflected prevalent Cold War thinking, and so did his movie, not entirely by what was said, but just as importantly by what was left out.

Viva Zapata! opened in New York on February 7, 1952, and in its first week approached a record-breaking gross of sixty-eight thousand dollars for the Rivoli Theater.[50] But met by mixed reviews and undermined by a lackluster promotional campaign, the film steadily lost audiences' interest. Kazan thinks Zanuck was relieved, if not anxious, to see it die. Not only had the producer lost faith in the movie as a potential moneymaker, but he had always feared repercussions from HUAC. In retrospect, Kazan believes that all during the production struggle Zanuck had been in touch with the government watchdogs.[51]

Apparently because they knew little of Emiliano Zapata and Mexico's Revolution, the reviewers concentrated on Brando's performance, rated from magnificent to mumbling and slouching.[52] *Time* found the movie a "muscular horse opera," but thought Zapata a "pretty tame cat."[53] *Commonweal* recognized that Steinbeck's script had slipped from the portrayal of a rebel determined to free people from dictatorship to a confused leader who wondered if violence wrought change.[54] Richard C. Coe of the *Washington Post* recognized the dilemma: how to handle a controversial revolutionary in a repressive national atmosphere. Zapata could not be excused, let alone praised, "for in these days of fear of freedom, to excuse a revolutionary is a dubious tack"—and he might have added, "if you intend to keep working." Coe thought the film had ducked the issue, that Steinbeck and Kazan had taken a massive mouthful they simply could not digest.[55]

Several reviewers challenged the historical accuracy of the movie without indicating they knew anything of Mexican history. One specialist on the subject, however, Professor Carlton Beals, took Kazan and Steinbeck to task in the *Saturday Review*. "I have ridden with the men of Morelos for months on end, slept on their straw mats, eaten their tortillas and chile and know the stuff of which they are made," said Beals, displaying his credentials. "The epic story of Zapata . . . cannot be told as a propaganda piece either for or against Communism, or by making his stark primitive career into a cream-puff of Gandhi hocus-pocus for school-boy platitudes about democracy and teen-age symbolism of a white horse." Fernando fit the image of no Mexican intellectual Beals said he knew, and he found the caricatures of Madero, Huerta, and Villa to be "poster-like portraits." Beals especially decried the movie's emphasis upon Zapata's renunciation of power, which he found historically indefensible and foreign to the rebel's genuine determination for land reform.[56] Beals, who has certainly been challenged on some of his interpretations of Mexican history, correctly insisted that Zapata never held the presidential power that the film allows him to reject.[57]

But such criticism misses the point. *Viva Zapata!* was never meant to recreate Mexico's Revolution but was instead constructed as a vehicle to clarion a message to post-World War II America. Kazan asserted that Steinbeck had worked with any number of versions of Zapata's activities. "John had to make choices and he made them with an eye to implementing his interpretation. . . . I thought John's angle had great value *for our thinking today* [emphasis added], and I was proud to direct it."[58] Kazan and Steinbeck were obviously more concerned with Stalinism than Zapatismo. Yet, even today the movie as Mexican history has its scholarly defenders. Harvard Professor John Womack, properly acclaimed for his 1969 biography of Zapata, finds the movie captures the aura of Zapatismo.[59] For other historians, myself included, it wrestles in an entertaining and provocative way with the contradictions and conservatism of the rebellion.

In sum, *Viva Zapata!* presents something of value about Mexico's Revolution, but much more importantly, it reflects Americans being enveloped by the Cold War, the frustrations of disoriented liberals, the impact of HUAC on the nation's culture, the business sense of Darryl F. Zanuck, the bedroom morals of Americans, the sensibilities of the Mexican government, Hollywood's early response to television, the country's mood toward social change, and undoubtedly a good deal more.

Certainly, much more, for in the midst of the turbulent 1960s *Viva Zapata!* experienced a resurgence approaching cult status among students and in theaters which catered to minority patrons. It became, and remains, recurring television fare in the United States, and elicited an extraordinarily popular rerun response in foreign theaters. Kazan says he has been vindicated, that Zapata appeals to disgruntled and rebellious people in the world.[60] So many members of the Old Left, like Kazan, are still searching for ideological peace within themselves. Yet the new Zapata phenomenon is significant. Why and in what manner do these audiences and their movements relate to this reluctant rebel? Historians can certainly continue their analysis of a changing America in *Viva Zapata!*

NOTES

1. William A. Langer and S. Everett Gleason, *The Challenge to Isolation, 1937–1940* (New York: Harper, 1952, published for the Council on Foreign Relations), p. 12.

2. Franklin Delano Roosevelt Library, Hyde Park, N.Y., FDR Personal Papers File 1945, Hays to Roosevelt, November 18, 1938.

3. Paul J. Vanderwood, "Image of Mexican Heroes in American Film" (Paper presented to American Historical Association, Washington, D.C., 1976), pp. 3–12.

4. Twentieth Century-Fox Studios, Los Angeles, Ca., Archive, File No. 2480, *Viva Zapata!*, box 1, various letters from Edgcomb Pinchon, December 1, 1938–June 1, 1939, Pinchon to Edwin Knopf of Metro-Goldwyn-Mayer, December 1, 1938. (Hereafter cited as Fox, *Viva Zapata!*, box number, file, correspondents, date.)

5. Fox, *Viva Zapata!*, box 1, various letters from Pinchon, Pinchon to Knopf, December 1, 1938.

6. Ibid.

7. Donald W. Rowland (comp.), *History of the Office of the Coordinator of Inter-American Affairs* (Washington, D.C.: Gov't. Printing Office, 1947), pp. 7–8.

8. Motion Picture Producers Association, Washington, D.C., *Viva Zapata!*, Addison Durland Memorandum, June 1, 1948. (Hereafter cited as MPPA, *Zapata*, correspondents, date.)

9. MPPA, *Zapata*, Durland Memorandum, June 1, 1948.

10. Personal interview with Jack Cummings, Los Angeles, August 17, 1976, and personal interview with Lester Cole, telephone, San Francisco, June 25, 1976.

11. "TRA Interviews Lester Cole," *Toward Revolutionary Art*, 1975, p. 3, and Cole interview, June 25, 1976.

12. Washington, D.C., National Archives, Department of State, Record Group 59, Decimal file 811.4061, Motion Pictures/11-547, Gerald M. Mayer, managing director of International Division of Motion Picture Producers Association to Secretary of State, November 5, 1947, and William T. Stone, director of Office of Information and Educational Exchange, to Mayer, [Nov., 1947].

13. Fox, Archive, Story Editor's Correspondence, *Viva Zapata!*, Inter-Office correspondence, Lew Schreiber to George Wasson, December 23, 1948, and Wasson to Francis Langton, June 29, 1949, and *Hollywood Reporter*, December 12, 1949, p. 5.

14. Fox, Archive, Contract Abstract File, *Zapata*, "Synopsis of Contract for Purchase of Literary Material," Agreement, February 1, 1951.

15. John Steinbeck, *Steinbeck, A Life in Letters*, Elaine Steinbeck and Robert Wallsten (eds.), (New York: Viking, 1975), p. 282.

16. Fox, *Viva Zapata!*, box 4, Inter-Office Correspondence, *Zapata* (Revised Screenplay of December, 1950), Darryl Zanuck to Elia Kazan and John Steinbeck, December 26, 1950, p. 1.

17. Personal interview with Elia Kazan, San Diego, Ca., October 6, 1976.

18. Kazan interview, October 6, 1976. Also, Steinbeck, *Letters*, "Steinbeck to Bo Beskow, November 19, 1948," p. 342; "Steinbeck to Elaine Scott, November 1, 1949," p. 382. Also, personal interview with Barbara McLean, who edited *Viva Zapata!*, Marina del Mar, Ca., August 17, 1976.

19. For original Steinbeck typescripts of *Viva Zapata!* see: University of Texas, Austin, Humanities Research Center, John Steinbeck Collection, "Zapata, Written for the Screen," by John Steinbeck, November 26, 1949; and "Zapata" by John Steinbeck, "Foreword: It will be explain [*sic*] that we have attempted to draw the essence of history and character, rather than exactness," [n.d.]; also, Fox, Archives, File No. 2480, *Viva Zapata!*, various boxes contain a succession of screenplays written, revised, and rewritten by Steinbeck and Kazan. For printed final shooting script, see: Robert E. Morsberger, *"Viva Zapata!," the Original Screenplay by John Steinbeck* (New York: Viking, 1975). For dialogue taken from moviola, consult Fox, *Viva Zapata!*, box 6.

20. Kazan interview, October 6, 1976. For Kazan's political thinking at the time *Viva Zapata!* was being produced, see: Elia Kazan, *Kazan on Kazan* by Michel Ciment (New York: Viking, 1974), pp. 83–101.

21. "Letters to the Editor," *New York Times*, October 17, 1976, Sec. 2, p. 28, Ronald Radosh/Louis Monashe letter.

22. Lillian Hellman, *Scoundrel Time* (Boston: Little, Brown, 1976), p. 98.

23. Fox, *Viva Zapata!*, box 3, "*Zapata*" Treatment, October 17, 1949, by Elia Kazan. "Notes on Zapata's Character" by Elia Kazan.

24. Elia Kazan, "Elia Kazan on *Zapata*," in "Letters to the Editor," *Saturday Review*, April 5, 1952, pp. 22–3.

25. Kazan interview, October 6, 1976.

26. University of Texas, Austin, Humanities Research Center, Steinbeck Collection, "*Zapata*, for Screen," November 26, 1949, pp. 160–61.

27. Fox, *Viva Zapata!*, box 6, "Dialogue Taken from Moviola," pp. 47–8.

28. University of Texas, Austin, Humanities Research Center, Steinbeck Collection "*Zapata*, for Screen," November 26, 1949, p. 175; also "*Zapata*" by John Steinbeck [n.d.], pp. 149–50.

29. Vanderwood's conclusion upon viewing movie *Viva Zapata!*

30. Fox, *Viva Zapata!*, box 4, Inter-Office Correspondence, Zanuck to Kazan and Steinbeck, December 26, 1950, p. 7.

31. *Ibid.*, pp. 7–8.

32. *Ibid.*, pp. 1–5.

33. Fox, *Viva Zapata!*, box 6, "Dialogue Taken from Moviola," p. 16.

34. Fox, *Viva Zapata!*, box 4, Inter-Office Correspondence, Zanuck to Kazan and Steinbeck, December 26, 1950, pp. 9–10.

35. *Ibid.*, p. 9.

36. *Ibid.*, pp. 10–11.

37. Kazan interview, October 6, 1976.

38. Fox, *Viva Zapata!*, box 4, Inter-Office Correspondence, Zanuck to Kazan and Steinbeck, December 26, 1950, pp. 16–18.

39. Fox, *Viva Zapata!*, box 5, "Memorandum of Conferences between Professor Sologuren, Doctor Barcia, Ralph de Lara, Colonel Jason Joy, Molly Mandeville," April 23, 25, May 2, 1951; "Mr. Zanuck's Comments on the Conference notes . . . ," May 2, 1951.

40. *Ibid.*

41. *Ibid.*

42. Kazan interview, October 6, 1976.

43. See note no. 19 for locations of relative screenplays.

44. Fox, *Viva Zapata!*, box 5, "Memorandum of Conferences . . . ," p. 25 (for conferences of April 23, 25); pp. 8–9 (for conferences of May 2), "Mr. Zanuck's comments . . . ," p. 10.

45. Fox, *Viva Zapata!*, box 4, "Zapata: Letter Dictated by Mr. Zanuck to M. Mandeville on Revised Screenplay of July 31, 1950," Zanuck to Steinbeck, August 10, 1950.

46. Fox, *Viva Zapata!*, Story Editor's Correspondence File, "Conference on Final Script of February 6, 1951 (with Messrs. Zanuck, Kazan, Richard Murphy)," Molly Mandeville (Zanuck) to F. D. Langton, Feb. 12, 1951; also box 6, "Dialogue Taken from Moviola," p. 46.

47. Fox, *Viva Zapata!*, box 4, "Zapata: Memorandum on Revised Screenplay of April 27, 1950 (dictated to Molly Mandeville by Darryl Zanuck)," Zanuck to Kazan and Steinbeck, May 3, 1950, p. 13.

48. For example, see MPPA, *Viva Zapata!*, Joseph I. Breen, director of Production Code Administration, to Colonel Jason S. Joy, Twentieth Century-Fox Film Production, February 12, 1951; May 25, 1951, and June 4, 1951

49. Fox, *Viva Zapata!*, box 4, Inter-Office Correspondence, Zanuck to Kazan and Steinbeck, December 26, 1950, p. 11.

50. "B'way Spurts; *Zapata* . . . ," *Variety*, February 13, 1952, p. 9.

51. Kazan interview, October 6, 1976.

52. *"Viva Zapata!* Is Action Drama at Fox," *Philadelphia Inquirer,* March 1, 1952, p. 15; *"Viva Zapata!* At Fifth Ave.," *Seattle Post-Intelligence,* March 19, 1952, p. 26; and "Movies," *Holiday,* May 2, 1952, p. 105.

53. "Cinema," *Time,* February 11, 1952, p. 92.

54. "The Screen," *The Commonweai,* February 29, 1952, p. 517.

55. *"Viva Zapata!* Opens at Palace," *Washington Post,* February 23, 1952, p. 8.

56. Carlton Beals, "Letters to the Editor," *Saturday Review,* May 24, 1952, pp. 25 and 28.

57. For an analysis of this point, see John Womack, *Zapata and the Mexican Revolution* (New York: Knopf, 1969), chapter 7.

58. Elia Kazan, "Letters to the Editor," *Saturday Review,* May 24, 1952, p. 28.

59. Morsberger, *Original Screenplay,* p. 139.

60. Kazan interview, October 6, 1976.

The Age of Conspiracy and Conformity:

Invasion of the Body Snatchers (1956)

STUART SAMUELS

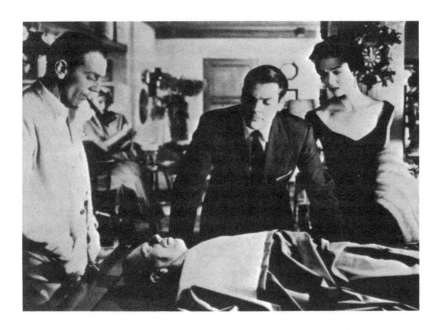

Dr. Miles Bennell (Kevin McCarthy) and Becky (Dana Wynter) ponder the meaning of the "body" found in his friend's home. The film is a statement about the collective paranoia of the times.

(Photo courtesy of Museum of Modern Art)

In what way can a seemingly absurd science fiction/horror film, *Invasion of the Body Snatchers*, give us insight into the history and culture of America in the mid-1950s? How is a film about people being taken over by giant seed pods "reflective" of this critical period in our history?

Films relate to ideological positions in two ways. First, they *reflect*, embody, reveal, mirror, symbolize existing ideologies by reproducing (consciously or unconsciously) the myths, ideas, concepts, beliefs, images of an historical period in both the film content and film form (technique). Secondly, films *produce* their own ideology, their own unique expression of reality. Films can do this by reinforcing a specific ideology or undercutting it.

All films are therefore ideological and political insomuch as they are determined by the ideology which produces them. Fictional characters are only prototypes of social roles and social attitudes; every film speaks to some norm. Some behaviors are deemed appropriate, others not. Some acts are condemned, others applauded. Certain characters are depicted as heroic, others as cowardly. Film is one of the products, one of the languages, through which the world communicates itself to itself. Films embody beliefs, not by a mystic communion with the national soul, but because they contain the values, fears, myths, assumptions, point of view of the culture in which they are produced.

While films relate to ideology, they also relate to specific historical and social events, most obviously when the content of a film deals directly with a subject that is identifiable in its own period. In the 1950s, for example, such films as *I Was a Communist for the FBI* (1951) and *My Son John* (1952) spoke to a society increasingly concerned with the nature of the internal communist threat. Similarly, in the previous decade such films as *The Best Years of Our Lives* (1946) attempted to analyze some of the problems and confusions of the immediate post-World War II period and *The Snake Pit* (1948) addressed a society trying to deal with the tremendous increase in the hospital treatment of the mentally ill. As far back as Griffith's *Intolerance* (1916), which relayed a pacifist message to a nation struggling to stay out of war, films have reflected society's attempts to come to grips with contemporary problems.[1]

Film "reflects" an agreed-upon perception of social reality, acceptable and appropriate to the society in question. Thus, in the 1950s when a conspiracy theory of politics was a widely accepted way of explaining behavior (being duped), action (being subversive), and effect (conspiracy), one would expect the films of the period to "reflect" this preoccupation with conspiracy. But *Invasion of the Body Snatchers* is not *about* McCarthyism. It is about giant seed pods taking over people's bodies. Indirectly, however, it is a *statement about* the collective paranoia and the issue of conformity widely discussed in the period.

The idea for the film came from Walter Wanger, the producer, who had read Jack Finney's novel of the same name in serial form in *Collier's Magazine* in 1955. Wanger suggested the project to his friend Don Siegel, who in turn assigned Daniel Manwaring to produce a screenplay from Finney's book.

The story of the film is contained within a "framing" device—a seemingly insane man, Miles Bennell (Kevin McCarthy), telling a bizarre story to a doctor and a policeman. In flashback we see Bennell's tale—of giant seed pods taking over the minds and bodies of the people of Santa Mira, a small town in California, where Bennell was the local doctor. Returning home after a medical convention, Miles finds the pretty little town and its peaceful inhabitants in the grip of a "mass hysteria." People seem obsessed by the conviction that relatives and friends are not really themselves, that they have been changed. Despite the outward calm of Santa Mira, there is a creeping contagion of fear and paranoia, of wives not knowing their husbands, children fleeing from parents.

Miles's friend Becky (Dana Wynter) struggles against this delusion, tends to dismiss it as improbable, but nevertheless finds her own Uncle Ira slightly changed: "There's no emotion in him. None. Just the pretense of it." The improbable becomes real when Miles's friend Jack calls him to report something fantastic: a semihuman body, without features, has been found on Jack's billiard table. From this point on events move rapidly. The unformed body is clearly growing into an exact duplicate of Jack, and in the greenhouse Miles stumbles upon giant seed pods, each containing a half-formed body. In Becky's basement Miles finds still another embryonic shape—this time a model of Becky herself. Now Miles believes the fantastic stories, and determines to escape and warn the world of this danger.

But escape is not simple. The town of Santa Mira has nearly been taken over by the pods, who while the inhabitants sleep form themselves into precise replicas of human beings—even-tempered, peaceful, but soulless automatons. Miles is terrified and drags Becky from her bedroom, to flee in his auto. But the town has now mobilized against them; the pod-people cannot allow the story to be told, and the "people" of Santa Mira organize to catch Miles and Becky. In a desperate escape attempt, they flee over the mountains, pursued by those who had once been their friends and neighbors.

The horror mounts when, in a tunnel, Becky succumbs to the pods. She falls asleep and soon her mind and body are taken over, cell by cell. In a moment of utmost panic, Miles looks into her eyes and realizes the awful truth. Continuing on alone, he comes to a highway where he makes wild attempts to flag down motorists who are terrified by his insane behavior. Eventually, he is picked up by the police, who naturally consider him mad, and taken to a hospital for medical examination. The doctors agree that he is psychotic, but then fate intervenes. An intern reports an accident to a truck from Santa Mira, and in a casual aside, he tells how the driver of the wreck had to be dug out from under a pile of strange giant seed pods. The truth dawns on the police inspector, who orders the roads to Santa Mira closed, and in the final shot tells his assistant to "call the FBI."

The political, social, and intellectual atmosphere of the era that created *Invasion* must be understood in light of several preoccupations: the "Red Menace," which crystallized around the activities of Senator Joseph McCarthy and the somewhat less spectacular blacklisting of figures in the communications and entertainment industry, who were seen as a nefarious, subversive element undermining the entire fabric of American society; learning to cope with the consequences of a modern, urban, technologically bureaucratized society; and the pervasive fear of atomic annihilation.[2] All these factors undermined the traditional American myth of individual action. The experience of the Depression, the rise and threat of totalitarianism, the loss of American insularity, the growth of technocracy all in one form or another challenged the integrity of the individual. It is therefore not surprising to note that film genres like science fiction or horror films proliferated in the 1950s. The central themes of these films show a preoccupation with depersonalization and dehumanization. Moreover, as Susan Sontag has suggested, it is by no means coincidental that at a time when the moviegoing public had for over ten years been living under the constant threat of instant atomic annihilation films of the 1950s should be concerned with the confrontation of death. As Sontag expressed it: "We live[d] under continued threat of two equally fearful, but seemingly opposed destinies: unremitting banality and inconceivable terror."[3] On the surface there existed a complacency that disguised a deep fear of violence, but conformity silenced the cries of pain and feelings of fear.

In response to the threats of social banality and universal annihilation, three concepts dominated the decade: (1) conformity, (2) paranoia, (3) alienation. Each concept had its keywords. *Conformity*: "silent generation," "status seekers," "lonely crowds," "organization men," "end of ideology," "hidden persuaders." *Paranoia*: "red decade," "dupes," "front organization," "blacklisting," "un-Americanism," "fifth column," "fellow travelers," "pinkos." *Alienation*: "outsiders," "beats," "loners," "inner-directed men," "rebels." For the most part, the decade celebrated a suburbanized, bureaucratized, complacent, secure, conformist, consensus society in opposition to an alienated, disturbed, chaotic, insecure, individualistic, rebel society. Each of those three concepts dominating the 1950s finds obvious expression in *Invasion of the Body Snatchers*. First—conformity.

During the 1950s a concern for respectability, a need for security and compliance with the system became necessary prerequisites for participation in the reward structure of an increasingly affluent society. Conformism had replaced individuality as the principal ingredient for success. This standard extended to all aspects of life. Tract-built, identical, tidy little boxlike ranch houses on uniform fifty-foot plots bulldozed to complete flatness were the rage. Conformity dictated city planning in the form of Levittowns, the same way it silenced political dissidents in Congress. Creativity meant do-it-yourself painting-by-numbers. One created great artistic masterpieces by following directions.

The concern with conformity grew out of a need to escape from confusion, fear, worry, tension, and a growing sense of insecurity. It was accentuated by a sense of rootlessness and increased mobility. Consensus mentality offered a refuge in an anxious and confusing world. It represented an attempt to shift the burden of individual responsibility for one's fate to an impersonal monolithic whole. Excessive conformity, as in the 1950s, was a salve to smooth over obvious conflict and turmoil. A country that emerged from war victorious around the globe feared internal subversion at home; a society powered by a new technology and a new structure (corporate bureaucracy) feared a loss of personal identity. In the White House was a person whose great appeal was that he represented a politics of consensus, classlessness, and conformism—Eisenhower.

By the time *Invasion* was released (May, 1956) the intensity of the drive for consensus politics had diminished—the Korean War had ended, McCarthy had been censored, Stalin was dead, the spirit of Geneva had thawed the Cold War, the imminent threat of atomic annihilation had subsided, witch hunting had lost its appeal, and the threat of internal subversion had lessened. But the context of fear was still active. The political reality might not seem as frightening, but the mind-set of the period was always ready at any moment to raise its repressive head. To many people, the fact that the enemy appeared less threatening only meant that he was better at concealing his subversion and that the eternal vigilance of good Americans had to be even more effective.

David Riesman's *The Lonly Crowd* (1955) spoke of a society obsessed by conformity.[4] His now-famous formulation about inner-directed and other-directed men, focuses on the same conflicts outlined by Siegel in *Invasion*. Miles Bennell is "inner directed"—a self-reliant individualist who has internalized adult authority, and judged himself and others by these internalized self-disciplined standards of behavior. The "pods" are "other-directed" beings whose behavior is completely conditioned by the example of their peers. While inner-directed individuals like Miles felt concern and guilt about violating their inner ideals—in fact, were driven by them —the other-directed pods had no inner ideals to violate. Their morality came from the compulsion to be in harmony with the crowd. Their guilt developed in direct proportion to how far they deviated from group consensus. The other-directed pods were uncritical conformists. It was no coincidence that the most popular adult drug of the 1950s was not alcohol or aspirin, pot or cocaine—but Miltown and Thorazine—tranquilizers.

The second basic concept in 1950s America, the natural corollary to the drive toward conformity, was the notion of conspiracy. Conformity is based on the idea that there is a clear-cut division between *them* and *us.* In periods of overt conflict, like wars or economic crises, the division between the good and the bad is obvious. But in periods of confusion, the identification of enemies becomes more problematic. Covert expressions of subversion are more common than overt challenges; the enemy attacks—whether real or imagined—through subversion and conspiracy rather than war. In the 1950s subversion seemed to be everywhere. Appearances were deceptive; to many, nothing was what it appeared to be. Schools named after American heroes like Jefferson, Lincoln, Walt Whitman, Henry George were rumored to be fronts for communists, calls for free speech were seen as pleas for communism, and racial unrest as being formented by party activists. To many, taking the Fifth Amendment in order not to incriminate oneself was just another way of disguising one's political treason.

Threats to social order in the 1950s were not so much associated with personal violence as with an indefinable, insidious, fiendishly cold undermining of the normal.[5] Conspiracy theories feed off the idea of the normal being deceptive. In *Invasion*, the pods, the alien invaders, take on the appearance of normal people. It becomes physically impossible to tell the difference between the aliens and the normals. In *Invasion* all forms of normalcy are inverted. Friends are not friends, "Uncle Ira" is not Uncle Ira, the police do not protect, sleep is not revivifying, telephones are no longer a way of calling for help but a device to tell the pod-people where the remaining non-pod-people are. Even the name of the town is paradoxical. Mira in Spanish means "to look," but the people of Santa Mira refuse to look; they stare blankly into the unknown.[6] A patina of normalcy hides a deep-seated violence. A man holds a giant seed pod and calmly asks his wife, "Shall I put this in with the baby?" "Yes," she replies, "then there'll be no more crying." In another scene, what appears to be a quiet Sunday morning gathering in the town square turns out to be a collection point where fleets of trucks filled with pods quietly dispense these "vegetables" to people who carry them to their cars and buses, ready to spread the invasion to neighboring towns. It is during a typical home barbeque among friends that Miles finds the pods in his greenhouse.

At the end of the film, when all avenues of help seemed closed, Miles and Becky, hiding in an abandoned cave, hear sweet, loving music—a Brahms lullaby. Miles decides that such beauty and feeling could not possibly be the singing of unemotional pods. He scrambles off to find out where this music is coming from—only to discover that its source is a radio in a large truck being loaded by robotlike people with seed pods destined for far-off towns. The familiar is fraught with danger. It is no wonder that Miles comes to the edge of madness, no wonder that he treats people with a paranoid suspicion. Paranoia becomes the logical alternative to podlike conformism.

Finally, conformism and conspiracy signaled a new age of personal alienation. From the very beginning of our history, one of the most persistent myths about American society has been the myth of natural harmony. The idea is derived from the notion made popular by Adam Smith and John Locke that there is a *natural* and harmonious relationship between the desires of individuals and the demands of social necessity, that individuals who act out of self-interest will automatically move the society as a whole in the direction of natural perfection. At the heart of this notion was the belief that nothing in the system prevented people from achieving their own individual goals, and that the traditional barriers of class, religion, and geography were absent in the American experience. The concept of natural harmony is further based on the belief of abundance.[7] Individual failure had to be due to personal shortcomings because a society of abundance offered opportunity to anyone capable of grasping it—conflict was not built into the system. People were basically good. Solutions were always within grasp. Control was inevitable. Progress was assured.

This underlying belief in natural harmony was one of the casualties of the post-1945 world. In the 1930s American films had portrayed people ordering their environment. "The people," the Mr. Smiths, the Mr. Deeds, the Shirley Temples, and the Andy Hardys saw to it that control and harmony were restored. Individual "good acts" reinforced "social good" in the desire to control life. In the 1940s the theme of conquest, control, and restoration of the natural was the underlining statement of war films. Commitments to courage, self-sacrifice, and heroism were shown instead of Senate filibusters, talks with Judge Hardy, or faith in "the people." Depictions of failure, helplessness, and feelings of inadequacy were introduced as muted themes in the postwar films. Although we had won the war, conquered the Depression, and tamed nature by splitting the atom, things seemed out of control in the 1950s as conflict emerged between the desire for personal autonomy and the pressures for collective conformity. Individual acts of heroism were suspect. Group work and group think were the ideals. Success was measured by how much individuals submerged themselves into some larger mass (society, bureaucracy) over which they had little individual control. The rewards of status, popularity, and acceptance came with conformity to the group. In the films of the period, people who did not sacrifice individual desires for general social needs were fated to die, commit suicide, be outcast, or simply go mad.

Popular books like Riesman's *The Lonely Crowd*, William Whyte's *The Organization Man*, and Vance Packard's *The Status Seekers* showed how the traditional model of the hard working, rugged individualist was being rejected for a world of the group—big universities, big suburbs, big business, and big media. Such harmony as existed resulted from the artificial ordering to an agreed upon surface norm.[8] After the scarcity of the Depression came the affluence of the 1950s—complete with its never-ending routine of conspicious consumption. Out of the victory for democracy and freedom came a society more standardized, less free, more conformist, and less personal. Out of splitting the atom came the threat of instant annihilation.

The mid-1950s films portrayed people trying desperately to ward off failure in the face of overwhelming destructive forces of nature (horror films), technology (science fiction films), and human imperfection (*film noir*). There were films about people being taken over or reincarnated: *The Search for Bridie Murphy* (1956), *I've Lived Before* (1956), *Back from the Dead* (1957), *The Undead* (1957), *Vertigo* (1956), *Donovan's Brain* (1953); about individuals in conflict with their societies: *High Noon* (1952), *The Phenix City Story* (1955), *No Place to Hide* (1956), *Not of this Earth* (1957); about superior forces beyond man's control: *Them* (1954), *Tarantula* (1956), *The Beast from 20,000 Fathoms* (1953), *This Island Earth* (1955), *Earth versus the Flying Saucers* (1956); about the apocalypse: *20,000 Leagues Under the Sea* (1954), *On the Beach* (1959),

The Thing (1951). In these films, the world seemed menacing, fluid, chaotic, impersonal, composed of forces which one seldom understood, and certainly never controlled. Fear is centered on the unknown, unseen terrors that lurk beneath the surface normality.[9]

Invasion's podism is depicted as a malignant evil, as a state of mind where there is no feeling, no free will, no moral choice, no anger, no tears, no passion, no emotion. Human sensibility is dead. The only instinct left is the instinct to survive. Podism meant being "reborn into an untroubled world, where everyone's the same." "There is no need for love or emotion. Love, ambition, desire, faith —without them, life is so simple." A metaphor for communism? Perhaps! But, more directly, podism spoke to a society becoming more massified, more technological, more standardized.

The motto of the pods was "no more love, no more beauty, no more pain." Emotionless, impersonal, regimented, they became technological monsters. But they were not the irrational creatures of blood lust and power—they were just nonhuman. They became tranquil and obedient. They spoke to the fear of the 1950s—not the fear of violence, but the fear of losing one's humanity. As Susan Sontag argued, "the dark secret behind human nature used to be the upsurge of the animal—as in *King Kong* (1933). The threat to man, his availability to dehumanization, lay in his own animality. Now the danger is understood to reside in man's ability to be turned into a machine."[10] The body is preserved, but the person is entirely reconstituted as the automated replica of an "alien" power.

The attraction of becoming a pod in the 1950s was all too real. But although dangling the carrot of conformity, *Invasion* opts ultimately for the stick of painful individuality. The possibility of moral uncertainty was the price we must pay for continued freedom. As Miles says: "Only when we have to fight to stay human do we realize how precious our humanity is." Podism, an existence without pain or fear or emotion, is seen as no existence at all. The fear of man becoming a machinelike organism, losing his humanity, was centered around the ambiguous dual legacy of an increasingly technological civilization. The atomic bomb was both a testament to man's increased control over his universe and a clear symbol of man's fallibility. *Invasion* mirrors this duality. It praises the possibility of a society without pain, yet it raises the spectre of a society without feeling. Security at what price?—the price of freedom and individualism. The rise of technology at what costs?—the cost of humanness itself. Although *Invasion* is ambiguous on this issue, demonstrating the positive effects of "podism" at the same time as condemning its consequences, this confusion, this ambiguity, is very much at the heart of the American cultural issues of the period—the internal conflict between the urge for conformity and the painful need for individuality, between an antiheroic loner and an institutionalized, bureaucratized system of mindless automated pods.

In his struggle to remain his own master, Miles fights against control by first falling back on the traditional notions inherited from the past. He appeals to friends—only to be betrayed. He appeals to the law—only to be pursued by it. He appeals to the system—only to be trapped by it. He appeals to love—only to be disappointed by losing it. All betray him. All become his enemy. Not because they are corrupt, or evil, but because they have become pods, because they have given up their individuality, their ability to choose.

If there is a 1950s vision of historical reality in *Invasion*, there is also a system of film technique designed to reinforce this vision. The language and technique of *Invasion* come out of the social reality of the period and speak directly to that context.

One of the major themes of life in the 1950s was the feeling of constraint—people feeling enclosed within boundaries. People were cut off from options, limited in their choices. There was a closing down of dissent, a shrinking of personal freedom. Silence became the acceptable response to oppression.

Invasion is a film about constraints. It is the story of a man whose ability to make sense of the world decreases and diminishes to the point of madness and frenzy. The film's action takes place within enclosed physical spaces and the physical spaces in the film induce a sense of isolation and constraint. The sleepy California town of Santa Mira is surrounded by hills. When Miles tries to escape he must run up a series of ladderlike stairs to flee the pod-people and reach the open highway that separates the town from the outside world. Miles and Becky are constantly running—in and out of small rooms, darkened cellars illuminated only by matches, large but empty nightclubs, miniature greenhouses, closets, low-ceilinged dens, abandoned caves. The giant seed pods are found in basements, closets, car trunks, greenhouses. The main actors are claustrophobically framed by doorways and windows photographed from low angles, and spend much of their time running down and up endless stairs, into locked doors, and beneath towering trees. The narrative structure of *Invasion* resembles a series of self-contained Chinese boxes and is designed to tighten the tension of the story at every step. Though Miles returns from his convention on a sunny morning and the film ends in a confused mixture of daylight and darkness, the main section of the film takes place in darkness—at night.

The whole film is enclosed within a framing device of prologue and epilogue. Siegel's original version had not included this frame, but the addition of a prologue and epilogue, making the film narrative appear as an extended flashback, has the unintended effect of constricting the narrative—itself contained in a rigidly enclosed time frame—even further. Within this framing device, Siegel also uses the technique of repeating a situation at the end of the film that mirrors a sequence presented at the beginning. In the final flashback episode, Siegel has Miles running in panic down the road and being pursued by a whole town of pod-people. This scene mirrors the opening scene when we see little Jimmy Grimaldi running down the road being pursued by his "podized" mother.

The effect of these devices is to keep the narrative tight in order to heighten tension and suspense. The use of flashback, prologue and epilogue, repeated scenes, interplay of lightness and darkness, all keep the narrative constrained within a carefully defined filmic space. The unbelievable tension is released only in the epilogue, when Miles finally finds someone who believes his story. The ending is not about the FBI's ability to counteract the threat of the pods but about the fact that Miles has finally made contact with another human—and that he is not alone. The film is more about being an alien, an outsider, an individualist, than about the "invasion" by aliens. When Dr. Bassett and his staff finally believe Miles's story, the enclosing ring of constraint is broken, and Miles collapses, relaxing for the first time in the film, knowing that at least he has been saved from a horror worse than death—the loss of identity. The final line—"Call the F.B.I."—is the signal that he is not alone and acts as an affirmative answer to the shout heard at the opening of the film—"I'm not insane." Up to the point when the doctor finally believes Miles's story, the film is actually about a man going insane.

Time is also a constant constraint on humanity, and Siegel

emphasizes the fact that time is running out for Miles. The whole film is not only a race against madness, but also against time—of time slipping away. Time in *Invasion* is circumscribed by the fact that sleep is a danger. Miles needs to escape Santa Mira before he falls asleep. He takes pills, splashes his and Becky's face in a constant battle to stay awake. Sleep is not comfort and safety but the instrument of death.

Siegel uses a whole arsenal of filmic techniques to reinforce the feelings of enclosure, isolation, and time running out. His shot set-ups focus on isolated action. People are photographed in isolation standing beneath street lamps, in doorways, alone at crowded railway stations. A background of black velvet darkness and a direct artificial light are used to highlight objects which in isolation take on an "evil clarity." In the film, objects are always illuminated, people's faces are not. Shadows dominate people's space and obscure personality. Diagonal and horizontal lines pierce bodies.

Darkness is combined with a landscape of enclosure to increase the feeling of fear. There is a stressed relationship between darkness and danger, light and safety. Those who wish to remain free of the pods must not only keep awake, but must constantly keep themselves close to direct light. For example, when Miles discovers Becky's pod-like double in the basement of her home, he hurries upstairs into her darkened bedroom and carries her out of the dark house into his car which is parked directly beneath a bright street lamp.

Tension in the film is not only created by lighting techniques and camera set-ups, but most significantly by the contrast in how the actors play their roles. Miles is frenzied, harried, hard-driving, always running. The robot-like, affectless pod people stare out at the camera with vacant eyes, openly unemotional, unbelievably calm, rational, logical. They appear to be normal, and Miles appears to be insane; however, the reverse is true. The pods' blank expression, emotionless eyes mask their essential deadness.

The whole film texture is based on the internal contrast between normal and alien. The hot dog stands, used-car lots, small office buildings, friendly cops, sleepy town square, and neighborhood gas stations only create the illusion of normalcy played against the mounting terror.

The mise-en-scène, lighting, acting styles, physical presence, props, and Carmen Dragon's unrelenting, spine-chilling musical score keep the audience in a constant state of tension. The same is true of the constant introjection of siren sounds, cuckoo clocks, screams in the middle of the night, and the use of distorting lenses, claustrophobic close-ups, juxtaposed long shots, and low-angled shots that establish a mood of vague disquiet. All help to create a basic tension between the normal and the fearful, the familiar and the sinister, and to result in a film designed to give the audience a sense of isolation, suspense, and feeling of constraint.[11]

Historians will debate the actual nature of the 1950s for a long time. But through the films of a period we can see how a particular society treated the period, viewed it, experienced it, and symbolized it. Few products reveal so sharply as the science fiction/horror films of the 1950s the wishes, the hopes, the fears, the inner stresses and tensions of the period. Directly or indirectly, *Invasion* deals with the fear of annihilation brought on by the existence of the A-bomb, the pervasive feeling of paranoia engendered by an increasing sense that something was wrong, an increasing fear of dehumanization focused around an increased massification of American life, a deep-seated expression of social, sexual, and political frustration resulting from an ever-widening gap between personal expectation and social reality, and a widespread push for conformity as an acceptable strategy to deal with the confusion and growing insecurity of the period. It is a film that can be used by historians, sociologists, and psychologists to delineate these problems and demonstrate the way American society experienced and symbolized this crucial decade.

NOTES

1. See Andrew Bergman, *We're In the Money: Depression America and Its Films* (New York, 1971); Richard Pelles, *Radical Visions and American Dreams: Culture and Social Thought in the Depression Years* (New York, 1973); Andrew Dowdy, *Movies Are Better Than Ever: Wide Screen Memories of the Fifties* (New York, 1973); Lawrence Alloway, *Violent America: The Movies, 1947–1964* (New York, 1971); Michael Wood, *America at the Movies* (New York, 1975); Robert Sklar, *Movie-Made America: A Cultural History of American Movies* (New York, 1975).

2. See David Caute, *The Great Fear: The Anti-Communist Purge Under Truman and Eisenhower* (New York, 1978); Fred J. Cook, *The Nightmare Decade: The Life and Times of Senator Joe McCarthy* (New York, 1971); Stefan Kanfer, *A Journal of the Plague Years* (New York, 1973) Michael

Paul Rogin, *The Intellectuals and McCarthy: The Radical Specter* (Cambridge, Mass., 1967); Dalton Trumbo, *The Time of the Toad: A Study of Inquisition in America* (New York, 1972); Robert Vaughn, *Only Victims: A Study of Show Business Blacklisting* (New York, 1972); David Zinn, *Post War America, 1945–1971* (New York, 1973); I. F. Stone, *The Haunted Fifties* (New York, 1963); John Cogley, *Report on Blacklisting*, 2 vols. (New York, 1956); Lawrence S. Wittner, *Cold War America: From Hiroshima to Watergate* (New York, 1974).

3. Susan Sontag, *Against Interpretation* (New York, 1966).

4. David Riesman, et al., *The Lonely Crowd: A Study of the Changing American Character* (Garden City, N.Y., 1955 ed.).

5. See Douglas T. Miller, Marion Nowak, *The Fifties: The Way We Really Were* (Garden City, N.Y., 1977).

6. The most famous congressional enactments of the period tried to legislate conformity. The McCarren-Internal Security Act, the establishment of a Subversive Activities Control Board, the increased activities of the House Un-American Activities Committee and the Senate Internal Security Committee all attempted to determine acceptable political behavior.

7. Op. cit., Riesman, *The Lonely Crowd*.

8. See Judith M. Kass, "Don Siegel" in *The Hollywood Professionals*, vol. 4 (New York, 1975); Charles T. Gregory, "The Pod Society Versus the Rugged Individualist," in *Journal of Popular Film*, vol. 1, no. 1 (Winter 1972), pp. 3–14; Brian Murphy, "Monster Movies: They Came from Beneath the Fifties," in *Journal of Popular Film*, vol. 1, no. 1 (Winter 1972), pp. 31–44; William Johnson, ed., *Focus on the Science Fiction Film* (Englewood Cliffs, N.J., 1972).

9. See Richard Hofstadter, *The Paranoid Style in American Politics* (New York, 1965).

10. See David Potter, *People of Plenty: Economic Abundance and American Character* (Chicago, 1954); Carl N. Degler, *Affluence and Anxiety, 1945–Present* (Glenview, Ill., 1968).

11. Stuart A. Kaminsky, "The Genre Director: The Films of Donald Siegel," in *American Film Genres: Approaches to a Critical Theory of Popular Film* (New York, 1974), pp. 174–202; Stuart A. Kaminsky, "On *Invasion of the Body Snatchers*," in *Cinefantastique*, vol. 2, no. 3 (Winter, 1973), pp. 16–23; Stuart A. Kaminsky, *Don Siegel: Director* (New York, 1974); Alan Lovell, *Don Siegel: American Cinema* (London, 1975).

The Pentagon and Hollywood:

Dr. Strangelove
or: How I Learned to Stop Worrying and Love the Bomb (1964)

LAWRENCE SUID

The contradiction between national expectations of peace and Pentagon actions brought the Armed Forces and their methods into question on the nation's motion picture screens.

(Photo courtesy of Museum of Modern Art)

Until the early 1960s, Hollywood generally portrayed the American military as infallible, noble, and all-conquering in its movies about war and the armed forces. Few people had any reason to question this image throughout the 1950s. The United States military had won a great victory in World War II. If Korea ended in a stalemate, most Americans attributed the standoff to political failures rather than any shortcomings within the armed forces. And during the Cold War, the military preserved the peace against an enemy who wanted to take over the world, at least according to the conventional teachings which bombarded the nation.[1]

By the time President Kennedy had come to office, however, the black and white delineation of the Free World versus the monolithic Communist World had become blurred. China and Russia were no longer allies. Tito was a friendly Communist. Khruschev had toured the United States and seemed less a cruel, ruthless dictator than a shrewd party politician. Despite the strains caused by the U-2 crisis, the Bay of Pigs invasion, and the Cuban missile crisis, the old images of Cold War confrontation seemed to be eroding away. The President initiated the Peace Corps, he met with the Russian Premier, negotiations began to limit nuclear bomb testing. The Cold War was finally thawing.

As the old perceptions of international power politics underwent change, so did the manner in which the nation perceived the military establishment. Before leaving office, President Eisenhower had warned of the dangers of the military-industrial complex. The Bay of Pigs fiasco was attributed at least in part to poor military planning and advice.[2] The military confrontation between the Soviet Union and the United States in October, 1962, brought the American people face to face with the reality of nuclear holocaust.[3] Perhaps for the first time since Hiroshima and Nagasaki, the nation had to examine the premises on which the military had preserved peace—the ever-present threat of massive atomic retaliation to an enemy attack.

Most people had accepted the atomic bombing of Japan as a wartime necessity. The subsequent Pacific testing in 1946, the development of the hydrogen bomb, the creation of the Strategic Air Command had all demonstrated the nation's commitment to preserving the peace through an overwhelming military strength.

The arms race became a necessary evil about which few people thought during the 1950s. Civil defense preparations, started after the war to provide protection against possible atomic attack, became all but forgotten following the abortive efforts to launch a massive bomb shelter construction program in the late 1950s.

While the threat of nuclear attack remained ever present, most people had come to ignore the danger, had forgotten about it, or perhaps simply had suppressed an image of destruction too horrible to contemplate. Consequently, the sudden confrontation with Russia in October, 1962, and the threat of nuclear missiles only ninety miles from United States shores shocked most Americans into an awareness of the continued danger that the bomb posed.[4]

When Russia "blinked" after going eyeball to eyeball with the United States's determination to prevent the installation of nuclear missiles in Cuba, the road to arms limitation seemed open. The signing of the Nuclear Test Ban Treaty in 1963 became the first visible sign that peace might be possible through negotiations rather than the continued reliance on the bomb.[5] Nevertheless, the military seemed to be doing business as usual, continuing to call for more bombs, more bombers, more submarines, and more missiles. As a result of this contradiction between national expectations and Pentagon actions, the armed forces found themselves and their methods the subject of question in Congress, in the news media, and for the first time on motion picture screens.

Over the years, few Hollywood movies had portrayed the military or American fighting men in less than a favorable light. Even in the films which contained a negative image, the fault invariably rested with one or two individuals, not the military as a whole. *Attack!* (1956), for one, showed an incompetent company commander kept in his job by a corrupt colonel because of his own postwar ambitions. But the movie made it clear that the military as a whole was not at fault. The soldier who ultimately kills the incompetent officer explains at one point, "The Army is not a mockery! The war is not a mockery! It's just this small part!"[6]

To ensure that even "this small part" appeared on the screen as seldom as possible, the armed forces regularly worked with film-makers on scripts submitted as part of requests for military assistance in the form of technical advice, men, and equipment. At least until the mid-1960s, few people in the film industry questioned the military's right to ask for changes in scripts or to turn down requests for help if the story was unacceptable. Daniel Taradash, who wrote the script for *From Here to Eternity* (1953), did not think the changes he made in transforming James Jones's novel into a screenplay constituted military censorship. Noting that he could not use Jones's "whore" and "fuck" because of the Motion Picture Production Code, he explained, "When you're writing a movie, you accept all kinds of limitations."[7]

Terry Sanders, the producer of *War Hunt* (1962), a small-budget, antiwar film, on the other hand, felt that the Army requirement of script approval on movies requesting assistance did constitute censorship: "Obviously the atmosphere of control and influence is censorship." Nevertheless, the producer did not consider the army's turndown of this request for help to be illegitimate: "Why the hell should they have given me cooperation? I don't feel badly that they turned us down at all. I centainly would have if I had been in their shoes."[8]

With the exception of an occasional *Attack!* or *War Hunt*, however, films about the military portrayed the armed forces positively. On their part, the services believed that the assistance they extended to filmmakers benefited the military or was in its best interest. In most cases, the movies aided recruiting or informed the public of the military's activities and procedures far better than other informational avenues. The military also found it was in its best interest to provide cooperation to a film like *From Here to Eternity* which did not offer any tangible benefit. By assisting, the army was able to obtain changes in the script which made the service's movie image better than its image had been in Jones's novel.[9]

Filmmakers, of course, had little reason not to submit positive scripts or, if necessary, to smooth the rough edges of unflattering portrayals. The military's successes on the battlefields in the two world wars and Korea provided successful models for screenwriters. Moreover, filmmakers usually did not know technical and procedural aspects of military life and so were willing to accept advice on improving the accuracy of scripts in order to insure a more authentic military ambience.

At the same time, all the major studios had long-standing and excellent relationships with the armed forces, in some cases dating back to the pre-World War I period. General Hap Arnold, for one, had recognized the value of military portrayals in motion pictures as a result of his appearance in the 1911 movie *Military Scout* and had subsequently helped arrange air corps assistance on such movies as *Wings* (1927) and *Air Force* (1943).[10] On their part, such leading Hollywood figures as Frank Capra, John Huston, George Stevens, John Ford, and Darryl Zanuck had served in uniform during World War II and had established friendships within the armed forces. Finally, armed forces assistance was a practical necessity not only to save filmmakers large amounts of money, but also to provide military equipment unavailable from other sources. To obtain aircraft carriers, planes, and tanks, Hollywood had no choice but to submit scripts which showed the military in a good light.

By the late 1950s, however, the film industry was changing. The old studio system had broken down under the onslaught of television. With its demise went Hollywood's traditional contacts with and respect for the military. The new independent producers, directors, and screenwriters like Terry Sanders and his brother Denis, Max Youngstein, James Harris, James Poe, and Stanley Kubrick were no longer beholden to the armed forces and their unsullied images. With the change in attitude toward the military that began to take place in the early 1960s, these filmmakers saw the possibility of finding markets for their antiestablishment, antimilitary movies.

Since World War II and Korea offered little material with which to make their statements, these filmmakers turned to the Cold War, peacetime military establishment and, more specifically, to the atomic bomb for their target. They found it provided a perfect symbol for criticism of war and the military without denying the real need for a strong armed forces.

During the 1950s, with the exception of a few science fiction movies, Hollywood had portrayed the bomb as the instrument that had brought peace to the world and had helped maintain it during the height of the Cold War. *Above and Beyond* (1952) had told the story of Paul Tibbets and the dropping of the first atomic bomb on Hiroshima which ended the war and so appeared as a positive good. *Strategic Air Command* (1955) portrayed Curtis LeMay's bomber force as the major deterrent to communist domination of the world.

Bombers B-52 (1957) provided the American people with further information about SAC and featured its newest weapons for winning the peace.[11]

Only at the end of the decade did Stanley Kramer's *On the Beach* (1959) suggest the other side of the bomb, that it might be the force which would destroy the world. Contending that Kramer's vision of doomsday was scientifically impossible, the Pentagon refused to provide the filmmaker with a nuclear submarine during the shooting of the picture.[12] Rejecting as it did the military's claim that the bomb had preserved peace during the 1950s, *On the Beach* opened the dialogue about the efficacy of using nuclear deterrents to prevent World War III.[13]

With the release of Kramer's film, Hollywood began to portray the bomb as having no socially redeeming features. In contrast to its earlier role as a peacemaker, filmmakers during the 1960s suggested that the bomb's only function was most likely the destruction of modern civilization. The armed forces had committed themselves to its use and so any criticism of the bomb would by its very nature be a criticism of the military and its reliance on destruction to do its job. In addition, having enjoyed a "good" press during most of the 1950s, the bomb offered filmmakers virgin territory in which to develop stories about its negative features. Finally, having lived for more than a decade under the tensions of a peace maintained through the threat of nuclear destruction, the American people were ready to look at the other side of the bomb and its relationship to the future of civilization.

On its part, the air force had always insisted upon a serious and factual presentation of its procedures, preparedness, and the competence of those who had their fingers on the switches of the nuclear arsenal. The service had used the films on which it assisted to inform the American people not only of SAC's potential, but also of how it guarded against accidental launchings of a nuclear attack. Consequently, the knowledge that Hollywood was preparing two films about accidental nuclear warfare moved Curtis LeMay to encourage Sy Bartlett to make *Gathering of Eagles* (1963) another in the line of peacetime SAC movies designed to show the American people that the Air Force was doing its job in a responsible manner.[14]

Gathering of Eagles conveyed its message well, reflecting the competence of two Academy Award winners in its screenwriter,

Robert Pirosh (*Battleground*), and its director, Delbert Mann (*Marty*). But however visually dramatic its images, the film broke no new ground, provided no new insights into the bomb or the men who controlled it. It was in fact a 1950s movie released in the 1960s to an audience no longer willing to accept the air force's story uncritically.[15] Consequently, its pseudo-documentary style and traditional message were overwhelmed by the brilliance of Stanley Kubrick's *Dr. Strangelove or: How I Learned to Stop Worrying and Love the Bomb* (1964).

Based on Peter George's 1958 novel *Red Alert*, Kubrick's film told the story of an air force general who orders a flight of B-52 bombers to attack Russia in hopes of triggering a war to wipe out the communist menace. If one such story was not enough, the air force also had to face a second film with the same basic plot. In *Fail Safe* (1964), based on the Eugene Burdick-Harvey Wheeler novel of the same name, a faulty computer rather than a deranged general initiates the strike force. As in *Dr. Strangelove*, neither the United States nor Soviet armed forces are able to stop all the bombers. One reaches Moscow and delivers its hydrogen bombs. While each film contends that the military does not truly control the bomb and so suggests that a nuclear accident is inevitable, the two movies approached their common thesis in diametrically opposite manners.

Dr. Strangelove took on not only the bomb, but military and government leaders, American and Russian alike, using satire to attack virtually everyone and everything. Kubrick peopled his film with incompetents, bigots, and warmongers, with the military characters bearing the brunt of the criticism. In contrast to the occasional attacks on a military character in earlier armed forces movies, in *Dr. Strangelove*, the system is questioned, as well as the premises on which it operates and the people who run it.

Initially, Kubrick did not set out to convey his message in a comic vehicle. Having made one major antimilitary statement in *Paths of Glory* (1957), he had become interested in the theme of "a nuclear war being started by accident or madness." Kubrick did not discover *Red Alert* until 1961, but decided almost immediately that it would serve as the basis for making his statement about the bomb. He first tried to follow the serious tone of the novel in working on the screenplay, but he soon found that each time he created a scene, it turned out to be comic. Kubrick later recalled, "How the hell could the President ever tell the Russian Premier to shoot down American planes? Good Lord, it sounds ridiculous."[16] As a result, the film turned into a satirical nightmare, a surrealistic portrayal of humans blundering through war rooms, carrying on absurd dialogues on a hot line, and committing sheer lunacy while the world moves quickly toward destruction.

It was most unlikely that the Pentagon would cooperate in making a film based on such images, but Kubrick unofficially approached the air force to "discuss" it any way. Apart from the portrayal of its officers as insane, bloodthirsty, and ludicrous, the service told the filmmaker that the misrepresentation in his script of the Positive Control safeguards against accidental nuclear war precluded any Pentagon assistance.[17] In contrast to General Ripper's one-man war in the movie, a SAC commander cannot order a single plane or rocket to undertake a nuclear bomb mission. Only the President or his surrogate has the attack code, which only he can relay to SAC Headquarters, which in turn issues the appropriate command. Given Kubrick's scenario, the air force had no basis on which even to begin discussions about possible cooperation.[18]

According to military officials, the Positive Control system could not be subverted; it was fail safe. Kubrick disagreed—he was making *Dr. Strangelove* to warn the nation about the possible dangers of the safeguard system. Consequently, literal accuracy of air force procedures had little relevance. He wanted to convey a message, not make a pseudo-documentary for the service *à la Strategic Air Command* or *Gathering of Eagles*. For the first time, therefore, the air force had to watch its men and its procedures portrayed in a manner which it felt was not only inaccurate, but which could seriously affect public perception of its activities and behavior.

Without military cooperation, Kubrick became the film's technical advisor, using knowledge gained from a youth spent watching war movies in New York City. He recreated a B-52 cockpit and cabin from magazine pictures and impressions gained from earlier SAC films. The war room was built out of his and the art director's imagination since no one had ever acknowledged the existence of an underground crisis center in the Pentagon, let alone released a picture of such a place. The sequences of the bomber in flight were produced by placing a ten-foot model of a B-52 in front of a moving matte made up of shots taken over the Arctic.[19] If the end result bore little resemblance to actual air force procedures or equipment, Kubrick was able to create an ambience which most people accepted as reality, even when presented within the framework of the film's comic motif.

Opening with a poetic, rhythmic sexual scene of a B-52 bomber being refueled in midair (the only "live" footage in the film), the movie unfolds in a rapid fire sequence of events that gives the audience no time to catch its breath. A SAC general orders a flight of bombers to attack Russia, the President informs the Soviet Premier of what has happened; the crew of the lead bomber prepares for its mission; the governments of both nations attempt to stop the attack both in the air and by trying to capture the insane general; efforts meet with failure; and one plane reaches its target. At the fade out, bombs go off like fireworks, filling the screen with mushroom clouds.

In producing his biting denouncement of man's inability to control the weapons of war, Kubrick used all manner of visual and verbal imagery. The sexual coupling of the two planes at the opening of the movie is followed at regular intervals by shots of a bomber flying gracefully, sensually toward its target over a snowcovered landscape. The beauty of the plane in motion contrasts starkly with the utter destructiveness of its mission. Yet, when the bombs go off, the explosions assume their own sensuality which Kubrick reinforces with the soothing sounds of a female vocalist singing, "We'll meet again, don't know where, don't know when, but I know we'll meet again some sunny day."[20]

One of Kubrick's skills as a filmmaker has always been his ability to mesh the visual with the aural, the image with the words and music. And in *Dr. Strangelove*, the visual effects of the movie receive reinforcement from language, from the music, and from the very names of the characters which help create their personalities. The demented SAC commander is Jack D. Ripper, the President is Merkin Muffley, the Russian Premier is Dimitri Kissof, the Russian Ambassador is de Sadesky, the Chairman of the Joint Chiefs of Staff is "Buck" Turgidson, the colonel in charge of storming General Ripper's headquarters at Burpelson Air Force Base is "Bat" Guano, the British officer assigned as Ripper's Executive Officer is Group Captain Mandrake. Finally, there is Dr. Strangelove himself, a "rehabilitated" Nazi scientist, whose character is developed both visually and verbally.

Strangelove makes his entrance into the underground Pentagon war room in a wheelchair. He speaks with the appropriate German accent and periodically experiences a problem with a bionic right arm that has a mind of its own. In moments of stress, Strangelove reverts to his Nazi background, addressing President Muffley as "Mein Führer," while desperately trying to restrain his arm from either giving a Nazi salute or strangling himself.

If any one scene captures the black humor of *Dr. Strangelove*, however, it comes when President Muffley calls Premier Kissof on the hotline to tell him of the impending disaster. After tracking the Premier down at his mistress's residence with the help of Ambassador de Sadesky ("Our Premier is a man of the people."), the President tries to explain what has happened:

> How are you? . . . Oh fine. Just fine. Look, Dimitri, you know how we've always talked about the possibility of something going wrong with the Bomb? . . . The Bomb? The HYDROGEN BOMB! . . . That's right. Well, I'll tell you what happened. One of our base commanders did a silly thing. He, uh, went a little funny in the head. You know, funny. He ordered our planes to attack your country . . . let me *finish* Dimitri.[21]

But there is nothing else to say. The deed has been done. General Ripper, a caricature of a right wing fanatic who is worried about the "commie plot" to fluoridate American drinking water and debilitate the people by threatening "the purity and essence of our natural fluids," has severed all communications with the outside world and he alone knows the recall code.

What follows resembles a tour through a Hollywood insane asylum. When General Turgidson starts wrestling with Ambassador de Sadesky who has been taking pictures of the underground command center, President Muffley remonstrates with both men: "You can't fight in here, this is the War Room." In arguing that the President should seize the opportunity and launch an all-out attack, General Turgidson admits, "I'm not saying we won't get our hair mussed." Going over their survival kits containing rubles, dollars, gold, Benzedrine, cigarettes, nylons, chocolate, chewing gum, prophylactics, and tranquilizers, one of the crewmen remarks, "I could have a pretty fine weekend with this in Vegas."

The crew is not going to Las Vegas, however, but to drop its bombs on a Russian missile site. Under other circumstances, the Russians might have been willing to accept such a loss if the attack was truly accidental. But the Soviets have built a Doomsday Machine, set to go off if any nuclear bomb explodes on Russian territory and generate enough radioactivity to make the earth uninhabitable for ninety-nine years. To have acted as a deterrent, however, the device had to be publicized. Dr. Strangelove notes with suitable irony: "the whole point of the Doomsday Machine is lost *if you keep it a secret! Why didn't you tell the world, eh?"* The Russian ambassador can only answer that Premier Kissof "loves surprises" and was going to announce it at the upcoming Party Congress.[22]

The only hope rests in destroying the SAC bombers or getting them to turn back. Burpelson Air Force Base is besieged by army units with the battle raging under a SAC billboard proclaiming: "Peace Is Our Profession." Inside, Mandrake alternately pleads with General Ripper to recall the planes and tries to figure out the proper recall sequence based on the General's rantings. When he finally does, after Ripper has killed himself to avoid torture, Mandrake tries to relay the information to the President by telephone. But the military lines are out and he has no money for the pay phone. The White House will not accept collect calls from an unknown group captain. In desperation, Mandrake pleads with Colonel Guano to shoot the lock from a Coke machine to get the needed change. But the officer recoils in horror: "That's private property."[23]

In the end, one plane eludes all Russian efforts to shoot it down and heads toward its target. In a seeming last minute reprieve, the bomb will not drop from the damaged bomb bay. In *Red Alert*, the bomb was damaged and did not go off. However, in the final grim moment of truth, Kubrick does not cop out. The pilot, Major Kong, an unreconstructed Texas cowboy, climbs onto the bomb, works it free, and rides it downward, yelling exuberantly and waving his Stetson as if on a bucking bronco rather than the instrument which will end the world. This paradox of pure joy juxtaposed with the vision of absolute destruction which immediately follows, symbolizes the two sides of *Dr. Strangelove*. On one hand, it produces side-splitting laughs. On the other, it creates horror at the thought of what lurks just around the corner.

As ridiculous and funny as the story appears on the screen, the threat to the world from nuclear accident still comes across as a plausible reality. Kubrick himself observed, "The greatest message of the film is in the laughs. You know, it's true. The most realistic things are the funniest." To Kubrick, *Dr. Strangelove* perhaps seemed realistic. He estimated he had read seventy books on the subject of the bomb and had maintained an extensive clippings file of relevant articles. He had also talked to such nuclear war strategists as Thomas Schelling and Herman Kahn, the author of *On Thermonuclear War* and *Thinking About the Unthinkable*. Consequently, he could believe that a "psychotic general" could unleash a flight of bombers against Russia and could maintain that "for various and entirely credible reasons, the planes cannot be recalled, the President is forced to cooperate with the Soviet Premier in a bizarre attempt to save the world."[24]

Dr. Strangelove does not portray reality, Kubrick notwithstanding. Instead, he produced a black satire, a genre which does not depend on reality to expose the foibles of man and his society. To succeed as satire, any social commentary must reach its intended audience, which Kubrick's film did do through the very quality of its script, its acting, and its directing.

Kubrick shot *Dr. Strangelove* in England to accommodate Peter Sellers who was indispensable to the film. The actor assumed the roles of President Muffley, Group Captain Mandrake, and Dr. Strangelove, managing to instill a unique personality in all three in a tour de force of character acting. If he did not completely steal the film, it was only because George C. Scott as General Turgidson and Sterling Hayden as General Ripper are equally superb. The actors, however, performed only within the structure that Kubrick created, manipulated, and directed. His interweaving of the visual and verbal images, the use of sound and music, the imaginative production values, all combined to produce a rare film experience, one that does not lose its impact even in an age where missiles have for the most part replaced bombers as the United States's first line of defense and where people have all but stopped thinking about accidental nuclear warfare.

When *Dr. Strangelove* was released in 1964, however, the Cuban missile crisis was still fresh in people's minds. B-52s still constituted the nation's primary strike force. Audiences could thus readily accept Kubrick's vision of the accidental launching of a nuclear attack even though Kubrick created his dramatic impact with what was, in fact, a story based on inaccurate premises and factual errors.[25] A SAC base commander had no means of ordering a flight of planes to attack Russia, the script's explanation of events notwithstanding. The attack code came down the chain of command from the President through SAC Headquarters in Omaha to base commanders to planes on the ground and in the air. Moreover the code was transmitted to air crews orally, not by means of a black box as shown in the movie. And the air force's fail safe mechanisms operated on the principle of positive control—the planes on their missions had to receive a direct order to launch its attack. The absence of such a command would automatically abort the mission. Unfortunately, at least for the air force and its image, few people either knew or had the time and concern to ascertain how SAC procedures worked. Therefore most viewers could readily suspend their disbelief and accept Kubrick's version of the system and its implied weaknesses. They might well emerge from the theater not only entertained, but also concerned over the future of the world, at least to the extent that any movie audience thinks seriously about such things.

To the degree that *Dr. Strangelove* was seen as making a serious statement, it did become the focus of discussion about the subject of accidental nuclear warfare. Lewis Mumford, for one, thought the film was "the first break" in the nation's "cold war trance." He observed:

> What has masked the hideous nature of our demoralized strategy of total extermination is just the fact that it has been the work of otherwise well-balanced, responsible men. . . . What the wacky characters in *Dr. Strangelove* are saying is precisely what needs to be said: this nightmare eventuality that we have concocted for our children is nothing but a crazy fantasy, by nature as horribly crippled and dehumanized as Dr. Strangelove himself.

Mumford rejected the criticism that the film was sick by suggesting that "what is sick is our supposedly moral, democratic country which allowed this policy to be formulated and implemented without even the pretense of open public debate."[26]

In contrast, Bosley Crowther in the *New York Times* found *Dr. Strangelove* "a bit too contemptuous of our defense establishment for my comfort and taste." He acknowledged that the film was "cleverly written and most skillfully directed and played." Moreover, he conceded it was a "devastating satire" which contained some "awfully funny" stuff, describing the initial phone conversation between President Muffley and Premier Kissof as a "simply delicious passage." Nevertheless, Crowther thought the "sportive speculation about a matter of gravest consequence seems more malicious than diverting, more charged with poison than wit."[27]

A second viewing of the film did not change Crowther's opinion that *Dr. Strangelove* did a disservice to the nation. He agreed that Kubrick's message might aid those people who were spreading the word about the potential danger of the bomb. However, he noted that the trouble with the film "as a thesis for mordant satire . . . is that it is based more on wild imagination than on basically rational truths." He said that Kubrick "goes beyond truths that are absurd and asks his audience to follow in a frightening and dangerous fantasy. He constructs a nightmare speculation upon an assumption of military and political flaws that are so fanciful and unsupportable by any evidence that they are beyond sober belief." To Crowther, making "a terrible joke" of the potential dangers of the bomb "is not only defeatist and destructive of morale. It is to invite a kind of laughter that is only foolish and hysterical."[28]

Other reviewers saw the film performing a more positive service. *Newsweek* called it "outrageous" and said it contained "low clowning." But the magazine also thought the film "suggests all too clearly that human society is not yet so well organized as to be able to afford such dangerous toys as hydrogen bombs." The reviewer thought that Kubrick's use of comedy to convey the message made his observation

> all the sharper, all the clearer, and that much better a film. . . . Kubrick, and his biting bitter satire, stands as eloquent testimony not only to the possibilities of intelligent comment in film, but to the great freedom which moviemakers have, even if most of them have not dared use it.[29]

If *Dr. Strangelove* had a failing as social commentary, the fault probably lay in Kubrick's very success as a filmmaker. Whatever the validity of his message/warning to the American people, much of its strength became lost in the audience's laughter. As *Newsweek* noted, the film was "side-splittingly funny."[30] As a result, more viewers undoubtedly remembered *Dr. Strangelove* for its entertainment, its comedy, its acting, and its directing than as a serious treatise on the dangers of the bomb and incompetent leadership.

The same could not be said of *Fail Safe*, which appeared later the same year. In contrast to *Dr. Strangelove*, Max Youngstein's film was a realistic, serious attempt to warn the American people of the dangers of accidental nuclear warfare. Given Kubrick's format, most viewers probably spent little time considering his method of launching the bomber attack—the portrayals of Generals Ripper and Turgidson undoubtedly did more damage to the military image than did the inaccurate account of the fail safe system. But *Fail Safe* purported to tell it like it was in the guise of a pseudo-documentary. As a result, more than in *Dr. Strangelove*, the portrayals in *Fail Safe* called the military establishment onto the carpet and questioned its methods and procedures in a way that few Hollywood military films had done up to that time.

While most people accepted *Fail Safe* as an exciting account of a potentially destructive nuclear accident, not even Youngstein considered it a work of art in the same category as *Dr. Strangelove*. The producer thought his company had turned out a "good picture," but conceded that Kubrick had "turned out a brilliant picture. It's as simple as that. . . . It was a brilliant type of black humor, so far ahead of its time."[31] Nevertheless, *Fail Safe* offered a greater chance of conveying its message to the American people because of its serious tone and seemingly accurate portrayal of military procedures and actions. Bosley Crowther observed in his *New York Times* review that unlike *Dr. Strangelove*, *Fail Safe* had in its favor that "it does not make its characters out to be maniacs and monsters and morons. It makes them out to be intelligent men trying to use their wits and their techniques to correct an error that has occurred through over-reliance on the efficiency of machines."[32]

Ultimately, of course, the military image, so long burnished by Hollywood movies, suffered not because of the negative portrayals in these two films but because military leaders and the nation itself had come to believe in the strength and infallibility of the armed forces, a image created in large part by movies. In Vietnam, the military suddenly discovered that it could not win the war in the final reel as John Wayne and his fellow actor/soldiers, sailors, fliers, and marines had been doing for more than forty years on the screen.

It was the defeat in Vietnam, not the General Rippers or Turgidsons that forced the American people to reexamine their unquestioned acceptance of the military establishment.

NOTES

1. There is a vast and steadily growing literature regarding the Cold War. Among the outstanding and long list of books on the problems of war, peace, and the military in postwar America, see Gar Alperovitz, *Atomic Diplomacy: The Use of the Atomic Bomb and the American Confrontation with Soviet Power* (New York, 1967) on the decision to use the atomic bomb in 1945. In *The Power Elite* (New York, 1956) sociologist C. Wright Mills made one of the earliest and still most cogent examinations of the military-industrial connection. A critical vision of the U.S. military, and its industrial component, is in Richard J. Barnet, *The Economy of Death* (New York, 1969), and, from the period of the film, Fred Cook's *The Warfare State* (New York, 1962). On the Cold War, see Norman Graebner, *Cold War Diplomacy, 1945–1960* (Boston, 1962), George F. Kennan, *Russia, the Atom and the West* (New York, 1958), and Walter LaFeber, *America, Russia and the Cold War, 1945–1966* (New York, 1967). For a look into a real-life confrontation, see Elie Abel, *The Missile Crisis* (New York, 1966).

2. Robert F. Kennedy, *Thirteen Days: A Memoir of the Cuban Missile Crisis* (New York, 1969), p. 112, and Arthur M. Schlesinger, Jr., *A Thousand Days* (Boston, 1965), pp. 250–297.

3. Kennedy, *Thirteen Days, passim*, Schlesinger, *A Thousand Days*, pp. 794–819.

4. *Ibid.*

5. Schlesinger, pp. 893–915.

6. Interview with Robert Aldrich, March 14, 1974. *Attack!* (1956), United Artists. Robert Aldrich, dir.; James Poe, SP.

7. Interview with Daniel Taradash, March 27, 1974.

8. Interview with Terry Sanders, August 17, 1975.

9. Interviews with Donald Baruch, Chief, Motion Picture Production Office, Audio/Visual Division, Directorate for Public Information, Department of Defense, March 22, 1973 to present.

10. General H. H. Arnold, *Global Mission* (New York, 1949), pp. 34–35. Interview with Col. Bruce Arnold, March 19, 1977.

11. Interviews with General Curtis LeMay, August 17, 1975, Beirne Lay, Jr., August 5, 1975, General Paul Tibbets, July 7, 1976, and Col. Ben Ostlind, August 21, 1975.

12. Interviews with Donald Baruch.

13. Interview with Stanly Kramer, February 8, 1974; *The Nation*, January 2, 1960, p. 20; *Commentary*, June 1960, pp. 522–523.

14. LeMay interview. Also interviews with Sy Bartlett, February 9, 1974, Robert Pirosh, March 5, 1974, and Delbert Mann, March 13, 1974.

15. *Newsweek*, July 22, 1963, p. 86; *Daily Variety*, June 4, 1963.

16. *New York Times*, April 21, 1963, Sec. II, p. 7; *Newsweek*, February 3, 1964, pp. 79–80; *Variety*, February 27, 1963, p. 11.

17. Arthur Ragen, *Image of the Military as Portrayed in Three Novels Made into Screenplays since 1958.* Unpublished M.A. thesis, Boston University, 1964.

18. Baruch interviews.

19. *Newsweek*, February 3, 1964, pp. 79–80; *New York Times*, April 21, 1963, Sec. II, p. 7.

20. *Dr. Strangelove or: How I Learned to Stop Worrying and Love the Bomb* (1964), Columbia Pictures, Stanley Kubrick, dir.; Terry Southern, Stanley Kubrick, SP.

21. *Ibid.*

22. *Ibid.*

23. *Ibid.*

24. *New York Times*, April 21, 1963, Sec. II, p. 7.

25. Alastair Buchan, director of the Institute for Strategic Studies, a non-governmental research group, said that Kubrick met with him in 1961 to discuss making a film about a nuclear accident. Buchan told the filmmaker that he thought it would be "unwise because he would not be able to describe precisely what precautions the United States or other nuclear powers take to guard against the danger of accident or false command." He also told Kubrick the picture would "mislead anxious people." After seeing the film, Buchan noted that few viewers "will be aware that the basis of the plot is a series of distortions even of the known facts about American control and safety procedures." *New York Times*, February 5, 1964, p. 29.

26. Cited in William L. O'Neill, *Coming Apart*, Quadrangle Books, New York, 1971, pp. 214–215.

27. *New York Times*, February 2, 1964, Sec. II, p. 1.

28. *Ibid.* February 16, 1964, Sec. 11, p. 1. The *Times* published reactions to Crowther's earlier review on p. 7 of Sec. 11, the same date.

29. *Newsweek*, February 3, 1964, p. 79.

30. *Ibid.*

31. Interview with Max Youngstein, April 5, 1974.

32. *New York Times*, September 16, 1964, p. 36. Far more than *Dr. Strangelove*, both the original novel, *Fail Safe*, and the movie on which it was based, stirred up debate over the efficacy of the Air Force's Fail Safe procedures. See Sidney Hook, *The Fail Safe Fallacy* (New York, 1963); Arthur Ragen, *Image of the Military as Portrayed in Three Novels*; Herman S. Wouk, "Book Review of *Fail Safe*," in *Air Force Magazine*, December, 1962, p. 81; and Lawrence Suid, *Guts and Glory: Great American War Movies* (Reading, Mass., 1978), chapter 10.

Hollywood, Nihilism, and the Youth Culture of the Sixties:
Bonnie and Clyde (1967)

LAWRENCE L. MURRAY

In this early encounter between Clyde Barrow (Warren Beatty) and Bonnie Parker (Faye Dunaway) the sexual overtones are stressed. The alienation of the young in the 1960s was comparable to the director's image of the 1930s.

(Photo courtesy of Museum of Modern Art)

The 1960s has not proven to be an epoch which readily lends itself to ease of analysis and comprehension. From the beginning, in the snow and cold of Washington when John F. Kennedy proclaimed that the torch had been passed, to its close in a hail of gunfire on a grassy knoll at Kent State University when the flame was extinguished, a montage of eclectic events transpired to assault the national consciousness. In the ongoing historical quest for simplifications and generalization, Jim E. Heath has arranged the disparate occurrences around the amorphous thesis that it was a "decade of disillusionment." Similarly, Andrew Kopkind and James Ridgeway sought to bring order from chaos by erecting a vague framework in which crisis was the common denominator. The most thorough study to date, that of William L. O'Neill, has fallen on the dramatic phrase "coming apart" as its descriptive theme.[1]

Although a more restricted endeavor, reconstructing the history of American film during that period is an equally elusive task. One can describe and catalog the significant movies as John Baxter has, but organizing and synthesizing all of the events, issues, and personalities into a cohesive whole has thus far not been attempted.[2] Whichever perspective is taken, contradictions abound. For example, attendance figures and box-office receipts inched forward and though the annual increments were not overwhelming, it was the first sustained forward movement since World War II. Yet audience surveys found that theater clientele constituted an ever more skewed sector of the population as nearly every viewer was under thirty. The studio system continued to falter and such corporate conglomerates as Gulf and Western and Transamerica absorbed Paramount and United Artists amidst rumors of renewed antitrust action. The symbiotic relationship between television and the movies, developed in the late 1950s, began to disintegrate as Hollywood was more and more being transformed into Television City. What had begun as cooperation ended in competition with the CBS announcement that it was establishing its own film division and the other networks following suit. There was a boom in new construction as over a thousand new theaters opened in the last half of the decade. But production continued to hover around 230 new releases yearly and exhibitors complained that there were not enough features to sustain their emporiums. The reorganization of the Motion Picture Association of

America under Jack Valenti and the imposition of a rating system with the collapse of the old Hays Code seemed to herald an opportunity for pursuing more mature and sophisticated themes. Such an assumption, however, was counterbalanced by demands for censorship of movies that were too violent and sexually explicit.[3] Amidst this welter of crosscurrents, *Bonnie and Clyde* (1967) appeared, one of the most discussed and controversial films of the decade. Few pictures have generated as much critical analysis, and the process continues a decade later.

Bonnie and Clyde was the creation of David Newman and Robert Benton.[4] While working as art director and editor respectively of *Esquire* in 1964, the two satirically-inclined writers collaborated on a screenplay. The appetite of these novices for such a venture was whetted by the profound filmic influence of "New Wave" directors, particularly François Truffaut and Jean-Luc Godard. Newman and Benton had been caught up in the euphoria of what *Cahiers du Cinema* termed "the furious springtime of world cinema," the transition of movies from a means of escape to a means of approaching a problem. As they recalled it, three factors coalesced to provide the immediate impetus. First was their belief that the mood of American society was in the process of change, that there was a shift in attitudes which they described in an article, "The New Sentimentality," published by *Esquire* in June, 1964. Second was their fascination with the revelations contained in a new book by John Toland, *The Dillinger Days.*[5] Finally, daily attendance at a month-long retrospective of Alfred Hitchcock pictures sponsored by the Museum of Modern Art convinced them to move forward with their scheme.

Of course, in a larger sense, as John Cawelti has noted, their script grew out of a "complex cultural and artistic background: the reality and legend of the historical Bonnie and Clyde, the American artistic tradition of the gangster film, and the new-wave French film."[6] In a comparable vein, film critic Tom Milne emphasized the reactive or responsive quality of *Bonnie and Clyde*, that it was an American reply to the stranglehold that French directors, notably Truffaut in *Shoot the Piano Player* (1960) and Godard in *Bande à Part* (1964), had on the gangster film genre.[7]

Developing a scenario about the exploits of Bonnie Parker and Clyde Barrow was a project with little likelihood of success. Neither

Newman nor Benton had any experience in screenwriting and were totally ignorant of how to compose a treatment. More importantly, the subject had been reworked several times by Hollywood: Fritz Lang in *You Only Live Twice* (1937), Nicholas Ray in *They Live By Night* (1948), James E. Lewis in *Gun Crazy* (1949), and William Witney in *The Bonnie Parker Story* (1958). The prospect that their script would ever be filmed was diminished further when the writers decided that they would accept only François Truffaut as the director and wrote with him in mind.

Their naiveté, *chutzpah* they called it, was substantially mitigated by well-connected friends. Two of them, equally ignorant of the movie business but enthusiastic about the sketchy treatment, thought that producing a movie would be exciting. They took out an option and provided working capital. Another acquaintance, Helen Scott of the French Film Office in New York, was also intrigued and she forwarded the treatment with her recommendation to her friend Truffaut. The director was captivated by what he read, and during a visit to America a month later spent three days with Benton and Newman offering constructive criticisms. However, he avoided committing himself. That they were not decisively rejected was embraced by the writers as a good omen. They left their jobs, journeyed to Texas to conduct research, and began drafting a shooting script.

For eighteen months, Benton and Newman floundered about in search of a director or possibly a studio when it briefly seemed that Truffaut might yet be available.[8] They were rejected at every turn; even Arthur Penn—the eventual director—refused to read the script as his schedule was full.[9] Frustrated, they authored a book which went unpublished, free-lanced several magazine articles, and scripted a musical play about Superman which ran four weeks on Broadway. While they were engaged in these other affairs, Warren Beatty contacted them and asked to read the scenario. He said his interest had been piqued during a conversation with Truffaut.

Beatty's reading convinced him that *Bonnie and Clyde* was a viable commodity, but he would only become involved if he owned the property. Benton and Newman allowed their initial agreement to lapse and sold an option to Beatty for $10,000, against a final payment of $75,000. The actor originally intended to find someone else who would actually produce the film while he played the lead role, but the exigencies of the situation led to him assuming both parts.[10]

The decision to engage Arthur Penn as the director was also Beatty's.[11] Penn initially was uninterested as he was involved in the early stages of *Little Big Man* (1970). Beatty's insistence and the attraction of the "outlaw" quality of Bonnie and Clyde meshed to convince him to participate.[12] Like Beatty, he was captivated by the relationship of the two figures to an era in which "the country was destitute, in the grip of a depression which was not only economic, but was also a state of mind." Bonnie and Clyde "were a product of their times," the director thought, "historical figures in the social-political situation. . . ."[13] Penn's major contribution to the screenplay was in developing more of a sense of the period and emphasizing the socioeconomic chaos. Additionally, he was responsible for placing a premium on the legendary quality, the mythical aspects. The director accurately perceived that the *zeitgeist* of the 1960s, the alienation of the young from standard social conventions, was quite comparable to his image of the 1930s. His intent was "to make a modern film whose action takes place in the past," to appeal to the sensibilities of a youthful audience caught in the throes of rebelliousness and challenge. He believed the allegory would be strengthened by giving increased attention to a time frame unfamiliar to the under-thirty generation.[14]

The scenario written by Benton and Newman drew primarily upon information contained in *The True Story of Bonnie and Clyde: As Told by Bonnie's Mother and Clyde's Sister* (Emma Parker and Nell Barrow Cowan), edited and compiled by Jan I. Fortune.[15] Other accounts were available, especially the voluminous newspaper reports, Frank Hamer's rendition of his killing of Bonnie and Clyde as recounted in Walter Prescott Webb's *The Texas Rangers*, and Toland's *The Dillinger Days*.[16] While these may have been consulted —Toland has accused them of utilizing material he discovered about John Dillinger and ascribing it to Bonnie and Clyde—the writers preferred the more subjective portrayal in spite of its obvious in-accuracies.[17] "We had decided early on that, for dramatic purposes, certain figures of considerable importance in true history had to be eliminated, certain adventures altered or dropped, certain facts ignored and certain legends adhered to [and] certain characters combined from many into one for the sake of simplification. . . ."

They were much more enthralled with listening "to the language patterns, the speech cadences, the colloquialisms, so as to insure absolute accuracy of dialog."

Shooting the film proved to be relatively simply. Penn performed masterfully in bringing the production in on time and within budget, 2.5 million dollars.[18] He and Beatty had only one disagreement, that relative to the casting of Bonnie's part. The producer had wanted his sister, Shirley MacLaine, while the director preferred Faye Dunaway.[19] Penn won that dispute as well as a more important one concerning editing the final cut. Over the objections of Jack Warner, whose company distributed the film, the director did the cutting in New York with his close associate Dede Allen. Penn believed that his previous difficulties in film had resulted from his lack of control over the final cut.[20]

The collaboration of Benton and Newman with Beatty and Penn worked exceedingly well.[21] The only problem centered around the sexual activities of Bonnie, Clyde, and C. W. Moss, a composite figure of several individuals who had been members of the gang. The original draft had them functioning as a *ménage-à-trois*, with Clyde unable to perform sexually without the stimulation of a third participant. Both Penn and Beatty worried about labeling the hero as a sexual deviant, feeling that such a characterization would turn audiences off and lead to the conclusion that every action he performed was done because he was a pervert. That there was some sexual dysfunction within the group, the exact nature of which was not known, was thought by Penn to be a vital element for the dynamics of the characters and their relationships. Eventually, a group decision emerged in which it was agreed that Clyde would be portrayed as impotent. Otherwise, "the collaboration between myself [Penn] and the scriptwriters was quite real"; "basically" it was their film.[22] Benton and Newman were more than satisfied, testifying that "it was the film we *all* wanted to make, the film Arthur Penn *did* make."

John Cawelti has identified what he felt to be two "major changes" between the original script and what was shot, but in doing so he failed to recognize that the initial screenplay was changed in cooperation with the writers. Furthermore no one expected religious adherence to the first draft. Most of what Penn and Beatty recommended was incorporated in revisions written by Benton and Newman themselves. The alterations were not fundamental; rather they amounted basically to deletions of what might be construed as extraneous material so as to tighten the narrative.[23]

The plot and narrative of *Bonnie and Clyde* are relatively easy to follow and understand, factors which no doubt contributed to its enormous popularity. The film opens with several photographs of the two principal characters and the period interspersed with the credits. After the final credit, two title cards containing brief biographical information appear, establishing the setting as Texas in 1931. The technique enhanced what many reviewers would call its "documentary-like" or "pseudo-documentary" quality. The cards dissolve into the bedroom of Bonnie Parker, who is sitting naked, involved in thought about the dull, unhappy life she is leading as a waitress in a small-town cafe. Her attention is distracted by a man who has come into her yard, apparently to steal her mother's car. Bonnie calls to him and then, drawn by some excitement or animal magnetism, quickly dresses and goes down to talk to him. The two walk into town, with Clyde Barrow deriding Bonnie's boring life while bragging about his daring, his prison background, and his gun. Taunted in turn by Bonnie, Clyde proves his courage by holding up a grocery store and the two roar off in a stolen car. Their escape is punctuated by rapid banjo music that gives the scene the quality of a Keystone Kop's escapade. Thrilled and sexually stimulated, Bonnie throws herself at Clyde only to discover that he is impotent. Though unable to satisfy her sexually, Clyde does come to dominate Bonnie through a combination of flattery and force of personality.

Two confused, ineffective robberies follow. The first is at a bank, but it fails and produces no cash. Angered and embarrassed, Clyde shoots out the windows. The second is the holdup—for food—of a grocery in which a butcher attacks Clyde with a meat cleaver. Clyde pistol-whips the man and finally shoots him to avoid his grasp. The affair befuddles him:

> Why'd he try to kill me? I didn't want to hurt him. Try to get some-thing to eat around here and some son-of-a-bitch comes up on you with a meat cleaver. I ain't against him. I ain't against him.

In these early stages, Penn has developed a farce that is hard to accept seriously. Ineptitude is at a premium. More importantly, criminal actions are attributed to accidents of circumstance and it is strongly indicated that they are not very malicious. On the contrary, the protagonists emerge as reasonably attractive—physically and psychologically—figures who are simply rebelling against the system. Vicarious identification by viewers is certainly possible.

Bonnie and Clyde bring C. W. Moss, a not-very-bright but hero-worshiping country boy, into their activities. With C. W. driving, they rob a bank. They brutally shoot a pursuing teller because of the stupidity of Moss who temporarily lodged the getaway vehicle between two parked cars. The gang is now subjected to a widespread manhunt. The emotions of the audience are wrenched by the wanton slaying of the teller and the vivid, realistic photography. (According to Penn's philosophy, "In film, when you show a death, it should have that shock effect." "The trouble with violence in most films is that it is not violent enough.") The seriocomic quality of the earlier episodes dissolves. Having been led to empathize with Bonnie and Clyde and to perceive them as likable people who have accidentally fallen into a life of crime, the audience is confused as to how to respond to the transition. The recurring banjo music becomes more macabre; *Bonnie and Clyde* is not the Keystone Kop comedy first assumed.

The frequency and intensity of the gang's violent behavior increases after Clyde's brother Buck and his wife Blanche join them in hiding. The police discover their location and attempt to capture them. The group narrowly escapes amidst a hail of gunfire with Blanche screaming hysterically and running about madly. Three policemen are killed, and the gang is marked for destruction. A Texas Ranger, Frank Hamer, is instructed to hunt them down.

The gang eludes the police for a while. They glory in the role of hunted celebrities, reading of their exploits in the papers. Yet the increasing pressure of flight creates tensions, particularly between Blanche and Bonnie. Increasingly Bonnie is becoming aware that their criminal behavior is just another destructive trap and at one point tries to flee. Clyde brings her back, however, and the two are drawn into an even closer relationship. After a desperate but futile attempt to recapture their old lives by attending a picnic with Bonnie's relatives, they realize that they cannot go back, that they have only one another. But a scene with Bonnie's mother in which the girl expresses her desire never to live more than a mile away revives the audience's sympathies for her and Clyde. This constant change in tone, from burlesque to pathos, from empathy to revulsion, marks the entire production. Viewers are constantly emotionally off balance, never knowing quite how to react for fear there will be a shift in the next scene.

The audience senses that the end is near when, after a second narrow escape, the gang is quickly trapped again; this time Buck is killed, Blanche captured, and both Bonnie and Clyde wounded. During the flight to sanctuary at the home of C. W. Moss, the fugitives are given food by a group of dispossessed Okies who appear in awe of their famous visitors. As in an earlier scene in which Clyde and an evicted farmer take turns shooting at a bank's notice of foreclosure, an attempt is being made to project the two criminals as "folk heroes" of the victims of the Depression, "well-known and even revered" was the opinion of the screenwriters. According to Penn, "the fact is when Bonnie and Clyde were killed, they were regarded as enormous folk heroes. . . ."[24]

While recovering on the Moss farm, Bonnie and Clyde finally are able to consummate their love. Ironically, just as they learn how to fulfill themselves in love rather than violence, they are betrayed to the police by C. W.'s father. Lured into an ambush, they die in a tremendous fusillade. In an extended scene shot by four cameras, each at different speeds, the bodies jerk and twist under the impact of the bullets. A piece of Clyde's head flies off as had happened in the assassination of John F. Kennedy, a conscious comparison by Penn.[25] The brutality of their execution exceeds anything done by the gang and the film closes, as it had opened, with the audience being drawn to the principals. The previous confusion of emotions is resolved in the final frames.

Bonnie and Clyde debuted in early August, 1967, as the leading American entry and opening night feature at an extravagant film festival in Montreal held in conjunction with Expo '67. *Variety* was unimpressed, panning the production for inconsistent direction and characterization, erratic performances, and an uneven tempo.[26] The dean of the nation's movie critics, Bosley Crowther of the *New York Times*, was scathing.[27] Lamenting that "Hollywood movie-makers seem to have a knack of putting the worst foot forward at international film festivals," he condemned the picture as "another indulgence of a restless and reckless taste and an embarrassing addition to the excess of violence on the screen." Insulted by the "wild, jazzy farce melodrama," he contended that it was historically inaccurate and criticized the audience for its tremendous burst of applause at the end. Formally reviewing *Bonnie and Clyde* a week later at the onset of its New York run, Crowther continued his tirade, launching what Andrew Sarris termed a "crusade that makes the 100-years-war look like a border incident."[28]

Crowther's effort to bury *Bonnie and Clyde* under a mountain of invective contrasted with the approach of other critics who rallied to its support, and hastened the end of a lengthy career. William Wolf judged it a "major artistic achievement," declaring that it was "a wonderfully authentic look at the 1930s." A similar opinion was voiced by Jacob Suskind who thought it "a documentary of a kind," that "you feel that you are actually witnessing history." Wilfred Sheed raved that it was best movie of the festival, that it was a veritable "W.P.A. mural of the thirties. . . ." Pleased that justice triumphed in the end, the National Catholic Office for Motion Pictures included it in its "Best of the Month" category.[29] Andrew Sarris devoted most of his review to chastising Crowther, accusing him of using the pages of the *Times* for a "personal vendetta" and of inciting the "lurking forces of censorship and repression with inflammatory diatribes. . . ." Sarris was particularly distressed because he believed the *Times* critic was in effect pandering to the emotions of those who were demanding "law and order," a racist euphemism in 1967 for those who wanted punishment meted out to the black community for the urban riots of the previous three years.[30]

The readership of the *Times* also responded to Crowther in a series of letters to the editor, and he promptly issued another ringing denouncement.[31] "Puzzled by the upsurge of passionate expressions of admiration and defense," he remained adamant in his opinion that the movie was a "deliberately buffoonized" miscarriage of history, "a cheating with the bare and ugly truth. . . ." Contemporary newspaper accounts were cited at length to buttress his opinions. Rather than silencing opponents with his "factual" rendition, Crowther only succeeded in eliciting a new ardor, and more letters deluged the *Times*.[32]

Virtual internecine war erupted when Vincent Canby permitted Arthur Penn to respond via an intreview. At a Montreal press conference, the director had previously addressed the complaint that *Bonnie and Clyde* was an exercise in gratuitous violence, and these comments were reprinted under the title "Private Integrity and Public Violence."[33] He now focused his attention on the issue of historical accuracy as well. Any errors, he said, might exist in "the small details, but not in the big ones." But more importantly,

> We weren't making a documentary, any more than Shakespeare was writing documentaries in his Chronicle plays. To some extent we did romanticize—but so, inevitably, does any storyteller. . . . We do not purport to tell the exact truth, but we do tell a truth.[34]

Pauline Kael endorsed Penn, asking "why [are there] so many accusations of historical inaccuracy, particularly against a work that is far more accurate historically than most and in which historical accuracy hardly matters anyway?" Throwing the point back at Crowther, Kael suggested "that when a movie so clearly conceived as a new version of a legend is attacked as historically inaccurate, it's because it shakes people a little." And, "*only* good movies . . . provoke attacks."[35]

Crowther's venomous insults made it awkward for others to offer negative commentaries without appearing either to be in league with him or to have succumbed to his rampant emotionalism. One critic who did embrace his posture was Page Cook, who noted that the film was "so incompetently written, acted, directed and produced it would not be worth noticing were a claque not attempting to promote the idea that its sociopathology is art." *Bonnie and Clyde*, she concluded, "was dementia praecox of the most pointless sort."[36] Joseph Morgenstern reflected the quandary of some when he called the movie "a squalid shoot-em-up for the moron trade," and then reversed himself after a second viewing.[37] An attempt by Richard Schickel was made to disentangle matters when he "invited all men of good will to join me here on the nice soft grass of the middle ground."[38]

That *via media* was most commonly exploited by persons who judged the production in the context of the American film heritage. *Bonnie and Clyde* would ultimately be compared with John Ford's *The Grapes of Wrath* (1940), John Frankenheimer's *The Manchurian Candidate* (1962), and Richard Brooks's *In Cold Blood* (1967), among others. The most successful and productive of those who sought a contextual framework within a comparative-historical analysis was Philip French. French penned a joint review of *Bonnie and Clyde* and Roger Corman's *The St. Valentine's Day Massacre* (1967), for he conceived of them as the "highwater marks" of two divergent streams of the gangster film genre.[39] Furthermore, they had given the genre a new lease on life, witness, he said, the British exhibitor who quickly rushed out a double bill of *Dillinger* (1945) and *Al Capone* (1959).

As French structured his argument, *The St. Valentine's Day Massacre* was from a vein of films set in the 1920s within a static, urban milieu occupied by ethnic types who were organized and successful and who engaged in violence to achieve specific ends. It was an heir to the classic gangster movies: Joseph Von Sternberg's *Underworld* (1927), Mervyn LeRoy's *Little Caesar* (1930), and William Wellman's *Public Enemy* (1931). Conversely, *Bonnie and Clyde* emerged from a smaller, but no less distinct collection of films rooted in the 1930s within a rural environment. The characters were native born, disorganized, and constantly on the move; when they resorted to violence, it was unpremeditated. It was a linear descendant of Max Nosseck's *Dillinger* (1945), Don Siegel's *Baby Face Nelson* (1957), and Roger Corman's *Machine Gun Kelly* (1957).[40]

All of the controversy surrounding *Bonnie and Clyde* enhanced its box-office appeal. The film grossed over 20 million dollars in paid rentals to the distributor—high for a year which included *The Graduate, Guess Who's Coming to Dinner, In the Heat of the Night*, and *Cool Hand Luke*. It soon catapulted into thirteenth place on the all-time list of financial successes. Critical acclaim in the form of Academy Award nominations followed. Put forward in ten categories, it won two Oscars, for supporting actress and cinematography, while *In the Heat of the Night* garnered the prize for best picture from both the industry and the New York film critics.

Bonnie and Clyde also ignited a clothing fad, the Bonnie and Clyde "look," first evidenced at the Paris opening but destined to spread under the careful direction of Warner Brothers publicists.[41] Theodora Van Runkle's costumes meshed perfectly with the movement by European designers to replace the mini-skirt with the maxi-dress.[42] The movie's theme song, "Foggy Mountain Breakdown" by Lester Flatt and Earl Scruggs, was soon in the "Top Ten," reaching number one in England. Nineteen-thirties music came into vogue and posters appeared as the country, if not the world, was swept by a fit of nostalgia.

The prevailing, but unsubstantiated, assumption at the time was that *Bonnie and Clyde* appealed to the young, the under-thirty crowd that normally populated the theaters. In London where it smashed all box-office records, Charles Marowitz reported that the film "captured the rollicking dream-life-cum-reality of thousands of young Britons." He connected viewing with the rise in drug usage: "There is an unmistakable affinity between the euphoria of L.S.D. and the kicks Bonnie and Clyde get from robbing banks."[43]

That *Bonnie and Clyde* was the province of the young has been accepted by most later observers too. According to John Gallagher and John Hanc,

> A good deal of the picture's financial success was the fact that late Sixties audiences related to the rootless alienation of the film's milieu. Bonnie and Clyde are rebels without a cause; Penn is exploiting characters which the so-called "youth movement" of the late Sixties turned into campy pop culture heroes, a theme he dealt with more explicitly in *Alice's Restaurant*.[44]

The connection with youthful viewers has been echoed by John Baxter who believed that "unable to find anything worthy of emulation in a society devoid of social purposes, the young audiences saw Penn's couple as saints for a disenchanted age. . . ."[45]

That *Bonnie and Clyde* would strike a nerve in adolescents and post-adolescents was intended by Benton and Newman. As described in their treatment,

> If Bonnie and Clyde were here today, they would be hip. Their values have been assimilated in much of our culture—not robbing banks and killing people of course, but their style, their sexuality, their bravado, their delicacy, their cultivated arrogance, their narcissistic insecurity, their curious ambition have relevance to the way we live now.

The theme of a 1930s "underworld" inhabited by heroes was quite comparable to the "underground" of the youth culture of the 1960s.[46]

The enormous financial return of *Bonnie and Clyde* suggests that while young people may have composed the bulk of its audiences, people of all ages must have found something attractive about it. Film critic-historian Richard Dyer McCann blithely wrote off its popularity at the time to a "shortage of first-rate films in 1967." William O'Neill ran to the other extreme with his contention that the film "rendered the spirit of the age more finely than any other picture, except perhaps *Dr. Strangelove*."[47]

Within those widely divergent evaluations was a broad spectrum of opinion. Arthur Penn attributed the success to the rhythm of the film and to a certain tragic cast that the two protagonists had; that there was a sense of two individuals not belonging to the life and times of a society in which they found themselves. "These are problems related to what young people feel in society now."[48] Penn also believed that the characters of Bonnie and Clyde as he portrayed them were such that blacks in an age of urban riots could also identify with them.[49] Robert Steele has reinforced Penn's point about rhythm whereas John Howard Lawson reiterated the theme of tragedy. According to Steele, "The fresh amalgam of domestic-comedy, Western, and gangster movie routines makes *Bonnie and Clyde* a dazzling picture, and something would be lacking in anyone who could keep from becoming deeply involved in it."[50] The tragic appeal, from Lawson's standpoint, emerged from his observation that "there is no doubt that the film is an attack on American society, linking the events of the Thirties with the continuing predominance of oppression, corruption and hypocrisy in the present."[51] Although distressed that such would happen, Charles Thomas Samuels thought that "the audience probably identifies with Bonnie and Clyde as surrogate social victims. . . ."[52] Equally fundamental was *Time*'s interpretation that "undeniably, part of the scandal and success . . . stems from its creative use of what has always been a good box-office draw: violence."[53]

Trying to determine with any degree of exactitude why a particular movie elicits an enthusiastic reaction is to pursue an elusive and illusive chimera. All producers and directors hope that their latest project will touch the collective consciousness, strike a responsive chord while communicating with the needs, concerns, and desires of society. Director Penn has testified that he had no idea while shooting *Bonnie and Clyde* that he was giving birth to what *Time* would call "the sleeper of the decade."[54]

The chaotic and increasingly divisive American scene in 1967 made it difficult to identify what would please the masses. That year witnessed the culmination of three consecutive "long, hot summers" of urban riots, and the separation between white and black America became more pronounced than ever. The antiwar movement divided the populace into hawks and doves who either supported President Lyndon Johnson and his continual escalations of the war in Vietnam or joined what Norman Mailer called the "armies of the night" and marched for peace. The "generation gap" between young and old became more extended as the youthful counterculture, "the flower children," harkened to Dr. Timothy Leary's admonition to turn on, tune in, and drop out.

That *Bonnie and Clyde* appealed to so many Americans can be attributed to two things. First, the violence offered an emotional catharsis for many, particularly because of its lifelike quality. Surrounded by carnage, barraged nightly on the televised news with the shock and fury of scenes from Newark to Hue, the filmic murder and mayhem presented a means for expunging confused feelings from the psyche. More importantly, counterpoints of humor and the frequent slapstick quality of the movie's violence made the subject more bearable. For others, the violence and its graphic depiction appealed to an unconscious bloodlust. The violence of films in 1967, so shocking that year for some, pales into insignificance when contrasted with what would follow: Sam Peckinpah's *The Wild Bunch* (1969), John Avildsen's *Joe* (1970), and Tom Laughlin's *Billy Jack* (1972). As *Bonnie and Clyde* has been praised for spawning a series of nostalgia films, for example, Sidney Pollack's *They Shoot Horses Don't They* (1969) and Peter Bogdanovich's *The Last Picture Show* (1971), so too must it receive a share of the "credit" for influencing the drift toward violence.

Second, *Bonnie and Clyde* did appeal to the spirit of the age, especially among youth. That zeitgeist can be summed up in the word nihilism. Some, such as Norman Mailer, may opt for existentialism as the dominant mood, but this writer believes that nihilism comes closer to capturing the essence of the period.[55] In the wake of an unending stream of domestic and foreign violence and the disintegration of the expectations raised during the Kennedy years, moral absolutism dissolved into moral relativism. The cultural bond of a shared value system eroded. This was particularly true among the young, many of whom opted for a countercultural existence often built around drugs and/or communal living.

But middle America also was experiencing an undermining of

long-held and cherished traditions.[56] In such a circumstance, as Robert Sklar has stated, "the emotional power of the film's anarchic individualism, its depiction of the awesome force of violent authority . . ." offered something that audiences understood.[57] To use a hackneyed favorite of movie critics, *Bonnie and Clyde* was "compelling." Its affront to traditional sensibilities afforded an opportunity for millions of outraged Americans to expell—vicariously—a welter of conflicting emotions.

Bonnie and Clyde would have been a success in nearly any period because of the quality of its production and the captivating nature of its screenplay. However, coming as it did, when it did, it rocketed to unforeseen heights. The picture, in its own way, addressed the needs, desires, and aspirations of a society replete with ambivalent feelings. It remains something of a "cult" film among the young, principally because those ambivalent feelings have as yet to be reconciled.

NOTES

1. Jim E. Heath, *Decade of Disillusionment: The Kennedy-Johnson Years* (Bloomington: University of Indiana Press, 1975); Andrew Kopkind and James Ridgeway, eds., *Decade of Crisis: America in the 60's* (New York: World Publishing Co., 1972); and William L. O'Neill, *Coming Apart: An Informal History of America in the 1960's* (Chicago: Quadrangle Books, 1971).

2. John Baxter, *Hollywood in the Sixties* (New York: A. S. Barnes, 1972).

3. Statistical data provided by the Motion Picture Association of America and the National Association of Theater Owners. Some of it may also be found in *Historical Statistics of the United States, Colonial Times to 1970.* 2 vols. (Washington, D.C.: Government Printing Office, 1975), I, pp. 400–01.

4. "The Shock of Freedom in Films," *Time*, December 8, 1967, p. 68, and D. Newman and R. Benton, "Lightning in a Bottle," in Sandra Wake and Nichola Hayden, eds., *The Bonnie and Clyde Book* (New York: Simon and Schuster, 1972), p. 13. Unless otherwise noted, all information about the development of the screenplay came from these sources.

5. New York: Random House, 1963.

6. John G. Cawelti, "Introduction: *Bonnie and Clyde:* Tradition and Transformation," in J. G. Cawelti, ed., *Focus on Bonnie and Clyde*, (Englewood Cliffs, N.J.: Prentice Hall, 1973), p. 2.

7. Tom Milne, "*Bonnie and Clyde*," *Sight and Sound* (Autumn, 1967), p. 204.

8. The screenplay was submitted to Truffaut who finally turned them down, but he did pass it along to Godard who was quite interested. Conflict with their producers and the director's haphazard plan to begin shooting immediately led to a collapse in negotiations. A viewing of *Pierrot le Fou* (1966) will

illustrate the influence reading the script for *Bonnie and Clyde* had on Godard.

9. Joseph Gelmis, *The Film Director as Superstar* (Garden City: Doubleday and Co., 1970), p. 223. Penn later claimed to have read the script, but rejected it because "it didn't sound very appetizing. . . ."

10. Curtis Lee Hanson, "Interview With Warren Beatty," *Cinema*, 3 (Summer, 1967), pp. 8–10. In assuming the dual role of producer-actor, Beatty was working on the assumption that "making a movie, no matter how you slice it, is the work of a committee." So far as he was concerned, the auteur theory was "bullshit." Ibid. Benton and Newman vigorously disagreed, and though they worked closely with the director, they ascribed the end result to him. Arthur Penn also subscribed to the auteur theory, while crediting Beatty and his actions for much of the commercial success.

11. Both Beatty and Penn agreed to accept deferred salaries. *Variety*, August 30, 1967. Penn's salary was to be 10 percent after the production grossed 8 million dollars. The eventual gross was 22.7 million dollars and the director's share amounted to 1,470,000 dollars. Only one of his four previous films had been a financial as well as critical success. *Variety*, January 8, 1975 and Gelmis, *Director as Superstar*, pp. 223 and 227.

12. Ibid. and Curtis Lee Hanson, "Interview With Arthur Penn," Cinema, 3 (Summer 1967), p. 12. Penn's fascination with the outlaw can be seen in his previous films, *The Left Handed Gun* (1958), his first picture, and *The Chase* (1966).

13. Ibid.

14. Jim Hiller, "Arthur Penn," *Screen*, 10 (Jan.–Feb., 1969), p. 12, *New York Times*, September 17, 1967, and Stanley Solomon, *Beyond Formula: American Film Genres* (New York: Harcourt, Brace and Jovanovich, 1976), p. 194. A close friend of Beatty's, Robert Towne, also assisted in rewriting parts of the script, though he is given screen credit as a "special consultant." Gelmis, *Director as Superstar*, pp. 223–4. See also Robert Towne, "A Trip With Bonnie and Clyde," *Cinema*, 3 (Summer, 1967), pp. 4–7. His exact contribution is uncertain, though he was called in only when the original writers had exhausted their ideas.

15. New York: Signet Books, 1968. The book was originally published under the title *Fugitives* (Dallas: The Texas Ranger Press, 1934). Ironically, their heirs unsuccessfully sued the filmmakers for what they thought to be libelous and slanderous treatment of their relatives.

16. Austin: University of Texas Press, 1935 and 1965. See also John H. Jenkins and Gordon Frost, *I'm Frank Hamer: The Life of a Texas Peace Officer* (Austin and New York: The Pemberton Press, 1968), one of the many attempts to capitalize on the commercial success of the movie.

17. John Toland, "Sad Ballad of the Real Bonnie and Clyde," *New York Times Magazine*, February 18, 1968, pp. 26–29. Toland's opinion, that "not only were they relatively minor figures in their day; they were in every sense of the word 'punks,' vicious and petty and despised even by their contemporaries in the criminal world," was hardly congenial with the image that Benton and Newman intended to project.

18. "The Shock of Freedom in Films," *Time*, December 8, 1967, p. 68.

19. Ibid., and André Labarthe and Jean-Louis Comolli, "*Bonnie and Clyde*: An Interview with Arthur Penn," *Evergreen Review*, 12 (June, 1968), p. 61. The interview was a translation of what had appeared in *Cahiers du Cinema* (December, 1967).

20. *Variety*, February 3, 1971. The basis of the article was a deposition Penn

had given emphasizing cutting and editing as "a critical part of a director's work" in a suit brought by Elaine May against Paramount Pictures. See also Jacob Atlas, "A Conversation with Arthur Penn," *Rolling Stone*, March 19, 1970, p. 37. Penn had left Hollywood for Broadway for five years after his objections to what Warner Brothers did to *The Left Handed Gun* (1958) in the editing process.

21. A complete screenplay, based on the original script and a comparison against a copy of the dialogue continuity and several viewings of the film, is provided by Wake and Hayden, in *The Bonnie and Clyde Book*, pp. 37–164. Cawelti, in *Focus on Bonnie and Clyde*, includes a script extract, pp. 151–65, a content outline, pp. 148–50, a plot synopsis, pp. 146–47, and, most importantly, an analysis of the changes between the original script and the film, pp. 138–45. Other overviews and evaluations are available in Robin Wood's *Arthur Penn* (New York: Praeger, 1969), pp. 72–91 and in Jim Cook's "*Bonnie and Cldye*," *Screen*, 10 (October, 1969), pp. 101–14.

22. Labarthe and Comolli, "Interview with Arthur Penn," *Evergreen Review*, 61 and Gelmis, *Director as Superstar*, p. 224.

23. J. G. Cawelti, "Changes and Revisions from the Original Script to Film," in J. G. Cawelti, ed., *Focus on Bonnie and Clyde*, pp. 142 and 144.

24. *New York Times*, September 17, 1967.

25. Labarthe and Comolli, "Interview with Arthur Penn," *Evergreen Review*, 63.

26. *Variety*, August 9, 1967.

27. *New York Times*, August 7, 1967.

28. Ibid., August 14, 1967, and *Village Voice*, August 31, 1967.

29. Clippings from *Cue*, n.d., *Montreal Gazette*, n.d., *Esquire*, November, 1967, p. 32 and *Variety*, September 13, 1967. Folder "*Bonnie and Clyde*," Clipping Collection, Museum of Modern Art, New York.

30. *Village Voice*, August 31, 1967.

31. *New York Times*, September 3, 1967. The nature and content of John Toland's "factual" study, "Sad Ballad of the Real Bonnie and Clyde," *New York Times Magazine*, February 9, 1928, pp. 26–29, suggests that it was solicited by Crowther to aid in his defense.

32. Ibid., September 10 and 17, 1967.

33. A. Penn, "*Bonnie and Clyde*: Private Morality and Public Violence," *Take One*, 1 (September, 1967), pp. 20–22.

34. *New York Times*, September 17, 1967. See also *Variety*, August 30, 1967, in which Penn is quoted as saying that he tried for "documentary authenticity" and that there was not a major incident that did not happen. In less heated circumstances some years later, Penn extended his remarks on the matter of historical accuracy, at least in the instance of Clyde Barrow's sexuality, by admitting "I don't know what the history books say. . . ." Gelmis, *Director as Superstar*, pp. 225–26.

35. P. Kael, *Kiss Kiss Bang Bang* (Boston: Little Brown and Co., 1968), p. 50. Originally published in the *New Yorker*, October, 1967. Albert Johnson thought the debate on historical accuracy was a moot one for "the 'legend' of Bonnie and Clyde is exactly what the movie was about." "*Bonnie and Clyde*," *Film Quarterly*, 21 (Winter, 1967–68), p. 47. From a different perspective, Vernon Johnson has chided the critics of violence, noting that "they find truth more unpalatable than fiction." *On Film, Unpopular Essays on a Popular Art* (Chicago: Quadrangle, 1972), p. 190.

36. *Films in Review*, 18 (October, 1967), p. 504.

37. *Newsweek*, August 21 and 28, 1967, pp. 66 and 82. His retraction, "The Thin Red Line," included a short history of violence in the movies for they give us "an historical perspective on violence. . . . In that context *Bonnie and Clyde* was an ideal laboratory for studying violence. . . ."

38. *Life*, October 13, 1967, p. 16. Schickel also would revise his generally negative opinion of the film, describing it as a "breakthrough," "the first of the new cult films for kids and helps establish the now infamous 'youth market.' " R. Schickel, *Second Sight, Notes on Some Movies, 1965–1970.* (New York: Simon and Schuster, 1972), p. 143.

39. Phillip French, "Incitement Against Violence," *Sight and Sound*, 37 (Winter, 1967–68), pp. 2–8.

40. Peter Collier disputed such an assertion: "Whatever else it is, *Bonnie and Clyde* is not a gangster movie. The film genre has seen its day. . . ." P. Collier, "The Barrow Gang: An Aftertaste," *Ramparts*, 6 (May, 1968), p. 18. Collier's position is weakened by his narrow definition of the genre which would be improved by a rereading of "The Gangster as Tragic Hero," by Robert Warshow in *The Immediate Experience* (Garden City: Doubleday and Co., 1962), pp. 127–35.

41. "*Bonnie and Clyde* 'Revives 30's Style,' " Warner Brothers Press Release, n.d., Folder "*Bonnie and Clyde*," M.O.M.A.

42. *Village Voice*, December 21, 1967. Pauline Kael has pointed out that the fashion change was really so much a charade as Faye Dunaway actually had "a sixties look." P. Kael, *Kiss Kiss Bang Bang*, p. 58.

43. *Variety*, September 20, 1967, and *Village Voice*, December 21, 1967. Not all of Europe, however, was taken by *Bonnie and Clyde*; it was banned in Norway because of its "brutality."

44. J. Gallagher and J. Hanc, "Arthur Penn's *Bonnie and Clyde*," n.d., n.s., Folder "*Bonnie and Clyde*," M.O.M.A. A similar opinion was expressed by Stephen Farber, "The Outlaws," *Sight and Sound*, 38 (Autumn, 1968), pp. 26–27.

45. Baxter, *Hollywood in the Sixties*, p. 35.

46. Benton and Newman, "Lightning in a Bottle," in Wake and Hayden, *Bonnie and Clyde Book*, p. 19.

47. O'Neill, *Coming Apart*, p. 217, and Heath, *Decade of Disillusionment*, p. 299.

48. Bernard Weintraub, "Director Arthur Penn Takes on General Custer," *New York Times Magazine*, December 21, 1969, p. 82.

49. Labarthe, and Comolli, "Interview With Arthur Penn," *Evergreen Review*, 63.

50. R. Steele, "The Good-Bad and Bad-Good in Movies," *The Catholic World* (May, 1968), p. 80.

51. J. H. Lawson, "Our Film and Theirs: *Grapes of Wrath* and *Bonnie and Clyde*," *American Dialogue*, 5 (Winter, 1968–69), p. 32.

52. C. T. Samuels, "*Bonnie and Clyde*," *The Hudson Review*, 1 (Spring, 1968), p. 16.

53. "The Shock of Freedom in Films," *Time*, December 8, 1967, p. 67.

54. Ibid., and J. Gelmis, *Director as Superstar*, p. 229.

55. Norman Mailer, "Kennedy—The Existential Hero," *Esquire* (November, 1960), pp. 46–55.

56. *Time*, July 7, 1967, pp. 16–22.

57. Robert Sklar, *Movie-Made America* (New York: Random House, 1975), p. 301. Sklar also believed that the enormous popularity of *Bonnie and Clyde*

"was, among other things, a small victory for the independent judgment of audiences against the guiding advice of mass journalism. . . ." Beatty would dispute that opinion as he has observed that while "establishment" critics did not understand his picture, younger ones did. He admitted that he "disobeyed" tradition and "broke a lot of rules," especially by mixing comedy and violence, but he believed that a new generation of film critics had greeted his work with enthusiasm. Jeffrey Lyons, "Interview with Warren Beatty," W.C.B.S. radio, Aug. 31, 1978.

The Blue Collar Ethnic in Bicentennial America:

Rocky (1976)

DANIEL J. LEAB

Hands bloodied from using a side of beef as a punching bag, Rocky
(Sylvester Stallone) is interviewed by a condescending TV news reporter.
The film's racism is not overtly stated, but it is vividly and visually
implicit.

(Photo courtesy of Museum of Modern Art)

The mood of the American people at the end of 1975 was gloomy. Earlier that year an "America-watcher" of long standing found it "perfectly logical" to assert that "the springs shall become silent, the seas polluted, and the atmosphere heated to a degree destructive of human life as we have found it."[1] Things did not seem to be going well for the United States in the 1970s.

The very foundations of the American Dream had been severely shaken during the first half of the decade: the Watergate crisis had resulted in the resignation of a President of the United States and criminal prosecution of high-ranking federal officials; the armed forces had been defeated in combat by an Asian people; the Arab oil embargo forced recognition that the United States no longer enjoyed unlimited natural resources; the economy floundered between the seemingly irreconcilable forces of increasing unemployment and inflation; a vocal and alien counterculture had challenged successfully various traditional values; "crime-in-the-streets" as well as rioting in the inner city and on campus threatened permanent damage to domestic tranquility; various minority groups through escalating, sometimes violent, demands seemed to have irreparably rent the fabric of American society. So dour, indeed, did everyday American life appear that in 1974 a positive and hopeful assessment of the United States in the 1970s characterized the decade thus far as "the age of the rip-off."[2]

Suddenly, in 1976, with the celebration of the two hundredth anniversary of the Declaration of Independence and the creation of the United States, the nation's mood changed perceptibly. Bicentennial America, almost overnight, put behind it Watergate, Vietnam, stagflation, and many other problems. The media—which for so long had highlighted the negative side of American life—now spoke of "the ongoing resilience of what used to be called The American Dream."[3] Even *U.S. News & World Report*, well known for its weekly prophecies of doom and analyses of the various malaises troubling the United States, now unabashedly declared that "nowhere on earth . . . do the hopes for the future appear more exciting than they do in the U.S., rich in spirit . . . power . . . and people."[4] A German observer of the American scene found that concern over America's problems had given way, at least for the moment, to celebration of the bicentennial.[5]

Rocky is an integral if somewhat unusual part of that bicentennial binge. Set in the white ethnic working-class slums of South Philadelphia, *Rocky* deals with such unappetizing aspects of current life in the United States as organized crime, professional boxing, media exploitation, and the hard-scrabble world of the working-class, blue-collar ethnic. Yet, even though dealing with the underside of contemporary America, *Rocky* is a celebration of the American Dream. Movie critic Frank Rich perceptively analyzed the film's wide appeal when he described *Rocky* as a "fairy tale" that "tapped the popular spirit of the present: . . . the old-fashioned, Bi-Centennial vision of America."[6]

At first glance the film's eponymous protagonist seems an unusual hero for bicentennial America. Rocky Balboa (Sylvester Stallone)—self-styled "The Italian Stallion"—is a dim-witted, fourth-rate, thirty-year-old club fighter of no particular distinction, except perhaps for the fact (of which he proudly boasts) that in ten years of fighting his nose has never been broken. Professional boxing has netted him nothing. He earns his keep working as a muscle man for Gazzo, a loan shark. Rocky's life is bleak. He seems to have no future. He lives alone, in squalor. Drunks, bums, and seedy layabouts line the streets of his rundown Philadelphia neighborhood. His friends and acquaintances are corrupt, moronic, or venal. Avuncular advice to a young teenage girl about "hanging out" at night "with them coconuts on the corner [older boys]" earns Rocky a derisive "Screw you, Creepo!!!"[7]

Whatever the drawbacks of Rocky's world, the film makes clear —in that peculiar cinematic shorthand so well understood by movie audiences all over the world—that although he may be a bum, he is a bum with heart. Rocky (to use one reviewer's exaggerated but apt words) is presented as "an innocent . . . an earth child from the streets of a slum."[8] He likes animals: his confidantes are two pet turtles named Cuff and Link. He cares about people: on a cold night he takes a drunkard out of the gutter and carries him into the corner saloon. He is not mean: even though ordered to break the thumb of one of Gazzo's clients, Rocky refrains from so doing.

Happenstance lifts Rocky out of his nether world. A bicentennial world heavyweight championship match has been scheduled for Philadelphia. A few weeks before the match, the contender is injured and the champion, Apollo Creed (Carl Weathers playing a nasty caricature of Muhammad Ali), decides that rather than scrap the intricate and profitable arrangements that already have been made, he will fight a "local boy." Creed chooses Rocky, in part because Rocky seems easily beatable, and in part because the champion believes that the "Italian Stallion" nickname should make good media copy and help maintain interest in the fight. A surprised Rocky is offered 150,000 dollars and a chance at the title. He accepts and trains to win. On the eve of the fight Rocky recognizes that he has been deceiving himself, but he resolves to prove his worth nevertheless by going the distance with Creed. And in a bruising, gritty, fifteen-round brawl Rocky does just that—even managing to knock down the champion several times. The decision goes to Creed, but Rocky has won personally, having proven that he is not "just another bum from the neighborhood."

As important as the title match for Rocky's growth in self-esteem is his romantic involvement with Adrian (Talia Shire), his friend Paulie's (Burt Young) painfully shy spinster sister. Adrian works in the pet shop that Rocky frequents. However, their first date comes about at the instigation of Paulie, who virtually orders Rocky to ask out Adrian and forces her to accept. Initially she appears on screen as an unattractive, mousey, withdrawn drudge who forlornly lives with and looks after her brother. But then Rocky takes her out, takes down her hair, takes off her glasses, and takes her to bed. As their romance blossoms she becomes a new person in the best traditions of Hollywood's Golden Age. And by the end of the film she has become a graceful, attractive, spirited young woman. After an argument with Paulie about his attempts to use Rocky, she moves out of her brother's home and in with the fighter. This concession to modern mores notwithstanding, the relationship between Rocky and Adrian is presented as sentimental and uplifting. In an age of sexually blatant movies, *Rocky*'s love scenes are discreet: the sexual overtones are there, but only romance is made explicit; nudity and copulation are left to the audience's imagination.

Rocky's story is essentially the work of Sylvester Stallone. He began writing it in the early spring of 1975. He was in his late twenties and after six years of brash effort seemed to have failed as an actor. His one big part had been in *The Lords of Flatbush*, a 1974 artistic success/commercial flop. The majority of his roles had been small and/or forgettable in movies like *The Prisoner of Second*

Avenue (1975), *Capone* (1975), and *Death Race 2000* (1975). He also had tried writing movie and television scripts but won little recognition—the major exception being a credit he earned for "additional dialogue" on *The Lords of Flatbush*.[9]

Stallone got the idea for *Rocky* after watching the March, 1975, title bout between Muhammed Ali and Chuck Wepner for the heavyweight championship. Wepner, "a guy on the skids" known as "the Bayonne Bleeder," not only managed to knock Ali down, but also (unlike most of the champion's previous opponents) almost went the distance—the fight being stopped nineteen seconds from the end of the fifteenth and final round.[10] Stallone and Gene Kirkwood, a "fledgling producer" (to use *Newsweek*'s description) had been discussing various movie possibilities before the Ali-Wepner match.[11] Inspired by the fight, Stallone in three and a half days of almost nonstop effort drafted the screenplay that became *Rocky*. An interesting sidelight to current moviemaking is Stallone's comment that this "script was about 122 pages long and went to more than 330 or 340 pages of revisions and we barely altered it from the original concept."[12] Kirkwood interested the independent producing team of Robert Chartoff and Irwin Winkler in Stallone's script. They in turn offered it to United Artists, who ultimately agreed to undertake the production. Shooting began in December, 1975.

Stallone was determined to play Rocky. The producers recognized the quality of the script but wanted a name star for the title role. They offered Stallone well over $100,000 to sell the script and "to bow out."[13] He refused, even though, as Kirkwood recalls, Stallone was "hard up for bucks": he had a bank balance of $106, a pregnant wife, and few other forseeable prospects.[14] Stallone later recalled telling his wife "if you don't mind going out in the backyard and eating grass, I'd rather burn this script than sell it to another actor."[15] She agreed, but the need to eat grass never arose. Stallone played Rocky. He won critical acclaim as well as Oscar nominations for his script *and* his performance—placing him in very select company, as only Orson Welles and Charlie Chaplin had received these dual nominations before.

Stallone made good media copy, and understandably he received far more publicity than anyone else connected with the film. However, as critic James Monaco pointed out, "while *Rocky* has been advertised as the protean conception of its star-writer, director

John Avildsen's contributions are essential to its success and should not be overlooked."[16] Avildsen has a flair for the kind of working-class milieu portrayed in *Rocky*. Indeed, he first came to prominence in 1970 as director and photographer of *Joe*, whose central character was also lower class—albeit very different from the good-natured Rocky. Joe was a foul-mouthed, beer-drinking, hippie-hating factory worker, who joined with an upper-middle-class "friend" to murder some Greenwich Village "drop outs." The film's phenomenal box-office success stemmed in part from Avildsen's ability to present Joe so realistically and dramatically that there were "recorded incidents of kids shouting 'We'll get you, Joe!' at the screen."[17] *Joe*'s success enabled Avildsen to escape making exploitation pictures such as *Turn On to Love*, and in the next few years he directed a variety of films, including the 1973 Paramount release *Save the Tiger*, whose star, Jack Lemmon, won the Oscar for Best Actor.[18]

Avildsen, noted for his economy and speed, shot *Rocky* in twenty-eight days (two under schedule) and did not overspend his budget. Critical response to Avildsen's direction of *Rocky* varied considerably. Pauline Kael found his approach to be "strictly-from-hunger."[19] Andrew Sarris asserted that Avildsen provided "no glow, no aura for his hero."[20] *Newsweek*'s Janet Maslin, on the other hand, maintained that the film had been "crisply directed."[21] In *Time*, Richard Schickel argued that in *Rocky* the director showed a "stronger naturalistic gift than in *Joe* or *Save the Tiger*."[22]

Certainly the film benefited from Avildsen's ability to capture the gritty atmosphere of South Philadelphia's garbage-strewn, joyless streets and seedy, worn, row houses. English critic Tom Milne waxed rhapsodic over Avildsen's ability to film the "extraordinary nocturnal landscapes of strangely dislocated urban geometry . . . in which the human figures seem both estranged and yet as much a natural part of the scene as the tenuously impermanent structures themselves." Milne argued that Avildsen and his cameraman had turned the Philadelphia exteriors "into something very close to a series of Magritte paintings."[23] Amidst all the justified praise for Stallone, it should be remembered that Avildsen won an Academy Award for his direction of *Rocky*.

Both the much-publicized genesis of the film and Stallone's insistence on playing Rocky had Horatio Alger overtones that appealed to bicentennial America. But the production of the film reflects no sentiment, only the hard-headed economic realities of the American movie industry in the 1970s. Chartoff and Winkler are not producers in the traditional sense; they are "packagers" and as such part of what the film journalist Axel Madsen has dubbed "the New Hollywood." They do not work with any one studio. They put packages together and then look to the studios for financing. As Chartoff has explained: "We go to Warner's and say 'Look, we have such and such a project that so and so is interested in . . . ; the whole thing can be made for so and so much money. . . .'" If Warner's is not interested, "United Artists, Columbia, or any of the other majors then look at it and say yes or no, sometimes no . . . or yes, if we can bring it down to such a figure."[24] Chartoff, a theatrical lawyer, and Winkler, a television agent, met "by accident," became one of the first independent producing teams in Hollywood in the mid-1960s, and prior to *Rocky* had produced eighteen movies, including such interesting ones as *Point Blank* (released by MGM in 1967) and such clinkers as the Charles Bronson melodrama *Breakout* (distributed by Columbia in 1975).[25]

After *Rocky* had proved itself, the head of West Coast production for United Artists gloated over "the excitement" provoked both by the film and by Stallone.[26] But when Chartoff and Winkler initially sought approval from United Artists to meet Stallone's demand that he himself play Rocky, the company set some hard conditions. The film's budget was cut almost in half to one million dollars; Stallone was to be paid a minimal salary of twenty thousand dollars (albeit also a percentage of the possible profits); Chartoff and Winkler had to guarantee to make up any budget overruns. Just before the film was released, Winkler told an interviewer "everyone sacrificed for potential profits. We hope it pays off—we think it will. . . ."[27]

And it did, probably far beyond his expectations. Financially the film turned out to be a bonanza, "one of the biggest movie winners of all time," according to *Newsweek*.[28] Its one-million-dollar budget was very modest in terms of 1975–76 feature film production, "peanuts in today's movie world," to use critic David Sterritt's clichéd but apt description.[29] By the end of April, 1977—five months after the film had been released—*Rocky* had grossed over fifty million dollars in the United States and Canada. And in August, 1977, *Variety* estimated that thus far *Rocky* had grossed over one hundred million dollars in the United States and Canada, and that the film still had considerable earning potential in those markets.[30] *Rocky* had proved to be one of the highest grossing films ever made, on a par in terms of impact and drawing power with films like *Gone With the Wind* (1939), *The Sound of Music* (1965), and *Jaws* (1975).

Critically, *Rocky* also scored a major triumph—albeit one less overwhelming than its box-office success. Film reviewers used words like "schmaltz" and "cliché" in discussing *Rocky*, and there was criticism of some aspects of the film in most reviews, but overall, few reviewers failed to respond positively to it.[31] Even the tough-minded and unsentimental Pauline Kael found much to praise in *Rocky*, and although alert to its shortcomings she described the film as "engaging" and "emotionally effective."[32] Vincent Canby of the *New York Times* was a notable exception to the generally favorable critical response; he found the film lacking in verve, seemingly fraudulent, and he thought it "never quite measured up."[33] But his comments had little effect. Rocky won a wide variety of awards, including ten Oscar nominations and three Academy Awards (Best Director, Best Picture, and Best Editing).[34]

To what can one attribute *Rocky*'s extraordinary commercial success and generally favorable critical reception? An extensive, hard-hitting, intelligent publicity campaign played a significant role. A seemingly untiring Stallone, for example, made himself available for interview after interview by representatives from every branch of the media.[35] Indeed, so ubiquitous was Stallone that one commentator claimed that Rocky's creator "has granted more interviews in recent months than any American short of Lillian Carter."[36] The *Variety* review of *Rocky*, written almost a month before the film went into release, noted that "the p.r. juggernaut is already at high speed."[37] And Vincent Canby in his *New York Times* review expressed uneasiness and displeasure at "the sort of highpowered publicity . . . that's been attending the birth of *Rocky*. . . ."[38] The extent of this high-powered publicity campaign is emphasized by the many echoes of Canby's attitude among reviewers. A trade journalist examining the selling of the film found that "whether rave, pan, or . . . 'no opinion,' review after review of *Rocky* tore into the crescendo of advance comment. . . ."[39]

Hype alone, however, cannot account for the wildly enthusiastic response that many movie audiences afforded the film. They cheered Rocky, booed Creed, and at the end of the film, with tears in their eyes, applauded the credits. Critic Roger Greenspun reported that "the two times I saw *Rocky* people in the audience stood up and cheered at the end."[40] Another reviewer detailed the reactions of an "Italian friend" at a screening of the film: "when the 'Italian Stallion' landed a savage right hook on the . . . chin of Apollo Creed . . . , my friend let out a 'Whoop' as if he had a week's salary riding on the punch."[41] Frank Rich expressed amazement at the number of usually blasé New York City moviegoers who after seeing *Rocky* left "the theater beaming and boisterous, as if they won a door prize rather than parted with the price of a first-run movie ticket, and they volunteer ecstatic opinions of the film to the people waiting on line for the next show."[42]

Viewing *Rocky* was an emotion-charged experience for many American moviegoers. The film touched "a live nerve with the public," as Frank Rich put it.[43] American audiences, influenced by the bicentennial's strong emphasis on the validity of the American Dream, had lost interest in downbeat themes, in bleak reality, in attacks on old-fashioned values—all subjects which as films of one sort or another had recently done well at the box office. Stallone rather perceptively touched on the changing interests of moviegoers in one of his many interviews: "I believe the country as a whole is beginning to break out of this . . . antieverything syndrome . . . this nihilistic, Hemingwayistic attitude that everything in the end must wither and die. . . ."[44]

In discussing *Rocky*'s appeal (as well as its positive outlook) reviewers and other commentators referred over and over again to the optimistic, idealistic, sentimental, 1930s movies of director Frank Capra. Even Avildsen announced that he was fond of the comparison: "Capra's my idol. I love the emotionalism and idealism in what he was doing. . . ."[45] Capra himself said about *Rocky*: "Boy, that's a picture I wish I had made."[46] But "Capra-corn" as evidenced by such films as *Mr. Deeds Goes to Town* (1936) or *Mr. Smith Goes to Washington* (1939) will not and should not serve as points of reference for *Rocky*. In the Capra productions, as film historian Richard Griffith has astutely pointed out, "a messianic innocent, not unlike the classic simpleton of literature . . . pits himself against the forces of entrenched greed . . . his gallant integrity in the face of temptation calls forth the good will of the 'little people' and through combined protest, he triumphs."[47] Rocky may be an innocent, but he is not messianic, and the "little people" he associates with are not the middle class on which Capra dotes. It is not surprising that Capra, when discussing his films at an AFI seminar in 1971, declared that Ralph Nader "would make a perfect Capra hero."[48] And Rocky certainly is not a Nader type.

Just as *Rocky* owed little to the Capra films, so too did it owe little to previous Hollywood treatments of boxing. These in the main had concentrated on exposing the ills of "the fight game." But *Rocky* had none of the bleak cynicism of *Champion* (1949), the oppressive social consciousness of *Golden Boy* (1939), the vicious corruption of *The Harder They Fall* (1956), or the sleazy hopelessness of *The Set-Up* (1949). However, *Rocky* does not exist in a vacuum. It does owe something to the ingratiating style of *Somebody Up There Likes Me*, the enthusiastic 1956 screen biography of one-time middleweight champion Rocky Graziano. And *Rocky*'s love story obviously owes something to *Marty*, the poignant 1955 film about two lonely people who expect never to find love, but come together. In one respect, however, *Rocky* is almost unique, and that is its working-class perspective.

As James Monaco has pointed out, "the intellectual, middle class establishment has always felt quite comfortable with films whose *subjects* were workers. . . ."[49] But *Rocky* is not presented from a middle-class point of view; the film speaks for the working class, albeit as columnist Pete Hamill acidly commented: "nobody calls it the working class any more . . . ; the bureaucratic, sociological phrase is white lower-middle class," sometimes referred to as "the ethnics."[50] *Rocky* obviously was palatable to the American middle class, but its success rests on the film's appeal to the white ethnic American (once succinctly described by a magazine writer as "perhaps the most alienated person" in the United States).[51] *Rocky* endorsed the ethnic's prejudices, deferred to his fantasies, and highlighted his life style.

The film's treatment of blacks accords with the racial attitudes that, in the view of many social scientists, govern the thinking of the white ethnic American. Their conventional wisdom holds that these white ethnics believe that they have "paid the costs" of

American society's attempts to redress black grievances, that "the poorest, least secure, least educated, and least tolerant" in the white community believe they have been sacrificed by a liberal elite anxious to insure "responsible social change."[52] And, it is argued, the ethnics bitterly resent this attempt at change. Thus, a sociologist surveying the attitudes of a group of blue-collar workers about contemporary America in the early 1970s argues that except for the Vietnam war "the most explosive issue was the demand for black equality." And in this context he quotes as representative a carpenter who angrily declared, "I realize that something has to be done for the black bastards, but I sure as hell don't want them living next to me. I don't care to work with them either."[53]

Rocky plays on these old prejudices and new fears. The film's racism is not overtly stated, but if not explicit, it is still vividly (and visually) implicit. At one point in the film Rocky is shown training in the meat-packing plant where Paulie works. He is training for the fight with Creed by using a carcass of beef as a punching bag, hitting the carcass until his hands are blood red from the juice of the meat. A local television station has sent a crew to film this unusual method of training. The reporter is an arrogantly glib, fashionably dressed, light-skinned black woman, who oozes condescension and contempt during her dealings with Rocky (and Paulie). In many ways she is an unpleasant burlesque of the female reporters found on television newscasts across the country. One can, of course, attribute her presence in the film to a hostility to television news programming or to the women's liberation movement. But one must also ask why a black woman, why that particular kind of arrogant black woman, who patronizes Rocky and Paulie. Here we must remember the words of a literary critic in dealing with another movie genre: "everything in a film is there because somebody wanted it there, although it is often hard to know why or even who that somebody was."[54]

That "somebody" must also claim credit for the nasty, smarmy depiction of Apollo Creed. In public Creed acts the clown, satirizing traditional American values. He enters the arena for his fight with Rocky to the tune of "Yankee Doodle Dandy," and he prances around the ring in an elaborate Uncle Sam costume before stripping to star-spangled trunks. If publicly Creed mocks the bicentennial, privately he expresses contempt for the American Dream and views public belief in it as one more means of making money. Explaining his choice of Rocky as a substitute for the injured challenger, a mocking Creed says "I'm sentimental, and lots of people in this country are just as sentimental." The articulate, well-groomed, business-minded Creed stands in obvious contrast to Rocky—so much so that as Andrew Sarris points out, the "Italian Stallion" becomes "the most romanticized Great White Hope in screen history."[55] Nor, despite over a decade of black heavyweight champions, should the White Hope feeling be ignored. Ali, for example, in his autobiography touches on "the racial issue" in boxing and asks "who put it there and who keeps it there." His answer is given by a veteran reporter who tells him, "they want your ass whipped in public, knocked down, ripped, stomped, clubbed, pulverized, and not just by anybody, but by a real Great White Hope."[56]

The makers of *Rocky* had a feel for ethnic America. Somber authenticity marks the film's settings indoors and out. The home of Paulie and Adrian, for example, is in a row house with a tiny front yard in a decayed inner-city neighborhood. The furniture is neat but worn, the rooms are small, the lamps are chintzy, the living room is dominated by an old television set. The outdoor Christmas decorations, or lack of them, on various houses are just right for South Philadelphia, or Hamtramck, or Corona, or any one of a hundred ethnic neighborhoods.

Paulie is presented as "pathetically brutish" (to use Judith Crist's apt phrase).[57] A picture of him in uniform on the mantel hints at his only and temporary escape from the neighborhood. Paulie desperately wants to get away from the meat-packing plant and almost pleadingly asks Rocky for an introduction to Gazzo the loan shark. Paulie feels he could certainly do as good a job for Gazzo as Rocky. Michael Novak has commented that one of the reasons for "the new ethnicity" is the "suppressed anger" of the white lower middle-class.[58] In a remarkable scene Paulie lets loose that anger, and stalking around his home strikes out wildly, viciously, forcefully with a baseball bat. He smashes doors, furniture, walls, as he rants against the dead-endedness of his life. Paulie, in Stallone's words, is "a symbol of the blue collar, disenfranchised, left-out mentality, a man who feels life has given him an unfair amount of cheap shots. . . ."[59]

But in the final analysis neither racism nor reality brought people to the box office in such large numbers. *Rocky* succeeded because of its mythic qualities which neatly dovetailed with the imagery that had been sold by the bicentennial. The sociologist Andrew Greeley has argued that "ethnicity has become almost fashionable."[60] But it was not that fashion which sold *Rocky*. The movie, as Frank Rich said, "can hold its own with Cinderella," as it sets forth that a bum can become a real contender overnight, that riches can come from nowhere, that hard work and the will to make good can still succeed in the United States, that "a shy and unattractive heroine can blossom into a worldly beauty by getting contact lenses and losing her virginity," and that happy endings still exist.[61] And it is to such myths that *Rocky*'s audiences responded so enthusiastically.

Historian William Hughes contends that the feature film does not just "reveal popular attitudes," but "like other forms of cultural expression, can reveal more than they intend."[62] *Rocky* is an excellent manifestation of this "covert-overt" approach to looking at feature films. On the surface it is a "fairy tale," and quite an ingratiating one at that. But *Rocky* also provides strong clues to the public mood in the United States in the mid-1970s. *Rocky* could do this because as a French commentator on American film points out, "the freedom of the Hollywood director is not measured by what he can openly do within the . . . system, but rather by what he can imply about American society in general. . . ."[63] John Avildsen wove Stallone's story into a richly textured film, shot through with social implications, reactionary as some of them may be.

The film itself and the public's response to it speak volumes about how Americans saw themselves in 1976. *Rocky* captured the mood of bicentennial America, a mood which saw the reaffirmation of many traditional values, including racial prejudices that seemed rejuvenated by the economic and social pressures of the 1970s. *Rocky* also highlighted America's changing attitude toward the white lower middle class and toward ethnic blue-collar America. Stallone hit at the core of the matter in his comments on audience response to the film: "when they're cheering for Rocky, they're cheering for themselves."[64]

NOTES

1. Gerald W. Johnson, *America Watching: Perspectives in the Course of an Incredible Century* (Owings Mills, Maryland: Stemmer House Publishers, 1976), p. 326.

2. Tad Szulc, *Innocents At Home: America in the 1970s* (New York: The Viking Press, 1974), p. 43. For a perceptive overview of contemporary America by a foreigner, see Robert Hargreaves, *Super Power: A Portrait of America in the 70s* (New York: St. Martin's Press, 1973).

3. "Our America," *Newsweek*, 4 July 1976, p. 32.

4. "As the Nation Turns 200 . . . ," *U.S. News & World Report*, 3 July 1976, p. 11.

5. Christian Hacke, "Rückblick auf 200 Jahre: Wege und Probleme der Weltmacht USA," *Das Parlament*, 7 August 1976, p. 1.

6. Frank Rich, "*Rocky* Hits a Nerve," *The New York Post*, 4 December 1976, p. 44.

7. Sylvester Stallone, *The Official Rocky Scrapbook* (New York: Grossett & Dunlap, 1977), p. 41; in addition to this scene there are several other excerpts from the screenplay in the *Scrapbook*.

8. Katie Kelly, "In this corner, a stunning *Rocky*," *The East Side Express*, 25 November 1976, p. 11.

9. Stallone, pp. 9–21, passim; Judy Klemesrud, " '*Rocky* Isn't Based on Me,' Says Stallone, 'But We Both Went the Distance,' " *The New York Times*, 28 November 1976, sec. 2, pp. 17, 48.

10. Joseph Valerio, "The Real *Rocky*," *The New York Post*, 29 January 1977, p. 23. In forty-seven previous fights, less than one-third of Ali's opponents had managed to last until the final round (Muhammad Ali with Richard Durham, *The Greatest: My Own Story* [New York: Random House, 1975], pp. 12–13). Gil Clancy, a trainer, felt that the film "wasn't too realistic" because, unlike Rocky, Wepner was not "a complete bum." At the time of the Ali fight Wepner according to Clancy "was ranked eighth in the world. . . ." (*Chelsea Clinton News*, 3 March 1977, p. 5).

11. "KO's Hollywood," *Newsweek*, 18 April 1977, p. 78.

12. Stallone, p. 32.

13. "KO's Hollywood," p. 78.

14. Louise Farr, "*Rocky*: It Could Be a Contender," *New York*, 18 October 1976, p. 72.

15. "Italian Stallion," *Time*, 15 November 1976, p. 44.

16. James Monaco, "The New Hoke," *Take One*, January, 1977, p. 36.

17. Gary Arnold, "*Joe*," in *Film 70/71*, ed., David Denby, (New York: Simon and Schuster, 1971), p. 43.

18. For background on Avildsen's career see *Focus on Film*, Spring, 1977, p. 58, Autumn, 1977, p. 17.

19. Pauline Kael, "The Current Cinema," *The New Yorker*, 29 November 1976, p. 154.

20. Andrew Sarris, "Takes," *The Village Voice*, 22 November 1976, p. 61.

21. Janet Maslin, "Knockout," *Newsweek*, 29 November 1976, p. 33.

22. Richard Schickel, "The Contender," *Time*, 13 December 1976, p. 97.

23. Tom Milne, "*Rocky*," *Monthly Film Bulletin*, April, 1977, p. 78.

24. Axel Madsen, *The New Hollywood: American Movies in the 70's* (New York: Thomas Y. Crowell, 1975), pp. 133, 135. See also, for a more favorable

assessment, Robert Lindsey, "The New Tycoons of Hollywood," *New York Times Magazine*, 7 August 1977, pp. 12–23.

25. "Dialogue On Film: Chartoff and Winkler," *American Film*, December–January, 1977, pp. 37–52, passim.

26. "Italian Stallion."

27. Farr, p. 72.

28. "KO's Hollywood," p. 71.

29. David Sterritt, *"Rocky*—once in a blue moon movie," *The Christian Science Monitor*, 22 November 1976, p. 27.

30. *Variety*, 27 April 1977, p. 12, 17 August 1977, p. 16. *Rocky* also did very well elsewhere in the world. By the beginning of August, 1977, it had grossed over twenty-four million dollars in thirty-one countries.

31. An index to the major reviews as well as substantial excerpts from them is to be found in *Film Review Digest*, 2 (Spring, Summer, 1977): 310–313, 422. See also Kathleen Carroll, "A Real Contender," *The New York Daily News*, 22 November 1976, p. 24; Lita Eliscu, *The SoHo Weekly News*, 18 November 1976, p. 32; Schickel, pp. 96–97.

32. Kael, pp. 154, 157.

33. Vincent Canby, *"Rocky*: Pure 30s Make Believe," *The New York Times*, 22 November 1976, p. 19.

34. Among the other awards garnered by *Rocky* was the selection both by the National Board of Review and the New York Film Critics Circle of Talia Shire as Best Supporting Actress of the Year for her depiction of Adrian (*Films in Review*, February, 1977, p. 65; *The New York Times*, 4 January 1977, p. 18).

35. These interviews were not just for U.S. consumption. I was a Fulbright lecturer at the University of Cologne just before *Rocky* opened in West Germany. And my first viewing of any part of the film came via German television which carried a voiceover translation interview with Stallone (filmed by a German TV crew in Hollywood) and dubbed scenes from the film.

36. Rich, p. 22.

37. "Rocky," *Variety*, p. 20.

38. Canby.

39. Stuart Byron, "Rocky and His Friends," *Film Comment*, 13 (January–February, 1977): 36.

40. Quoted in *"Rocky,"* (*UA/16 Images*, September–October, 1977, p. 2.

41. Bob Rosen, "Underdog's Uppercut," *The Villager*, 25 November 1976, p. 10.

42. Rich, p. 42.

43. Ibid.

44. David Sterritt, "The man behind *Rocky*," *The Christian Science Monitor*, 13 January 1977, p. 12. Stallone's perceptions were not always that acute, and sometimes they were downright foolish. Commenting on his three-and-a-half-day stint in drafting a script, Stallone said: "I'm astounded by people who take 18 years to write something. That's how long it took that guy to write *Madame Bovary*. And was that ever on a best seller list? No. It was a lousy book and it made a lousy movie." (Guy Flatley, "At the movies," *The New York Times*, 24 September 1976, sec. 2, p. 6).

45. Jerry Oster, *"Rocky* road to a long limbo," *New York Daily News*, 4 January 1977, p. 39.

46. "KO's Hollywood," p. 71.

47. Richard Griffith, *Frank Capra*, New Index Series, no. 3 (London: British Film Institute, c. 1950), p. 5.

48. "Frank Capra: 'One Man—One Film,'" *Discussion*, No. 3 (Washington, D.C.: American Film Institute, 1971), p. 18. See also Frank Capra, *The Name Above the Title: An Autobiography* (New York: Macmillan, 1971) and Leland A. Pogue, *The Cinema of Frank Capra* (London: The Tantivy Press, 1975), which has a good bibliography.

49. Monaco, p. 32.

50. Pete Hamill, "The Revolt of the White Lower-Middle Class," in *The White Majority: Between Poverty and Affluence*, ed. Louise Kapp Howe (New York: Random House, 1970), p. 11.

51. Peter Schrag, "The Forgotten American," *Harper's Magazine*, August, 1969, p. 27.

52. Richard F. Hamilton, "Black Demands, White Racism, and Liberal Alarms," in *Blue Collar Workers: A Symposium on Middle America*, ed. Sar A. Levitan (New York: McGraw Hill, 1971), p. 130.

53. E. E. LeMasters, *Blue Collar Aristocrats: Life Styles at a Working Class Tavern* (Madison: University of Wisconsin Press, 1975), p. 187. A sensitive and perceptive as well as angry view of how Italian-Americans have and are faring in the United States is Richard Gambino, *Blood of My Blood: The Dilemma of the Italian-Americans* (Garden City, New York: Doubleday, 1974).

54. Jack Shadoian, *Dreams and Dead Ends: The American Gangster/Crime Film* (Cambridge: The MIT Press, 1977), p. xi.

55. Sarris.

56. Ali, pp. 299, 307.

57. Judith Crist, "Rocky," *Saturday Review*, 27 November 1977, p. 41.

58. Michael Novak, *Further Reflections on Ethnicity* (Middletown, Pennsylvania: Jednota Press, 1977), p. 82.

59. Stallone, p. 26. For a many-faceted overview of "The World of the Blue Collar Worker" see the special issue of *Dissent*, Winter, 1972.

60. Andrew M. Greeley, *Why Can't They Be Like Us? America's White Ethnic Groups* (New York: E. P. Dutton, 1975), p. 15. Father Greeley believes that "ethnicity may not be 'in' exactly, but it's not as 'out' as it used to be."

61. Rich, p. 44.

62. William Hughes, "The evaluation of film as evidence," in *The Historian and Film*, ed. Paul Smith (Cambridge, London, New York: Cambridge University Press, 1976), p. 71. See also Marc Ferro, *Analyse de film, analyse de sociétés: une source nouvelle pour l'histoire* (Paris: Classiques Hachette, 1975), and Michal Bruun Andersen, *et al.*, *Film Analyser: Historien i filmen* (Copenhagen: Røde Hane, 1974).

63. Jean-Loup Bourget, "Social Implications in the Hollywood Genres," *Journal of Modern Literature*, 3 (April, 1977): 200.

64. Sterritt, "The man behind *Rocky*."

Fragments of War:
Platoon (1986)

LAWRENCE W. LICHTY
AND
RAYMOND L. CARROLL

The gritty realism of *Platoon* is evident in the faces of its protagonists: rear l to r: Charlie Sheen, Tom Berenger, and Willem Dafoe; front l to r: Francesco Quinn and Kevin Dillon. (Photo courtesy Museum of Modern Art/ Film Stills Archive)

As Lawrence Suid has noted earlier in this volume, the Hollywood image of war, at least of Americans in battle, was nearly always very positive. Many of those films begin with the training of a single unit—very rigorous but, as is demonstrated at the end of the film, necessary and life saving—and follow it into battle. American troops were heroic; the enemy fanatical. Our men were reluctant soldiers more interested in the girl back home, their families, and baseball than they were in international politics. A number of early films about the war in Vietnam fit that pattern.

There was a tremendous increase in the number of war films—most about combat—just after the United States entered World War II and again during the war in Korea. But there was no similar spurt of war film production from 1963 as more and more American troops served, and died, in Southeast Asia.[1]

There have been few major theatrical films that dealt with the American fighting man in Vietnam. This void was, in part, responsible for the tremendous reception of Oliver Stone's *Platoon*. No earlier Vietnam feature film was so narrowly focused on the plight of the "grunt." That point is clearly made by a brief review of three previous films that deal primarily with men fighting in Vietnam, each of which detour to propaganda, silliness, and a dark personal muddle. The first after the big buildup of American troops was a John Wayne depiction that was more a Western than a film about the war Americans were watching each night on TV news.

In August, 1965, just after President Johnson promised to provide General Westmoreland with the troops he needed to fight the war, Art Buchwald observed: "Every war deserves a war movie and the Vietnamese War is no exception. . . . We have a part for John Wayne, as the tough paratrooper colonel." But Buchwald quotes a fictitious studio head to explain that there are other troubles:

"No one knows how to tell the South Vietnamese from the Viet Cong. They all look alike."

"Our research indicates the Viet Cong are always smiling and looking friendly."

"The Defense Department is against it. They say they don't want to show American soldiers attacking a South Vietnamese village because the Americans are in South Vietnam to protect the villages and not to attack them. We had a great scene when the paratroopers couldn't find any Viet Cong, so they burned every straw hut to the ground."

The studio, as parodied by Buchwald, wants to have Frank Sinatra show the Communists that they will be kicked out of South Vietnam by explaining to his Vietnamese girlfriend why we are there. But the Defense Department says GIs aren't supposed to fraternize with Vietnamese women. And so Buchwald has his studio head conclude:

> "Defense said if they have to fight a different kind of war we should be willing to make a different kind of war picture."[2]

Between 1965 and 1975—from the landing of American combat troops to the final withdrawal of Americans from Saigon—the only major American film about combat in Vietnam was John Wayne's *The Green Berets* (1968). It was argued that the Pentagon would not cooperate and that the studios were afraid that protests about the war had made the subject "boxoffice poison."[3]

But almost as Buchwald predicted, John Wayne did write President Johnson in late 1965 suggesting a movie based on the Robin Moore book published earlier that year. The book related stories of the Special Forces, but the movie is more like a typical Western. James Lee Barrett, the screen writer, said that "the film makes wide departures from the book—but stops short of going on a propaganda foray."[4] Most viewers would probably not agree. A subplot with a reporter was introduced into the movie to make the political points Wayne wanted. At the beginning of the film the newspaperman (David Janssen) asks, "Why is the United States waging this ruthless war?" Sergeant Muldoon (Aldo Ray) argues the case, shows captured Chinese Communist weapons, and explains that most of the press doesn't give any of the arguments *for* the war. By the end of the film the reporter, who went to see for himself, has changed, and is fighting side by side with the troops. But he argues that if he did write how he feels now, he would be out of a job. The film's producer, and star's son, Michael Wayne observed:

> I'm not making a picture about Vietnam, I'm making a picture about good against bad. I happened to think that that's true about Vietnam but even it isn't as clear as all that. That's what you have to do to make a picture. It's all right, because we're in the business of selling tickets.[5]

The critics were harsh, calling it "cliché ridden," "dull," "stupid," "rotten and false in every detail," "foolish," "vile and insane," "absurd and blundering," and so on. But it sold tickets. British journalist John Pilger said it was "so unwittingly silly that it was funny."[6] That is surely true if one expects a film to approach a truthful representation of the way a war is fought, or the issues involved. Yet Pilger also noted that when he saw the movie in the summer of 1968, at a theater in the South, many in the audience cheered.

The world premiere was June 19, 1968—after the Tet offensive, Lyndon Johnson's declaration that he would not run again, and the beginning of peace talks in Paris. In March 1968 a majority of Americans thought it had been a mistake to send troops to Vietnam and 56 percent agreed with the statement that the best thing would be to "stop the bombing and the fighting and gradually withdraw from Vietnam." As more Americans were killed, and there seemed to be no progress in spite of the statements of optimistic officials, support for the war had declined steadily since Wayne's letter to President Johnson in December 1965.[7]

The film cost six million dollars, according to Warner Brothers (7.7 million dollars according to Michael Wayne); with distributions and other costs it added up to more than ten million. By the end of 1968 Warner Brothers said it had earned nearly eleven million and was one of the most successful of its releases in the past five years—compared to twenty-six million for *Bonnie and Clyde* released a year earlier. However, a decade later *Variety* listed the film's total rentals at only 9.75 million dollars, compared to more than twenty-two million for *Bonnie and Clyde* by that time.[8]

Not until five years after the last American combat troops and POWs came home were there other films dealing with the combat experience.[9] The first to be released was based on a script by a nineteen-year-old student at Yale, and its producer said it would be like *Battle Cry* or *Battleground*. But *The Boys of Company C* (1978), advertised as "Vietnam as it really was," was a silly copy of *M*A*S*H* (1970) with a soccer game substituted for football at the end. One critic concluded:

> The best thing to be said for this blithering, disjointed chronicle of a group of Marine recruits from boot camp to combat duty (of a sort) in Vietnam is that it scrapes the bottom. It will require truly subterranean ineptitude to sink lower. . . . [This film] gets the heralded cycle of Vietnam movies off to such a flying catastrophe that everything that follows is bound to look relatively respectable.[10]

But meanwhile, attention was already directed at the promised *Apocalypse Now* (1979), which industry analysts thought would be a "critical test of whether the wounds of war have healed enough for American audiences to pay money to relive the painful experience."[11]

Francis Ford Coppola frequently boasted that he was "the only one making a picture about Vietnam."[12] But because of numerous delays that generated nearly as much print as the final film, it was the last in the 1977–78 cycle. Yet it was really the first combat movie since *Green Berets* more than ten years earlier. Production began in March 1976, stopped and was resumed in August of that year—taking 167, then 230 shooting days. The budget was announced as ten, twelve, seventeen, and finally about thirty-one million dollars. When it finally did come out, CBS correspondent Morley Safer observed that it reminded him of "Vietnam only in the sense that they tried to win it with money."[13]

Coppola had asked the Pentagon for support but the Department of the Army was not interested. After much anticipation, the film was first publicly shown as "a work in progress" and as such received a great deal of publicity. *Variety* and *Newsweek* both said it was "worth the wait." The trade weekly called it alternatively "brilliant and bizarre" and the newsweekly said it was "extraordinarily powerful."[14] It was also previewed in Los Angeles with a questionnaire from Coppola inviting viewers to "help me finish the film"[15] by describing favorite or disliked scenes and providing suggestions for the ending. Indeed, compared to the 70mm limited theater version, the 35mm print does include, under the credits, an additional ending as the jungle hideout of the mad Colonel Kurtz (Marlon Brando) is bombed to bits.

When it was finally released in August 1979 most critics were not kind. Vincent Canby argued that in many scenes it did live up to its title,

> disclosing not only the various faces of war but also the contradictions between excitement and boredom, terror and pity, brutality and beauty. . . .
>
> When it is thus evoking the look and feelings of the Vietnam War, dealing in sense impressions for which no explanations are adequate or necessary, [it] is a stunning work.[16]

Yet, Coppola's film is really two movies—one about the many absurdities of the Vietnam War, the other the bizarre story borrowed from Joseph Conrad's *Heart of Darkness*, James Frazer's *The Golden Bough*, and even T. S. Eliot's *The Waste Land*.[17] Many of the incidents on the trip up the river show the "real" Vietnam with reasonable allowances for exaggeration and contraction. Patrols were startled by tigers and other animals in the jungle. While there is no record of surfing in Vietnam, one navy commander did arrange for his men to water-ski behind patrol boats and loud speakers did broadcast music and propaganda to the enemy from helicopters. And when, in the midst of this, Lieutenant Colonel Kilgore (Robert Duvall) says: "I love the smell of napalm in the morning . . . the smell of gasoline smells like victory"—that is only an echo of General George S. Patton, Jr., describing his men after battle as "bloody good killers."[18] There were many tours by beautiful women, like those in the film from *Playboy*, but no riots. At one point on the trip up the river Willard (Martin Sheen) and his men stop a sampan when a Vietnamese woman moves too quickly to protect something. All the Vietnamese in the boat are killed: the lone survivor is the small puppy she tried to shield. This scene is frighteningly real to anyone who witnessed men on river patrol boats conduct just such searches.

Most of the rest is a "profoundly anticlimactic intellectual muddle"[19] and "a ruinously pretentious and costly allegorical epic."[20] Coppola knew that himself, saying: "The movie is a mess—a mess of continuity, of style—and most important, the ending neither works on an audience or philosophical level."[21] But critic Frank Rich said more:

> In its cold, haphazard way, "Apocalypse Now" does remind us that war is hell, but that it is not the same thing as confronting the conflicts, agonies and moral chaos of this particular war. . . . The Vietnam War was a tragedy. "Apocalypse Now" is but this decade's most extraordinary Hollywood folly.[22]

As a study of filmmaking, celebrity, or egotism *Apocalypse Now* may be worthy of note.[23] For one who wishes to understand Vietnam it has very limited value.

In September 1967 Oliver Stone reported for duty in Vietnam as a member of the 2d Platoon, Bravo Company, 3d Battalion, 25th Infantry. He served in two other units and was wounded twice. In 1976, the year he arrived in Hollywood, Stone wrote a screenplay about his comrades and their war.

> "Platoon" in many ways is a chapter in his autobiography. The character of Chris Taylor has the psyche of Oliver Stone, and when the director is asked a question, he will sometimes refer the interviewer to his screenplay for the answer.[24]

At nineteen Stone quit Yale, taught in a Vietnamese school, then served in the Merchant Marine, and worked on a novel in Mexico— all before the army and Vietnam. In 1969, after Vietnam and a scrape with the law over marijuana possession, he enrolled in the New York University film program where he studied with Martin Scorsese.

After moving to Hollywood in 1976 he was the writer or coauthor of a number of scripts including *Conan the Barbarian* and *Midnight Express*, for which he won an Academy Award. Even with that success he struggled for years to get the script based on his Vietnam experiences produced. Apparently, it was the dedication of the Vietnam Memorial in Washington, DC that was, or symbolized, a turning point. The change was marked by increased sales of books about the war, two TV documentary series, and a willingness for those who knew and those who wanted to know to talk about the war. Yet it would take financing (two-thirds of the money) from Britain to get it made. For those and other unknown reasons, the timing was right. The film was released for a short run to qualify for the Oscars in December 1986, and when it opened generally in January 1987 a very good publicity campaign, much press attention, and word of mouth made it a very successful motion picture.[25] By mid-February it had become the top-grossing film, and remained so for several weeks.

Like Stone, Chris Taylor (Charlie Sheen) arrives in Vietnam in September 1967. As he disembarks a troop carrier plane, he passes body bags and seasoned soldiers so dirty and tired they look dead. On patrol Sergeant Barnes (Tom Berenger) argues with Lieutenant Wolfe (Mark Moses) who is portrayed as a wimp. Chris, the greenhorn, has to learn on his own—the more experienced grunts rarely help and do not trust newcomers. Out on ambush a black GI falls asleep on guard duty, there is a firefight, and Taylor is wounded.

Out into the jungle—it is January 1, 1968—Sergeant Elias (Willem Dafoe) enters a tunnel to find an enemy hospital and emerges in a hooch. They move up a river toward a village to find a GI missing from their outfit tied to a tree, tortured, and killed. Arriving in the village they see a civilian (enemy?) running away, and he is shot. A GI trips over a cooking pot. A pig is shot. Civilians come out of one of the holes and an explosive charge is thrown in. Bunny (Kevin Dillon) uses his rifle butt to smash an old (retarded?) man's skull. Prisoners are rounded up, Sergeant Barnes shoots a woman, kids cry.

To this point, many who saw the film and served in Vietnam were noting how realistically the frustrations are portrayed.[26] It was clearly the milestone movie for the evocation of jungle combat. Yet, everything in the film happens so fast. The images are so rich, the action compacted—even in several viewings it cannot all be absorbed. It seems to trivialize what is happening. There is the danger that the actions of the men do not seem motivated and some of the audience will withdraw in disgust.

Sergeant Barnes interrogates an old woman and an older man. Growing impatient he grabs a young girl and holds a pistol to her head. Sergeant Elias approaches and seemingly in a single motion asks what is going on and smashes Barnes in the face. They fight. The lieutenant orders a village burned and blown up. When he stops a rape, Chris is called a homosexual and spat upon.

Later the same day—the climactic battle of the film is based on a real battle of New Year's Day, 1968—after an artillery barrage that drives the enemy back, Elias pursues the enemy. Barnes stalks and shoots Elias. But he lives and flees, running in the open in front of enemy soldiers. The action is observed from a helicopter over the battlefield. This scene looks as though it is faked. In fact it is so phony looking that it reduces the credibility of the rest of the movie.

Later Barnes taunts and disdainfully urges his own men to kill him. The firefight continues the next day and is even more ferocious: the captain faces annihilation of his company class in an air strike on his positions, Junior is bayoneted in the throat several times, and Bunny is killed when his foxhole is overrun. Barnes is wounded and tries to kill Taylor just as an air strike comes in. At dawn Chris Taylor finds Barnes still alive and shoots him. At the end all enemy dead are bulldozed into a bomb crater and the wounded Americans are evacuated.

Occasionally Chris Taylor narrates his story in voice-over from letters to his grandmother. Without this continuity the film might be hopelessly muddled. Much of the swirling confusion seems a deliberate attempt to capture the reality of a surreal experience. Neither we nor Taylor are given any information to help understand why the men in the platoon are so abusive toward one another—especially the new members of the group. This is not the "group-at-war" genre war-combat film. War here is depicted from the perspective of the individual. We experience his confusion and disorientation from beginning to end. As he is evacuated his narration concludes:

> I think now, looking back, we did not fight the enemy, we fought ourselves. And the enemy was in us.
>
> The war is over for me now, but it will always be there, for the rest of my days, as I'm sure Elias will be, fighting with Barnes for . . . "possession

of my soul." There are times since then I've felt like a child born of those two fathers.

But be that as it may, those of us who did make it have an obligation to build again, to teach to others what we know, and to try with what's left of our lives to find a goodness and a meaning to this life.

This same dichotomy is required for understanding the two parts of this one film. One is an incredibly contracted but realistic visualization of what it was "really" like for some men in Vietnam.[27] For those who were there, and even for those who watched at home, the images are incredibly vivid and evocative.

- A GI pulls another dead soldier over himself to hide.[28]
- On night ambush, a GI falls back asleep as the enemy sneaks up.
- Smoking drugs through the barrel of a shotgun.[29]
- Hooches set on fire with a lighter and flame throwers.[30]
- GIs wounding themselves to get out of battle.
- GI cuts ear off dead enemy.[31]
- Enemy bodies staked and buried.[32]

As Vincent Canby put it:

The movie is a succession of found moments. It's less like a work that's been written than one that has been discovered, though, as we all probably know, screenplays aren't delivered by storks.[33]

Here then for the first time in a theatrical film about Vietnam is the "small war" fought by the ordinary grunt. Literally the only settlement shown during the film was the village that is burned and many of its civilians killed. There are no dramatic shots of choppers in flight. Except for one complaint about the bureaucrats in Washington who made them fight the war with one hand tied, the only "politics" discussed is a gripe about preferential treatment given other soldiers. After the village is burned and civilians killed Sergeant Elias can only say that he believed in the war in 1965 "but now it just bugs me." The platoon's war is not for ideology but for survival. They are draftees, living in fear, counting the days they are "short."

These are finely drawn characterizations developed by the writer-director and the actors—especially with the aid of the technical adviser. The actors and extras went through "twelve unique days of hard, no-slack field training."[34]

Second, it is also a melodrama. Anne Tayler Fleming argues that the My Lai-like destruction of the village and its people is the "shining moment of truth" in the film. But when the bad soldier kills the good soldier, and young Taylor must avenge, how are we to think about heros or murderers? Thus, she argues that the film is no less sentimental about the Vietnam war than its predecessors,

> no less full of the old notion, [that] war is the ultimate male romance. War is the place where men got to learn about themselves and each other. That is the enduring myth Oliver Stone is not ready to let go of, nor judging from the huge success of this film, are many of the rest of us.[36]

All artists manipulate history. *Platoon*, as art, can be judged by others. The main questions we want to ask here are these: What is the film's value in helping us understand some of what actually happened in 1967–68? What did it mean at the time to Oliver Stone and his fellow grunts, and how, if at all, had their thoughts changed when it came to making a film in 1985? Finally, what can all this mean to viewers of the film in 1988 and beyond?

Those who lived through combat like this understand how accurately parts of this film catch the fevered pitch of battle. *Platoon* can help others who were in Vietnam but only heard of such experiences, who saw only occasional glimpses of this in news reports and documentaries, or for whom this is all new, to understand the frustrations and madness of men under such conditions. *Platoon* can allow us to imagine what that kind of combat was like and perhaps, with that insight, to read other documents and sources in a more illuminating light.

But without the context provided by personal experience, will others—it is too easy to say younger people who did not experience our time—turn away? Many have seen it, but, as writer Charles Krauthammer has asked, how many can understand it?

> A filmmaker is not obliged to give context. It is perfectly legitimate to choose a narrow focus. But he should not then pretend to a cosmic message, such as the narrator's conclusion that in Vietnam the enemy was us.
> War is hell, and "Platoon" does hell well. That is a considerable achievement. What "Platoon" does not do, despite its pretensions, is tell us anything more than that.[36]

The men of the platoon are draftees living in fear counting the number of days they have left. They carry with them the flaws in character that so typify ordinariness, existing unfettered by conventions in force "back in the world." The believability of these characters is the film's strength, which magnifies its greatest weakness. Sergeant Barnes is the manifestation of man's most ignoble instincts unchecked. The brooding and brutal Barnes seems to have wrenched his destiny from fate where the others—the ordinary ones—seemed propelled by a milieu that catches them up and overwhelms their inhibitions. Courage and restraint took on much different meanings in "the Nam."

Control—or its abandoment—permeates the film. Some of the characters seem predisposed to unconscionable behavior. Others are pushed to hysteria by horrific circumstances.

For Bunny, the loud, not-very-bright, working-class kid who drinks beer and listens to country music, war is hell—except the good parts. He summarizes:

> I like being here. You get to do what you want, nobody fucks with you. The only worry you got is dying. If that happens you won't know about it anyway.

The central figure in *Platoon* is Chris Taylor, the college dropout. We see in him perceptiveness and indecisiveness. He is neither good nor bad. He is not held up for admiration nor reviled for his conduct. His role is to "be there," to act as surrogate for you and me.

In the end this is not a film in which the classic notion of "justice" is carried out when protagonist and antagonist come to a showdown. It is a nasty ending. In the ambiguity of war (or are we to believe it was only the Vietnam War?) Chris Taylor's cool execution of Barnes is depicted as justice. Viewers may dismiss that act as inevitable, assuming that Sergeant Barnes would unhesitatingly kill Taylor. Thus, the ending of the film plays out the film's greatest flaw. In Sergeant Barnes, Stone's film has succumbed to the temptation of a Francis Ford Coppola sort of treatment of a universal madness personified in an individual. Neither Colonel Kurtz nor Sergeant Barnes have human frailties that are truly comprehensible.

That flaw is all the more regrettable since the totality of the madness of the war, and what it did to the human beings who populated the platoon, was so finely drawn and credibly conveyed.

We are *not* asking that just one film tell the whole story of the Vietnam War. No film, novel, or history book can do that. But more than any other feature film to date *Platoon* demands that the viewer experience what is portrayed on the screen.

Nor do we find fault with the film because it is not the final word on Vietnam. This is a Vietnam War story from the perspective of Oliver

Stone, which carries more credence in its telling by virtue of his having served there. The writer-director makes no pretense of dealing with the gamut of events and places that was Vietnam; instead he limits his account to that of a single platoon serving like Stone in War Zone C in a place the Americans called the HoBo Woods, 1967–68. It is, Stone says, "one reality."[37]

Yet *Time* for a cover story on January 26, 1987, went overboard announcing "Viet Nam as It Really Was" causing former Marine and *Washington Post* writer Henry Allen to retort:

> This is silly and decadent, this willful confusion of life and art. And it's dangerous. War is too wildly stupid, glorious, hideous, huge and human for us to think that art can tell us what it really is. War is a little like God— when we start thinking we understand it, we're heading for trouble.[38]

NOTES

1. There are a number of picture books, listings, and analyses of war films; for example, see: Ken D. Jones and Arthur F. McClure, *Hollywood at War: The American Motion Picture and World War II* (New York: A. S. Barnes and Co., 1973); John Dowling, *War Peace Film Guide*, Third Edition (Chicago: World Without War Publications, 1980); Roger Manvell, *Films and the Second World War* (New York: A. S. Barnes and Co., 1974); Lawrence H. Suid, *Guts & GLory: Great American War Movies* (Reading, MA: Addison-Wesley Publishing Company, 1978); Jeanine Basinger, *The World War II Combat Film* (New York: Columbia University Press, 1986); Brock Garland, *War Movies* (New York: Facts on File Publications, 1987); and Clayton R. Koppes and Gregory D. Black, *Hollywood Goes to War: How Politics, Profits & Propaganda Shaped World War II Movies* (New York: The Free Press, 1987).

For Vietnam films specifically also see: Julian Smith, *Looking Away: Hollywood and Vietnam* (New York: Charles Scribner's Sons, 1975) and Gilbert Adair, *Vietnam on Film: From "The Green Berets" to "Apocalypse Now"* (New York: Proteus Publishing Co., 1981). A convenient short summary of television and newspaper coverage, as well as films, is in: David E. Bonior, Steven M. Champlin, and Timothy S. Kolly, *The Vietnam Veteran: A History of Neglect* (New York: Praeger Publishers, 1984).

For general information on the war itself see: George C. Herring, *America's Longest War: The United States and Vietnam 1950–1975* (New York: John Wiley & Sons, 1979, 2nd Edition Temple University Press, 1986) and Stanley Karnow, *Vietnam: A History* (New York: The Viking Press, 1983). There are a number of collections of documents and anthologies, two useful ones are: Steven Cohen, *Vietnam: Anthology and Guide to a Television History* (New York: Alfred A. Knopf, 1983) and Peter Braestrup, *Vietnam as History* (Washington, DC: University Press of America, 1984).

Among the many Vietnam documentaries are two thirteen-hour series now available on home video cassette: *Vietnam: A Television History* (PBS, 1983) and *Vietnam: The Ten Thousand Day War* (syndicated, 1982). Several CBS documentaries and a number of *CBS*

Evening News film stories are also available in the series *The Vietnam War with Walter Cronkite* (CBS Video Library).

2. Art Buchwald, "War Is What?," *Washington Post*, August 12, 1965.

3. "Pentagon Fears Fictional Angling; Hence, No Vietnam War Features," *Variety*, May 10, 1967, p. 7 and "Studios Reject Viet Scripts," *Film Daily*, January 8, 1968, p. 1. In addition to Suid's book see: Russell E. Shain, "Effect of Pentagon Influence on War Movies, 1948–1979," *Journalism Quarterly*, 49:2 (Winter 1972), pp. 641–7.

4. *Film Daily*, p. 5.

5. Quoted in *Esquire*, May 1968.

6. John Pilger, "Why the Deer Hunter Is a Lie," *New Statesman*, March 16, 1979, p. 353.

7. John E. Mueller, *War, Presidents and Public Opinion* (New York: John Wiley & Sons, 1973); see especially pp. 52–65 and 90.

8. Felix Kessler, "Green Berets, Rapped as 'Vile, Insane' Film Is 'Boffo' at Box Office," *Wall Street Journal*, July 3, 1968; "Glory," *New Yorker*, June 29, 1968; " 'Berets' Brings in the Green," *Wisconsin State Journal* (New York Times News Service), January 20, 1969; "Army's Film Help Rapped for Cost," *Wisconsin State Journal* (UPI), June 27, 1969; "All-Time Rental Champs," *Variety*, May 17, 1978, p. 123.

9. We refer here, of course, only to major studio, widely distributed feature motion pictures. Maybe the most bizarre of all little noted features was *The Losers* (1970), which also had the working title *Hell's Angels in Vietnam*, about a motorcycle gang that tries to free an American agent held in Cambodia. They used motorcycles, of course, that were armored and that had mounted machine guns.

There were also many documentaries on TV, but few that spent extended time in combat with American soldiers. Among the network-produced documentaries mostly about the ground combat experience were: *Daring Americans: Letters from Vietnam* (ABC, September 10, 1964), *I Am a Soldier* (ABC, May 8, 1966), and *World of Charlie Company* (CBS, July 14, 1970). Two produced primarily by independents but shown on network TV were: *Anderson Platoon* (CBS, April 4, 1967) and *Hill 943* (CBS, June 4, 1968). The best depiction of American soldiers in combat is *A Face of War* (Eugene Jones, 1968). Other documentaries (not national TV network) that also spent considerable time showing or describing the GI fighting situation were: *Mills of the Gods* (Canadian Broadcasting Corporation, December 5, 1965; NET, May 2, 1966); and *Interviews with My Lai Veterans* (1970). A documentary very critical of the US involvement that was frequently shown (often to raise money by peace groups) on campus during the war was *In The Year of the Pig* (1969).

The only documentary to get much distribution in theaters was *Hearts and Minds* (1974). Accepting an Oscar in 1975 the producers said it was ironic that this was happening just as Vietnam was being "liberated"—causing a big fuss at the ceremony.

10. Gary Arnold, " 'Boys in Company C': First Bomb in the Vietnam War Movie Cycle," *Washington Post*, February 9, 1978, p. B13.

11. "Viet War Films Get Marching Orders," *Variety*, August 10, 1977, p. 7. Also: Lee Grant, "War Sells; Vietnam Is In," *Los Angeles Times*, March 2, 1977, pp. 4, 6; "After Long Study, Movie Maker Finds a New War to Fight," *Wall Street Journal*, November 1, 1977, p. 1; Henry Allen, "And Now, by Popular Demand: The Real Vietnam War," *Washington Post Magazine*, January 29, 1978, pp. 13–16; and Randy Sue Coburn, "Now, from the Folks Who Brought You Hollywood, Here Comes—Vietnam!," *Washington Star*, January 13, 1978, pp. E1, E8.

12. George McArthur, "Coppola Storms Philippines for Re-Creation of Viet War," *Los Angeles Times Calendar*, June 6, 1976, p. 37.

13. *CBS Sunday Morning*, discussion with Charles Kuralt, Ed Bradley, and Morley Safer, August 19, 1979.

14. Film Reviews, *Variety*, May 16, 1979, p. 21; Charles Michener, "Finally, 'Apocalypse Now,' " *Newsweek*, May 28, 1979, p. 100.

15. David Denby, " '8½' Now: Coppola's Apocalypse," *New York*, May 28, 1979, p. 101.

16. Vincent Canby, "The Screen: 'Apocalypse Now,' " *New York Times*, August 15, 1979.

17. John Tessitore, "The Literary Roots of 'Apocalypse Now,' " October 21, 1979, and Tony Chiu, "Francis Coppola's Cinematic 'Apocalypse' Is Finally at Hand," *New York Times*, August 12, 1979, p. 2:1.

18. *ABC Evening News*, August 1, 1968.

19. Ibid.

20. Quoted in Gary Arnold, "Mangled Revelations: 'Apocalypse,' at Last," *Washington Post*, October 3, 1979, p. B12.

21. Ibid.

22. Frank Rich, "The Making of a Quagmire," *Time*, August 27, 1979, p. 57.

23. Eleanor Coppola. *Notes* (New York: Simon & Schuster, 1979). Excerpted in Eleanor Coppola, "Diary of a Director's Wife," *New York Times Magazine*, August 5, 1979, p. 31. For an interesting analysis, see also William A. Hagan, "*Apocalypse Now* (1979): Joseph Conrad and the Television War," in Peter C. Rollins, ed. *Hollywood as Historian* (Lexington: University Press of Kentucky, 1983), pp. 230–45.

24. Michael Norman, " 'Platoon' Grapples with Vietnam," *New York Times*, December 21, 1986, Sec. 2, p. 17.

25. See especially, "Platoon," *Time*, January 26, 1967, cover story, pp. 54–61.

26. To understand the film better we recommend: Dale Reich, "One Year in Vietnam: A Young Soldier Remembers," *Wisconsin Magazine of History*, Spring 1981; Frederick Downs, *The Killing Zone* (New York: W. W. Norton, 1978); Francis J. West, *Small Unit Action in Vietnam Summer 1966* (New York: Arno Press, 1967); F. J. West, Jr., *The Village* (New York: Harper & Row, 1972); Ronald J. Glasser, *365 Days* (New York: George Braziller, 1971); Tim O'Brien, *If I Die in a Combat Zone* (New York: Dell Publishing, 1974); Al Santoli, *Everything We Had* (New York: Ballantine Books, 1981); Mark Baker, *Nam* (New York: William Morrow and Company, 1981); Wayne Karlin, et. al., *Free Fire Zone* (New York: McGraw-Hill, 1973); Samuel Vance, *The Courageous and the Proud* (New York: W. W. Norton, 1970); James Webb, *Fields of Fire* (Englewood Cliffs, NJ: Prentice-Hall, 1978); *The Short-Times's Journal*, No. 1, 9–10/80, Winter Soldier Archive; and Ron Kovic, *Born on the Fourth of July* (New York: Pocket Books, 1976); among others. The order of these articles and books is arranged to provide specific information about GIs in Vietnam—such as arriving, first patrol, mines, etc.—in the order in which these appear in *Platoon*.

27. How realistic was argued in a number of printed interviews with vets, in letters to the editors of newspapers, and in opinion columns. David Halberstam and Bernard E. Trainor, "Two Who Were There View 'Platoon': The Correspondent [and] The Marine Officer," *New York Times*, March 8, 1987; James P. Sterba, "In Vietnam, 1 Platoon Grunt Equaled 8 Remington Raiders," *The Wall Street Journal*, February 27, 1987; Carole Kass, "Veterans Disagree on 'Platoon's' Picture of War," *Richmond Times-Dispatch*, April 12, 1987; Phil McCombs, "Veterans, Reliving the Pain," *Washington Post*, January 16, 1987; Richard Cohen, "The Nightmare of 'Platoon,' " *Washington Post*, February 3, 1987, p. A21; Colman McCarthy, "Why Teens Should See 'Platoon,' " *Washington Post*, February 7, 1987, A21; Michael Kinsley, "From 'Rambo' to 'Platoon,' " *Washington Post*, February 18, 1987, p. A19; Harold Evans, "Parable in the Jungle," *U. S. News & World Report*, March 2, 1987, p. 78; John C. Shoemaker, "A Real-Life Platoon," *The Wall Street Journal*, March 19, 1987, p. A35; R. Emmett Tyrrell, Jr., " 'Platoon' Another Fantasy," *Washington*

Post, April 7, 1987, A17; and Andy Rooney, " 'Platoon'—An Impressive, Flawed Film," *Chicago Sun-Times*, April 4, 1987, p. 14.

28. As Jack Smith did on ABC-TV November 24, 1965 and in Specialist 4/C Jack P. Smith, "Death in the Ia Drang Valley," *Saturday Evening Post*, January 28, 1967.

29. Shown in a report by Gary Shepard on *CBS Evening News*, November 13, 1970.

30. Morley Safer report from Cam Ne *CBS Evening News*, August 5, 1965.

31. On *CBS Evening News*, reported by Don Webster October 9, 1967.

32. Robert Shackne, December 11, 1967, *CBS Evening News*.

33. Vincent Canby, "Film: The Vietnam War in Stone's 'Platoon,' " *New York Times*, December 19, 1986, sec. 3, p. 12.

34. Jay Sharbutt, "The Grunts' War, Take 1," *Los Angeles Times Calendar*, May 25, 1986, p. 32.

35. Anne Taylor Fleming, *MacNeil-Lehrer News Hour*, PBS, February 11, 1987.

36. Charles Krauthammer, " 'Platoon' Chic," *Washington Post*, February 20, 1987, p. A19.

37. Stone Phillips, "Platoon," *20/20*, ABC-TV, March 26, 1987, and Oliver Stone speech to the National Press Club, Washington, DC, C-SPAN, April 18, 1987. Following *Platoon* there were, of course, a number of other Vietnam films—*Full Metal Jacket, Hamburger Hill, Hanoi Hilton, Good Morning Vietnam*, and the TV series *Tour of Duty*.

38. Henry Allen, "Why We Aren't in Vietnam," *Washington Post*, January 25, 1987, p. 25. Hollywood probably confuses reality and its movies much more than the general public does. That point was made clear in a recent article about the trend of movies of the 1960s. "Analyst Stuart Byron says the problem in making these pictures will be in finding a way to make the period look different from the way it looked at the time": in Anne Thompson, "Hollywood Cautiously Embraces the Sixties," *Chicago Tribune*, August 13, 1987, Sec. 5, p. 11A.

Notes on Contributors

John E. O'Connor is Professor of History at New Jersey Institute of Technology. He is editor of *American History/American Television: Interpreting the Video Past* (Ungar, 1983) and of the quarterly journal *Film & History*. His other books include: *William Paterson: Lawyer and Statesman, 1745–1806* (Rutgers University Press, 1979); *I Am a Fugitive From a Chain Gang* (University of Wisconsin Press, 1981); and *The Hollywood Indian* (New Jersey State Museum, 1983). "The Historian and the Moving-Image Media," the National Endowment for the Humanities funded project that he designed and directed for the American Historical Association, has resulted in a two-hour video compilation that is cross-referenced to his *Teaching History With Film and Television* (American Historical Association, 1987), and *Image as Artifact: The Historical Analysis of Film and Television* (forthcoming in 1988).

Martin A. Jackson, co-founder of the Historians Film Committee, taught history and film studies at the State University of New York and at New Jersey Institute of Technology. He lives in New York City where, among other interests, he continues to contribute to several publications as a free-lance writer.

Raymond L. Carroll, Associate Professor of Broadcast and Film Communication at the University of Alabama, teaches courses in broadcast programming and news analysis and is graduate program coordinator. He was editor of *Feedback* for the Broadcast Education Association. He has written a number of articles on the history of the television documentary.

Thomas Cripps is Professor of History at Morgan State University in Baltimore. His combined interest in film and television and his specialty in black history are reflected in his *Slow Fade to Black: The Negro in American Film* (Oxford University Press, 1977); *Black Film as Genre* (Indiana University Press, 1978) and *Black Shadows on the Silver Screen*, an award-winning film (Post-Newsweek television, 1975). His "Movies, Race and World War II," *Prologue*, XIV (Summer, 1982), was awarded the Charles Thompson Prize.

David H. Culbert is Professor of History at Louisiana State University, Baton Rouge. His *Mission to Moscow* was published by the University of Wisconsin Press in 1980. He is Editor-in-Chief of the five-volume *Film Propaganda in America: A Documentary History* (Greenwood Press, 1988). The documentary film, *Huey Long*, for which he served as Associate Producer and Director of Historical Research, won the Erik Barnouw Prize from the Organization of American Historians in 1985. He is currently president of the International Association for Audio-Visual Media in Historical Research and Education.

Michael T. Isenberg teaches history at the U. S. Naval Academy. His *War on Film: The American Cinema and World War I (1914–1941)* appeared in 1981. *Puzzles of the Past: An Introduction to Thinking About History* came out in 1985, and *John L. Sullivan and His America* was published in 1988.

Garth Jowett has a Ph.D. in History from the University of Pennsylvania, and is a Professor in the School of Communication, University of Houston, where he served as Director for five years. His special interests are the history of communications, propaganda, and popular culture. He is author of *Film: The Democratic Art* (Little, Brown, 1976), a detailed social history of movie-going in America, as well as *Movies as Mass Communication* (Sage, 1981), and *Propaganda and Persuasion* (Sage, 1986) with Victoria O'Donnell. He has recently completed a book on culture and communication, and his work in progress is a social history of television.

Daniel J. Leab is Professor of History at Seton Hall University. His publications include numerous articles and books among them: *A Union of Individuals: The Formation of the American Newspaper Guild* (Columbia University Press, 1970), *From Sambo to Superspade: The Black Experience in Motion Pictures* (Houghton Mifflin, 1976), and *The Labor History Reader* (University of Illinois Press, 1982). He is editor of the journal *Labor History*.

Lawrence W. Lichty is Professor of Radio/Television/Film Northwestern University. He was Director of Media Research for *Vietnam: A Television History* (PBS, 1983) produced at WGBH, Boston. The thirteen-hour documentary series was honored with the George Foster Peabody Award, the du Pont-Columbia University Award, and six national Emmys.

Lawrence L. Murray has published and spoken widely on the interrelationship of film and history. His particular interest in film as a pedagogical resource is addressed in *The Celluloid Persuasion*, which was published by Eerdmans in 1979. He is currently pursuing other interests in the Washington, D.C. area.

Peter C. Rollins is Professor of English at Oklahoma State University where he teaches film and American Studies. He has published widely on related themes in such journals as *American Quarterly*, *The Journal of Popular Film*, and *Film & History*, and is editor of *Hollywood as Historian: American Film in a Cultural Context* (University Press of Kentucky, 1983). His award-winning film, *Will Rogers' 1920's* (Churchill Films) is available for rental from the Oklahoma State University AV Center. His recent work has been on the production of documentaries on such subjects as Vietnam, poverty, and the New Left.

Stuart Samuels taught the history of film at the University of Pennsylvania from 1967 to 1981. He is the author of *Midnight Movies* (1983) and currently produces videos, TV shows, and feature films in New York City.

Robert Sklar, Professor of Cinema Studies at New York University, is the author of *Movie-Made America: A Cultural History of American Movies* (1975). He is a member of the Editorial Board of *Cineaste* magazine, a film quarterly, and an editorial adviser to *Film & History*. His essays on television have been collected in *Prime Time: Life On and Behind the Television Screen* (1980).

June Sochen is Professor of History at Northeastern Illinois University in Chicago where she teaches courses in American Cultural as well as Women's History. She has edited or written ten books, most recently *Enduring Values: Women in Popular Culture* (1987).

Lawrence H. Suid combines special interests in the history of film, the American military, and space exploration. His *Guts and Glory: Great American War Movies* (Addison-Wesley) appeared in 1978. He has recently completed a history of the Armed Forces Radio and Television Services and is currently working on a history of the image and reality of manned space flight.

Paul J. Vanderwood teaches history at San Diego State University where he combines his special interests in Latin American history and film. His books include: *Disorder and Progress: Bandits, Police and Mexican Development* (University of Nebraska Press, 1981), and *Juarez* (University of Wisconsin Press, 1982). *Border Fury: A Picture Postcard Report on Mexico's Revolution and U.S. Preparedness Along the Border, 1910–1917* will be published by University of New Mexico Press in 1988.

Film Credits and Rental Sources

1. *Way Down East* (1920) 107 minutes black & white silent
   with Lillian Gish and Richard Barthelmess
   directed by D. W. Griffith   rental: Audio-Brandon Films
2. *The Big Parade* (1925) 130 minutes black & white silent
   with John Gilbert and Renee Adoree
   directed by King Vidor   rental: Films Incorporated
3. *Scar Of Shame* (1929) 65 minutes black & white silent
   with Harry Henderson and Lucia Moses
   produced by Oscar Micheaux   rental: Standard Film Service
4. *Public Enemy* (1931) 84 minutes black & white sound
   with James Cagney and Jean Harlow
   directed by William Wellman   rental: Audio-Brandon Films
5. *Steamboat 'Round the Bend* (1935) 80 minutes black & white sound
   with Will Rogers and Irwin S. Cobb
   directed by John Ford   rental: Films Incorporated
6. *Drums Along the Mohawk* (1939) 105 minutes color sound
   with Henry Fonda and Claudette Colbert
   directed by John Ford   rental: Films Incorporated
7. *Mission To Moscow* (1943) 124 minutes black & white sound
   with Walter Huston and Ann Harding
   directed by Michael Curtiz   rental: United Artists 16
8. *The Best Years Of Our Lives* (1946) 170 minutes black & white
   sound
   with Frederick March, Dana Andrews, Myrna Loy
   directed by William Wyler   rental: Audio-Brandon Films
9. *Red River* (1948) 133 minutes black & white sound
   with John Wayne and Montgomery Clift
   directed by Howard Hawks   rental: United Artists 16
10. *Viva Zapata!* (1952) 113 minutes black & white sound
    with Marlon Brando and Anthony Quinn
    directed by Elia Kazan   rental: Films Incorporated
11. *Invasion of the Body Snatchers* (1956) 80 minutes black & white
    sound

with Kevin McCarthy and Dana Wynter
directed by Don Siegel   rental: Ivy Films

12. *Dr. Strangelove*   (1964)   93 minutes   black & white   sound
with Peter Sellers, George C. Scott and Sterling Hayden
directed by Stanley Kubrick   rental: Columbia Pictures

13. *Bonnie and Clyde*   (1967)   111 minutes   color   sound
with Warren Beatty and Faye Dunaway
directed by Arthur Penn   rental: Warner Brothers

14. *Rocky*   (1976)   121 minutes   color   sound
with Sylvester Stallone and Talia Shire
directed by John Avildsen   rental: United Arists 16

15. *Platoon*   (1986)   120 minutes   color   sound
with Tom Berenger, Willem Dafoe, Charlie Sheen
directed by Oliver Stone.   Presently unavailable in 16mm. Available in
videotape from HBO HOME VIDEO or VESTRON VIDEO.

Film Distributors: the companies listed below specialize in the rental of 16mm films. Prices vary depending upon the intended use of the film so that the prospective renter should study the catalog carefully and understand fully his/her responsibility before ordering a film for classroom purposes. Please note also that some of the films listed here may be available from more than one rental source; substantial savings can often be achieved by comparing prices and availability from several companies or film libraries.

Audio-Brandon Films
34 MacQuesten Parkway South
Mount Vernon, N.Y. 10550

Columbia Pictures
711 Fifth Avenue
New York, N.Y. 10022

Films Incorporated
440 Park Avenue South
New York, N.Y. 10016

Ivy Films
165 West 46th Street
New York, N.Y. 10036

United Artists 16
729 7th Avenue
New York, N.Y. 10019

Warner Brothers Inc.
Non-Theatrical Division
4000 Warner Boulevard
Burbank, Calif. 91505

For Further Reading

Abrash, Barbara, and Janet Sternberg, editors, *Historians & Filmmakers: Toward Collaboration*. New York: The Institute for Research in History, 1983.

Aldgate, Anthony. *Cinema and History: British Newsreels and the Spanish Civil War*. London: Scholar Press, 1979.

Arnheim, Rudolf. *Film As Art*. Berkeley: University of California Press, 1957.

Balio, Tino. *United Artists: The Company Built By the Stars*. Madison: University of Wisconsin Press, 1976.

Balio, Tino, editor. *The American Film Industry*. Revised Edition. Madison: University of Wisconsin Press, 1985.

Barsam, Richard Meran. *Non-Fiction Film: A Critical History*. New York: E.P. Dutton, 1973.

Barsam, Richard Meran, editor. *Non-Fiction Film Theory and Criticism*. New York: E.P. Dutton, 1976.

Barnouw, Erik. *Documentary: A History of the Non-Fiction Film*. New York: Oxford University Press, 1983.

Behlmer, Rudy. *Inside Warner Brothers (1935–1951)*. New York: Viking, 1985.

Benson, Susan Porter, Steven Brier and Roy Rosenzweig, editors. *Presenting the Past: Essays on History and the Public*. Philadelphia: Temple University Press, 1986.

Bergman, Andrew. *We're In the Money: Depression America and its Films*. New York: Harper and Row, 1971.

Biskind, Peter. *Seeing is Believing: How Hollywood Taught Us to Stop Worrying and Love the Fifties*. New York: Pantheon, 1983.

Bordwell, David, Janet Staiger, and Kristin Thompson. *The Classical Hollywood Cinema: Film Style and Mode of Production to 1960*. New York: Columbia University Press, 1985.

Burns, E. Bradford. "Conceptualizing the Use of Film to Study History." *Film & History*, Vol. IV (December, 1974), pp 1–11.

Burns, E, Bradford. *Latin American Cinema: Film and History*. Los Angeles: UCLA Latin American Center, 1978.

Cripps, Thomas. *Slow Fade to Black: The Negro in American Film, 1900–1942*. New York: Oxford University Press, 1977.

Ferro, Marc. "1917: History and Cinema." *Contemporary History*, Vol. III (October, 1968), pp 45–61.

Fielding, Raymond. *A Technological History of Motion Pictures and Television*. Third Edition. Berkeley: University of California Press, 1979.

Fledelius, Karsten, and Kaare Rübner Jorgenson, Niels Skyum-Nielson, and Erik H. Swiatek. *Studies in History, Film and Society I: History and the Audio-Visual Media*. Copenhagen: Eventus, 1979.

———. *The American Newsreel*. Norman: University of Oklahoma Press, 1972.

Gomery, Douglas, and Robert C. Allen. *Film History: Theory and Practice*. New York: Knopf, 1985.

Gomery, Douglas. *The Hollywood Studio System*. New York: St. Martins, 1986.

Griffin, Patrick. "The Making of *Goodbye Billy*." *Film & History*, Vol. II (May, 1972), pp 6–10.

Isaksson, Folke, and Leif Furhammar. *Politics and Film*. New York: Praeger, 1971.

Isenberg, Michael T. *War on Film: The American Cinema and World War I*. Rutherford, New Jersey: Fairleigh Dickinson University Press, 1981.

Jacobs, Lewis, editor. *The Documentary Tradition: From "Nanook" to "Woodstock."* New York: Norton, 1971.

Jarvie, Ian. *Movies and Society*. New York: Basic Books, 1970.

Jowett, Garth. *Film: The Democratic Art*. Boston: Little, Brown, 1975.

Jowett, Garth, and James M. Linton. *Movies as Mass Communication*. Beverly Hills: Sage, 1980.

Jowett, Garth, and Victoria O'Donnell. *Propaganda and Persuasion*. Beverly Hills: Sage, 1986.

Koppes, Clayton R. and Gregory D. Black. *Hollywood Goes to War: How Politics, Profits and Propaganda Shaped World War II Movies*. New York: Free Press, 1987.

Kracauer, Sigfried. *From Caligari to Hitler: A Psychological History of the German Film*. Princeton: Princeton University Press, 1957.

Leab, Daniel J. *From Sambo to Superspade: The Black Motion Picture Experience*. Boston: Houghton Mifflin, 1975.

Leab, Daniel J., "Writing History With Film: Two Views of the 1937 Strike Against General Motors by the UAW," *Labor History,*. Vol. XXI (Winter, 1979–80), pp 102–12.

Maltby, Richard. *Harmless Entertainment: Hollywood and the Ideology of Consensus*. Metuchen, NJ: Scarecrow, 1983.

Marsden, Michael, John G. Nachbar, Sam L. Grogg, Jr., editors. *Movies as Artifacts: Cultural Criticism of Popular Film*. Chicago: Nelson Hall, 1982.

Mast, Gerald, and Marshall Cohen. *Film Theory and Criticism: Introductory Readings*. Second Edition. New York: Oxford University Press, 1979.

Mast, Gerald, editor. *The Movies in Our Midst: Documents in the Cultural History of Film in America*. Chicago: University of Chicago Press, 1982.

May, Larry. *Screening Out the Past: The Birth of Mass Culture and the Motion Picture Industry*. New York: Oxford University Press, 1980.

Mellencamp, Patricia, and Philip Rosen. *Cinema Histories, Cinema Practices*. Frederick, MD: University Publications of America, 1983.

O'Connor, John E., editor. *Film and the Humanities*. New York: The Rockefeller Foundation, 1977.

Pettit, Arthur G. *Images of the Mexican American in Fiction and Film*. College Station, Texas: Texas A & M University Press, 1980.

Peyton, Patricia, editor. *Reel Change: A Guide To Social Issue Films*. San Francisco: The Film Fund, 1979.

Pitts, Michael. *Hollywood and American Reality: A Filmography of Over 250 Motion Pictures Depicting U.S. History*. Jefferson, NC: McFarland, 1984.

Pronay, Nicholas, and Derek W. Spring. *Propaganda, Politics and Film, 1918–1945*. London: Macmillan, 1982.

Pronay, Nicholas, Betty R. Smith, and Tom Hastie. *The Use of Film in History Teaching.* London: The Historical Association, 1972.

Reader, Keith. *Cultures on Celluloid.* London: Quartet Books, 1981.

Raack, Richard C. "Clio's Dark Mirror: The Documentary Film in History," *The History Teacher,* Vol. VI, No. 1 (1972), pp 109–18.

———. "Historiography and Cinematography: A Prolegomenon to Film Work for Historians," *Journal of Contemporary History,* Vol. XVIII (July, 1983), pp 411–38.

Reimers, K.F. and H. Friedrich, editors. *Studies in History, Film and Society III: Contemporary History in Film and Television.* Munich: Verlag Ölschläger, 1982.

Rollins, Peter C. "The Making of Will Rogers' 1920s," *Film & History,* Vol. VII (January, 1977), pp 1–5.

———, editor. *Hollywood as Historian: American Film in Cultural Context.* Lexington: University of Kentucky Press, 1983.

Short, Kenneth R.M., editor. *Feature Films as History.* Knoxville: University of Tennessee Press, 1981.

Short, Kenneth R.M., editor. *Film and Radio Propaganda in World War II.* Knoxville: University of Tennessee Press, 1983.

Short, Kenneth R.M., and Karsten Fledelius, editors. *Studies in History, Film and Society II: History and Film: Methodology, Research, Education.* Copenhagen: Eventus, 1980.

Sklar, Robert. *Movie-Made America: A Cultural History of American Movies.* New York: Random House, 1975.

Smith, Julian. *Looking Away: Hollywood and Vietnam.* New York: Scribner's, 1975.

Smith, Paul, editor. *The Historian and Film.* Cambridge: Cambridge University Press, 1976.

Sorlin, Pierre. *The Film In History.* Totowa, NJ: Barnes and Noble, 1981.

Suid, Lawrence H. *Guts and Glory: Great American War Movies.* Boston: Addison-Wesley, 1978.

Taylor, Richard. *The Politics of the Soviet Cinema, 1917–1929.* Cambridge: Cambridge University Press, 1979.

Toplin, Robert Brent. "The Making of Denmark Vesey's Rebellion." *Film & History,* Vol. XII (September, 1982), pp 49–56.

Walkowitz, Daniel. "Visual History: The Craft of the Historian Filmmaker," *The Public Historian,* Vol. VII (Winter, 1985), pp. 53–64.

Welch, David. *Propaganda and the German Cinema, 1933–1945.* New York: Oxford University Press, 1983.

Woll, Allen L., and Randall M. Miller. *Ethnic and Racial Images in American Film and Television: Historical Essays and Bibliography.* New York: Garland, 1987.

Wollen, Peter. *Signs and Meaning in the Cinema.* Bloomington: Indiana University Press, 1969.

Wood, Robin. *Hollywood From Vietnam to Reagan.* New York: Columbia University Press, 1986.

Wood, Michael. *America in the Movies.* New York: Basic Books, 1975.

Wright, Will. *Sixguns and Society: A Structural Study of the Western.* Berkeley: University of California Press, 1975.

Index